The Smart Life Revolution

This book explores the integration of Artificial Intelligence (AI) across areas such as IoT, big data, healthcare, business, economics and security, and improving the quality of life (QoL) in smart cities today.

By looking in depth at the different application areas of AI, the reader learns about the broad and impactful ways AI is transforming our world, its profound influence in enhancing service efficiency, personalisation, accessibility and fostering both scientific and social advancement. The editors consider the importance of bridging theory and practice by offering a practical understanding of how key AI technologies can be applied in real-world scenarios for QoL. By covering both foundational concepts and advanced applications with case studies and practical examples, this approach ensures the reader obtains a comprehensive understanding of the technologies and their impact. An innovation mindset is emphasised with discussion about the challenges, opportunities, future trends and potential research directions to prepare readers for ongoing technological advancements. The book takes an interdisciplinary approach by integrating knowledge from computer science, engineering and social sciences, to offer a holistic view of technology's role in society.

This book serves as a valuable resource for both undergraduate and postgraduate students in the study of AI applications in society. The book may be used by researchers and communities to identify the different challenges associated with key technologies for building new applications for improving the quality of life in smart cities.

The Smart Life Revolution

Embracing AI and IoT in Society

Edited by
Connie Tee
Thian Song Ong
Md Shohel Sayeed

CRC Press
Taylor & Francis Group
Boca Raton London New York

CRC Press is an imprint of the
Taylor & Francis Group, an **informa** business

Designed cover image: Web Large Image (Public)

First edition published 2025
by CRC Press
2385 NW Executive Center Drive, Suite 320, Boca Raton FL 33431

and by CRC Press
4 Park Square, Milton Park, Abingdon, Oxon, OX14 4RN

CRC Press is an imprint of Taylor & Francis Group, LLC

© 2025 selection and editorial matter, Connie Tee, Thian Song Ong, and Md Shohel Sayeed; individual chapters, the contributors

ISBN: 978-1-032-83405-4 (hbk)
ISBN: 978-1-032-83408-5 (pbk)
ISBN: 978-1-003-50919-6 (ebk)

DOI: 10.1201/9781003509196

Typeset in Palatino
by SPi Technologies India Pvt Ltd (Straive)

Contents

About the Editors

Connie Tee serves as a professor at the Faculty of Information Science and Technology at Multimedia University. Her research interests cover the areas of computer vision, image processing and machine learning. She has published more than 100 scientific international publications in these areas.

Thian Song Ong works at the Faculty of Information Sciences and Technology (FIST), Multimedia University. His research interests include machine learning and biometric security. He has published more than 80 articles in internationally refereed journals and conferences and is a senior member of IEEE.

Md Shohel Sayeed has been a member of Multimedia University since 2001, and now he serves as a professor under the Faculty of Information Science and Technology. His core research interest is in the area of Biometrics, big data and artificial intelligence. He is a senior member of IEEE.

Contributors

Afizan Azman is an associate professor in the School of Computer Science, Taylors University. His research interests include data mining, cognitive science and machine learning. He has published 35 journals, 10 conference proceedings and 4 book chapters.

Umar Ali Bukar holds a BSc degree in business IT, MSc. In computer network management, and a PhD in Information Systems. He is a postdoctoral research fellow at Multimedia University, Malaysia. His research spans crisis informatics, generative AI, data analytics, machine learning and systematic literature reviews.

Lee-Ying Chong, a senior lecturer at the Faculty of Information Science and Technology, Multimedia University, Malaysia, specialises in machine learning, pattern recognition and biometric authentication. Her research focuses on developing innovative, data-driven solutions to address challenges in security and artificial intelligence applications.

Siew-Chin Chong, assistant professor and deputy dean in the Faculty of Information Science & Technology, Multimedia University (Malaysia), specialises in machine learning and biometric security. With extensive publications, she has also served as editorial board member for journals and technical chair for international conferences.

Kah-Ong Michael Goh, associate professor at Multimedia University (Malaysia), specialises in pattern recognition, image processing, video analytics and computer vision, particularly multimodal biometrics. He has published in top journals like *Scientific Reports*, *Pattern Recognition Letters* and *Image and Vision Computing*.

Ying Han Pang is an associate professor in the Faculty of Information Science and Technology, at Multimedia University, Malaysia. Her research interests include human activity recognition, machine learning, deep learning and data analytics.

Hamza Ibrahim is a BTech graduate in Computer Science Education from Abubakar Tafawa Balewa University, works with Bread of Hope, supporting out-of-school children. His research focuses on blockchain, cybersecurity, AI, machine learning and 6G, exploring innovative solutions to address real-world challenges.

Sharifah Noor Masidayu Sayed Ismail is currently a PhD candidate and a lecturer at the Faculty of Information Science and Technology (FIST), MMU. Her research explores the use of artificial intelligence to detect cardiovascular diseases via physiological signals. Her research interests include affective computing, AI, signal processing and geriatric diseases.

Yee Jian Chew is a lecturer at the Faculty of Information Science and Technology, Multimedia University, Malaysia. His research interests include forest fire and cybersecurity. Notable work: *A Review of Forest Fire Combating Efforts, Challenges and Future Directions in Peninsular Malaysia, Sabah, and Sarawak.*

Check-Yee Law is a senior lecturer at the Faculty of Information Science and Technology, Multimedia University, Melaka Campus, Malaysia. She has published in educational technology, computing education, user-centred design and data visualisation. She conducts research and development activities in the domain of information systems, human–computer interaction and data analytics.

En Lee is a PhD candidate in the Faculty of Information Science & Technology (FIST) at Multimedia University, specialising in machine learning and socio-economic fields. His focus is on integrating machine learning and economic models to analyse poverty and inequality issues.

Yvonne Lee is an assistant professor at Multimedia University, Malaysia. Her research interests are the digital economy, social capital and development economics with a focus on gender and income inequality.

Meng-Chew Leow received his PhD from Multimedia University. His research interest is in game-based learning, specifically in role-playing game-based learning. He is also interested in system science, practical spirituality and philosophy. Her notable publications include works on usability study and e-learning.

Lim Jing Yee is a PhD candidate in Artificial Intelligence at Multimedia University Malaysia. Her research primarily focuses on data science, deep learning and machine learning, with a particular emphasis on predictive modelling, time-series analysis and decision-making in data-driven environments.

Jashila Nair Mogan is a senior lecturer in the Faculty of Information Science and Technology, Multimedia University. Her research interests include artificial intelligence, computer vision, deep learning and gait recognition. She has published six journals and three conference proceedings.

Lee-Yeng Ong received a PhD degree in computer vision and is currently working as an assistant professor at Multimedia University, Malaysia. Her research interests include object tracking, data science and big data analytics. Her notable publications include works on skeleton-based human pose estimation and Kalman filtering.

Shih Yin Ooi is an associate professor at the Faculty of Information Science and Technology, Multimedia University, Malaysia. Her research interests include machine learning, cybersecurity and environmental security. She led the FRGS-funded project "Spatio-Temporal Forest Fire Predictive Modelling with Random Forest and Deep Learning Variants".

Siti Fatimah Abdul Razak is an assistant professor in the Faculty of Information Science and Technology, Multimedia University. Her research interests include vehicle safety applications, machine learning, Internet of Things, information systems development, and educational technology. She has published 43 journals and 45 conference proceedings and 2 book chapters. She is also a registered professional technologist with the Malaysian Board of Technologist and a member of the International Association of Engineers.

Yong-Wee Sek is a distinguished researcher at Universiti Teknikal Malaysia Melaka. His expertise spans across technology adoption, information systems, e-learning and smart farming. He is also a reviewer for *IEEE Access, F1000, and Brain Informatics*. He has published in renowned journals including *IEEE Access*, *IET Computer Vision* and *AI Open*.

Avenaish Sivaprakasam is currently a network engineer at Ace Team Networks Sdn Bhd, Malaysia. He graduated from Multimedia University with a bachelor's degree majoring in Data Communication and Networking. His research interests include IoT, machine learning and embedded devices.

Radhwan Sneesl holds a BSc degree in computer science from the University of Basrah and an MSc degree in AI and distributed computing from the West University of Timisoara. He is pursuing a PhD at Universiti Putra Malaysia, focusing on IoT, smart campuses, data analytics and technology adoption.

Joon Liang Tan is an assistant professor at the Multimedia University, Malaysia. He has published 27 journals, of which 23 are Q1/Q2 WoS journals. He is actively pursuing NGS-based (genomics, transcriptomics, exomics, metagenomics) Bioinformatics research, focusing on machine learning/AI, phylogenomics and evolution.

Pei-Sze Tan is a PhD candidate at Monash University Malaysia, focusing on human face analysis, affective computing and causal inference. Her research emphasises fairness and causality in micro-expression analysis, resulting in two publications in prestigious venues, ICASSP and APSIPA.

Yee-Fan Tan is a PhD candidate at Monash University Malaysia, specialising in computational neuroscience. His research focuses on deep generative models for human brain functional and structural connectomes. He has published multiple papers in leading conferences, including ICIP, ICASSP and ISBI.

Min-Er Teo, currently pursuing a PhD degree at the Faculty of Information Science & Technology (FIST), Multimedia University, Melaka, Malaysia. Her current research interests include 2.5D face recognition, 2.5D geometric feature processing, pattern recognition and deep learning.

Arif Ullah is currently doing a postdoc with the Centre for Intelligent Cloud Computing, Multimedia University. He is a dedicated academic and researcher with a robust background in Computer Science. He earned his PhD from Universiti Tun Hussein Onn Malaysia (UTHM) where he developed a hybrid algorithm for energy-efficient virtual machine load balancing in cloud computing. His research interests include machine learning, deep learning, IoT, cloud computing, evolutionary algorithms and database systems.

Bello Sani Yahaya holds a PhD in Business Administration and expertise in IT and marketing. Bello has a multidisciplinary background spanning banking, education and economic forecasting using neural networks. His technical certifications in networking and data analysis further enhance his analytical expertise.

Chia-Hong Yap, a Computer Science (AI) graduate from Multimedia University, has experience in website development and object detection projects. Skilled in AI applications, he combines technical expertise with a strong academic foundation, demonstrating a history of excellence in his studies.

Lim Ke Yin is currently pursuing her PhD in Information Technology at the Faculty of Information Science and Technology, Multimedia University (MMU), Malaysia. Her research interests include machine learning, deep learning, Internet of Things and embedded devices.

Sumendra Yogarayan is a senior lecturer in the Faculty of Information Science and Technology, Multimedia University. He graduated from Multimedia University (MMU) with a PhD in Information Technology in 2023. His research and teaching interests include intelligent transportation systems, wireless communication, ad hoc networks, machine learning, Internet of Things, embedded device and sensors. He has published 47 journals, 18 conference proceedings and 6 book chapters.

Li Wen Yow is currently a postgraduate student at the Multimedia University, Malaysia. With her background in bioinformatics, she focuses her research on the application and development of machine learning techniques for genomic analyses.

1

Resilience Thinking Artificial Intelligence Integration Framework

Umar Ali Bukar and Radhwan Sneesl

Introduction

Society is rapidly moving towards an era of coexistence between humans and artificial intelligence (AI). This technological advancement is revolutionising various industries, including healthcare, education, finance and transportation, by enhancing the accuracy and efficiency of numerous tasks. However, alongside these benefits, AI also raises significant ethical concerns, creating a complex ethical landscape across different sectors (Tippins et al., 2021; Gaur & Sahoo, 2022; Li et al., 2022; Guleria et al., 2023; Dwivedi et al., 2023; Salloum, 2024; Bukar et al., 2024b, 2024c, 2024d, 2024a). When used efficiently and effectively, AI solutions have the potential to optimise quality of life, foster innovation and reduce environmental pressures. The continuous integration of AI into our daily lives has led to the development of solutions designed to improve user convenience and satisfaction. Tools like ChatGPT and Bard are examples of AI technologies that demonstrate the capability to interact and respond like humans. Today, AI is recognised as a key driver of the future, significantly influencing the development of smart cities and intelligent living environments.

The term "artificial intelligence" is a buzzword that describes a complex intelligent system that behaves or answers like a human, or that is associated with both a property or quality to perform this certain capability (Samoili et al., 2020; Gabriel, 2020; Legg & Hutter, 2007). An intelligent system refers to an advanced computer system that can gather, analyse and respond to data from its environment, and can learn from experience and adapt accordingly. As a result of its capability, AI has become a strategic area of importance and is identified as a potential key driver of economic development, as highlighted in the European strategy on AI (Samoili et al., 2020). Similarly, AI has become a priority for national governments across various countries, resulting in the formulation of dedicated AI strategies. However, discussing

DOI: 10.1201/9781003509196-1

AI necessitates considering various aspects, this chapter aims to provide an overview of the global AI landscape, focusing particularly on the concept of resilience in the face of rapid AI advancements and how resilience can be used to counter the development of AI effectively.

Accordingly, the chapter introduces the concept of resilience as a critical framework for navigating the AI landscape and ensuring a sustainable future. Resilience, in this context, refers to the ability of systems and societies to absorb, adapt to and transform in response to the changes introduced by AI technologies. This concept was motivated by existing work (Bukar et al., 2024b) through the concept of Risk, Reward, Resilience (RRR) framework (Robert, 2023). The RRR framework suggests that merely considering risk or reward in isolation when creating or introducing policy is insufficient; policymakers must internalise both elements and understand how they interact with and impact resilience over time. This understanding is crucial for determining the likelihood of survival and success in a sustainable society due to AI advancements. While risk, reward and resilience are interconnected, this chapter discusses resilience thinking as the central focus when considering the societal impacts of AI.

Background

The progression of AI brings with it a myriad of ethical concerns that extend beyond what many could have imagined, prompting numerous stakeholders to call for a reassessment of AI initiatives (Tippins et al., 2021; Gaur & Sahoo, 2022; Li et al., 2022; Guleria et al., 2023; Dwivedi et al., 2023; Salloum, 2024; Bukar et al., 2024b, 2024c, 2024d, 2024a). Historically, technological advancements have often sparked significant concerns. For instance, the introduction of cars led to the development of seatbelts to curtail accidents (Robertson, 1996; Cohen & Einav, 2003), electricity brought about rigorous regulations to ensure safety (Huber, 1986; Alonzo, 2009), and the advent of printers and social media raised issues regarding misinformation (Bertot et al., 2012; Posetti & Matthews, 2018), leading to the creation of new norms, laws and institutions to mitigate these risks. Drawing from past experiences with technology, it becomes clear that to address the challenges posed by AI tools, there is a need to establish norms, regulations, practices and institutions designed to ensure society can withstand potential threats from AI, a concept referred to "resilience" in this chapter. Hence, "resilience" is not just about surviving disruptions but also about thriving amidst them. It is about building systems and societies that can adapt to new challenges and leverage them as opportunities for growth and innovation. In the context of AI, resilience involves the capacity to absorb the ethical and operational challenges posed by AI, adapt to these changes, and transform societal structures to better integrate AI in a way that aligns with human values and goals. As AI tools continue to evolve and impact various practices, resilience thinking becomes essential. As a result, the proceeding discusses the AI architecture, applications and integration, as well as the Resilience Thinking Artificial Intelligence Integration Framework.

AI Architecture

The framework of AI Architecture is shown in Figure 1.1, devised from the work of Dong et al. (2020) where AI acts as a critical component within various domains of modern society, such as safety, healthcare, education, legislation, environment, and politics or government (see AI application areas in Figure 1.2 and AI Integration in Figure 1.3). These interdisciplinary factors can either constrain or promote the development of AI systems, reflecting the interconnected nature of AI in societal progress. The core structure of AI Architecture is composed of three layers surrounding the stakeholders: infrastructure layer, technology layer and service layer. The outermost layer

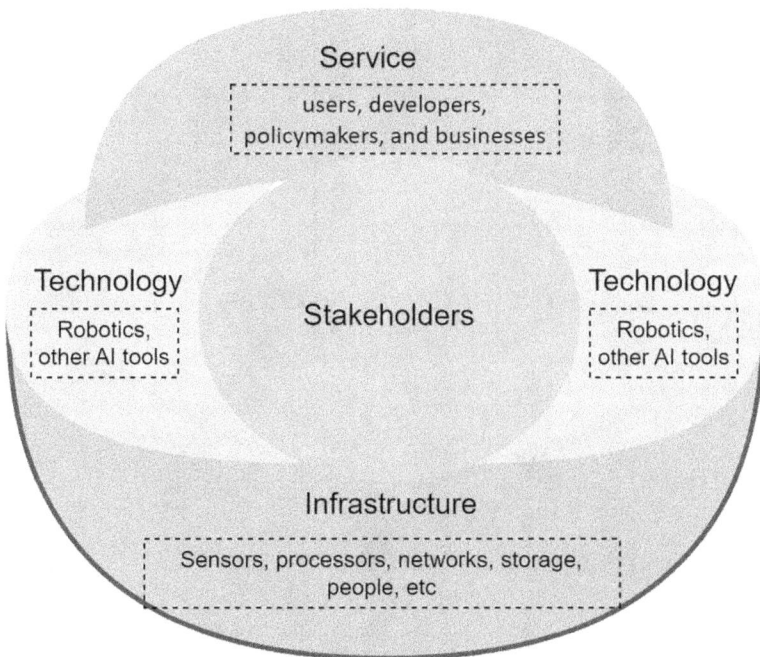

FIGURE 1.1
The AI Architecture, emphasising its foundational layers, stakeholder interactions, and how AI services are structured to meet diverse needs within society.

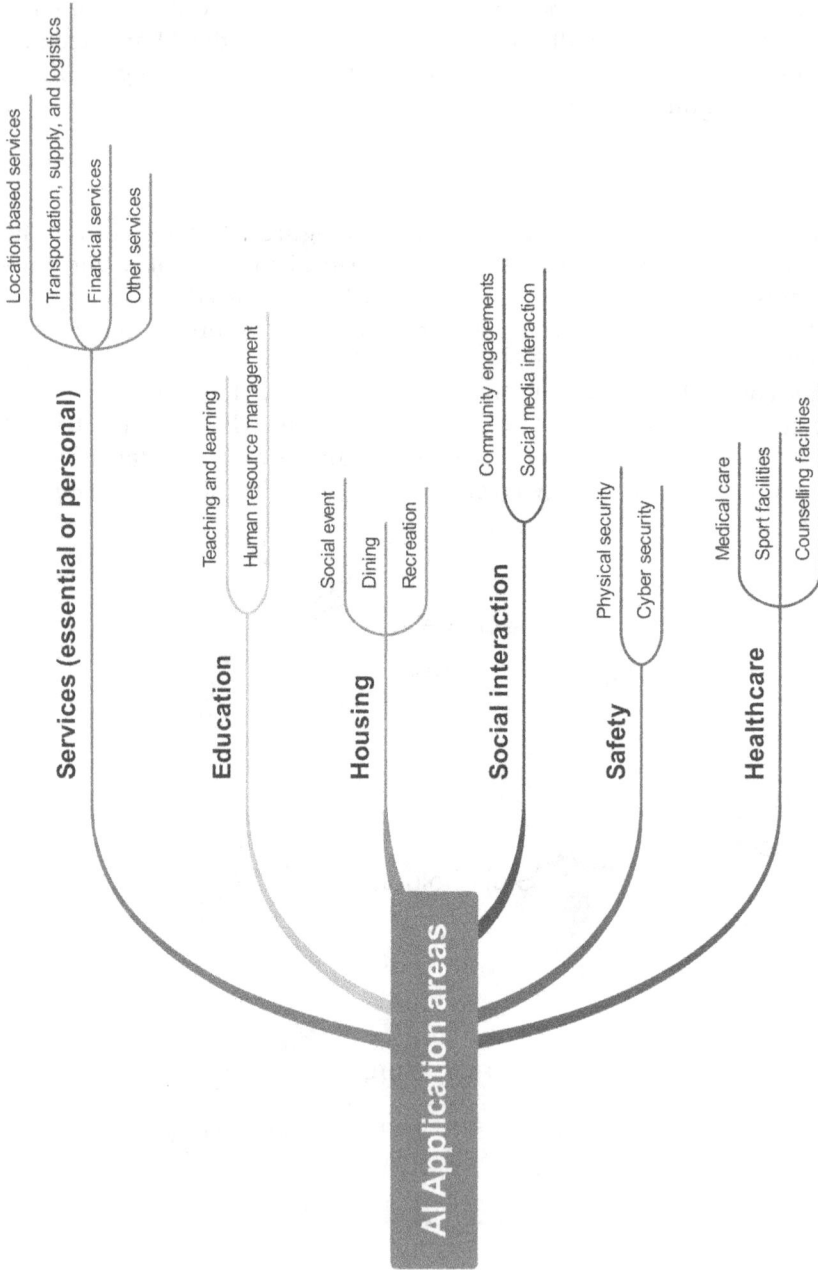

FIGURE 1.2
Perspectives of AI Applications Areas in the Society.

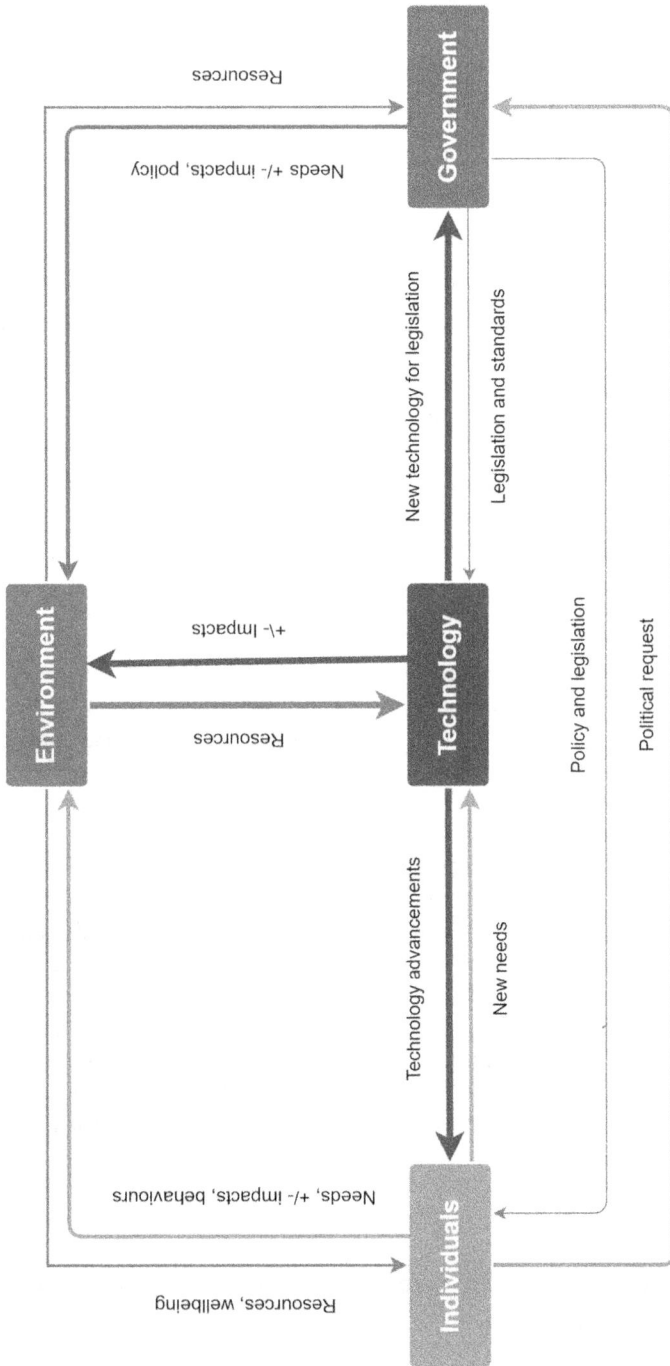

FIGURE 1.3
Schematic representation of the agents and their roles towards the development of AI: The diagram represents the roles and interactions between technology, individuals, government and the environment, and it places more emphasis on the feedback loops and systemic impacts, which align with AI's transformative role in society.

provides the underlying infrastructure essential for AI systems, while the innermost layer includes elements that directly interact with stakeholders. The framework places stakeholders at the centre, signifying that while not all AI system activities directly connect with them, they should be designed with the stakeholders' interests as the focal point. The specific needs of the stakeholders and the three layers of AI Architecture are further elaborated in the following paragraphs.

AI Stakeholders

The planning, development, maintenance and deployment of AI systems involve multiple stakeholders, including users, developers, policymakers, businesses and society at large. Feedback from these stakeholders is vital for the evolution of AI development. Given the diverse roles and contributions of each stakeholder group, it is crucial to fully understand their perspectives to maximise the value and potential of AI. The needs and contributions of each type of stakeholder within AI systems can vary, and an inclusive approach ensures that AI solutions are both robust and aligned with societal needs.

Infrastructure Layer

A strong and adaptable infrastructure is essential for AI development, as it forms the foundation for the other layers. This infrastructure must include both technological components (such as computing power, data storage and communication networks) and human resources (engineers, data scientists and system architects) who design, build and maintain AI systems. The required infrastructure might involve cloud-based solutions, distributed networks, high-performance computing clusters and data centres, ensuring that AI systems can operate efficiently and at scale. New AI infrastructures could be built from scratch for emerging applications, allowing developers to integrate cutting-edge AI technologies from the beginning. Alternatively, existing infrastructures can be retrofitted to support AI functionalities, leveraging the current systems while introducing upgrades that balance cost, performance and scalability. This phased approach is crucial for organisations transitioning from traditional systems to AI-enabled architectures, ensuring that resources are allocated effectively to achieve the desired level of AI capability.

Technology Layer

The technology layer is the intermediary between the infrastructure and the direct applications of AI-facilitated services. Although it may not engage stakeholders directly, it plays a critical role in enabling AI systems to function smoothly. This layer includes algorithms, models, and data processing technologies that form the backbone of AI systems. By leveraging this layer, AI applications can transform traditional processes and overcome obstacles such as limitations in speed, accuracy and scale. Accordingly, the implementation of AI technologies will vary based on specific applications and contexts, as different environments and industries have unique requirements. For instance, AI systems deployed in healthcare may focus on predictive diagnostics and personalised medicine, while those in transportation may emphasise real-time navigation and autonomous systems. The effective deployment of AI technology depends on optimising resources, ensuring privacy and enhancing security while addressing budgetary and operational constraints.

Service Layer

The service layer comprises the AI applications that directly interact with stakeholders. In this context, AI systems should be designed to meet diverse stakeholder needs while achieving their primary objective such as delivering improved and more efficient services. The stakeholder-centred approach in AI systems means that services must be tailored to the specific use cases and preferences of individuals, businesses and organisations. Understanding stakeholder requirements involves gathering data through surveys, user feedback and real-world case studies, which inform the ongoing refinement and development of AI services. Moreover, the primary aim of AI services is to enhance the performance and outcomes across sectors. Whether it is improving customer experiences in e-commerce, streamlining processes in manufacturing, or optimising decision-making in government, AI services should be evaluated based on their ability to contribute directly or indirectly to achieving the desired outcomes. This requires careful assessment of the risks, benefits and potential impacts of each AI service and addressing different aspects of stakeholder needs.

AI Applications

The primary objective of any AI system is to enhance human life by delivering more efficient, personalised and intelligent services. AI is no longer just a buzzword; it has become an integral part of our daily lives, influencing diverse sectors such as transportation, healthcare, banking, retail, entertainment and e-commerce. As highlighted by Min-Allah and Alrashed (2020), various services and applications are now revolutionising intelligent and smart solutions, offering unprecedented advancements in service delivery. Significant projects, like enabling secure electronic transactions through cashless payments and e-wallet systems using smart cards and devices, have become defining features of modern living, powered by AI technologies. These innovations streamline daily interactions and facilitate convenience on a broad scale. With the rapid pace of technological progress, even intelligent solutions quickly become outdated. Many institutions are now incorporating AI-based services, such as facial recognition systems, into their operations. An example is live audio translation services, which enhance accessibility in conferences, theatres and public spaces. Accordingly, data derived from social interactions and networking platforms can be analysed for insights, driving intelligent decision-making. The ultimate goal of any society is to enhance the quality of life and well-being, making AI solutions essential for optimising daily activities and improving public services.

Real-time data fed to AI-powered dashboards enables organisations to make informed, data-driven decisions. AI technologies can also be integrated with existing physical infrastructure to deliver enhanced services. For example, AI-enabled surveillance cameras in buildings can predict structural durability, helping determine when maintenance is required. Also, smart occupancy tracking helps monitor building usage and improves safety during emergencies by providing real-time data on the number of people in a specific location. This can be crucial in disaster situations like fires, tsunamis or earthquakes, allowing for efficient recovery planning, particularly if vulnerable individuals or valuable resources are present. Similarly, AI attendance systems in schools can use smart classroom cameras to automatically mark students' presence, improving efficiency by saving time and streamlining resources for better use. For real-time decision-making, AI-driven systems can be employed across various sectors. For instance, in public spaces, AI-based navigation tools can assist individuals in finding routes or services, while personalised notifications can be sent to citizens about changes in local events or infrastructure updates. Likewise, public safety can be enhanced through AI-powered surveillance systems, such as smart cameras capable of real-time threat detection and analysis. To ensure these applications maintain user trust, the implementation of privacy-preserving AI technologies is crucial. Blockchain-based approaches are gaining traction for safeguarding data integrity and privacy, particularly in smart cities and other AI-integrated communities. These methods provide transparent and secure ways to handle sensitive information without compromising individual rights.

All the core application areas of AI are essential components of a well-functioning AI-powered ecosystem. Insights gained through AI applications can aid governments and organisations in strategic planning. For instance, AI in transportation systems can issue alerts to commuters about service schedules and provide statistical analysis of traffic flow, usage patterns and peak times. Similarly, updates regarding changes in public services or events can be delivered in real time through AI-powered platforms. In addition, smart mobility is one of the leading features of AI-driven societies, generating vast amounts of data from ride-sharing services, public transport and traffic management systems. This data can be harnessed for resource optimisation, smoother traffic flow and more effective public service delivery.

AI can also support services such as utility payments, food deliveries and medical services, streamlining everyday tasks. Moreover, AI-driven analytics can foster better social interactions in both physical and digital spaces. By using facial recognition technologies, public behaviour data can be collected and analysed to offer insights that improve community services, safety measures and engagement strategies. Figure 1.2 illustrates how AI supports various areas within a broader societal context, enabling a more connected, secure and efficient community.

Integration of AI

The integration of AI into society is revolutionising the way individuals, businesses and governments operate, creating a more connected and data-driven world. AI technologies are being embedded across diverse sectors, transforming processes, enhancing efficiency and offering innovative solutions to complex societal challenges. This profound shift makes AI more deeply intertwined with everyday life, impacting decision-making, governance and human interactions, which brings both opportunities for growth and the need for careful consideration of its ethical and societal implications. Vinuesa et al. (2020) schematically illustrate the complex interplay between AI and society, as depicted in Figure 1.3, which represents the key agents and their roles in shaping the development of AI, highlighting the dynamic relationships between individuals, technology, government and the environment. The use of thicker arrows in the diagram denotes areas of faster change or more significant influence, emphasising the rate of transformation within certain interactions.

Accordingly, technology, including AI systems and their developers, serves as a primary driver of change, influencing how individuals work, communicate and interact with both each other and their environment. This influence extends to the government, where new technological advancements prompt the need for updated regulations, piloting and testing frameworks to ensure safe and ethical deployment. Additionally, technology developers actively engage with governments through lobbying efforts and policy influence, influencing changes in regulatory initiatives. The interaction between individuals and technology is bidirectional. On one hand, technical developments shape people's daily lives by introducing new tools and systems that alter their behaviour and decision-making processes. On the other hand, individuals create new demands and challenges that push the boundaries of technological innovation, requiring developers to design solutions that address these evolving needs.

Moreover, the government plays a crucial role by enacting legislation and standards to regulate the responsible use of technology. This ensures that AI and other technologies are developed and deployed in ways that benefit society while minimising potential risks. As societal needs shift, individuals increasingly call upon governments to introduce new laws and policies that reflect the evolving technological landscape and address emerging ethical concerns related to AI. Similarly, the environment is an integral component of the AI-society interaction. It provides the natural resources necessary for the development and operation of technology, from raw materials for manufacturing AI systems to the energy required for data processing and storage. At the same time, technology has a direct impact on the environment, both positively (e.g., through the development of AI solutions that mitigate climate change) and negatively (e.g., through the environmental costs of manufacturing and energy consumption).

Moreover, individuals and governments affect the environment through their decisions, actions, and policies. Governments may implement environmental regulations aimed at minimising the ecological impact of AI technologies, while individuals' consumption patterns and technological choices shape demand for resources and influence environmental sustainability. In particular, the environment, acting as the underlying foundation for all interactions, also represents the planetary boundaries, which are the ecological limits within which humanity and technology must operate to maintain a balanced and sustainable ecosystem. The feedback loops between technology, individuals, government and the environment illustrate the complex interdependencies, where advancements in one domain trigger changes in others. This interaction underscores the need for a holistic approach to AI development, such as RTAIF, which is the central focus of this chapter, where technological progress is aligned with social, ethical and environmental considerations to ensure a sustainable future.

Resilience Thinking AI Framework

This section discusses the theoretical framework of the resilience ability of the individual and society as a result of AI integration. The resilience framework can be visualised as a concentric model, where each layer represents a different level of people or organisation resilience to AI integration. These layers are interconnected but can create resilience independently or in combination (Roberts, 2023). Accordingly, at the innermost circle is the absorption. This layer represents the core ability of people and organisations to withstand the challenges posed by AI without significant changes. The absorption layer emphasises stability and immediate response mechanisms that help maintain the status quo. Secondly, adaptation is positioned at the middle circle layer, surrounding the absorption layer. This signifies the ability of people and organisations to adjust and modify their operations and structures in response to AI integration. Adaptation represents flexibility and learning, highlighting how people can change incrementally to better suit new conditions. Thirdly, at the outer circle lies the transformation, which represents the capability of people or organisations to undergo fundamental changes, rethinking and reshaping their core structures and processes. This layer emphasises innovation and long-term strategic changes that can lead to a more resilient future.

Moreover, the white double-edge arrows show the progression from one stage to another, as well as indicate feedback loops, demonstrating that people and organisations can move back and forth between stages as they evolve and face new challenges. Finally, the uttermost layer consists of the external environment, which represents external factors that influence resilience. This could include economic conditions, regulatory frameworks, technological advancements and societal megatrends. Accordingly, Figure 1.4 illustrates the Resilience Thinking AI Integration Framework, known as RTAIF, with its three core components: Absorption, Adaptation and Transformation. Each concentric circle represents a different level of resilience, highlighting how people and stakeholders can respond and evolve in the face of AI existence. Nevertheless, people's resilience as a result of AI integration and usage is built on dynamic capacities that enable people and society to navigate and thrive amidst change. These capacities, as illustrated in Figure 1.4, are essential for maintaining functionality and ensuring continuity in the face of continuous integration of AI, which are seen as threats to society with myriads

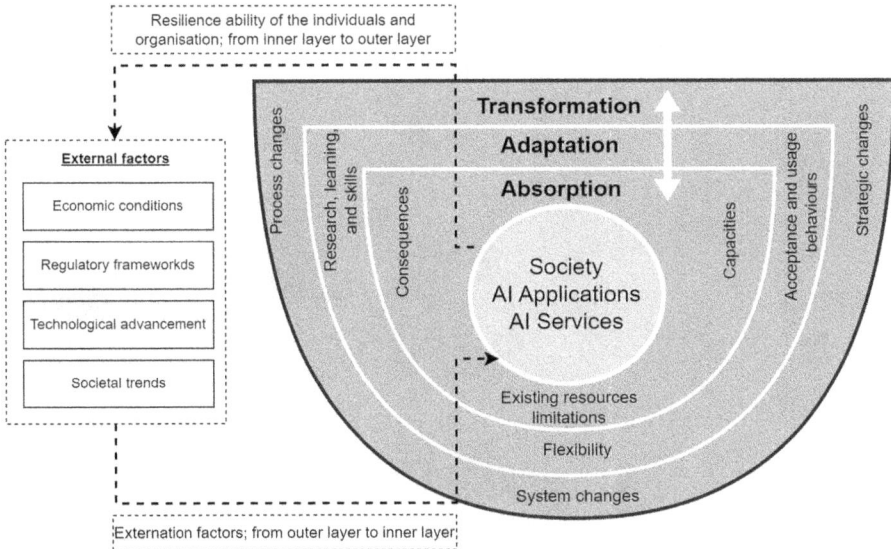

FIGURE 1.4
Resilience Thinking AI Integration Framework (RTAIF), illustrating the three core components; absorption, adaptation and transformation and how external factors influence them.

of ethical concerns. Each of these drivers plays a crucial role in shaping the resilience of the people and society, allowing individuals to withstand, adjust to and evolve from the challenges posed by AI integration in various sectors.

Absorption

Absorption is the first line of resistance that individuals and society exhibit within the resilience framework concerning AI. It represents the ability to withstand the challenges posed by AI without experiencing significant negative consequences. This capacity involves maintaining core functions and structures despite AI integration in various sectors, effectively protecting against immediate impacts. Individuals or organisations with strong absorption capabilities can manage AI-related ethical concerns without substantial changes to their operations or structure. This may involve utilising existing resources (such as experts and detection tools), capacities, and strategies (like policies) to mitigate the potential effects of AI. Accordingly, absorption serves as the foundational layer in the resilience framework, reflecting the capacity of individuals, organisations and societies to handle the immediate impacts of AI while preserving stability. This concept emphasises the ability to sustain core functions and structures in the face of disruptions and ethical concerns brought about by AI integration.

Accordingly, absorption is a key component of the technology integration model, as illustrated in Figure 1.5. Similar to other technologies, the integration of AI involves three stages: adoption – the initial use of the technology in specific contexts; diffusion – the spread of technology across different settings and users; and absorption – the widespread adoption of technology

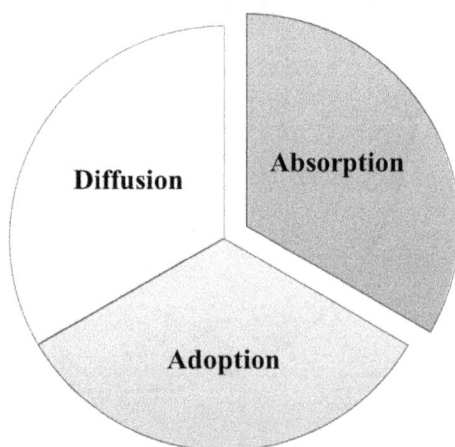

FIGURE 1.5
The three Elements of the Technology Integration Model.

across diverse contexts (Davis, 1989; Rogers, 2014; Venkatesh & Davis, 2000; Ali et al., 2023). The absorption of AI technology is influenced by various factors such as system, organisational, and regional infrastructure, connectivity status, and social and cultural similarities between regions (Ali et al., 2023). The idea of absorption within the resilience framework thus encompasses a broad range of examples and perspectives, highlighting the importance of enduring and managing the initial impacts of AI without major adverse effects. A few examples of absorption across various sectors are discussed as follows:

- Absorption was observed by some universities or academic journals that have introduced strategies to identify AI-generated submissions, and they have also updated their academic integrity codes to explicitly address AI misuse, demonstrating their absorption capacity.
- A hospital that introduces an AI-based diagnostic tool might initially encounter resistance from staff concerned about job security or the accuracy of AI predictions. However, through proper training, transparent communication and gradual implementation, the hospital can absorb these concerns, allowing staff to see AI as a complementary tool rather than a threat.
- A bank using AI to detect fraudulent transactions might face challenges such as false positives or privacy concerns. However, by continuously refining the bank's AI algorithms and maintaining transparency with customers about data use and protection, the bank can absorb these issues without significant disruptions to its business operations or customer trust.
- A manufacturing factory introducing AI-powered robots for assembly line work might face initial pushback from workers fearing job losses. However, using a phased approach to integration, offering retraining programmes and involving employees in the transition process, the company can absorb these concerns and maintain a stable workforce.
- The recent EU AI Act that aims to harmonise rules on AI by following a "risk-based" approach is the first global AI Act, which set a global standard for AI regulation. This helps prevent misuse while still allowing the beneficial aspects of AI, such as enhanced public safety, to be realised.

Adaptation

Adaptation goes a step further than absorption by allowing individuals or organisations to respond proactively to the ethical issues and concerns associated with AI integration. Unlike absorption, which aims to maintain the status quo, adaptation involves making changes that enable individuals and organisations to continue functioning, albeit in a modified form. This capacity is essential, especially given the enduring presence of AI and the ongoing coexistence between AI and humanity, which necessitates continuous adjustments. Moreover, adaptation is marked by flexibility and the ability to modify existing practices, strategies and structures to suit new conditions. It requires learning from past experiences, recognising emerging patterns and implementing changes that enhance the individual and organisation's ability to cope with ongoing or future challenges. Adaptive communities are characterised by their ability to pivot and reconfigure resources and processes to align with changing circumstances. A key strategy in adaptation is conducting research and generating knowledge to understand the behaviours of AI users and their integration, thereby fostering the development of more responsible AI. As a crucial aspect of the resilience framework, adaptation extends beyond simply absorbing the impacts of AI integration. It involves actively adjusting to new circumstances by altering behaviours, strategies and structures to better align with the evolving technological landscape. This proactive approach enables individuals, organisations and societies not only to cope with AI-related challenges but also to harness AI's benefits more effectively.

The typical adaptation policy cycle (Leitner et al., 2020) is presented in Figure 1.6. The end goal is to enhance people and organisation adaptive capacity, strengthen resilience and reduce individual vulnerabilities due to AI integration. Given the impact of AI integration, the question is not whether

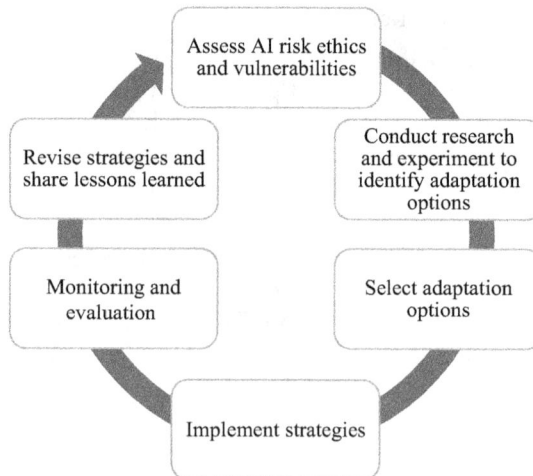

FIGURE 1.6
Adaptation Policy Cycle for AI Integration.

adaptation is necessary, but what are the adaptation options to increase public resilience. The discussion of adaptation within the resilience framework can reveal how various sectors apply these principles in practice and gain insight into how they adjust to the ever-changing technological environment enabled by AI. A few examples are covered in the following:

- Universities that have faced challenges with Gen-AI tools (ChatGPT, Gemini, etc.) generated content (such as essays written by AI tools) might adapt by shifting from traditional written assignments to more interactive, discussion-based assessments. They might also incorporate AI literacy into their curricula, teaching students not only how to use AI tools effectively but also how to critically assess AI-generated information for biases and inaccuracies.

- A hospital might adapt to the introduction of AI diagnostic tools (Google DeepMind's Streams, Zebra Medical Vision, etc.) by changing its workflow to include AI-assisted diagnosis as a preliminary step, followed by human review.

- Financial institutions might adapt to AI's capabilities by incorporating machine learning algorithms into their fraud detection systems, which adaptively learn from new fraud patterns to prevent losses.

- A manufacturing plant might adapt to AI integration by reconfiguring its assembly lines to include AI-powered robots while retraining human workers for roles that require more complex decision-making and oversight.

- A government might adapt to the rise of AI surveillance technologies by introducing new privacy laws that protect citizens' rights while allowing for the beneficial use of AI in public safety (e.g., GDPR, COPPA, EU AI Act).

Transformation

Transformation represents the highest level of resilience to AI integration within society. This stage involves fundamentally altering how individuals, organisations and societies operate, not just to absorb and adapt to changes but to emerge stronger and better equipped for the future. Transformation is about rethinking and reshaping to create new pathways and opportunities, often driven by a desire to address the root causes of AI's ethical issues and build long-term resilience. Characterised by profound and systemic change, transformation is a strategic, proactive process aimed at reinventing how people and organisations function and what they prioritise. This capacity requires visionary leadership, innovative thinking and a willingness to challenge and change existing norms, practices and policies. Accordingly, transformative actions are typically bold and comprehensive, addressing not only immediate ethical concerns but also underlying vulnerabilities and opportunities for growth. This process necessitates deep, systemic changes that fundamentally alter existing structures, behaviours and mindsets. It demands a strategic and forward-looking approach, coupled with a readiness to challenge and reform established norms.

Figure 1.7 presents six necessary conditions for successful transformation for an individual or organisation (Murty and Gorur, 2023). The first condition is communication, emphasising that transparent communication facilitates open, bilateral conversations between leadership and employees, fostering trust and collaboration. Secondly, a change in mindset is essential for digital transformation, requiring individuals to constantly question and challenge current ways of working and to learn new processes and skills. Thirdly, to be adaptable means to embrace new ways of working and to be comfortable in uncomfortable situations, responding flexibly to change. Moreover, people with the right mindset are crucial to transformation success, as they can change practices based on evidence, challenge the status quo, and align with the mission. In addition, selecting appropriate tools and technologies involves understanding the organisation's needs, ensuring efficiency and being open to changing tools as needed. Finally, process improvement argues that identifying and addressing gaps in processes is essential for maintaining high-quality outputs, requiring continuous improvement.

Numerous examples across various sectors illustrate how AI integration has driven transformational change in society, fundamentally altering how

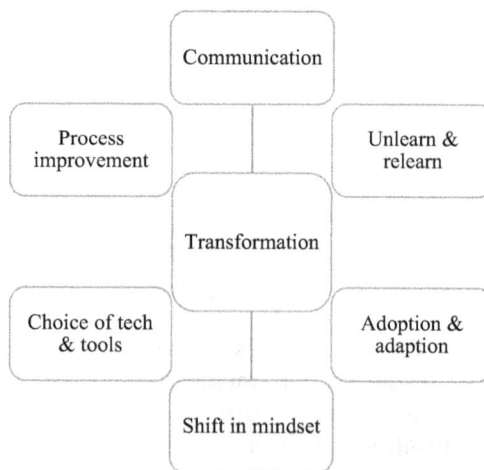

FIGURE 1.7
Six Conditions for Successful Transformation in AI Era.

various sectors are operating and positioning for future success. These examples are briefly explained in the following:

- In education, universities and schools might shift from traditional, knowledge-based curricula to competency-based education that emphasises critical thinking, creativity, and emotional intelligence skills that AI cannot easily replicate. This transformation encourages students to engage in higher-order thinking, problem-solving and ethical reasoning, which are crucial in a world where AI handles routine tasks.

- Healthcare systems are transformed by leveraging AI for predictive analytics to identify at-risk patients and intervene before health issues become severe. This approach shifts the focus from reactive to proactive care, using AI to analyse large datasets and identify patterns that human practitioners might miss.

- Financial institutions might transform by using AI to provide personalised financial advice, leveraging algorithms to analyse customers' spending habits, risk profiles and financial goals. AI can also be used to enhance fraud detection and cybersecurity, transforming the way banks protect customer data and transactions.

- Manufacturing companies can adopt AI-driven automation and robotics, moving towards a "smart factory" model. This transformation goes beyond merely replacing human workers with robots; it involves reengineering production lines to optimise efficiency, reduce waste and enhance product quality.

- Governments could transform by adopting AI to enhance public service delivery, using machine learning algorithms to analyse data and identify areas for improvement in healthcare, education and social services.

Conclusion

The integration of AI into society is inevitable, bringing both opportunities and challenges. This chapter discusses AI architecture, providing insights into key components such as stakeholders, infrastructure, technology and the service layer. Various AI applications are explored across sectors like education, housing, and essential and personal services. Additionally, the chapter examines the interaction between various elements in AI integration, represented by key agents and their roles in shaping AI development. It highlights the dynamic relationships between individuals, technology, government and the environment. Furthermore, this chapter conceptualised a framework, focusing on resilience to better prepare for and adapt to the transformative effects of AI technologies. Emphasising resilience enables societies to not only withstand the challenges posed by AI but also to harness these challenges as catalysts for growth and innovation, paving the way for a sustainable future. The drivers of resilience – absorption, adaptation and transformation – provide a concept for understanding and building resilience amidst AI challenges. The components are not mutually exclusive but rather complementary processes that can occur simultaneously or sequentially, depending on the nature of the issues and challenges and the context of the sectors.

In particular, the absorption within the resilience framework is about readiness and robustness. It involves leveraging existing resources, capacities, and strategies to buffer against the immediate impacts of AI. By enhancing knowledge, connectivity and flexibility, individuals, organisations and societies can develop stronger absorption capacities, enabling them to handle the challenges posed by AI integration effectively. The ability to absorb AI disruptions without substantial alterations to core functions or structures is essential for ensuring a smooth transition into a future where AI plays a central role in various aspects of life. Secondly, adaptation in the context of AI resilience is about more than just coping with change; it's about proactively evolving to thrive in an AI-integrated world. It requires flexibility, the ability to learn from past experiences, and the willingness to modify existing practices and strategies to meet new challenges head-on. By fostering an environment that encourages adaptation, societies can build resilience and ensure that they are not only prepared for the future but also capable of leveraging AI's full potential to drive innovation, efficiency, and positive change. Finally, transformation represents the highest level of resilience, enabling societies to not just survive but thrive in the face of AI integration. The transformation requires a fundamental rethinking of how individuals, organisations and systems operate, focusing on long-term sustainability, ethical considerations and inclusive growth. By embracing transformation, societies can harness the full potential of AI, turning challenges into opportunities and building a future that is resilient, equitable and innovative.

References

Ali, S. S., Kaur, R., & Khan, S. (2023). Identification of innovative technology enablers and drone technology determinants adoption: a graph theory matrix analysis framework. *Operations Management Research*, 16(2), 830–852.

Alonzo, R. J. (2009). *Electrical codes, standards, recommended practices and regulations: an examination of relevant safety considerations*. William Andrew.

Bertot, J. C., Jaeger, P. T., & Hansen, D. (2012). The impact of polices on government social media usage: Issues, challenges, and recommendations. *Government Information Quarterly*, 29(1), 30–40.

Bukar, U. A., Sayeed, M. S., Razak, S. F. A., Yogarayan, S., & Amodu, O. A. (2024b). An integrative decision-making framework to guide policies on regulating ChatGPT usage. *PeerJ Computer Science*, 10, e1845.

Bukar, U. A., Sayeed, M. S., Razak, S. F. A., Yogarayan, S., Amodu, O. A., & Raja Mahmood, R. A. (2024a). Text analysis on early reactions to ChatGPT as a tool for academic progress or exploitation. *SN Computer Science*, 5(4), 366.

Bukar, U. A., Sayeed, M. S., Razak, S. F. A., Yogarayan, S., & Sneesl, R. (2024c). *Decision-making framework for the utilization of generative artificial intelligence in education: A case study of ChatGPT*. IEEE Access.

Bukar, U. A., Sayeed, M. S., Razak, S. F. A., Yogarayan, S., & Sneesl, R. (2024d). Prioritizing ethical conundrums in the utilization of ChatGPT in education through an analytical hierarchical approach. *Education Sciences*, 14(9), 959.

Cohen, A., & Einav, L. (2003). The effects of mandatory seat belt laws on driving behavior and traffic fatalities. *Review of Economics and Statistics*, 85(4), 828–843.

Davis, F. D. (1989). Perceived usefulness, perceived ease of use, and user acceptance of information technology. *MIS Quarterly*, 13, 319–340.

Dong, Z. Y., Zhang, Y., Yip, C., Swift, S., & Beswick, K. (2020). Smart campus: definition, framework, technologies, and services. *IET Smart Cities*, 2(1), 43–54.

Dwivedi, Y. K., Kshetri, N., Hughes, L., Slade, E. L., Jeyaraj, A., Kar, A. K., … & Wright, R. (2023). Opinion Paper: "So what if ChatGPT wrote it?" Multidisciplinary perspectives on opportunities, challenges and implications of generative conversational AI for research, practice and policy. *International Journal of Information Management*, 71, 102642.

Gabriel, I. (2020). Artificial intelligence, values, and alignment. *Minds and Machines*, 30(3), 411–437.

Gaur, L., & Sahoo, B. M. (2022). Explainable AI in ITS: Ethical concerns. In *Explainable artificial intelligence for intelligent transportation systems: Ethics and applications* (pp. 79–90). Cham: Springer International Publishing.

Guleria, A., Krishan, K., Sharma, V., & Kanchan, T. (2023). ChatGPT: ethical concerns and challenges in academics and research. *The Journal of Infection in Developing Countries*, 17(09), 1292–1299.

Huber, P. (1986). Electricity and the environment: In search of regulatory authority. *Harvard Law Review*, 100, 1002.

Legg, S., & Hutter, M. (2007). Universal intelligence: A definition of machine intelligence. *Minds and Machines*, 17, 391–444.

Leitner, M., Mäkinen, K., Vanneuville, W., Mysiak, J., Deacon, A., Torresan, S., … & Prutsch, A. (2020). *Monitoring and evaluation of national adaptation policies throughout the policy cycle*. Publications Office of the European Union.

Li, F., Ruijs, N., & Lu, Y. (2022). Ethics & AI: A systematic review on ethical concerns and related strategies for designing with AI in healthcare. *Ai*, 4(1), 28–53.

Min-Allah, N., & Alrashed, S. (2020). Smart campus—A sketch. *Sustainable Cities and Society*, 59, 102231.

Murty, S., & Gorur, S. (2023, July 20). Six necessary conditions for a successful digital transformation. *Thoughtworks*.

Posetti, J., & Matthews, A. (2018). A short guide to the history of 'fake news' and disinformation. *International Center for Journalists*, 7(2018), 2018.

Roberts, A. (2023). Risk, reward, and resilience framework: integrative policy making in a complex world. *Journal of International Economic Law*, 26(2), 233–265.

Robertson, L. S. (1996). Reducing death on the road: the effects of minimum safety standards, publicized crash tests, seat belts, and alcohol. *American Journal of Public Health*, 86(1), 31–34.

Rogers, E. M., Singhal, A., & Quinlan, M. M. (2014). Diffusion of innovations. In *An integrated approach to communication theory and research* (pp. 432–448). Routledge.

Salloum, S. A. (2024). AI Perils in Education: Exploring Ethical Concerns. *Artificial Intelligence in Education: The Power and Dangers of ChatGPT in the Classroom*, 669–675.

Samoili, S., Lopez, C., Gomez, G. E., De, P. G., Martinez-Plumed, F., & Delipetrev, B. (2020). AI watch. *Defining Artificial Intelligence*.

Tippins, N. T., Oswald, F. L., & McPhail, S. M. (2021). Scientific, legal, and ethical concerns about AI-based personnel selection tools: a call to action. *Personnel Assessment and Decisions*, 7(2), 1.

Venkatesh, V., & Davis, F. D. (2000). A theoretical extension of the technology acceptance model: Four longitudinal field studies. *Management Science*, 46(2), 186–204.

Vinuesa, R., Azizpour, H., Leite, I., Balaam, M., Dignum, V., Domisch, S., … & Fuso Nerini, F. (2020). The role of artificial intelligence in achieving the sustainable development goals. *Nature Communications*, 11(1), 1–10.

2

Alertness Analytics: AI-Enhanced Detection of Driver Fatigue and Intoxication

Sumendra Yogarayan, Siti Fatimah Abdul Razak, Jashila Nair Mogan, Afizan Azman and Avenaish Sivaprakasam

Introduction

Road safety is a critical global concern, with driver fatigue and intoxication accounting for a significant portion of traffic accidents (Maqbool et al., 2019; Hayley et al., 2021). According to the World Health Organization (WHO), approximately 1.3 million people die annually due to road traffic crashes, with drowsy driving and alcohol impairment being major contributors. In Asia, particularly in countries like Malaysia, the issue is especially alarming (Sohail et al., 2023; Ahmed et al., 2023; Jamaludin et al., 2021). The Malaysian Institute of Road Safety Research (MIROS) reports that driver fatigue is involved in 20–30% of road accidents in the country, while alcohol-related crashes constitute around 23% of traffic fatalities (Razak et al., 2022; Yusof et al., 2023).

According to an NHTSA study, teenage drivers are inherently at a greater risk for crashes and fatal crashes than all other age groups (Ferreira et al., 2024). Figure 2.1 shows that teen drivers have the highest involvement rate in fatal crashes of any other age group. On the other hand, according to Penland (2023), the study detailed that alcohol was detected in 40.7% of the related teen drivers, and 44% of the drivers were found to be positive for alcohol use. Figure 2.2 depicts that teen drivers were the most common victims of fatalities associated with alcohol consumption. Figure 2.3 shows the primary cause of road accidents in Malaysia as reported by Kurnia Insurance.

Traditional measures, such as breathalyser tests and manual checks, offer limited effectiveness in addressing these issues in real time. They typically react after a problem has already occurred, making them inadequate in preventing accidents (Khamis et al., 2023). The integration of artificial intelligence (AI), specifically deep learning, presents an advanced solution. By utilising large datasets, deep learning models can analyse a range of inputs

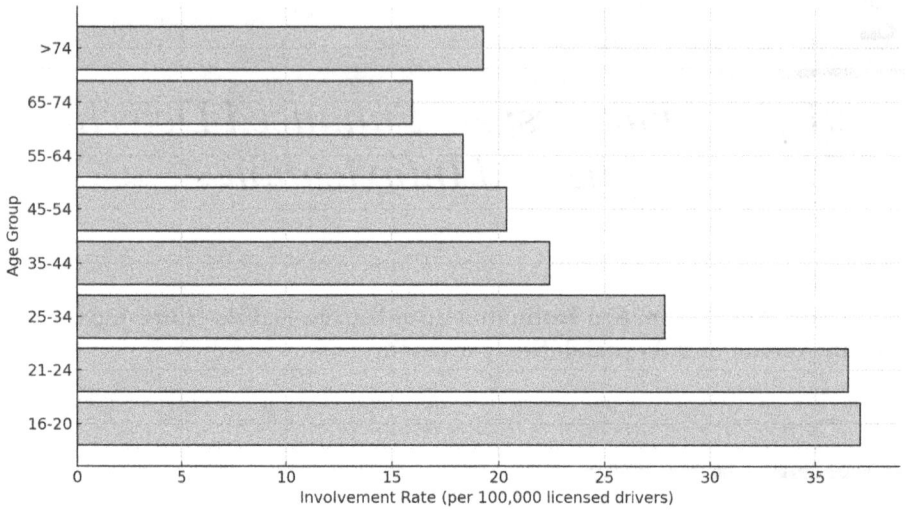

FIGURE 2.1
Fatal Crashes by Age Group (Duddu et al., 2019).

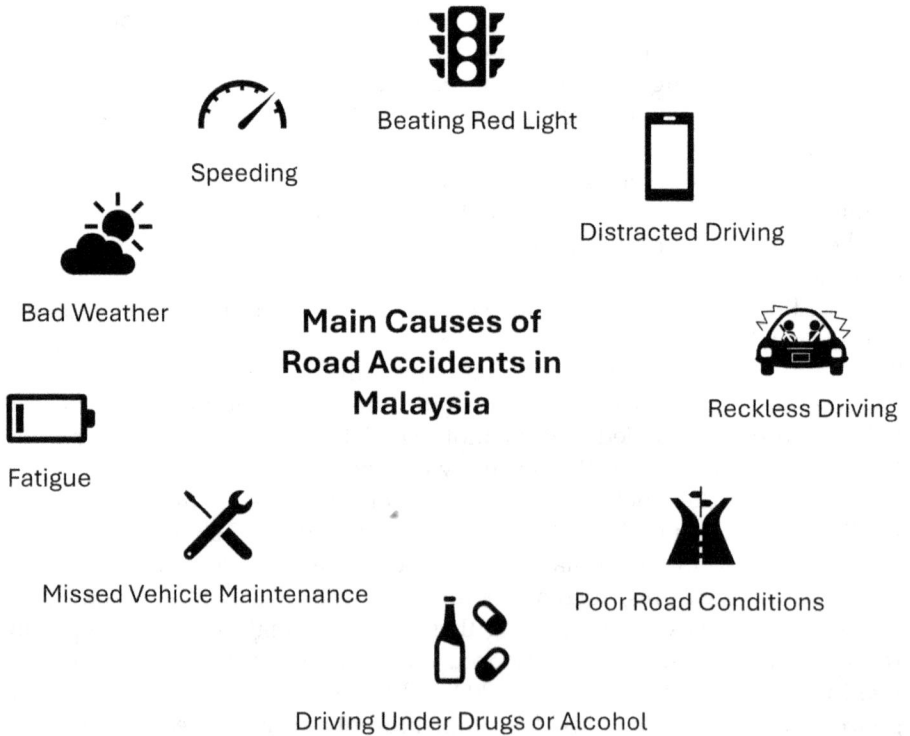

Speeding

Beating Red Light

Distracted Driving

Bad Weather

Main Causes of Road Accidents in Malaysia

Reckless Driving

Fatigue

Missed Vehicle Maintenance

Poor Road Conditions

Driving Under Drugs or Alcohol

FIGURE 2.2
Alcohol Positive Victims by Age Group (Papalimperi et al., 2019).

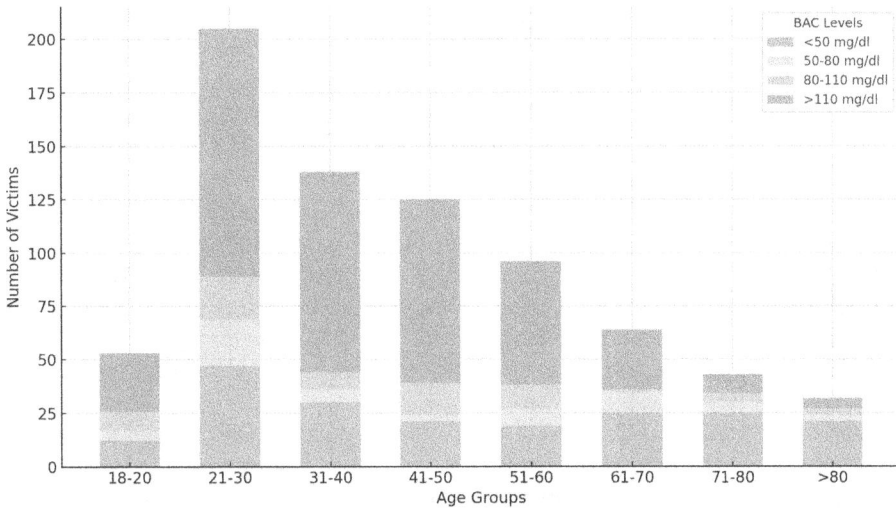

FIGURE 2.3
Primary Cause of Road Accidents in Malaysia (Kurnia Insurance, 2022).

from facial recognition data and eye movement patterns to subtle behavioural cues enabling the detection of fatigue and intoxication with high accuracy (Govindaraj et al., 2024; Debbarma et al., 2024; Liang et al., 2020).

The global push towards smarter and safer driving environments centres on the proactive capabilities of AI-driven systems (Rajput et al., 2024; Sarker, 2024; Jagatheesaperumal et al., 2024). By predicting unsafe situations before they become critical, these technologies move the focus from reactive measures to preventive strategies (Torbaghan et al., 2022; Fu et al., 2021). As AI continues to evolve, its application in real-time driver monitoring holds great potential to reduce accident rates and improve road safety.

In this chapter, we will explore the capabilities of deep learning in detecting driver drowsiness and intoxication, the challenges involved, and the impact these technologies can have, particularly in Malaysia. The discussion will focus on how AI can transform road safety by enabling intelligent, responsive and preventative driving systems for a safer future.

Literature Review

Causes of Driver Fatigue

Fatigue has numerous causes, both physiological and environmental. Internally, lack of quality sleep, sleep disorders (e.g., insomnia, sleep apnoea), and extended wakefulness are the primary drivers of drowsiness

(Silverman et al., 2022; Pérez-Carbonell et al., 2022). Externally, factors such as long driving hours, nighttime driving, poor road conditions and high stress levels contribute significantly to fatigue. The time of day is also crucial; most fatigue-related accidents occur between midnight and early morning, coinciding with dips in the circadian rhythm, where alertness is naturally low (Dinges, 2020; Magaña et al., 2021; Goldenbeld et al., 2023). Additionally, the literature points out that lifestyle choices such as poor diet, insufficient breaks during long trips and consumption of stimulants like caffeine can influence fatigue levels. These factors are particularly relevant in commercial transportation, where drivers are often pushed to meet tight deadlines under challenging conditions (Al-Mekhlafi et al., 2020; Sharma et al., 2024).

When an individual is fatigued, the communication between brain cells becomes less effective, leading to impairments in visual perception, physical reflexes and memory. These impairments are particularly dangerous in the context of driving, as fatigue significantly reduces a driver's ability to operate a vehicle safely. Fatigue can lower attentiveness and make drivers less alert to potential hazards on the road, putting them at greater risk of accidents (Ren et al., 2023; Delhomme & Gheorghiu, 2021; Peters et al., 2021). It also slows reaction times and impairs decision-making abilities, meaning drivers may take longer to respond in critical situations (Abd-Elfattah et al., 2015; Tornero-Aguilera et al., 2022). Additionally, fatigue can cause drivers to drift out of their lane or follow other vehicles too closely, increasing the likelihood of collisions. Drivers may also experience inconsistent speed control, unintentionally speeding up or slowing down without realising it. Furthermore, fatigue diminishes a driver's tolerance for other road users, potentially leading to frustration or aggression (Plămădeală, 2022; Soares et al., 2020; Wang et al., 2022).

In extreme cases, fatigue can lead to microsleep, brief periods of sleep lasting between three and five seconds, which occur without the driver realising it. These episodes are particularly dangerous when driving and are a major cause of fatigue-related crashes, where drivers run off the road due to their inability to react in time. Accidents resulting from microsleep are often severe, as the driver is typically unable to take any action to avoid or mitigate the crash (Bowen et al., 2020; Pham et al., 2021; Cori et al., 2021; Mahajan & Velaga, 2021). Signs of driver fatigue include difficulty concentrating, frequent yawning or blinking, difficulty keeping one's head up, drifting out of lanes and increased irritability or aggression towards other drivers. Recognising these signs is critical for preventing fatigue-related accidents on the road. Figure 2.4 provides a visual representation of the common signs of driver fatigue.

Intoxicated Driving and Its Overlap with Fatigue

Alcohol consumption is another leading cause of traffic accidents, with intoxicated driving contributing to over 25% of global road fatalities according to the WHO (Kassym et al., 2023). In Malaysia, stricter regulations have

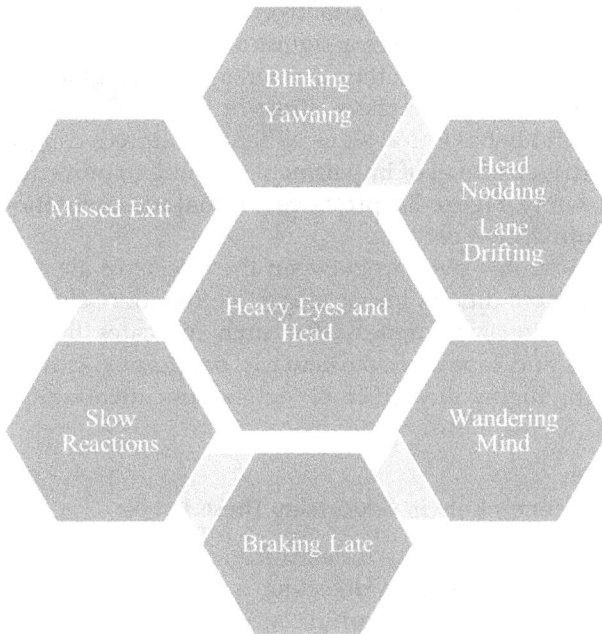

FIGURE 2.4
Common signs of driver fatigue.

been implemented in recent years, yet the issue persists. MIROS reported that despite enforcement efforts, alcohol-related crashes remain a significant problem, particularly during holiday seasons and in rural areas where enforcement is more challenging (Ferreira et al., 2024). When a driver is impaired, several physiological and behavioural signs can indicate diminished driving ability. Increased blood flow to the face, for instance, is a common indicator of intoxication or impairment, which can be detected through thermal imaging or facial monitoring systems (Azadani & Boukerche, 2021; Davoli et al., 2020). Changes in heart rate also signal impairment, with fluctuations often linked to alcohol or drug consumption, stress or fatigue (Wang & Shao, 2022; Siepmann et al., 2022). Elevated heart rates may indicate heightened anxiety, while reduced heart rates may signal drowsiness or relaxation, both of which can impair a driver's response to road conditions.

Eye behaviour is another crucial indicator, with impaired drivers often exhibiting slower blink rates, prolonged eye closure, or difficulty maintaining focus. These behaviours can severely reduce the driver's ability to track objects or react to changes in the driving environment (Ishaque et al., 2021). Additionally, changes in head position and body posture are key markers of impairment. Drivers may display a slouched posture, irregular head movements or difficulty maintaining an upright position, all of which suggest a lack of motor coordination or attentiveness (Alam et al., 2021; Qu et al., 2024). Finally, respiratory rate is a significant indicator of impairment. An altered breathing pattern, whether accelerated or irregular, can reflect the influence of intoxicating substances, stress or fatigue (Musicant et al., 2022). These physical and behavioural signs, when monitored, can provide critical insights into a driver's level of impairment, helping to prevent accidents and improve road safety. Figure 2.5 provides a visual representation of the common signs of intoxicated driving.

There is considerable overlap between the effects of alcohol intoxication and fatigue. Both conditions impair cognitive function, slow reaction times and reduce situational awareness. Research indicates that the combined effect of alcohol and fatigue is particularly dangerous; drivers under both influences exhibit highly unpredictable behaviours, increasing the likelihood of accidents.

Artificial Intelligence's Role in Addressing These Issues

Artificial Intelligence's capacity to learn from huge amounts of data allows for continuous improvement in detecting driver impairment (Davoli et al., 2020). Studies show that deep learning models can achieve higher accuracy

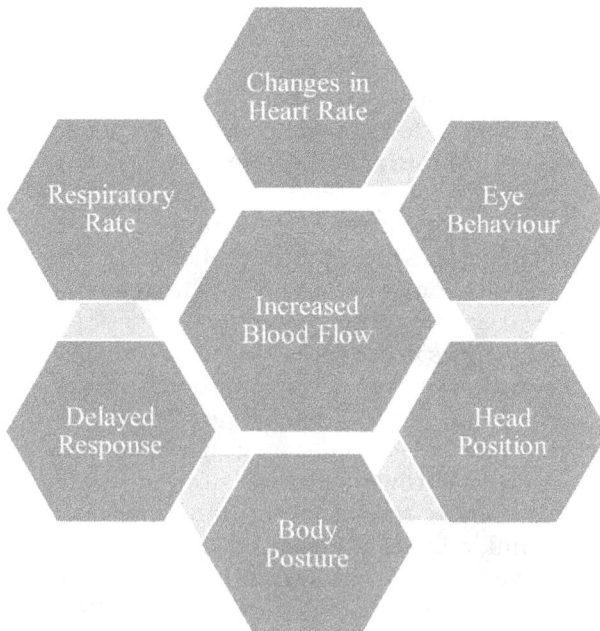

FIGURE 2.5
Common Signs of Intoxicated Driving.

in detecting drowsiness and alcohol impairment, significantly enhancing road safety. The literature also discusses the real-world application of such systems. For instance, some advanced driver assistance systems (ADAS) are already incorporating AI-powered fatigue and intoxication detection in commercial fleets, with early results showing a 30% reduction in fatigue-related incidents (Alkinani et al., 2020; Herath & Mittal, 2022). In Malaysia, several pilot programmes have been initiated to evaluate AI-enhanced monitoring systems in public transportation and logistics (Alvi et al., 2020). These systems are designed to not only detect impairment but also automatically adjust vehicle controls, such as limiting speed or safely bringing the vehicle to a stop if a driver shows signs of drowsiness or intoxication (Singh & Kathuria, 2021).

Indicators of Fatigue and Intoxicated Driving

The accurate detection of driver fatigue and intoxication relies on identifying a wide array of behavioural, physiological and cognitive indicators (Saleem et al., 2023; Fu et al., 2024). These indicators are crucial inputs for models designed to monitor driver alertness and predict potential impairment. This section elaborates on key indicators commonly discussed in the literature, focusing on how deep-learning models leverage these signals to provide real-time assessments.

Facial Expressions and Eye Movement Metrics

Percentage of Eye Closure (PERCLOS): One of the most reliable indicators of drowsiness, PERCLOS measures the proportion of time the eyes are at least 80% closed over a given period (Salvati et al., 2021). Studies indicate that as fatigue levels rise, the percentage of eye closure increases, making it a strong predictor of drowsiness (Dziuda et al., 2021).

Blinking Rate and Duration: Fatigue causes changes in blinking patterns, typically resulting in slower and more frequent blinks (Lapa et al., 2023; Islam et al., 2019). AI systems use cameras to track these metrics and identify irregularities indicative of drowsiness. For instance, prolonged blinks lasting over 100 milliseconds are a key sign of reduced alertness.

Gaze Tracking and Eye Movement: Sudden deviations in eye movement, such as drifting away from the road or fixating for too long on a single spot, are signs of both fatigue and intoxication (Xu et al., 2018; Safarov et al., 2023). AI models trained on gaze patterns can detect when a driver's attention is wavering or when they are becoming distracted.

Head Position and Body Posture

Head Nodding and Drooping: A common sign of severe drowsiness is the involuntary nodding of the head (Ansari et al., 2021; Doudou et al., 2020).

AI systems use in-cabin cameras to monitor head tilt angles, detecting the characteristic "jerk" motion as the head falls forward and then suddenly rises. Consistent head nodding is a critical indicator that a driver is nearing a microsleep episode.

Leaning or Slouching Posture: Fatigue often leads to changes in body posture, such as slouching or leaning excessively to one side. Intoxicated drivers may also exhibit unsteady posture, indicating a loss of control (Inkeaw et al., 2022; Lee et al., 2020). AI systems can track body movements and posture changes to assess the level of alertness.

Steering Behaviour and Vehicle Control

Lane Positioning and Drifting: One of the earliest signs of driver impairment is an inability to maintain a stable lane position (Khattak et al., 2021). Research has shown that both fatigued and intoxicated drivers tend to drift out of lanes more frequently, leading to erratic or corrective steering behaviour (Vinckenbosch et al., 2020). AI models analyse lane departure frequency and vehicle positioning in real time, providing alerts if a driver veers too often or fails to correct their path.

Steering Wheel Movements: Irregular steering patterns, such as sudden jerks or overly smooth corrections, can indicate a decline in alertness (Li et al., 2021b). Fatigued drivers may exhibit delayed or inconsistent responses when steering, while intoxicated drivers may overcorrect or struggle to keep the vehicle straight (Li et al., 2021a). Deep learning models can monitor steering input for signs of these behaviours, allowing for timely intervention.

Reaction Times and Cognitive Response

Response to External Stimuli: Drowsy or intoxicated drivers exhibit slower response times when reacting to traffic signals, pedestrians or sudden obstacles (Shahverdy et al., 2020; Zheng et al., 2021). AI systems assess reaction time by analysing delays between when a stimulus (like a red light) is presented and when the driver takes action. A noticeable lag in response is flagged as a sign of reduced cognitive function.

Inconsistent Speed Control: Fatigued or intoxicated drivers often have difficulty maintaining a consistent speed, leading to frequent acceleration and deceleration. This erratic control over vehicle speed is another indicator of potential impairment (Khattak et al., 2020). AI algorithms track speed variations to identify abnormalities and can trigger warnings if sudden changes occur without clear external causes.

Physiological Indicators

Heart Rate and Heart Rate Variability (HRV): Changes in heart rate and HRV can be strong indicators of driver alertness. Fatigue generally leads to a lower heart rate and reduced HRV, while intoxication may cause irregular spikes (Lu et al., 2022; Razak et al., 2024). Wearable sensors and in-cabin systems equipped with infrared or optical sensors can monitor these metrics and feed the data into AI models that assess driver conditions.

Breath and Skin Conductance: Intoxicated drivers often display changes in breath patterns (e.g., slowed or irregular breathing) and increased skin conductance due to alcohol's physiological effects (Saleem et al., 2023; Khattak et al., 2020). AI systems can integrate data from breath sensors or even thermal cameras to assess these changes, adding another layer of detection for alcohol impairment.

Behavioural Indicators

Yawning Frequency: Frequent yawning is a direct and visible sign of drowsiness (Zhang et al., 2021; Raman et al., 2018). AI systems can use facial recognition to detect repeated yawns, which are often associated with the early stages of fatigue.

Hand Movements and Coordination: Both fatigue and alcohol impairment can affect fine motor control, leading to uncoordinated hand movements (Brown, 2024; Yan & Abas, 2020). AI systems track hand positions and steering control, detecting shaky or unstable movements that indicate a driver's reduced alertness.

Related Works

The field of driver fatigue and intoxication detection has seen a surge in research efforts, especially with deep learning models. Numerous studies have focused on developing systems capable of identifying early signs of driver impairment using multi-modal approaches, such as computer vision, physiological monitoring and behaviour analysis. This section reviews 30 significant research papers that have contributed to this area, highlighting the different techniques and methodologies proposed by various authors.

Priyanka et al. (2024) suggested an approach to enhance driver drowsiness detection accuracy and reduce false alarms. The study proposed a model integrating Stacked CNN with LSTM architecture, utilising ReLU activation and MaxPooling layers. The study utilises a dataset comprising 183 hours of driving data, categorised into vehicle-related, facial-related and biosignal data. The effectiveness of the proposed methods was evaluated using performance metrics such as recall, accuracy, F1-score and precision. The CNN with LSTM model achieved a 96% accuracy rate in detecting drowsiness, showcasing its potential for real-time applications in manual and automated driving. Nevertheless, the challenge of interpersonal variability in physiological data, particularly EEG recordings, may affect the accuracy of fatigue detection. This variability can impact, as individual differences in physiological responses to fatigue may lead to inconsistent detection results.

Balwante et al. (2024) proposed an approach utilising YOLO v5 algorithm and OpenCV, to detect signs of driver fatigue through facial expressions and head movements. Besides, the study also integrates the proposed work on Arduino hardware to clarify driver's state through audible alarms and LED notifications. The study involved collecting data capturing various driving behaviours, particularly signs of drowsiness such as yawning and eye closure, using camera modules connected to Arduino. The evaluation focuses on accuracy, efficiency, real-world applicability and the integration of the system with Arduino hardware, ensuring it meets practical deployment standards. The study shows that the system successfully processes real-time video streams, generating alerts with low latency. However, the effectiveness of the drowsiness detection system can be influenced by various environmental factors, such as lighting conditions, road vibrations and background distractions.

Salbi et al. (2024) presented a driver assistance system utilising image processing and computer vision to detect signs of driver fatigue in real time. The study involves capturing the driver's face using a camera connected to Raspberry Pi 4 Model B, which processes the images using Python algorithms and Open CV libraries. The system monitors various indicators of driver fatigue, including eye closure, yawning and head orientation. Upon detecting signs of drowsiness, the system activates visual and audible alarms to alert the driver. The system achieved an accuracy rate of 93% in calculating the Eye Aspect Ratio (EAR) and Mouth Aspect Ratio (MAR), which are critical for detecting signs of driver fatigue. Nonetheless, the processing delays due to the Raspberry Pi sequential algorithm execution indicate a need for more powerful hardware or parallel processing solutions.

Paul et al. (2024) proposed an algorithm for driver drowsiness and distraction using image-based methods that focus on facial and body landmarks. The algorithm employs a camera module to monitor driver behaviour, focusing on facial detection, eye closure, yawning and head posture, with a stopwatch class to measure time intervals for accurate detection. The study created a custom dataset of 501 images, capturing both drowsy and non-drowsy states from various angles to ensure training for the detection algorithm. The study reports a detection accuracy of 91.8% in identifying driver drowsiness and distraction using the proposed algorithm. Nevertheless, the study acknowledges that the threshold values used for detecting drowsiness may not be universally effective. Different individuals have varying eye types, which means the threshold for Eye Aspect Ratio (EAR) might be too high for some, causing false alerts, or too low for others, resulting in missed drowsiness detection.

Cichocka and Ruminski (2024) proposed a CNN-based model trained on facial images, where the study aims to enhance detection accuracy compared to existing methods. The study utilises RGB camera video data, a yawning detection dataset and a new dataset of 112 images, capturing both open- and closed-eye conditions. The method uses EAR and MAR to calculate using specific geometric ratios derived from facial landmarks, establishing threshold values for effective fatigue detection. The developed method for detecting driver drowsiness achieved an average accuracy of 92% for eye detection and 82% for yawning. Some challenges were noted, such as variations in yawning movements and lighting conditions affecting detection accuracy. There were instances of misclassification, particularly in distinguishing between open and closed eyes, highlighting areas for potential optimisation. Table 2.1 provides a summary of the methodologies, key data, performance metrics and challenges encountered in each study of driver fatigue detection.

Bonela et al. (2023) developed a deep learning algorithm called ADLAIA that classifies alcohol inebriation status based on speech. Audio clips were transformed into Mel spectrograms, allowing the use of deep learning models pre-trained on image data for better prediction accuracy. ADLAIA was trained on a publicly available German Alcohol Language Corpus, comprising 12,360 audio clips. The model's effectiveness was measured using UAR and accuracy across different BAC thresholds (0.05%, 0.08%, 0.10%, 0.12%), allowing for a comprehensive analysis of its classification capabilities. ADLAIA achieved a notable classification performance, correctly identifying a significant number of sober and inebriated audio clips while also revealing areas of misclassification. However, the dataset's imbalanced class distribution and the presence of multiple voices in audio clips may pose challenges for accurate classification.

Sonule and Raman (2024) presented an approach to detect and classify the driver's blood alcohol concentration (BAC) levels in real time. The study utilises Support Vector Machine (SVM) classification to categorise the driver's BAC levels into predefined risk groups. The system employs Internet of Things (IoT) connectivity to facilitate the real-time transmission of data from in-car breathalyser devices to a central monitoring system. The breathalyser system integrates various sensors, including infrared spectroscopy and fuel cells, to ensure precise BAC measurements. The SVM classifier demonstrated remarkable accuracy in classifying BAC levels, with an overall accuracy rate of 89%. The effectiveness of the breathalyser system may be influenced by environmental factors such as temperature and humidity where it could potentially impact the accuracy of alcohol detection.

Kannan et al. (2024) proposed a deep learning model, named Smart AVDNet, designed to detect alcohol consumption through facial analysis. The Smart AVDNet employs a two-level checking system: the first level uses a fuzzy-based HOG-SSD approach to analyse the driver's eye and mouth,

TABLE 2.1

Summary of Existing Study on Driver Fatigue

Study	Methodology	Data Used	Accuracy/ Performance	Challenges
Priyanka et al. (2024)	Stacked CNN with LSTM architecture, ReLU activation, MaxPooling layers	183 hours of driving data (vehicle, facial, biosignal data)	96% accuracy	Interpersonal variability in physiological data affecting accuracy, particularly in EEG recordings
Balwante et al. (2024)	YOLO v5 algorithm and OpenCV with Arduino hardware integration	Real-time data capturing signs of drowsiness (yawning, eye closure) via camera modules on Arduino	Effective real-time processing, low latency	Environmental factors (lighting, road vibrations, background distractions) impacting system performance
Salbi et al. (2024)	Image processing and computer vision using Raspberry Pi and OpenCV	Camera capturing facial indicators of fatigue (eye closure, yawning, head orientation)	93% accuracy for EAR and MAR detection	Processing delays due to Raspberry Pi hardware limitations
Paul et al. (2024)	Image-based methods using facial and body landmarks	Custom dataset of 501 images capturing drowsy and non-drowsy states	91.8% accuracy for drowsiness and distraction detection	Varying eye types causing ineffective EAR threshold detection
Cichocka and Ruminski (2024)	CNN-based model trained on facial images using RGB video data	112 images capturing open and closed eye conditions, yawning detection dataset	92% accuracy for eye detection, 82% for yawning detection	Variations in yawning and lighting conditions leading to misclassification

while the second level utilises ROI-based CNN techniques to assess chin and cheek features. The model is trained using the IMDB-WIKI dataset, which contains over 500,000 images with age labels, although it primarily consists of facial images rather than those from dashboard cameras. The proposed model's accuracy rate of 99.39% and F1 score of 99.04% highlight its superior performance compared to existing methods. The study highlights difficulties in detecting the skin tone of Asian individuals using cheek and chin features. This limitation suggests that the model may not be equally effective across different ethnic groups, potentially affecting its accuracy and fairness.

Keshtkaran et al. (2024) proposed a computer vision technique to identify intoxication based on observable biobehavioural changes in drivers. The study involved 60 participants, selected to represent various levels of alcohol impairment, capturing a wide range of driving behaviours and physiological responses. The participants engaged in a simulated driving scenario that involved navigating through a city environment with moderate to high traffic. Breath samples were collected using calibrated breathalysers to ensure accurate BAC measurements. The study employed a machine learning model to detect BAC thresholds using facial features captured by standard RGB cameras. The system could identify alcohol intoxication impairment with an accuracy of 75% for BAC levels as low as 0.05 g/dL. However, the current system relies on manually crafted features, which may limit its adaptability and performance.

Doniec et al. (2024) explored the use of electrooculography (EOG) signals from smart glasses to monitor driver intoxication, leveraging machine learning techniques to analyse eye movement patterns. The study involved participants aged 20 to 23 years, with a mean and median age of 21, providing a focused demographic for the analysis of EOG signals. A driving simulator was used to assess driver performance across nine routes while participants wore JiNS MEME smart glasses and drunk vision goggles simulating varying levels of intoxication. Among the machine learning algorithms tested, Bagged Trees achieved the highest accuracy of 79% in classifying the EOG data. However, the study's sample size is notably small, consisting of only nine participants. This limited sample size can affect the generalisability of the findings and may not adequately represent the broader population. Table 2.2 presents an overview of the methodologies, datasets, performance outcomes and challenges identified in each of the studies.

Discussion

The application for detecting driver fatigue and intoxication brings numerous benefits but also introduces significant challenges. This section provides a balanced overview of these advantages and challenges, which must be considered when developing and deploying such technologies.

Advantages

Real-Time Monitoring and Detection

AI-based systems provide continuous, real-time monitoring, allowing for instant detection of fatigue or intoxication. Traditional methods, such as

TABLE 2.2

Summary of Existing Study on Driver Impairment

Study	Methodology	Data Used	Accuracy/ Performance	Challenges
Bonela et al. (2023)	Deep learning algorithm (ADLAIA) classifies alcohol inebriation based on speech	12,360 audio clips from the German Alcohol Language Corpus	High classification performance, notable accuracy at BAC thresholds (0.05%, 0.08%, 0.10%, 0.12%)	Imbalanced class distribution, presence of multiple voices in audio clips
Sonule and Raman (2024)	SVM classifier with IoT-connected in-car breathalyser system	Real-time BAC data from breathalyser devices (infrared spectroscopy, fuel cells)	89% accuracy	Environmental factors such as temperature and humidity affecting breathalyser accuracy
Kannan et al. (2024)	Deep learning model (Smart AVDNet) with HOG-SSD and ROI-based CNN techniques	IMDB-WIKI dataset of 500,000 facial images	99.39% accuracy, 99.04% F1 score	Skin tone detection issues, particularly among Asian individuals, affecting fairness and accuracy
Keshtkaran et al. (2024)	Computer vision technique detecting biobehavioural changes in drivers	Data from 60 participants in a driving simulator, BAC measurements using breathalysers	75% accuracy at detecting BAC levels of 0.05 g/dL	Manual feature crafting limiting adaptability and performance
Doniec et al. (2024)	EOG signal analysis using smart glasses and machine learning	EOG data from JiNS MEME smart glasses, driving simulator with 9 participants	79% accuracy using Bagged Trees model	Small sample size of 9 participants, limiting generalisability of the findings

breathalysers or manual observation, are often limited to periodic checks, missing gradual impairment that develops over time. By integrating deep learning models, these systems can process visual, behavioural and physiological data streams simultaneously, enabling rapid responses before critical driving errors occur.

High Accuracy and Reliability

Advances in AI, particularly deep learning, have significantly improved the accuracy of detecting fatigue and intoxication. Multi-modal approaches that analyse facial expressions, steering behaviour and physiological signals yield high detection rates, often exceeding 90%. For instance, combining indicators like PERCLOS, head nodding and irregular steering patterns enables robust predictions, reducing false positives and enhancing system reliability.

Adaptability and Learning Over Time

Deep learning models can be trained on huge datasets, allowing them to recognise complex patterns that static systems might miss. Moreover, these systems improve over time as they process more data, enabling better adaptability to different driver behaviours, conditions and environments. This self-learning capability allows AI models to adjust to individual driver profiles, minimising detection errors and enhancing user trust.

Seamless Integration with Advanced Driver Assistance Systems (ADAS)

AI-enhanced detection systems can be easily integrated into modern ADAS platforms, creating a comprehensive safety solution. This integration allows the system to trigger corrective actions, such as activating lane-keeping assistance, reducing vehicle speed or alerting emergency contacts. In more advanced cases, the vehicle might even take control to avoid a potential accident if the driver is unresponsive.

Scalability and Cost Efficiency

Once trained, AI models can be scaled across different vehicles and environments with minimal additional cost. The data-driven nature of these systems makes them adaptable to various makes and models, whether in personal vehicles, commercial fleets or public transportation. This scalability presents an opportunity to deploy these technologies widely, enhancing road safety on a large scale.

Challenges

Data privacy and Ethical Concerns

AI systems often require access to sensitive data, including facial images, physiological readings and behavioural patterns. The collection, storage and processing of this data raise concerns about driver privacy and data security. Ensuring that the system complies with data protection regulations while maintaining transparency and user control is a critical challenge for developers.

False Positives and Negatives

Despite high accuracy, no detection system is perfect. False positives (incorrectly identifying impairment) can lead to unnecessary interventions, frustrating drivers and potentially reducing their willingness to use the system. Conversely, false negatives (failing to detect impairment) pose serious safety risks, as undetected fatigue or intoxication could result in accidents. Striking the right balance between sensitivity and specificity remains an ongoing challenge.

Variability in Individual Responses and Conditions

Fatigue and intoxication indicators can vary significantly among individuals. Factors such as age, health conditions, tolerance levels, and even cultural differences affect how symptoms manifest. Additionally, environmental factors like lighting, weather conditions and vehicle type can impact detection accuracy. Developing models that account for these variables while maintaining generalisability is complex and requires extensive data collection and testing.

System Dependence and Over-Reliance

There is a risk that drivers may become overly reliant on these systems, leading to complacency. If drivers assume that the system will always alert them before it's too late, they may neglect their responsibility to stay alert. This over-reliance could paradoxically undermine road safety, especially if drivers fail to recognise situations where the system may not function optimally, such as in low visibility or technical malfunctions.

Integration with Legacy Vehicles and Infrastructure

Implementing AI-based detection systems in older vehicles poses practical challenges. Retrofitting existing cars with the necessary sensors, cameras and processing units can be costly and complex. Furthermore, older vehicles may lack the necessary computational resources or connectivity to support real-time AI processing, limiting the effectiveness of these solutions for a significant portion of the global vehicle fleet.

Legal and Regulatory Barriers

The regulatory landscape surrounding AI and driver monitoring systems is still evolving. Governments and transportation authorities are yet to fully standardise guidelines on acceptable accuracy levels, system interventions and data usage. Moreover, liability issues in cases where the system fails to prevent an accident are unresolved. Manufacturers and developers must navigate these legal uncertainties as they seek to commercialise their solutions.

Conclusion

The increasing prevalence of road accidents due to driver fatigue and intoxication underscores the need for solutions in automotive safety. AI-enhanced detection systems, driven by deep learning, offer a promising approach to addressing these challenges by providing real-time monitoring, high accuracy and adaptive learning capabilities. By analysing different data streams, including facial features, behavioural patterns and physiological signals, these systems can identify early signs of impairment, enabling timely interventions that enhance road safety. Despite the advantages, such as improved accuracy, scalability, and integration with Advanced Driver Assistance Systems (ADAS), several challenges remain. Privacy concerns, false detections, individual variability and the complexities of integrating these systems into older vehicles must be carefully addressed. Additionally, regulatory and legal uncertainties present obstacles to the widespread adoption of AI-based driver monitoring solutions. For the future, ongoing research and development will be essential in refining these systems, improving their reliability, and ensuring their adaptability across different driving environments and demographics. Collaboration between automotive manufacturers, AI developers and policymakers will also be crucial to establishing clear guidelines and standards that balance technological innovation with ethical considerations.

Acknowledgements

We would like to express our sincere gratitude to the anonymous reviewers for their invaluable feedback and insightful comments. We would like to also extend our heartfelt thanks to our research centre, whose support and resources have been instrumental in the development of this research.

References

Abd-Elfattah, H. M., Abdelazeim, F. H., & Elshennawy, S. (2015). Physical and cognitive consequences of fatigue: A review. *Journal of Advanced Research*, 6(3), 351–358, doi: 10.1016/j.jare.2015.01.011

Ahmed, S. K., Mohammed, M. G., Abdulqadir, S. O., El-Kader, R. G. A., El-Shall, N. A., Chandran, D., … & Dhama, K. (2023). Road traffic accidental injuries and deaths: A neglected global health issue. *Health Science Reports*, 6(5), e1240, doi: 10.1002/hsr2.1240

Alam, L., Hoque, M. M., Dewan, M. A. A., Siddique, N., Rano, I., & Sarker, I. H. (2021). Active vision-based attention monitoring system for non-distracted driving. *IEEE Access*, 9, 28540–28557, doi: 10.1109/ACCESS.2021.3058205

Alkinani, M. H., Khan, W. Z., & Arshad, Q. (2020). Detecting human driver inattentive and aggressive driving behavior using deep learning: Recent advances, requirements and open challenges. *IEEE Access*, 8, 105008–105030, doi: 10.1109/ACCESS.2020.2999829

Al-Mekhlafi, A. B. A., Isha, A. S. N., & Naji, G. M. A. (2020). The relationship between fatigue and driving performance: A review and directions for future research. *Journal Of Critical Review*, 7(14), 134–141, doi: 10.31838/jcr.07.14.24

Alvi, U., Khattak, M. A. K., Shabir, B., Malik, A. W., & Muhammad, S. R. (2020). A comprehensive study on IoT based accident detection systems for smart vehicles. *IEEE Access*, 8, 122480–122497, doi: 10.1109/ACCESS.2020.3006887

Ansari, S., Naghdy, F., Du, H., & Pahnwar, Y. N. (2021). Driver mental fatigue detection based on head posture using new modified reLU-BiLSTM deep neural network. *IEEE Transactions on Intelligent Transportation Systems*, 23(8), 10957–10969, doi: 10.1109/TITS.2021.3098309

Azadani, M. N., & Boukerche, A. (2021). Driving behavior analysis guidelines for intelligent transportation systems. *IEEE Transactions on Intelligent Transportation Systems*, 23(7), 6027–6045, doi: 10.1109/TITS.2021.3076140

Balwante, S. S., Kolhe, R., Pingale, N. K., & Chandel, D. S. (2024). Drowsiness Detection System: Integrating YOLOv5 Object Detection with Arduino Hardware for Real-Time Monitoring. *International Journal of Innovative Research in Computer Science & Technology*, 12(2), 59–66, doi: 10.55524/ijircst.2024.12.2.9

Bonela, A. A., He, Z., Nibali, A., Norman, T., Miller, P. G., & Kuntsche, E. (2023). Audio-based deep learning algorithm to identify alcohol inebriation (ADLAIA). *Alcohol*, 109, 49–54, doi: 10.1016/j.alcohol.2022.12.002

Bowen, L., Budden, S. L., & Smith, A. P. (2020). Factors underpinning unsafe driving: A systematic literature review of car drivers. *Transportation Research Part F: Traffic Psychology and Behaviour*, 72, 184–210, doi: 10.1016/j.trf.2020.04.008

Brown, L. (2024). Individuals With Motor Control and Motor Function Disorders. In *Clinical Exercise Pathophysiology for Physical Therapy* (pp. 465–496). Routledge.

Cichocka, S., & Ruminski, J. (2024, July). Driver fatigue detection method based on facial image analysis. In *2024 16th International Conference on Human System Interaction (HSI)* (pp. 1–6). IEEE, doi: 10.54254/2755-2721/57/20241332

Cori, J. M., Downey, L. A., Sletten, T. L., Beatty, C. J., Shiferaw, B. A., Soleimanloo, S. S., ... & National Transport Commission Heavy Vehicle Driver Project Team. (2021). The impact of 7-hour and 11-hour rest breaks between shifts on heavy vehicle truck drivers' sleep, alertness and naturalistic driving performance. *Accident Analysis & Prevention*, 159, 106224, doi: 10.1016/j.aap.2021.106224

Davoli, L., Martalò, M., Cilfone, A., Belli, L., Ferrari, G., Presta, R., ... & Plomp, J. (2020). On driver behavior recognition for increased safety: a roadmap. *Safety*, 6(4), 55, doi: 10.3390/safety6040055

Debbarma, T., Pal, T., & Debbarma, N. (2024). Prediction of Dangerous Driving Behaviour Based on Vehicle Motion. *Procedia Computer Science*, 235, 1125–1134, doi: 10.1016/j.procs.2024.04.107

Delhomme, P., & Gheorghiu, A. (2021). Perceived stress, mental health, organizational factors, and self-reported risky driving behaviors among truck drivers circulating in France. *Journal of Safety Research*, 79, 341–351, doi: 10.1016/j.jsr.2021.10.001

Dinges, D. F. (2020). The nature of sleepiness: Causes, contexts, and consequences. In *Eating, sleeping, and sex* (pp. 147–179). Routledge, doi: 10.1201/9780203771570-10

Doniec, R. J., Piaseczna, N., Duraj, K., Sieciński, S., Irshad, M. T., Karpiel, I., ... & Grzegorzek, M. (2024). The detection of alcohol intoxication using electrooculography signals from smart glasses and machine learning techniques. *Systems and Soft Computing*, 6, 200078, doi: 10.1016/j.sasc.2024.200078

Doudou, M., Bouabdallah, A., & Berge-Cherfaoui, V. (2020). Driver drowsiness measurement technologies: Current research, market solutions, and challenges. *International Journal of Intelligent Transportation Systems Research*, 18, 297–319, doi: 10.1007/s13177-019-00199-w

Duddu, V. R., Kukkapalli, V. M., & Pulugurtha, S. S. (2019). Crash risk factors associated with injury severity of teen drivers. *IATSS research*, 43(1), 37–43, doi: 10.1016/j.iatssr.2018.08.003

Dziuda, Ł., Baran, P., Zieliński, P., Murawski, K., Dziwosz, M., Krej, M., ... & Bortkiewicz, A. (2021). Evaluation of a fatigue detector using eye closure-associated indicators acquired from truck drivers in a simulator study. *Sensors*, 21(19), 6449, doi: 10.3390/s21196449

Ferreira, S., Vikneswary Suresh, M., Sulaiman, M. F., Al-Haji, G., Comi, A., Wah, Y. C., ... & Van Minh, N. (2024). *The ASIASAFE road safety handbook: the best practices in traffic safety between Europe–Indonesia*, Faculty of Engineering of the University of Porto, Malaysia, and Vietnam, doi: 10.24840/978-972-752-320-7

Fu, S., Yang, Z., Ma, Y., Li, Z., Xu, L., & Zhou, H. (2024). Advancements in the Intelligent Detection of Driver Fatigue and Distraction: A Comprehensive Review. *Applied Sciences*, 14(7), 3016, doi: 10.3390/app14073016

Fu, Y., Li, C., Yu, F. R., Luan, T. H., & Zhang, Y. (2021). A survey of driving safety with sensing, vehicular communications, and artificial intelligence-based collision avoidance. *IEEE Transactions on Intelligent Transportation Systems*, 23(7), 6142–6163, doi: 10.1109/TITS.2021.3083927

Goldenbeld, C., van Schagen, I., & Davidse, R. (2023). Fatigue-related consequences on road crashes. In *The Handbook of Fatigue Management in Transportation* (pp. 81–95). CRC Press, doi: 10.1201/9781003213154-9

Govindaraj, M., Asha, V., Katingeri, M. M., Manvanth, L. J., Ch, M. R. P., & Mathew, J. C. (2024, February). Deep Learning for Real-Time Drowsiness Onset Detection. In *2024 International Conference on Integrated Circuits and Communication Systems (ICICACS)* (pp. 1–7). IEEE, doi: 10.1109/ICICACS60521.2024.10498276

Hayley, A. C., Shiferaw, B., Aitken, B., Vinckenbosch, F., Brown, T. L., & Downey, L. A. (2021). Driver monitoring systems (DMS): The future of impaired driving management? *Traffic Injury Prevention*, 22(4), 313–317, doi: 10.1080/15389588.2021.1899164

Herath, H. M. K. K. M. B., & Mittal, M. (2022). Adoption of artificial intelligence in smart cities: A comprehensive review. *International Journal of Information Management Data Insights*, 2(1), 100076, doi: 10.1016/j.jjimei.2022.100076

Inkeaw, P., Srikummoon, P., Chaijaruwanich, J., Traisathit, P., Awiphan, S., Inchai, J., ... & Theerakittikul, T. (2022). Automatic driver drowsiness detection using artificial neural network based on visual facial descriptors: pilot study. *Nature and Science of Sleep*, 1641–1649, doi: 10.2147/NSS.S376755

Ishaque, S., Khan, N., & Krishnan, S. (2021). Trends in heart-rate variability signal analysis. *Frontiers in Digital Health*, 3, 639444, doi: 10.3389/fdgth.2021.639444

Islam, A., Rahaman, N., & Ahad, M. A. R. (2019). A study on tiredness assessment by using eye blink detection. *Jurnal Kejuruteraan*, 31(2), 209–214, doi: 10.17576/jkukm-2019-31(2)-04

Jagatheesaperumal, S. K., Bibri, S. E., Huang, J., Rajapandian, J., & Parthiban, B. (2024). Artificial intelligence of things for smart cities: advanced solutions for enhancing transportation safety. *Computational Urban Science*, 4(1), 10, doi: 10.1007/s43762-024-00120-6

Jamaludin, A. S., Abidin, A. N. S. Z., Roslan, A., Shahril, R., Azmi, A. H., Abdullah, N. A. S., … & Kassim, K. A. A. (2021). Malaysian road traffic crash data: Where do we stand now. *Journal of Modern Manufacturing Systems and Technology*, 5(2), 88–94, doi: 10.15282/jmmst.v5i2.6593

Kannan, E. P., Shunmugathammal, M., Barskar, R., & Thomas, L. (2024). Smart AVDNet: alcohol detection using vehicle driver face. *Signal, Image and Video Processing*, 1–14, doi: 10.1007/s11760-024-03222-0

Kassym, L., Kussainova, A., Semenova, Y., Kussainov, A., Marapov, D., Zhanaspayev, M., … & Bjørklund, G. (2023, March). Worldwide prevalence of alcohol use in non-fatally injured motor vehicle drivers: a systematic review and meta-analysis. In *Healthcare* (Vol. 11, No. 5, p. 758). MDPI, doi: 10.3390/healthcare11050758

Keshtkaran, E., von Berg, B., Regan, G., Suter, D., & Gilani, S. Z. (2024). Estimating Blood Alcohol Level Through Facial Features for Driver Impairment Assessment. In *Proceedings of the IEEE/CVF Winter Conference on Applications of Computer Vision* (pp. 4539–4548), doi: 10.1109/WACV57701.2024.00448

Khamis, A. A., Idris, A., Abdellatif, A., Mohd Rom, N. A., Khamis, T., Ab Karim, M. S., … & Abd Rashid, R. B. (2023). Development and performance evaluation of an iot-integrated breath analyzer. *International Journal of Environmental Research and Public Health*, 20(2), 1319, doi: 10.3390/ijerph20021319

Khattak, A. J., Ahmad, N., Wali, B., & Dumbaugh, E. (2021). A taxonomy of driving errors and violations: Evidence from the naturalistic driving study. *Accident Analysis & Prevention*, 151, 105873, doi: 10.1016/j.aap.2020.105873

Khattak, A. J., Arvin, R., Chakraborty, S., Melton, C., & Clamann, M. (2020). Driver impairment detection and safety enhancement through comprehensive volatility analysis (No. CSCRS-R23). *Collaborative Sciences Center for Road Safety*, https://rosap.ntl.bts.gov/view/dot/56547

Kurnia Insurance. (2022). Road accidents in Malaysia: Top 10 Causes & Prevention. Retrieved from https://www.kurnia.com/blog/road-accidents-causes

Lapa, I., Ferreira, S., Mateus, C., Rocha, N., & Rodrigues, M. A. (2023). Real-time blink detection as an indicator of computer vision syndrome in real-life settings: an exploratory study. *International Journal Of Environmental Research and Public Health*, 20(5), 4569, doi: 10.3390/ijerph20054569

Lee, S., Kim, M., Jung, H., Kwon, D., Choi, S., & You, H. (2020). Effects of a motion seat system on driver's passive task-related fatigue: An on-road driving study. *Sensors*, 20(9), 2688, doi: 10.3390/s20092688

Li, R., Chen, Y. V., & Zhang, L. (2021b). A method for fatigue detection based on Driver's steering wheel grip. *International Journal of Industrial Ergonomics*, 82, 103083, doi: 10.1016/j.ergon.2021.103083

Li, Z., Chen, L., Nie, L., & Yang, S. X. (2021a). A novel learning model of driver fatigue features representation for steering wheel angle. *IEEE Transactions on Vehicular Technology*, 71(1), 269–281, doi: 10.1109/TVT.2021.3130152

Liang, Y., Samtani, S., Guo, B., & Yu, Z. (2020). Behavioral biometrics for continuous authentication in the internet-of-things era: An artificial intelligence perspective. *IEEE Internet of Things Journal*, 7(9), 9128–9143, doi: 10.1109/JIOT.2020.3004077

Lu, K., Dahlman, A. S., Karlsson, J., & Candefjord, S. (2022). Detecting driver fatigue using heart rate variability: A systematic review. *Accident Analysis & Prevention*, 178, 106830, doi: 10.1016/j.aap.2022.106830

Magaña, V. C., Pañeda, X. G., Garcia, R., Paiva, S., & Pozueco, L. (2021). Beside and behind the wheel: Factors that influence driving stress and driving behavior. *Sustainability*, 13(9), 4775, doi: 10.3390/su13094775

Mahajan, K., & Velaga, N. R. (2021). Sleep-deprived car-following: Indicators of rear-end crash potential. *Accident Analysis & Prevention*, 156, 106123, doi: 10.1016/j.aap.2021.106123

Maqbool, Y., Sethi, A., & Singh, J. (2019). Road safety and road accidents: an insight. *International Journal of Information and Computing Science*, 6, 93–105.

Musicant, O., Richmond-Hacham, B., & Botzer, A. (2022, October). Estimating Driver Fatigue Based on Heart Activity, Respiration Rate. In *Lindholmen Conference Centre & online October 19–20, 2022* (p. 78), doi: 10.3390/s23239457

Papalimperi, A. H., Athanaselis, S. A., Mina, A. D., Papoutsis, I. I., Spiliopoulou, C. A., & Papadodima, S. A. (2019). Incidence of fatalities of road traffic accidents associated with alcohol consumption and the use of psychoactive drugs: A 7-year survey (2011-2017). *Experimental and Therapeutic Medicine*, 18(3), 2299–2306, doi: 10.3892/etm.2019.7787

Paul, A., Shaha, A., Mukherjee, A., & Sen, A. (2024, March). An Image Processing Approach to Enhance Driver Distraction and Drowsiness Detection Algorithm. In *2024 3rd International Conference for Innovation in Technology (INOCON)* (pp. 1–9). IEEE, doi: 10.1109/INOCON60754.2024.10511409

Penland, G. (2023). *Teen driving and car accident statistics*. BMW Law Group. Retrieved from https://bmwlawgroup.com/teen-driving-car-accident-statistics/

Pérez-Carbonell, L., Mignot, E., Leschziner, G., & Dauvilliers, Y. (2022). Understanding and approaching excessive daytime sleepiness. *The Lancet*, 400(10357), 1033–1046, doi: 10.1016/S0140-6736(22)01018-2

Peters, S. E., Grogan, H., Henderson, G. M., López Gómez, M. A., Martínez Maldonado, M., Silva Sanhueza, I., & Dennerlein, J. T. (2021). Working conditions influencing drivers' safety and well-being in the transportation industry:"on board" program. *International Journal of Environmental Research and Public Health*, 18(19), 10173, doi: 10.3390/ijerph181910173

Pham, N., Dinh, T., Kim, T., Raghebi, Z., Bui, N., Truong, H., … & Vu, T. (2021). Detection of microsleep events with a behind-the-ear wearable system. *IEEE Transactions on Mobile Computing*, 22(2), 841–857, doi: 10.1109/TMC.2021.3090829

Plămădeală, V. (2022). Driving tiredness–the end enemy of the driver. *Journal of Engineering Sciences*, doi: 10.3390/ijerph19073909

Priyanka, S., Shanthi, S., Kumar, A. S., & Praveen, V. (2024). Data fusion for driver drowsiness recognition: A multimodal perspective. *Egyptian Informatics Journal*, 27, 100529, doi: 10.1016/j.eij.2024.100529

Qu, F., Dang, N., Furht, B., & Nojoumian, M. (2024). Comprehensive study of driver behavior monitoring systems using computer vision and machine learning techniques. *Journal of Big Data*, 11(1), 32, doi: 10.1186/s40537-024-00890-0

Rajput, R. S., Dhoni, P. S., Patel, R., Karangara, R., Shende, A., & Kathiriya, S. (2024). AI-Driven Innovations. In *Cari Journals USA LLC* (p. 84). ISBN 9914746152.

Raman, K. J., Azman, A., Arumugam, V., Ibrahim, S. Z., Yogarayan, S., Abdullah, M. F. A., ... & Sonaimuthu, K. (2018, May). Fatigue monitoring based on yawning and head movement. In *2018 6th International Conference on Information and Communication Technology (ICoICT)* (pp. 343–347). IEEE, doi: 10.1109/ICoICT.2018.8528759

Razak, S. F. A., Ali, M. A. A. U., Yogarayan, S., & Abdullah, M. F. A. (2022, July). IoT based alcohol concentration monitor for drivers. In *2022 4th International Conference on Smart Sensors and Application (ICSSA)* (pp. 86–89). IEEE, doi: 10.1109/ICSSA54161.2022.9870947

Razak, S. F. A., Ismail, S. N. S., Bin, B. H. B., Yogarayan, S., Abdullah, M. F. A., & Kamis, N. H. (2024). Monitoring Physiological State of Drivers Using In-Vehicle Sensing of Non-Invasive Signal. *Civil Engineering Journal*, 10(4), 1221–1231, doi: 10.28991/cej-2024-010-04-014

Ren, X., Pritchard, E., van Vreden, C., Newnam, S., Iles, R., & Xia, T. (2023). Factors associated with fatigued driving among Australian truck drivers: a cross-sectional study. *International Journal of Environmental Research and Public Health*, 20(3), 2732, doi: 10.3390/ijerph20032732

Safarov, F., Akhmedov, F., Abdusalomov, A. B., Nasimov, R., & Cho, Y. I. (2023). Real-time deep learning-based drowsiness detection: leveraging computer-vision and eye-blink analyses for enhanced road safety. *Sensors*, 23(14), 6459, doi: 10.3390/s23146459

Salbi, A., Gadi, M. A., Bouganssa, T., Hassani, A. E., & Lasfar, A. (2024). Design and implementation of a driving safety assistant system based on driver behavior. *International Journal of Artificial Intelligence*, 13(3), 2603–2613, doi: 10.11591/ijai.v13.i3.pp2603-2613

Saleem, A. A., Siddiqui, H. U. R., Raza, M. A., Rustam, F., Dudley, S., & Ashraf, I. (2023). A systematic review of physiological signals based driver drowsiness detection systems. *Cognitive Neurodynamics*, 17(5), 1229–1259, doi: 10.1007/s11571-022-09898-9

Salvati, L., d'Amore, M., Fiorentino, A., Pellegrino, A., Sena, P., & Villecco, F. (2021). On-road detection of driver fatigue and drowsiness during medium-distance journeys. *Entropy*, 23(2), 135, doi: 10.3390/e23020135

Sarker, I. H. (2024). AI-driven cybersecurity and threat intelligence: cyber automation, intelligent decision-making and explainability. *Springer Nature*, doi: 10.1007/978-3-031-54497-2

Shahverdy, M., Fathy, M., Berangi, R., & Sabokrou, M. (2020). Driver behavior detection and classification using deep convolutional neural networks. *Expert Systems with Applications*, 149, 113240, doi: 10.1016/j.eswa.2020.113240

Sharma, I., Marwale, A. V., Sidana, R., & Gupta, I. D. (2024). Lifestyle modification for mental health and well-being. *Indian Journal of Psychiatry*, 66(3), 219–234, doi: 10.4103/indianjpsychiatry.indianjpsychiatry_39_24

Siepmann, M., Weidner, K., Petrowski, K., & Siepmann, T. (2022). Heart rate variability: a measure of cardiovascular health and possible therapeutic target in dysautonomic mental and neurological disorders. *Applied Psychophysiology and Biofeedback*, 47(4), 273–287, doi: 10.1007/s10484-022-09572-0

Silverman, S. A., Thorpy, M. J., & Ahmed, I. (2022). Sleepiness, Fatigue, and Sleep Disorders. In *Sleep and Neuropsychiatric Disorders* (pp. 101–140). Singapore: Springer Nature Singapore, doi: 10.1007/978-981-16-0123-1_6

Singh, H., & Kathuria, A. (2021). Analyzing driver behavior under naturalistic driving conditions: A review. *Accident Analysis & Prevention*, 150, 105908, doi: 10.1016/j.aap.2020.105908

Soares, S., Monteiro, T., Lobo, A., Couto, A., Cunha, L., & Ferreira, S. (2020). Analyzing driver drowsiness: From causes to effects. *Sustainability*, 12(5), 1971, doi: 10.3390/su12051971

Sohail, A., Cheema, M. A., Ali, M. E., Toosi, A. N., & Rakha, H. A. (2023). Data-driven approaches for road safety: A comprehensive systematic literature review. *Safety Science*, 158, 105949, doi: 10.1016/j.ssci.2022.105949

Sonule, V., & Raman, R. (2024, May). In-Car Breathalyzer Systems for Enhanced Road Safety Through SVM Classification and IoT Connectivity. In *2024 International Conference on Advances in Modern Age Technologies for Health and Engineering Science (AMATHE)* (pp. 1–5). IEEE, doi: 10.1109/AMATHE61652.2024.10582130

Torbaghan, M. E., Sasidharan, M., Reardon, L., & Muchanga-Hvelplund, L. C. (2022). Understanding the potential of emerging digital technologies for improving road safety. *Accident Analysis & Prevention*, 166, 106543, doi: 10.1016/j.aap.2021.106543

Tornero-Aguilera, J. F., Jimenez-Morcillo, J., Rubio-Zarapuz, A., & Clemente-Suárez, V. J. (2022). Central and peripheral fatigue in physical exercise explained: A narrative review. *International Journal of Environmental Research and Public Health*, 19(7), 3909.

Vinckenbosch, F. R. J., Vermeeren, A., Verster, J. C., Ramaekers, J. G., & Vuurman, E. F. (2020). Validating lane drifts as a predictive measure of drug or sleepiness induced driving impairment. *Psychopharmacology*, 237, 877–886, doi: 10.1007/s00213-019-05424-8

Wang, X., Liu, Q., Guo, F., Xu, X., & Chen, X. (2022). Causation analysis of crashes and near crashes using naturalistic driving data. *Accident Analysis & Prevention*, 177, 106821, doi: 10.1016/j.aap.2022.106821

Wang, X., & Shao, D. (2022). Human physiology and contactless vital signs monitoring using camera and wireless signals. In *Contactless Vital Signs Monitoring* (pp. 1–24). Academic Press, doi: 10.1016/B978-0-12-822281-2.00008-1

Xu, J., Min, J., & Hu, J. (2018). Real-time eye tracking for the assessment of driver fatigue. *Healthcare Technology Letters*, 5(2), 54–58, doi: 10.1049/htl.2017.0020

Yan, X., & Abas, A. (2020). Preliminary on Human Driver Behavior: A Review. *International Journal of Artificial Intelligence*, 7(2), 29–34, doi: 10.36079/lamintang.ijai-0702.146

Yusof, N. M., Karjanto, J., Hassan, M. Z., Sulaiman, S., Ab Rashid, A. A., Jawi, Z. M., & Kassim, K. A. A. (2023). Effect of road darkness on young driver behaviour when approaching parked or slow-moving vehicles in Malaysia. *Automotive Experiences*, 6(2), 216–233, doi: 10.31603/ae.8206

Zhang, Y., Han, X., Gao, W., & Hu, Y. (2021). Driver Fatigue Detection Based On Facial Feature Analysis. *International Journal of Pattern Recognition and Artificial Intelligence*, 35(15), 2150034, doi: 10.1142/S0218001421500348

Zheng, L., Sayed, T., & Mannering, F. (2021). Modeling traffic conflicts for use in road safety analysis: A review of analytic methods and future directions. *Analytic Methods in Accident Research*, 29, 100142, doi: 10.1016/j.amar.2020.100142

3

Traffic Analysis and Smart Traffic Management Using YOLO

Chia-Hong Yap, Kah-Ong Michael Goh, Check-Yee Law
and Yong-Wee Sek

Introduction

Transportation is essential in our daily lives because it provides us access to services and daily activities such as employment, entertainment, education and social events. In Malaysia, while public transport such as buses and trains are available, private vehicles such as cars and motorcycles remain the popular modes of transport for most Malaysians. Reasons include a lack of pedestrian walkways that connect to public transport facilities (Azzman Abdul Jamal, n.d.), not well-connected public transportation system (Tong, 10:25:00+08:00, 2017), poor planning and execution of public transport (Herald, 2022), and private vehicles offer shorter travelling time and are more convenient (Kamba et al., 2007). Almost every Malaysian will buy their own vehicle if they can afford it, either a motorcycle or a car. It is not uncommon for a family in Malaysia to own more than one private vehicle. The demand for motorised transport in Malaysia especially motorcycles and cars is in an upward trend (Azzman Abdul Jamal, n.d.). In recent years, the number of vehicles has been increasing, and this has led to an increasing number of road accidents. This can be seen from the road crash data collected in Malaysia from the year 2010 to 2019 (Ministry of Transport Malaysia, 2023). Road accidents are a global issue. According to the World Health Organization (WHO), it is a fact that nearly 1.3 million people die in road traffic crashes each year (World Health Organization, 2022). Among the causes of road injury and crashes are reckless driving, engineering factors and environmental aspects (Akmalia Shabadin et al., 2021). Road accidents not only cause financial loss but physical injuries, emotional trauma, disability and in a serious case, loss of life. The devastating consequences bring significant impacts to individuals, families, communities and society (Zafar, 2023). Therefore, it is important to take steps to mitigate or prevent road accidents. To this end, the Intelligent

Transport System (ITS) has been introduced to minimise traffic problems and to increase traffic efficiency (Ashokkumar et al., 2015). Traffic incident detection is an important study in the field of Intelligent Transport System (ITS) (Qureshi & Abdullah, 2013), and vehicle detection algorithms play an essential role in this aspect.

This research project uses the You Only Look Once version 5 (YOLOv5) algorithm for 2D vehicle detection to identify the vehicle in the images, whereas the YOLO3D algorithm is trained with the Kitti dataset for 3D vehicle detection to draw a 3D bounding box around the identified vehicle. The Residual Network (ResNet) architecture is one of the techniques employed in 3D vehicle detection to determine the front side of the vehicle to detect the moving direction of the vehicle. Besides that, this method is also able to detect illegal road activities and provide statistics on vehicles for decision-making to be made by the relevant authorities. The objectives of this project are to study the existing techniques and methods for traffic incident detection, develop methods to detect the incident that occurs on the scene using artificial intelligence (AI) approaches such as to detect the vehicle moving on the opposite direction of the road, and generate analytics representation on the incidental data for decision-making purposes. Section "Literature Review" presents the literature review of object detection techniques. Section "Proposed Solution" describes the proposed vehicle detection techniques. The experiment results and discussion are presented in Section "Experimental Results and Discussion". The research work is concluded in Section "Conclusion".

Literature Review

Object Detection

Object detection is a technology in computer vision that allows computer systems to understand and analyse visual data. It is often used to find the instance of objects in an image or video. Object detection can be applied to applications such as surveillance cameras and dashboard cameras. It can identify the object from the video scenes captured by the camera, including but not limited to people, cars, or animals. In this detection technology, a bounding box will be drawn around the object detected. This bounding box is used to help locate and identify the detected objects in an image. It is represented by a rectangular area and is defined by 4 coordinates. Nowadays, object detection technology has been widely used in autonomous driving (Khatab et al., 2021), surveillance, image search and other fields (Deng et al., 2020).

Object detection based on machine learning and deep learning typically can produce a meaningful result. It can help us recognise and locate the objects within seconds. Some object detection models are trained by using large labelled datasets and they are available online. The trained models learn to recognise the features to distinguish different object classes and even its behaviours. This can help us to solve problems in our lives such as detecting the moving direction of the car in the autonomous vehicle system or to detect human and animal actions from a surveillance camera.

However, there are some limitations in object detection that need to be addressed. The first limitation is that object detection methods may not be able to recognise and localise an object when it is occluded by another object. The second limitation involves the noise of the object appearance such as complex background that could affect the accuracy of detection. The complex background will make the identification of the object boundary difficult to identify a relevant object in the image. Besides that, the training of an effective object detection model requires a large training dataset and an abundance of processing resources (Lin et al., 2015). While creating datasets is a heavy workload, the training of detection models can be limited if the processing resources are lacking.

According to C. Liu et al. (2018), object detection algorithms can mainly be divided into two methods: the traditional method and deep learning method. The deep learning method is further divided into two categories. The first category is object detection based on region proposal that includes Region-based Convolutional Neural Network (RCNN) (Girshick et al., 2014), Spatial Pyramid Pooling (SPP-net), Fast Region-based Convolutional Network (Fast-RCNN) and Faster Region-based Convolutional Neural Network (Faster-RCNN) (Ren et al., 2016). The other category is object detection based on regression, for example, Single Shot Detector (SSD) (W. Liu et al., 2016) and You Only Look Once (YOLO). The difference between the two categories is region proposal-based algorithm generates region proposal network first and then classifies these region proposals whereas the regression-based algorithm conducts these processes at the same time.

You Only Look Once (YOLO)

YOLO (Redmon et al., 2016) is a deep learning method and popular object detection algorithm in computer vision. YOLO can use the neural network to provide a real-time object detection service based on deep learning. YOLO is faster than the traditional object detection method. It is not similar to the traditional object detection methods that use multi-stage pipelines. The YOLO algorithm is able to perform object detection with a single neural network in one evaluation. YOLO assumes object detection as a regression problem of spatially separated bounding boxes and it will predict class probabilities directly based on the bounding boxes. Each of the bounding boxes is responsible for detecting the object that stays within its boundary. YOLO makes a prediction based on the bounding box coordinates and calculates the class probability for each of the detected objects.

According to (Du, 2018), YOLO selects GoogLeNet as the base network but not VGG-16 because GoogLeNet has a faster rate of forwarding transport computation versus precision than VGG-16. YOLO is popular in object detection because of its speed. YOLO has a breakthrough in the max speed limit of CNN with excellent accuracy. The fastest speed of YOLO has achieved a result with 155 frames per second (FPS) with a mean average precision (mAP) of 78.6. Also, YOLO can reason and encode the contextual information of the image. Therefore, it is less likely to predict false positives in the background. However, it is difficult to generalise to objects with new or unusual aspect ratios. Besides that, the loss function for the small bounding boxes and large boxes is still imperfect. In the subsequent versions of YOLO, such as YOLOv2 and YOLOv3, the architecture of the YOLO algorithm has been improved and some of the limitations have been resolved.

Residual Neural Network (ResNet)

Residual Neural Network (ResNet) (He et al., 2016b) is an artificial neural network, and it is a popular architecture in computer vision tasks. According to (He et al., 2016a), the author developed an approach to address the degradation problem by introducing a deep residual learning framework. The identity shortcut connection in the ResNet allows the model to skip one or more layers without adding any extra parameter and computational complexity to the model. The formula of F(x)+x as in Figure 3.1 can be realised by the feedforward neural networks with shortcut connections. A shortcut connection will simply perform the identity mapping and add the output to the output of the stacked layers. This approach can train the network on a thousand layers without compromising its performance.

There are many variants architecture in ResNet that have the same concept but different numbers of layers. The first ResNet architecture is the Resnet-34, which is a residual neural network that is transformed from a plain network

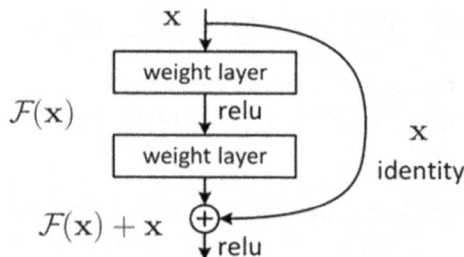

FIGURE 3.1
Building block.

by using shortcut connections. The plain network is mainly inspired by VGG (Visual Geometry Group) neural networks (VGG-19) with 3×3 filters whereas the ResNet has fewer filters and lower complexity. Besides that, there are two simple rules that need to be followed. First, the layers must have the same number of filters when there is the same output feature map size. Second, the number of filters should be twice the feature map size to preserve the time complexity per layer.

YOLO3D

YOLO3D is also known as You Only Look Once 3D. YOLO3D is an extension of the YOLO algorithm that is designed to detect objects in a 3D point cloud. The other YOLO algorithm that focuses on 2D object detection can only detect and draw the 2D bounding boxes. As for the YOLO3D, it is an extension of the YOLO architecture with the third dimension and is able to perform object detection in 3D space with an additional dimension. The architecture of YOLO3D is composed mainly of 2D and 3D object detection techniques.

According to (Ali et al., 2018), the author worked to extend the YOLOv2 (Redmon & Farhadi, 2016) model. It is based on the one-shot regression meta-architecture from the 3D perspective image space and be extended to a 3D bounding box from the LiDAR (Light Detection and Ranging) point cloud. The LiDAR point cloud is a collection of 3D points that are captured by a LiDAR sensor. There are several approaches that have been carried out to reach this objective. The following is the explanation of each approach.

Firstly, the bird-view of the 3D LiDAR point cloud was fed to the input convolution channel. The network architecture should follow the YOLO's meta-architecture and be adjusted to match the LiDAR inputs. The bird-view grid map was created from the point cloud projection, and it was not only simply flattening the 3D data into 2D data. Secondly, the point cloud projection extracted features such as density or elevation and used them as pixel values to obtain a 2D image. Two grid maps were created from the projection. The first grid map contained the maximum height, and each pixel value represented the highest point for that pixel. The second grid map contained the density of the points in which the higher the value in the pixel, the more points would be associated with this pixel.

Next, the Yaw Angle Regression was calculated and used to identify the orientation of the bounding boxes, from the range of $-\pi$ to π. The range of the bounding box has been standardised to be from -1 to 1 and the model was adjusted to predict the orientation of the bounding box via a single regressed number. After that, the K-means clustering was used to calculate the Anchor. This Anchor was used as the reference template for the detection, and it handled the entire range of the bounding box in the training dataset. The YOLOv2 model was trained with images that have the same high variability

TABLE 3.1

Validation Results

Label	Precision	Recall
PEDESTRIAN	44.00%	39.20%
CYCLIST	65.13%	51.10%
CAR	94.07%	83.40%

for the bounding boxes of an object class due to most of the cars having similar shapes and sizes. Therefore, the clustering method was suitable to be used in the calculation of the anchors. As there was no high variability in box dimensions within the same object class in the bird-view grid maps, the Anchor was calculated based on the average box dimension of each object class.

Besides that, the models used were based on the YOLOv2 architecture with some changes. They changed the down-sampling in max-pooling layer from 32 to 16 and removed the skip-connection from the model. Kitti dataset was used to train the model. It provided point cloud data that was projected in 2D space. There were a total 150 of training iterations performed. The learning rate for the training of model started from 0.00001 and was slowly increased to 0.0005. This is because if using a larger learning rate at the beginning, the model will diverge.

The result of the proposed architecture is shown in Table 3.1. The model can detect all the object classes based on the 2 channels bird-view input and has successfully achieved a real-time performance of 40 frames per second on the Titan X GPU (Titian X Graphics Processing Unit). The size of the validation dataset is about 40% of the Kitti training dataset size, and the precision for pedestrian is 44.00%, precision for cyclist is 65.13% and precision for car is 94.07%, respectively.

Proposed Solution

Dataset

In this research, two datasets used include the dataset used for training a custom YOLOv5 model and the Kitti dataset. The dataset used to train and test the YOLOv5 model must fulfil some criteria. Firstly, it is important to search for a suitable place to take videos. This means the video should have a high viewing angle so that all the road scenes can be fully recorded in the video. Secondly, it is recommended to record the video in front of the traffic light so that some traffic rules such as the moving direction of a vehicle and

Car	DontCare	Pedestrian	Van	Cyclist	Truck	Misc	Tram	Person_sitting
28742	11295	4487	2914	1627	1094	973	511	222

FIGURE 3.2
3D types of objects in the Kitti dataset.

making U-turn can be recorded in the video. Besides that, the video must be taken from different angles of the road and at different time periods (morning, afternoon, evening, and night).

The Kitti dataset (Andreas Geiger et al., 2017) that was used to train the model in this research consisted of the training images, label files for the images and the calibration files. The total number of these files is 7481. Figure 3.2 shows the labels (object class) that were labelled in the Kitti dataset. They were the data included in the label files. There were nine classes of objects in the dataset (Zhang, 2019/2023). In this research, the focus is on vehicles. So, only three objects were selected from this dataset. They were the car, van and the truck. There were 28742 cars, 2914 vans and 1094 trucks, respectively. Based on these numbers, the car has a better detection performance as compared to the other two classes of vehicles.

Labelling and Classifying Images

The collected video data were converted into images frame by frame through the scene video filter in the VLC media player. After that, the vehicles in the images were selected and each was labelled with a square box and then were classified based on vehicle classes. The process of labelling and classifying the images is called annotation. This is the preparation work required before starting to train our own custom object detection model with the YOLOv5 algorithm. In this step, the graphical image annotation tool – LabelImg (HumanSignal, n.d.) was used. It is essential to complete the annotation process. The annotation step is to create a bounding box around the vehicles in the image and assign a class to them based on the type of the vehicle. We then saved these data in text files. Once the annotation process is completed, it is ready for the detection model training.

Training and Testing of YOLOv5 Detection Model

The purpose of training and testing the detection model is to let the detection model accurately detect the vehicle, surround the vehicle with a 2D bounding box, identify the vehicle type, and label it with the type of vehicle. All the training and testing processes were conducted in the Google Collab as it provided a free GPU to run the Python code without any setup. Before starting the training, we cloned the repository of specific YOLOv5 method from the GitHub website.

Once the repository had been cloned, the pre-trained dataset would temporarily be saved inside the Google Collab folder. We then trained the object detection model with the pre-trained dataset. This object detection model can detect objects in a video or an image. The output video or output image is a 2D object bounding box around the detected object. These detected objects are based on the classes that had been trained in the pre-trained dataset.

Besides that, we can build a custom object detection model with more object classes (more than three object classes: car, van and truck). To do this, the class file (the text files as mentioned in Section "Labelling and Classifying Images") needs to be customised during the training process so that a detection model can be built based on the class file. The output of detection will be likely the same as the previous output, that is, a 2D object bounding box around the detected object but with different class labels around the bounding box.

Create 3D Model of Vehicle

Due to the small size of the custom dataset for the 2D detection model, a pre-trained model was chosen for 3D model building. The purpose of building a 3D model is to identify the front and back of the vehicle, the moving directions of the vehicle and to detect the behaviours of the vehicle such as illegally moving forward or backward.

YOLO3D and the Kitti dataset were used to build the 3D model based on the pre-trained 2D detection model from YOLOv5. For the YOLO3D algorithm, the original code was obtained from the GitHub website that is owned by Ruhyadi (Mousavian et al., 2017) (Ruhyadi, 2022/2023). Several setups were required in order to start running this YOLO3D detection model on our computer. Firstly, an environment in anaconda with the python version 3.8.16, setuptools version 58.0.4, cuda version 11.1 (NVIDIA Developer, n.d.) and pytorch version 1.9.0+cu111 (PyTorch, n.d.) was created. It is important to make sure that the cuda matches with the pytorch version or otherwise an error might occur.

Two pre-trained models were generated by using different regression models – ResNet18 and VGG11. They were used to identify the front and back of the vehicle based on the 2D bounding box that performed the detection by using the YOLOv5 model. The estimated output was postulated to surround the detected vehicles with a 3D bounding box and to identify the front view of the vehicles. However, both pre-trained models did not perform well in drawing 3D bounding box for the detected vehicles. We then performed some steps and training to improve the model performance.

Through the observation and testing, the 2D detection performed reasonably good and the 2D bounding boxes correctly surrounded the vehicles in the images. Nevertheless, there were some problems with the 3D detection.

This means the two pre-trained models need some further training. We then manipulated several parameters to train the model. We made changes to the learning rates for both regression models in the training. We then observed the performance of the model based on the training loss. We obtained a smaller range between the minimum and maximum training loss. This indicates a better performance of the model.

We also cropped the test image size into smaller rectangular sizes, for the width to be longer than the height to improve the model performance. This process helps to reduce the noise in the image and focus on the vehicles we want to detect. Although this way will reduce the number of vehicles in an image, it will produce a better detection result. Figure 3.3 shows the detection result of using the cropped image.

Vehicle Behaviour Detection

We then observed the performance of the model based on the training loss. We obtained a smaller range between the minimum and maximum training loss. This indicates a better performance of the model.

We also cropped the test image size into smaller rectangular sizes, for the width to be longer than the height to improve the model performance. This process helps to reduce the noise in the image and focus on the vehicles we want to detect. Although this way will reduce the number of vehicles in an image, it will produce a better detection result. Figure 3.3 shows the detection result of using the cropped image. After improving the performance of the 3D detection model, we proceeded to develop vehicle behaviour detection. Videos were used for this process. This is because it is impossible to determine the behaviour of a vehicle in an image in which the vehicle in an image is stationary and does not move. Based on the vehicles in a video, we split the video into a list of consecutive frames. We then determined the behaviour of the vehicle by comparing the location of the vehicle in the current frame

FIGURE 3.3
3D detection after training by using cropped image.

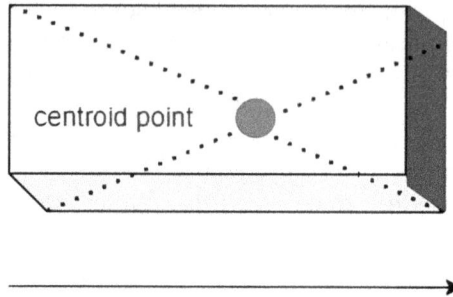

FIGURE 3.4
Centroid point of a vehicle.

and previous frame to determine whether the vehicle is moving forward or backward. It is important to note that the code from the author, Ruhyadi, can only run 3D detection on the images. So, a new detection way is needed for the 3D detection to be performed on a video.

Besides that, we also compared the location of the vehicle in each of the frames. A centroid point was drawn and saved to recognise the centre of the detected vehicle (see Figure 3.4). The centroid point can be obtained from the four points of the bounding box in the 2D detection. Through this centroid point, the movement of the vehicle can easily be tracked in the video and the action of the vehicle can be determined. Before comparing the centroid point between two frames, it is important to find the two centroid points that have the closest distance. Although this method may help us to find that these two points belong to the same vehicle, it does not always work correctly. For example, when there are too many vehicles in the video, it may cause the method to find a point belonging to another vehicle. This is a problem that needs to be solved in the future.

The expected result of the detection is to be able to determine whether the vehicle is moving forward or backward. To reach this result, the alpha value is used for detection. The 3D bounding box with the alpha value can help to determine the front of the vehicle. Through some observations, it is possible to know the directions of the vehicles based on different alpha values. In Figure 3.5, the vehicle with negative alpha value is shown on the upper half side of the figure. The value of alpha is from the range 0 to −3, as the orientation of the vehicle changes, the alpha value changes accordingly. In contrast, the vehicle that has a positive alpha value is shown on the lower half part, with the alpha value ranging from 0 to 3.

After confirming the direction of the vehicle, the process of determining whether the vehicle is moving forward or backward can be started through comparing the centroid point of the vehicle and its alpha value in the current frame and the previous frame. This moving direction detection is based on 3D detection. If the 3D detection is wrongly predicted, it may lead to wrongly

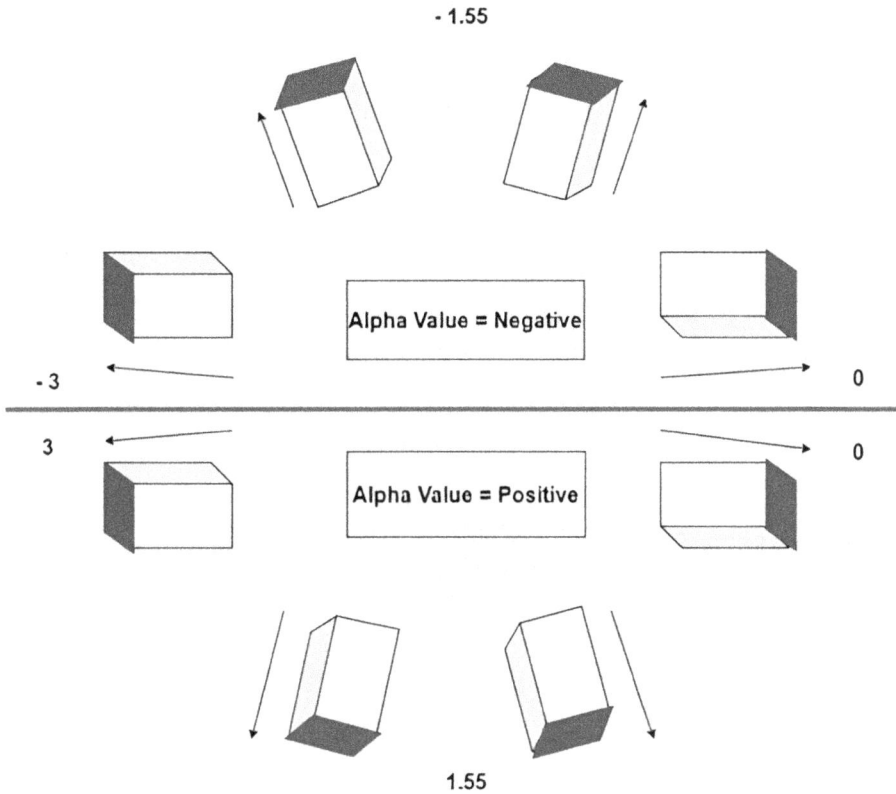

FIGURE 3.5
Alpha values versus vehicle directions.

determining the moving direction. For example, a vehicle with an alpha value on 1.05, which is the 3D bounding box labelled number 1 in Figure 3.6, the moving direction can be determined by comparing the coordinate X of the centroid point in current frame with the coordinate X of the centroid point in the previous frame. If the coordinate X of the vehicle in the current frame is greater than the coordinate X in the previous frame, the vehicle is moving forward. On the contrary, if coordinate X of the vehicle in the current frame is smaller than the coordinate X in the previous frame (Figure 3.7), the vehicle is moving backward. This is the method to determine the action of vehicle in this research project.

After that, a rule can be set to restrict the detection of vehicle movement when running the 3D detection in the video. There are four types of restrictions that were applied in this project. We named these restrictions based on the direction of the clock hand such as 3 o'clock, 6 o'clock, 9 o'clock and 12 o'clock. We can set the restriction before starting the detection, that is, set

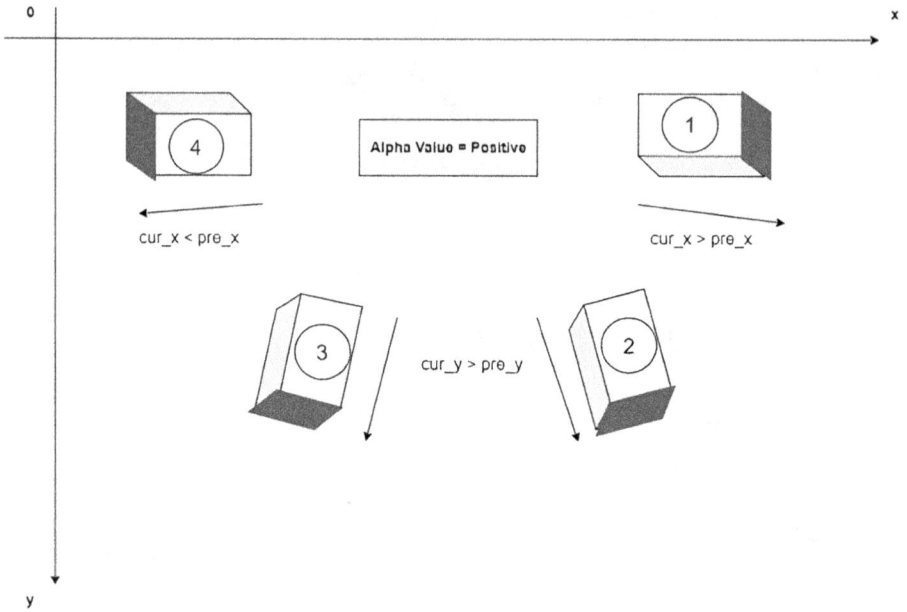

FIGURE 3.6
Vehicle with positive alpha value.

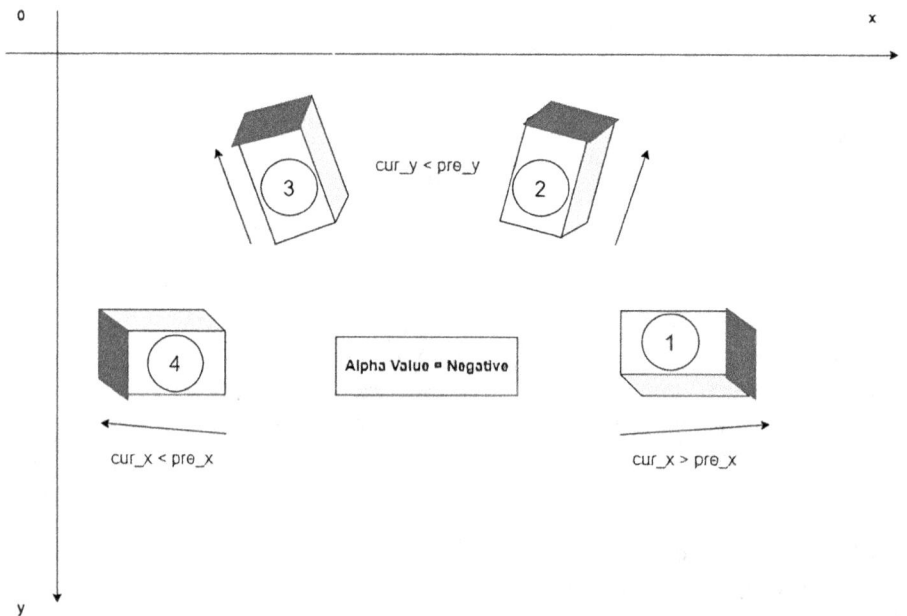

FIGURE 3.7
Vehicle with negative alpha value.

FIGURE 3.8
An example of "No Restriction" detection.

FIGURE 3.9
An example of detection result when restriction is set to 3.

3 for the 3 o'clock direction, set 6 for the 6 o'clock direction, set 9 for the 9 o'clock direction, and set 12 for the 12 o'clock direction. The default setting for the detection refers to no restriction is applied, and the result is as shown in Figure 3.8. One can manually set the restriction before starting the detection by selecting any one restriction type as mentioned above. For example, if the restriction is set to 3, moving in the direction of 3 o'clock is prohibited. Figure 3.9 shows an example of this restriction in which a vehicle was heading towards the 3 o'clock direction, and the detection model successfully detected it and the text "Not Allowed" was displayed in the detection scene.

Experimental Results and Discussion

3D Detection Evaluation

A set of testing data that involved 105 cropped images was used to test the selected model. This testing focuses on detecting the correct orientation of the vehicle. This means the 3D bounding box must be correctly drawn to determine the front of a vehicle. To test this, we manually observed and checked that the 3D bounding boxes were drawn correctly, the number of true results was used to calculate the accuracy of the model. To avoid counting mistakes due to human errors, we performed three times of detection checks. Each time the detection produced a total of 311 detections. We then calculated the average accuracy based on the three detection tests. Table 3.2 presents the results. The accuracy for the selected model inference on cropped images is 82.21%.

Table 3.3 shows the results when the 3D detection was performed directly on the original size images. In this testing, a dataset that consisted of 105 original images was tested and it produced a total of 354 detections. In this testing, only a few detections correctly determined the orientation of vehicle and drew the 3D bounding box. For the false detection, it included the bounding box that was completely wrong and could not be observed by humans. The accuracy of applying the 3D detection on the original images is 32.30%. It shows poor performance as compared to using cropped images. This indicates that cropped images can help us improve the accuracy of 3D detection. It is important to note that with the cropped images, the total number of detections that occurred in testing was also reduced. This is because we had cropped the interest object from the image and other not necessary objects were removed.

TABLE 3.2

Results of 3D Detection On Cropped Images

| | 3D Detection for Vehicle | | | |
	True	*False*	Accuracy	Total
DETECTION TEST 1	251	60	80.71%	311
DETECTION TEST 2	257	54	82.64%	
DETECTION TEST 3	259	52	83.28%	
	AVERAGE ACCURACY		82.21%	

TABLE 3.3

Results of 3D Detection On Original Images

| | 3D Detection for Vehicle | | | |
	True	*False*	Accuracy	Total
DETECTION TEST 1	109	245	30.79%	354
DETECTION TEST 2	117	237	33.05%	
DETECTION TEST 3	117	237	33.05%	
	AVERAGE ACCURACY		32.30%	

Table 3.4 shows the performance when running the 3D detection at night-time. In each test, 200 frames were extracted from a video to evaluate the nighttime 3D bounding box drawing. From the table, the accuracy for detection test 1 is 21.27%, detection test 2 is 14.47%, detection test 3 is 64.95% and detection test 4 is 54.68%.

Evaluation of Forward and Backward Moving Directions

The performance of the model in detecting the direction of vehicle movement was evaluated. Some testing videos that contained vehicles with different alpha values were tested and the accuracy rates were calculated after the testing. All the testing videos were cropped based on higher accuracy we obtained from the previous 3D detection evaluation result. Each video was checked for 200 frames for the vehicle movement (moving forward) with a correct 3D bounding box of vehicles. From Table 3.5, the accuracy of running the movement direction detection in forward test 1 video is 76.96%, forward test 2 video is 68.16%, forward test 3 video is 62.99% and forward test 4 video is 69.75%.

Table 3.6 shows the results when the 3D detection was performed on the cropped videos with backward moving direction. Each video was checked for 200 frames and the accuracy was calculated based on the number of correctly predicted frames. The accuracy of running the backward movement direction detection in test 1 video is 100.00%, test 2 video is 31.00%, test 3 video is 64.94% and test 4 video is 73.08%.

TABLE 3.4

Results of 3D Detection On Night View

| | 3D Detection for Vehicle | | | |
	True	*False*	Accuracy	Total
DETECTION TEST 1	57	211	21.27%	268
DETECTION TEST 2	11	65	14.47%	76
DETECTION TEST 3	415	224	64.95%	639
DETECTION TEST 4	374	310	54.68%	684

TABLE 3.5

Moving Forward Detection Testing

| | Detection For Going Forward | | | |
	True	*False*	Accuracy	Total
FORWARD TEST 1	304	91	76.96%	395
FORWARD TEST 2	167	78	68.16%	245
FORWARD TEST 3	160	94	62.99%	254
FORWARD TEST 4	113	49	69.75%	162

TABLE 3.6

Moving Backward Detection Testing

	Detection for Going Backward			
	True	*False*	Accuracy	Total
BACKWARD TEST 1	304	0	100.00%	395
BACKWARD TEST 2	167	69	31.00%	245
BACKWARD TEST 3	160	27	64.94%	254
BACKWARD TEST 4	113	21	73.08%	162

TABLE 3.7

Detection Results of Restricted Moving Directions

	Detection for Restrict Moving Direction			
	True	*False*	Accuracy	Total
RESTRICTION 3	32	13	71.11%	45
RESTRICTION 6	193	25	88.53%	218
RESTRICTION 9	8	2	80.00%	10
RESTRICTION 12	232	80	74.36%	312

Evaluation of Restricted Moving Direction

This testing is mainly to evaluate if a vehicle is moving in a restricted moving direction. We tested the model by selecting 1 restriction from the 4 types of restrictions that have been mentioned in Section "Vehicle Behaviour Detection". For the first test, the restriction type was set to 3 for the detection model to check for vehicles that moved to the right. In this case, vehicles that moved to the right were counted as true and were detected as "not allowed" and vice versa. We repeated the test by setting the restriction to 6 (moving down the road), 9 (moving left), and 12 (moving up the road), respectively. The accuracy we obtained for Restriction 3 is 71.11%, for Restriction 6 is 88.53%, for Restriction 9 is 80%, and for Restriction 12 is 74.36%. The accuracy obtained indicates that the detection model performs well in detecting restricted moving directions.

Conclusion

In summary, this traffic incidental detection system uses the YOLOv5 algorithm to build the 2D object detection model, which can identify and surround the vehicle with 2D bounding box and label the class of vehicle. The

3D object detection model of the vehicle has been trained using the YOLO3D algorithm and the Kitti dataset. This 3D detection model can identify the front of the vehicle with an accuracy of 82.21% by using a cropped image. Besides that, it can track the moving direction of a vehicle. The accuracy of detecting forward and backward moving directions is 69.47% and 67.26%, respectively. In addition, it can also detect the illegal moving direction of a vehicle with an average accuracy of 78.5%.

Nevertheless, the model has some limitations. First, the image or video needs to be cropped into a smaller rectangular size to get a better 3D detection performance. Second, the forward and backward moving directions detection of the vehicle and the restricted moving direction detection are processed according to the results obtained from the 3D detection. While the 3D detection is wrong, it will affect the forward and backward moving directions detection and the restricted moving direction detection.

Despite the limitations, this traffic incidental detection model is useful to detect traffic incidents in time and this can reduce or avoid the occurrence of secondary accidents. This could potentially save more lives and properties. The capability of the detection model to detect the illegal behaviours of the vehicle in the video could help the relevant department formulate a better road planning blueprint and to make plausible decisions that would benefit the community. In the future, this work could be improved by adding more training data to improve the model's accuracy and performance. More illegal behaviours detection such as illegal turning and over-speed driving can be added to the model.

Acknowledgement

This work was supported by the TM R&D Fund (Project no. RDTC/221054 and SAP ID: MMUE/220023) and MMU IR Fund (Project ID MMUI/220041).

References

Akmalia, Shabadin, Hamidun, Rizati, Roslan, Azzuhana, Harun, Nur Zarifah, Rahim, Sharifah Allyana Syed Mohamed, Jamaludin, Nurulhuda, Ishak, Siti Zaharah, & Kassim, Khairil Anwar Abu. (2021). *Identification of crash determinants involving students at school area in Selangor.* Malaysian Institute of Road Safety Research (MIROS). https://miros.gov.my/xs/page.php?id=1086

Ali, W., Abdelkarim, S., Zahran, M., Zidan, M., & Sallab, A. E. (2018). *YOLO3D: End-to-end real-time 3D Oriented Object Bounding Box Detection from LiDAR Point Cloud* (No. arXiv:1808.02350). arXiv. https://doi.org/10.48550/arXiv.1808.02350

Geiger, Andreas, Lenz, Philip, & Urtasun, Raquel. (2017). The KITTI Vision Benchmark Suite. https://www.cvlibs.net/datasets/kitti/eval_object.php?obj_benchmark=3d

Ashokkumar, K., Sam, B., Arshadprabhu, R., & Britto. (2015). Cloud Based Intelligent Transport System. *Procedia Computer Science, 50*, 58–63. https://doi.org/10.1016/j.procs.2015.04.061

Jamal, Azzman Abdul. (n.d.). Public transport flaws, the downfall of Malaysia's walking culture? | MalaysiaNow. Retrieved falseOctober 10, 2023, from https://www.malaysianow.com/news/2022/09/03/public-transport-flaws-the-downfall-of-malaysias-walking-culture

Deng, J., Xuan, X., Wang, W., Li, Z., Yao, H., & Wang, Z. (2020). A review of research on object detection based on deep learning. *Journal of Physics: Conference Series, 1684*(1), 012028. https://doi.org/10.1088/1742-6596/1684/1/012028

Du, J. (2018). Understanding of Object Detection Based on CNN Family and YOLO. *Journal of Physics: Conference Series, 1004*(1), 012029. https://doi.org/10.1088/1742-6596/1004/1/012029

Girshick, R., Donahue, J., Darrell, T., & Malik, J. (2014). *Rich feature hierarchies for accurate object detection and semantic segmentation* (No. arXiv:1311.2524). arXiv. https://doi.org/10.48550/arXiv.1311.2524

He, K., Zhang, X., Ren, S., & Sun, J. (2016a). Deep Residual Learning for Image Recognition. *2016 IEEE Conference on Computer Vision and Pattern Recognition (CVPR)*, 770–778. https://doi.org/10.1109/CVPR.2016.90

He, K., Zhang, X., Ren, S., & Sun, J. (2016b). *Identity Mappings in Deep Residual Networks* (No. arXiv:1603.05027). arXiv. https://doi.org/10.48550/arXiv.1603.05027

Herald, T. (2022, July 17). Public Transport in Malaysia: The Good, the Bad, and What Could be Better. *TLMUN Herald.* https://medium.com/tlmun-herald/public-transport-in-malaysia-the-good-the-bad-and-what-could-be-better-2d18fec734db

HumanSignal. (n.d.). GitHub—HumanSignal/labelImg: LabelImg is now part of the Label Studio community. The popular image annotation tool created by Tzutalin is no longer actively being developed, but you can check out Label Studio, the open source data labeling tool for images, text, hypertext, audio, video and time-series data. Retrieved falseOctober 10, 2023, from https://github.com/HumanSignal/labelImg

Kamba, A. N., Rahmat, R. A. O. K., & Ismail, A. (2007). Why Do People Use Their Cars: A Case Study In Malaysia. *Journal of Social Sciences, 3*(3), 117–122. https://doi.org/10.3844/jssp.2007.117.122

Khatab, E., Onsy, A., Varley, M., & Abouelfarag, A. (2021). Vulnerable objects detection for autonomous driving: A review. *Integration, 78*, 36–48. https://doi.org/10.1016/j.vlsi.2021.01.002

Lin, T.-Y., Maire, M., Belongie, S., Bourdev, L., Girshick, R., Hays, J., Perona, P., Ramanan, D., Zitnick, C. L., & Dollár, P. (2015). *Microsoft COCO: Common Objects in Context* (No. arXiv:1405.0312). arXiv. https://doi.org/10.48550/arXiv.1405.0312

Liu, C., Tao, Y., Liang, J., Li, K., & Chen, Y. (2018). Object Detection Based on YOLO Network. *2018 IEEE 4th Information Technology and Mechatronics Engineering Conference (ITOEC)*, 799–803. https://doi.org/10.1109/ITOEC.2018.8740604

Liu, W., Anguelov, D., Erhan, D., Szegedy, C., Reed, S., Fu, C.-Y., & Berg, A. C. (2016). SSD: Single Shot MultiBox Detector. In *Computer Vision - European Conference on Computer Vision (ECCV) Lecture Notes in Computer Science* (Vol. 9905, pp. 21–37). https://doi.org/10.1007/978-3-319-46448-0_2

Ministry of Transport Malaysia. (2023). Road Accidents and Fatalities in Malaysia. https://www.mot.gov.my/en/land/safety/road-accident-and-facilities

Mousavian, A., Anguelov, D., Flynn, J., & Kosecka, J. (2017). *3D Bounding Box Estimation Using Deep Learning and Geometry* (No. arXiv:1612.00496). arXiv. https://doi.org/10.48550/arXiv.1612.00496

NVIDIA Developer. (n.d.). *CUDA Toolkit 11.1 Downloads*. NVIDIA Developer. Retrieved falseOctober 10, 2023, from https://developer.nvidia.com/cuda-downloads

PyTorch. (n.d.). Installing Previous Versions of Pytorch. Retrieved falseOctober 10, 2023, from https://www.pytorch.org

Qureshi, K., & Abdullah, H. (2013). A Survey on Intelligent Transportation Systems. *Middle-East Journal of Scientific Research, 15*, 629–642. https://doi.org/10.5829/idosi.mejsr.2013.15.5.11215

Redmon, J., Divvala, S., Girshick, R., & Farhadi, A. (2016). *You Only Look Once: Unified, Real-Time Object Detection* (No. arXiv:1506.02640). arXiv. https://doi.org/10.48550/arXiv.1506.02640

Redmon, J., & Farhadi, A. (2016). *YOLO9000: Better, Faster, Stronger* (No. arXiv:1612.08242). arXiv. https://doi.org/10.48550/arXiv.1612.08242

Ren, S., He, K., Girshick, R., & Sun, J. (2016). *Faster R-CNN: Towards Real-Time Object Detection with Region Proposal Networks* (No. arXiv:1506.01497). arXiv. https://doi.org/10.48550/arXiv.1506.01497

Ruhyadi, D. (2023). YOLO For 3D Object Detection [Python]. https://github.com/ruhyadi/YOLO3D (Original work published 2022)

Tong, L. C. (10:25:00+08:00, 2017). Public transport is more than 'big toy' infrastructure. *Malaysiakini*. https://www.malaysiakini.com/news/395737

World Health Organization. (2022, June 20). Road traffic injuries. https://www.who.int/news-room/fact-sheets/detail/road-traffic-injuries

Zafar, S. (2023, May 9). 10 Effects Of Road Accidents | Devastating Consequences. https://www.hseblog.com/effects-of-road-accidents/

Zhang, H. (2023). Dtc-KITTI-For-Beginners [Python]. https://github.com/dtczhl/dtc-KITTI-For-Beginners (Original work published 2019)

4

Revolutionising Agriculture with AI

Siti Fatimah Abdul Razak, Sumendra Yogarayan, Lim Ke Yin,
Sharifah Noor Masidayu Sayed Ismail and Arif Ullah

Introduction

In recent years, the agricultural industry has demonstrated significant changes with the application of smart agriculture and Agriculture 5.0 (Melesse et al., 2024). Traditional methods are being minimised and optimised with the introduction of advanced technologies. As a result, the dependencies on human labour are reduced and more farming practices have been automated. By harnessing advanced technologies like comprehensive simulations, the transformations are not limited to physical improvements; they also provide valuable information and a deeper understanding of various aspects within the industry. However, the challenges of developing robust technologies for agricultural tasks are considerable due to the complexity of field-based processes (Abdul Razak et al., 2024). These processes involve numerous factors, such as plant variability, soil conditions, environmental factors, technological parameters and various influencing variables. The industry would benefit from a comprehensive simulation of the entire agricultural process. Integration of as many of these influencing factors as possible would lead to optimised agricultural outputs and improved decision-making throughout the system. Hence, the concept of Digital Twins (DT) is introduced in Agriculture 5.0 which emphasises soil health, biodiversity and sustainable agricultural practices.

Grieves (2005) introduced DT as a system which consists of three components, that is, physical system, virtual system and interconnection of physical and virtual system. The data and information flow between the physical and virtual system is known as twinning. Since then, there are various definitions of DT in the literature as in Table 4.1. For instance, one of the previous studies defines DT as accurate digital replicas of physical objects, processes, or services (Pylianidis et al., 2021). Digital twins (DTs) commonly rely on the feedback loop between the physical and virtual system which requires

DOI: 10.1201/9781003509196-4

TABLE 4.1

Definitions of Digital Twins

Source	DT definition	Main aspects/components
Grieves (2005)	A system which connects a physical and virtual system through a two-way data communication or loop known as twinning.	i. Physical system ii. Virtual system iii. Interconnection of the virtual and physical system via data and information.
Elijah et al. (2021)	The creation of a virtual entity which replicates a physical entity either physical assets, products or services.	i. The physical systems (physical, communication, cloud server, and application server layers) ii. The virtual system (interface, model and data layers) iii. The process model iv. The business model
Pylianidis, Osinga, and Athanasiadis (2021)	A dynamic virtual representation of a physical object or system that uses real-world data, simulation, or machine learning models combined with data analysis to enable understanding, learning, and reasoning. DT provides intuitive insights to answer what-if questions.	i. Physical system ii. Virtual system iii. Physical and virtual system coupling iv. Data analysis
Sharma et al. (2022)	A digital duplicate of an existing physical entity.	i. Elementary (physical asset, digital asset, information flow between physical and digital asset) ii. Imperative (IoT devices, integrated time continuous data) iii. Machine learning iv. Security of data and information flow v. DT performance evaluation
Attaran and Celik (2023)	A simulation model that acquires data from the field and triggers the operation of physical devices.	Internet of Things (IoT), ArtificialIntelligence (AI), Extended Reality (XR) and Cloud technologies for DT main aspects: i. data acquisition ii. data modelling iii. data application

(Continued)

TABLE 4.1 (CONTINUED)

Definitions of Digital Twins

Source	DT definition	Main aspects/components
Symeonaki, Maraveas, and Arvanitis (2024)	A bidirectional data and information flow between physical and virtual system.	i. Physical system with monitoring and sensing capabilities. ii. Virtual system incorporated with data mining, processing and AI/ML analytics. iii. The twinning which enables interconnection between the physical and virtual system.
Tagarakis et al. (2024)	A virtual representation of physical objects or systems with bidirectional, fully integrated data flows.	i. data acquisition ii. data modelling iii. data application
Melesse et al. (2024)	A single system which combines sensors, computing power, communication tools, and executions to manage the whole life cycle of a product.	i. Physical asset ii. Virtual testing platform iii. Intelligence layer

strong data connectivity to create a virtual representation of the physical system and produce valuable insights (Tagarakis et al., 2024).

Innovative advancements in farming practices are made possible with the integration of real-time data collection from multiple sources including historical data, in-field sensors, livestock equipped with biological sensors, environmental and climate data. DT enables accurate replication of the physical farm in the virtual system. This allows comprehensive simulations to be conducted which facilitates enhancements or redesign of existing farming practices to address current challenges and demand of the agricultural domain (Peladarinos et al., 2023). The DT can be grouped into 4 types based on the application as illustrated in Figure 4.1. Nevertheless, maintaining an accurate and up-to-date digital twin for agricultural tasks is a major challenge especially since the processes rely heavily on natural conditions such as soil conditions, weather and seasonal variations. This is where AI techniques can be utilised. By employing AI algorithms, data collection, integration and processing from multiple sources can be automated. These algorithms are capable of efficiently handling large volumes of real-time data, ensuring that the digital twin accurately reflects the current state of the farm.

Furthermore, literature review reveals that the integration of artificial intelligence (AI) can enhance the capabilities of DT. For instance, AI can be used to optimise the analytics model within the virtual system for classification and regression tasks (Kreuzer et al., 2024). AI methods can be implemented to enhance data pre-processing and quality which is fundamental to producing

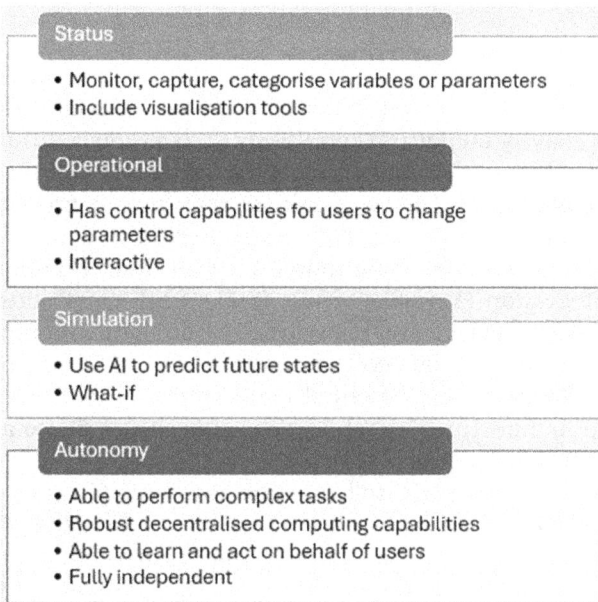

FIGURE 4.1
Types of digital twins.

reliable predictions (Emmert-Streib, 2023). AI empowers the virtual system to intelligently replicate and create realistic physical farm environments (Pexyean et al., 2022). In the absence of AI, it will be challenging to process multidimensional use case-specific data from various sources and generate data-driven insights which are actionable on the actual environment (Mihai et al., 2022). For instance, DTs often use controllers that combine ontologies, ML and deep learning techniques to facilitate decision-making based on IoT data using advanced algorithms that leverage the most up-to-date user information. By utilising time-series data, a user's DT can suggest measures to manage or mitigate potential risks, such as droughts that can affect crop well-being and output. This involves assessing irrigation efficiency and addressing issues with farm machinery, plant production equipment, or post-harvest transportation/storage equipment. In such cases, DTs can alert stakeholders to warning signs or swiftly take action to minimise adverse impacts on crop production (Nasirahmadi & Hensel, 2022). Hence, AI and ML incorporated DTs have the potential to enhance agricultural productivity and assist with precision agriculture operations (Melesse et al., 2024).

Therefore, this chapter presents the potential of AI-powered digital twins in agriculture, focusing on their capabilities, benefits and challenges. The following section includes the applications of AI-enhanced DTs for agriculture.

Fundamentals of Digital Twins in Agriculture

Agriculture is an industry that is both highly complex and dynamic. The processes rely heavily on natural conditions such as soil conditions, weather and seasonal variations. Moreover, the DTs for agriculture primarily focus on the various elements of the agricultural production process. Five main classes of DT in agriculture are energy consumption analysis, system failure analysis and prediction, real-time monitoring, optimisation or update, and technology integration (Verdouw et al., 2021). Each class aims to digitally capture and solidify agricultural knowledge by utilising different production models, system rules and data collections (Nie et al., 2022). Hence, although digital twin technology has potential benefits for agriculture, most of the modelling and architectures are still in the conceptual phase and have not been implemented yet (Wang, 2024).

In a recent study, Barbie, Hasselbring and Hansen (2024) define DT prototypes as the software prototype of a physical twin where the configurations are equal, but the connected sensors or actuators are emulated using existing data. In a previous study, Ghandar et al. (2021) explored the development and implementation of a decision support system for urban agriculture using digital twin technology. Sensor data and simulation model provides real-time feedback for a case study on aquaponics, a sustainable method of raising fish and plants in a mutually beneficial environment. In a separate study, Howard et al. (2021) present a comprehensive framework for DT designed specifically for commercial greenhouses. The primary goals of this framework are to optimise management strategies and reduce energy consumption by effectively modelling and balancing multiple interconnected system variables. The authors provide a high-level overview of the DT's functionalities and describe it as a powerful tool that leverages internet-of-things technology, agent-based modelling, and artificial intelligence to facilitate modelling, control and optimisation processes.

Chaux, Sanchez-Londono and Barbieri (2021) present an architecture for DTs in controlled environment agricultural systems, focusing on greenhouses. They also offer a case study to illustrate this architecture. The proposed design comprises six technology layers, that is, the physical greenhouse, a controller, gateway, data storage, intelligence, and the DT layer. These DTs utilise both current and historical data to assess different crop treatments and climate control strategies provided by the intelligence layer. By incorporating predictions for future climate conditions, energy consumption, and projected crop growth and yields, along with recommendations for optimal crop treatment and climate control strategies, the DTs provide valuable insights.

A conceptual DT architecture for agriculture is presented in Figure 4.2. The physical system refers to elements like crops, soil, irrigation systems or

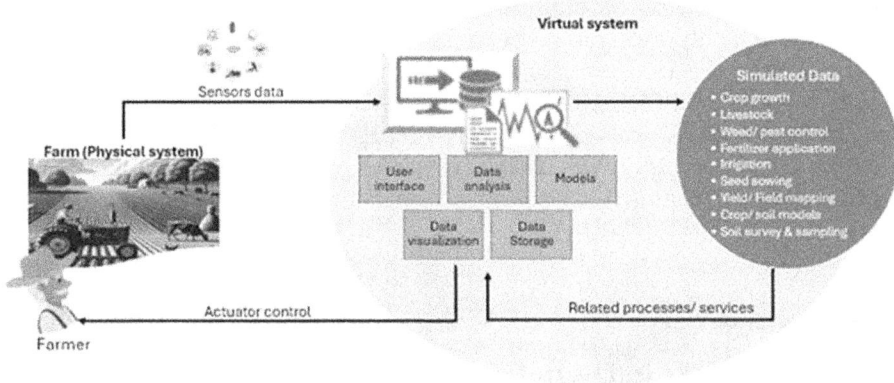

FIGURE 4.2
Conceptual digital twin architecture for agriculture.

livestock. To collect and receive data from these physical objects, in-field sensors and actuators are required to monitor and control various variables and processes in agricultural activities such as humidity, pH level, temperature, nutrients, pest infestation, soil depletion and weather impacts. Data from sensor or sensing devices will be transmitted to the virtual system which consists of the user interface, data models, analysis, storage and visualisation. The virtual system replicates a field's characteristics including the field size and shape, topography, soil types, sunlight exposure, planting patterns, drainage and cultivation history. The specific connection components used may vary depending on factors such as the source, type and volume of data, data transfer rate and speed, as well as the minimum delay between data acquisition and feedback. Generally, DT in agriculture is implemented using simulation which creates a real-time representation of a field's current state, helping farmers closely monitor crops, soil, and weather to understand plant growth patterns, evaluate resource needs and react to crop diseases. Hence, simulated data will be produced to provide real-time feedback to the farmers, depending on the agricultural activities such as weed/pest control, soil sampling, crop growth, etc. For instance, the real-time feedback can be daily for the farmer to monitor plant irrigation and nutrients. It can also be seasonal where it facilitates farmers in their planting and harvesting strategies.

The farmers shall monitor the DT using devices where they will be able to access the history or make predictions based on real-time data from sensors. They will also be able to switch on physical systems like fertilising and watering the plants. According to Catala-Roman et al. (2024), these capabilities will enable the farmers to make data-driven decisions which will optimise their farming practices and ensure environmentally sustainable operations. In addition, DTs can serve as educational tools, providing interactive and immersive experiences for students and professionals to learn about sustainable farming techniques and resource management. Even though DT has the potential to be used extensively in various spatial and temporal scales, with different levels of complexity based on its components and the desired functionality, the agricultural applications of DT have not yet demonstrated their added value (Pylianidis et al., 2021). Details on the implementation of DT for agricultural activities are often limited or absent (Bali and Singh 2024).

Integration of AI in Digital Twins for Agriculture

According to Alves et al. (2019), researchers in the agricultural area have adopted artificial intelligence, machine learning and deep-learning algorithm models for various purposes. Traditional machine learning approaches such as neural network, support vector machines, random forest, Bayesian algorithm are among the common approaches used to model state and behaviour characteristics from agricultural data (Dihan et al., 2024). Hence, as AI is adopted in agriculture, there will also be a natural progression towards the adoption of DT technologies (Smith, 2018). From the literature, there has been an increasing amount of work on the DT concept which demonstrates a similar trend with studies related to AI, cyber-physical systems and Internet of Things (Bali & Singh, 2024; Jones et al., 2020). AI techniques are suggested for data processing and analytics to optimise processes and predict potential problems that may not be discovered in the physical system (Nasirahmadi & Hensel, 2022).

Using AI, ML and sensor data, DTs can gather information about physical models and create accurate virtual representations. The models and data of the physical world are represented in a virtual system. This virtual world can include various concepts, such as processing, simulation, software, machine learning, data mining and AI models (Nasirahmadi & Hensel, 2022). The AI algorithms will allow specific DT to address a wider range of issues on the farm using predictive capabilities (Kreuzer et al., 2024).

Moreover, AI algorithms can be employed to automate the collection, integration and processing of data from various sources. These algorithms can efficiently handle large volumes of real-time data, ensuring that the digital twin remains accurate and reflects the current state of the farm (Emmert-Streib, 2023). This facilitates knowledge transfer among farmers, researchers and stakeholders, allowing them to better understand complex agricultural processes (Catala-Roman et al., 2024). Emmert-Streib (2023) highlighted that AI has six significant roles in DT. The performance of the virtual system can be optimised with AI model optimisation including creating and updating AI models, generative modelling, performing data analytics and predictive

analytics as well as facilitating decision-making through quantitative summarisation and visualisations. The author also highlighted that one AI technique is not limited to only one role in a DT (Figure 4.3).

On the other hand, Niggemann et al. (2021) introduced AITwin, a reference
model comprising three key components: a causality model, a prediction-
enabled closed-loop model, and a synchronised data model. These models
align with three categories of ML knowledge compilation methods: distance-
to-normal ML (anomaly detection), extrapolation ML (optimisation and self-
configuration) and symbolic AI (logic-based models). The primary goal of
this proposed model is to eliminate unnecessary duplication of modelling
work and facilitate the reuse and sharing of computed results within cyber-
physical systems, with a particular emphasis on the concept of DT. Figure 4.4
shows the AITwin model.

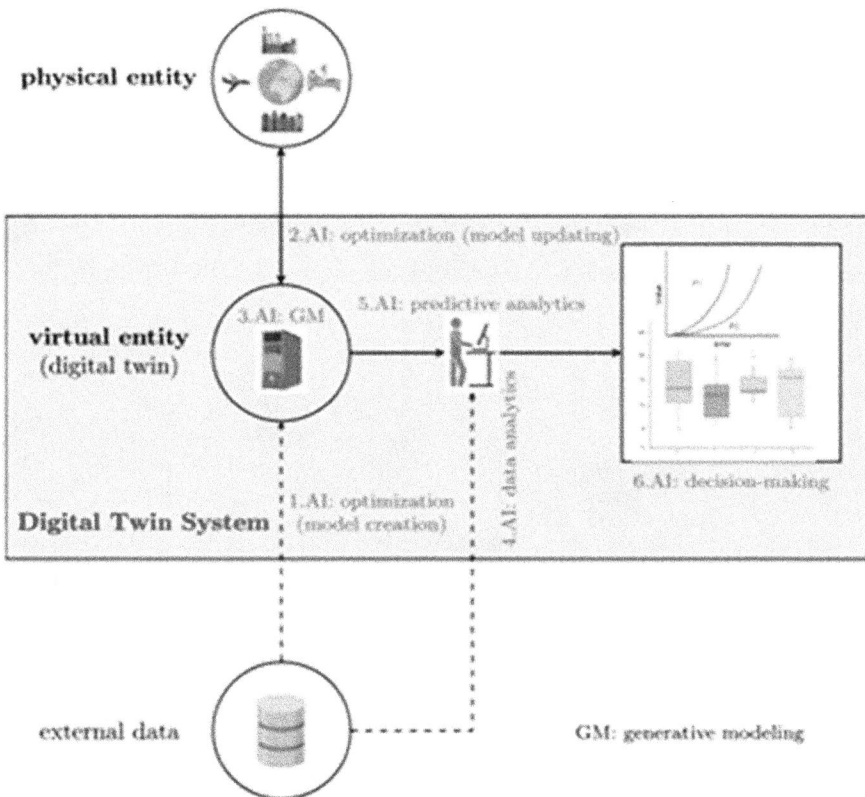

FIGURE 4.3
AI role in DT for agriculture.

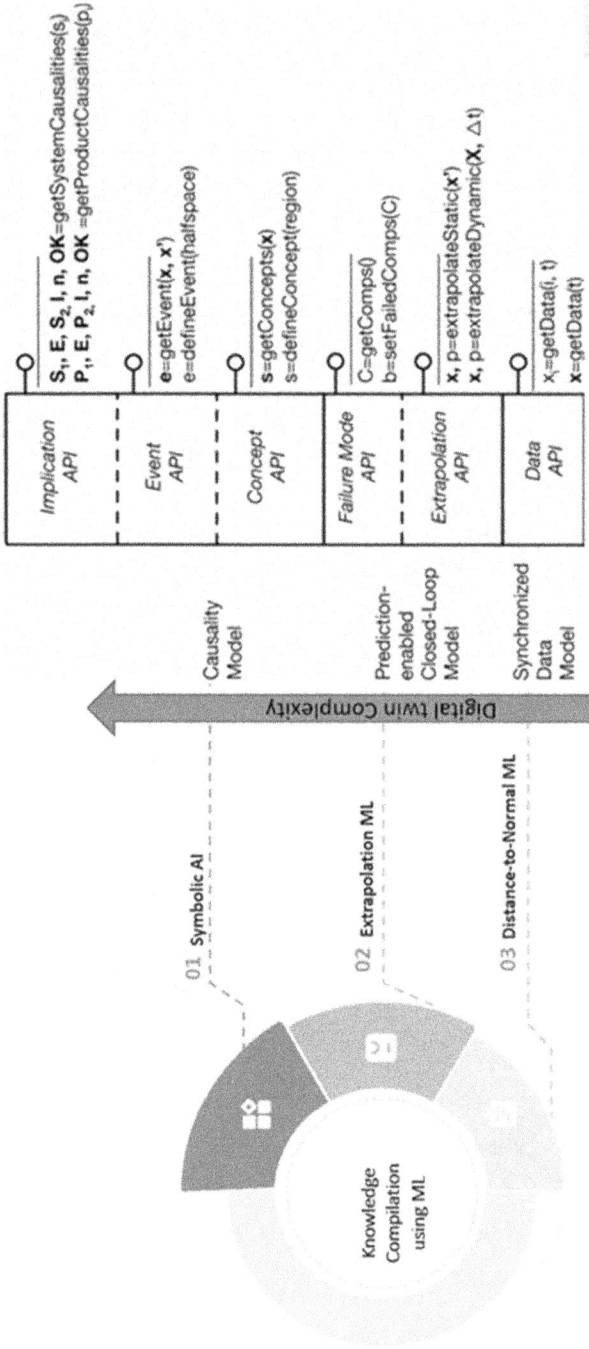

FIGURE 4.4

The Digital Twin AI reference model.

Applications of AI-Powered Digital Twins in Agriculture

Greenhouse Control

Advanced greenhouses are equipped with computer-controlled environmental control, consisting of a network of actuators and sensors to protect crops from the outside environment (Jans-Singh et al., 2020). Every object in the greenhouse, including plants, containers, greenhouse sections and equipment, has the potential to be virtualised and controlled remotely. Digital Twins have the potential to significantly enhance control capabilities for growers. They allow for immediate action to be taken in the event of anticipated deviations and enable the simulation of interventions using real-life data (Ariesen-Verschuur et al., 2022).

Earlier in the year 2018, the first Autonomous Greenhouse Challenge took place to investigate the use of state-of-the-art AI algorithms for cucumber production in existing commercial greenhouse. The aim of the experiment was to maximise net profit and minimise resource use, while controlling greenhouse crop growing remotely. Artificial training data was employed for the participants to develop their own AI algorithms. These algorithms include supervised and unsupervised approach, reinforcement machine learning (Dynamic Regression, Deep Reinforcement Learning DRL, Deep Deterministic Policy Gradient DDPG, Generative Adversarial Networks GAN, Convolutional Neural Networks CNN, Recurrent Neural Networks RNN). The authors concluded that AI-assisted or managed greenhouse production such as Artificial Neural Networks is competitive with experienced manual growers and can even outperform them in potentially improving crop production (Hemming et al., 2019).

Hemming et al. (2020) presented the results of the second Autonomous Greenhouse Challenge which was conducted to use AI algorithms in greenhouse cherry tomato production. A digital twin model of a virtual greenhouse was utilised to analyse various climate and crop management strategies in terms of net profit, yields and resource use. Participants combined AI algorithms such as long-short-term memory (LSTM), bidirectional LSTM (BiLSTM) and reinforcement learning algorithms with conditional (rule based) decisions and expert policies based on historical recorded or empirical data for either climate or crop growing strategies or both. The authors concluded that even though there are opportunities to control crop growth autonomously, the participating team still includes humans in the decision loop.

Howard et al. (2021) present ongoing research on optimising greenhouse production using multi-agent systems and Digital Twin technology. The study focuses on a simulation model powered by the AI simulation platform AnyLogic. This model examines the impact of optimising production scheduling, plant growth, energy consumption and cost simultaneously. The

Digital Twin considers influential factors like production deadlines, quality evaluation, heating requirements, gas and electricity prices, and weather forecasts.

Petropoulou et al. (2023) explored the potential of computer vision and deep learning algorithms in automating operational decisions for lettuce greenhouse production. Factors such as yield, product prices, resource utilisation, and greenhouse occupancy costs were considered to determine climate and crop management strategies that would maximise net profit.

Rahman et al. (2024) proposed a smart greenhouse control framework which utilised the IBM Watson IoT platform. The framework consists of the physical layer, fog layer and cloud layers. Within the cloud layer, there are seven sub-blocks which supports real-time processing, data storage, data analytics, rule engine, AI and machine learning, DT and user interface. Traditional machine learning approaches including Artificial Neural Networks (ANNs), Random Forest (RF), Support Vector Machine (SVM), and Adaptive Boosting (AdaBoost) were trained to automate the smart greenhouse control processes such as monitoring and adjusting the environment temperature and activate the irrigation system.

Crops Management

Publications that focused on developing digital twin methodology in crops management were divided into three categories including mathematical (physics-based), data-driven, and ontological multi-agent models (Melesse et al., 2024).

Kampker et al. (2019) proposed an automated method to calibrate the machine for harvesting potatoes. The authors claimed that the machine can identify the most suitable configuration for potato harvesters to minimise potato damage due to late harvest. They utilised sensors data, information from other related variables and machine learning for this purpose.

Li, Zhu and Wang (2022) investigated crop growth quality parameters to monitor crop growth based on plant leaves images. They proposed a method to reconstruct 3D leaves from a single view plant growth DT system. In addition to Resnet, differentiable render was utilised to enhance feature extraction and combine features with 3D positions. Prediction results and 3D evaluation indicators were also presented.

Kim and Heo (2024) developed a DT for mandarins based on data sourced using an Open API from approximately 185,000 hectares across Jeju Island. The automatic machine learning (AutoML) algorithm was implemented to predict the fruit size and sugar content based on the predictors including time (week and month), weather variables (temperature, humidity, and air pressure), frequency of agricultural practices (thinning, mulching, spraying, fertilisation, and pruning) and the orchard index. The orchard index was identified as the most influential predictor, followed by air pressure, for both sugar content and fruit size. In addition, the AutoML algorithm identified the stacked ensemble model as the best model.

Crop growth data which are manually recorded by farmers are prone to errors. Hence, in a previous study, Jans-Singh et al. (2020) used a random forest algorithm to impute missing temperature data based on outside weather data, the hour of the day, and neighbouring sensor data. In this view, the completed dataset can be used for the development of an urban-integrated hydroponic farm digital twin.

Zohdi (2024) developed a DT framework to simulate forestry management which consists of various growing and interacting plants. Genetic algorithm was employed to determine an optimal set of parameters for agricultural canopy surface growth including the number of plants, ground spacing between plants, initial seedling size, etc.

Livestock Management

In the year 2021, Neethirajan and Kemp proposed a theoretical DT system reference architecture to predict the behaviour of farm animals such as piglets. The architecture includes remote and wearable sensors for gathering data from farm animals, cloud servers, AI models for predictions and user interface (Neethirajan & Kemp, 2021). Later, Neethirajan (2022) conceptually explores how animals communicate their emotions through vocalisations, body movements, facial expressions and posture. The real-time data on the emotions of farm livestock will be gathered by implementing a sensor data processing pipeline in a DT model. This pipeline includes data processing, modelling and simulation phases, ultimately leading to the reporting and prediction of cattle's emotional states based on their tail movements, facial expressions and body posture. Compared to traditional methods which can cause fear, frustration and distress in farm animals, AI technologies offer a solution by enabling the recognition of cattle states. This empowers animal caregivers and ethologists to better understand animal behaviour and optimise their well-being and productivity.

Aquaponics

Ghandar et al. (2021) explored an agent model for decision support in a Digital Twin of an aquaponic-based production system. A selection of machine learning algorithms including Linear Regression (LR), Support Vector Regression (SVR), CART Decision trees (DT) and the ensemble method XGBoost with decision trees was implemented. As a proof of concept, tests were performed using data from a 3-month period to predict fish growth and plant growth in a real-life aquarium. The authors concluded that a model-based simulation could provide certain benefits over machine learning approaches, especially in low-data situations.

An intelligent fish farming DT infrastructure was presented by Ubina et al. (2023) to facilitate four services including automatic fish feeding, aquarium environment monitoring, monitoring fish growth and health. A prototype was developed to represent the virtual system with monitoring interfaces via web and mobile devices. YOLOv4 was utilised to detect fishes from video segments. The fish images from the detection were converted using Mask-RCNN which is one of the instance segmentation techniques and afterwards converted into 3D objects. The fish growth estimation was conducted using the video interpolation CNN and calculated using regression curve formula which was formulated by aquaculture experts. In addition, the authors also implemented the Fast-SCNN model to predict net damage before it actually happens. The Fast-SCNN was also used to predict and analyse water quality by detecting green algae in the aquarium.

Other Farming Practice

Johannsen, Senger and Kluss (2021) designed and developed a DT for urban beekeeping decision support. The authors embedded IoT and web applications to monitor bee hives and provide information for beekeepers and bee farmers community. The virtual space consists of autonomous agents which

TABLE 4.2

Summary of previous work

Authors	Area	DT Status	AI Approach	AI Role in DT
Han et al. (2022)	Livestock	Prototype	long short-term memory (LSTM) neural network	Prediction
Ghandar et al. (2021)	Aquaponics	Prototype	Linear Regression (LR), Support Vector Regression (SVR), CART Decision trees, XGBoost with decision trees	Prediction
Li et al. (2022)	Farm	Simulation	Resnet	Prediction
(Zohdi, 2024)	Forestry	Simulation	Genetic Algorithm	Forest canopy growth prediction
(Ubina et al., 2023)	Aquaculture	Prototype	YOLOv4 Mask-RCNN Fast-SCNN	Fish growth prediction, net damage prediction and water quality prediction
(Rahman et al., 2024)	Greenhouse	Simulation	Artificial Neural Networks, Random Forest, Support Vector Machine, AdaBoost	Monitoring greenhouse environment

employ machine learning and data fusion techniques for modelling entities based on different data sources including data from sensors and German weather service data.

Implementation Challenges for AI-Powered DT in Agriculture

Agriculture is a complex field and rely on a wide variety of data sources, such as soil, weather, plant health and machinery. It is also influenced by numerous environmental factors. Integrating these datasets accurately can be challenging due to their incompleteness, noise and lack of standardisation. Moreover, the use of artificial intelligence technology in agriculture heavily relies on vast amounts of data, but obtaining high-quality data is a major challenge in the future. Some crops or local farming practices may not have sufficient historical or real-time data to effectively model in a digital twin.

Additionally, the acquisition of agricultural data in the real world is limited by the growth cycle of crops, and the complex methods and lengthy acquisition periods pose significant challenges for researchers. Since different types of crops and their varying growth cycles have distinct growth states, the agricultural analysis model cannot be universally applied. Besides, most studies focus only on acquiring and analysing agricultural data at a surface level. They have yet to explore the underlying laws of agricultural production and lack in-depth analysis of error patterns that connect theory and practice.

To accurately model biological processes such as plant growth, soil microbiology and disease propagation, advanced AI techniques are necessary. However, these techniques may struggle to fully capture the complexity involved. Factors like regions, seasons, crop types, production environments and operating methods all contribute to determining the effectiveness of intelligent technologies. Researchers must gather and integrate different types of data comprehensively to model agricultural objects or systems, which can be a complex and time-consuming process.

Digital twins need to continuously update their virtual models by processing real-time data gathered from sensors, drones or satellite imagery. However, this process requires substantial computational resources, especially for large-scale farms. Additionally, delays in processing can compromise the accuracy of decision-making. Scaling digital twin models to various agricultural landscapes is challenging due to variations in climate, soil type, crop variety and farming practices. Consequently, it becomes difficult to generalise digital twins across regions. While digital twins offer real-time simulation capabilities throughout the product lifecycle and can even integrate the entire supply chain, there are interoperability issues when connecting data information collected, aggregated and exchanged between different suppliers, manufacturers and customers in a virtual space. Furthermore, fusing digital twin models developed using different architectures, technologies, interfaces, communication protocols, models and data can present challenges. Therefore, the development of standard-based interoperability for digital twin applications is a significant challenge in digital twin technology with the imposed high costs (Figure 4.5).

Conclusions

This study presents previous studies which have contributed to integrating AI techniques or approaches in the design of DT for agriculture. The AI roles in the DT design are mostly to monitor, detect or predict sets of variables which contributes to improving farming practices. Generally, the contribution of AI to digital twins' implementation is not without any challenges. The

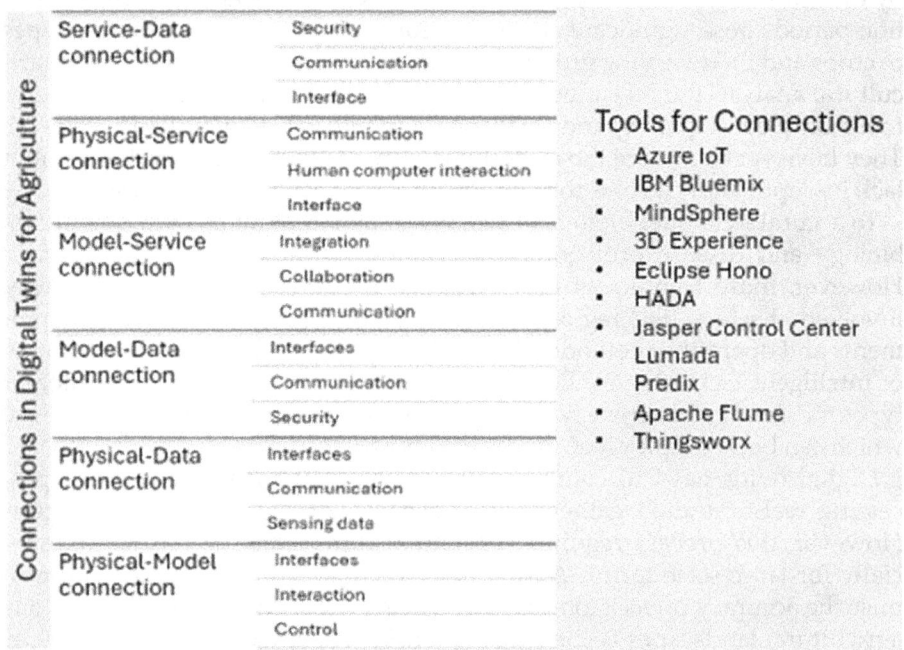

FIGURE 4.5
Connections in DT for agriculture.

amount and quality of acquired data will influence the AI model creation and updates. Furthermore, the AI model for each DT depends on the unique goals of each DT. From the literature, most DT in agriculture can be classified as either conceptual or proof-of-concept. Transforming legacy system to a DT-based system requires data standardisation, addressing privacy and security issues, high set-up costs, stable and continuous data connectivity, etc. Hence, the deployment of DT may be slow down without strong support from all stakeholders. Moreover, multiple technologies and tools are required to appropriately replicate a physical farm to a virtual state. Various models need to be developed to create the farm environment including multi-source, multi-dimension and heterogeneous data which maybe from historical data, farmer's knowledge, wind and sunlight direction, etc.

Acknowledgements

We would like to express our sincere gratitude to the anonymous reviewers for their invaluable feedback and insightful comments. We would like to also extend our heartfelt thanks to our research centre, whose support and resources have been instrumental in the development of this research.

References

Abdul Razak, S. F., Yogarayan, S., Sayeed, M. S., & Mohd Derafi, M. I. F. (2024). Agriculture 5.0 and explainable AI for smart agriculture: A scoping review. *Emerging Science Journal, 8*(2), 744–760. https://doi.org/10.28991/ESJ-2024-08-02-024

Alves, R. G., Souza, G., Maia, R. F., Anh, L. H. T., Kamienski, C., Soinenen, J.-P., Aquino-Jr, P. T., & Lima, F. (2019). A digital twin for smart farming. *2019 IEEE Global Humanitarian Technology Conference (GHTC)*, 1–4.

Ariesen-Verschuur, N., Verdouw, C., & Tekinerdogan, B. (2022). Digital Twins in greenhouse horticulture: A review. *Computers and Electronics in Agriculture, 199*. https://doi.org/10.1016/j.compag.2022.107183

Attaran, M., & Celik, B. G. (2023). Digital twin: Benefits, use cases, challenges, and opportunities. *Decision Analytics Journal, 6*. https://doi.org/10.1016/j.dajour.2023.100165

Bali, M. K., & Singh, M. (2024). Farming in the digital age: AI-infused digital twins for agriculture. *Proceedings - 2024 3rd International Conference on Sentiment Analysis and Deep Learning, ICSADL 2024*, 14–21. https://doi.org/10.1109/ICSADL61749.2024.00009

Barbie, A., Hasselbring, W., & Hansen, M. (2024). Digital twin prototypes for supporting automated integration testing of smart farming applications. *Symmetry*, *16*(2). https://doi.org/10.3390/sym16020221

Catala-Roman, P., Navarro, E. A., Segura-Garcia, J., & Garcia-Pineda, M. (2024). Harnessing digital twins for agriculture 5.0: A comparative analysis of 3D point cloud tools. *Applied Sciences (Switzerland)*, *14*(5). https://doi.org/10.3390/app14051709

Chaux, J. D., Sanchez-Londono, D., & Barbieri, G. (2021). A digital twin architecture to optimize productivity within controlled environment agriculture. *Applied Sciences (Switzerland)*, *11*(19). https://doi.org/10.3390/app11198875

Dihan, M. S., Akash, A. I., Tasneem, Z., Das, P., Das, S. K., Islam, M. R., Islam, M. M., Badal, F. R., Ali, M. F., Ahamed, M. H., Abhi, S. H., Sarker, S. K., & Hasan, M. M. (2024). Digital twin: Data exploration, architecture, implementation and future. In *Heliyon* (Vol. 10, Issue 5). Elsevier Ltd. https://doi.org/10.1016/j.heliyon.2024.e26503

Elijah, O., Rahim, S. K. A., Emmanuel, A. A., Salihu, Y. O., Usman, Z. G., & Jimoh, A. M. (2021). Enabling Smart Agriculture in Nigeria: Application of Digital-Twin Technology. *2021 1st International Conference on Multidisciplinary Engineering and Applied Science, ICMEAS 2021*. https://doi.org/10.1109/ICMEAS52683.2021.9692351

Emmert-Streib, F. (2023). What is the role of ai for digital twins? *AI (Switzerland)*, *4*(3), 721–728. https://doi.org/10.3390/ai4030038

Ghandar, A., Ahmed, A., Zulfiqar, S., Hua, Z., Hanai, M., & Theodoropoulos, G. (2021). A decision support system for urban agriculture using digital twin: A case study with aquaponics. *IEEE Access*, *9*, 35691–35708. https://doi.org/10.1109/ACCESS.2021.3061722

Grieves, M. W. (2005). Product lifecycle management: the new paradigm for enterprises. *International Journal of Product Development*, *2*(1–2), 71–84. https://doi.org/10.1504/ijpd.2005.006669

Han, X., Lin, Z., Clark, C., Vucetic, B., & Lomax, S. (2022). AI based digital twin model for cattle caring. *Sensors*, *22*(19). https://doi.org/10.3390/s22197118

Hemming, S., de Zwart, F., Elings, A., Petropoulou, A., & Righini, I. (2020). Cherry tomato production in intelligent greenhouses-sensors and AI for control of climate, irrigation, crop yield, and quality. *Sensors (Switzerland)*, *20*(22), 1–30. https://doi.org/10.3390/s20226430

Hemming, S., De Zwart, F., Elings, A., Righini, I., & Petropoulou, A. (2019). Remote control of greenhouse vegetable production with artificial intelligence—greenhouse climate, irrigation, and crop production. *Sensors (Switzerland)*, *19*(8). https://doi.org/10.3390/s19081807

Howard, D. A., Ma, Z., Veje, C., Clausen, A., Aaslyng, J. M., & Jørgensen, B. N. (2021). Greenhouse industry 4.0 – digital twin technology for commercial greenhouses. *Energy Informatics*, *4*. https://doi.org/10.1186/s42162-021-00161-9

Jans-Singh, M., Leeming, K., Choudhary, R., & Girolami, M. (2020). Digital twin of an urban-integrated hydroponic farm. *Data-Centric Engineering*, *1*(2). https://doi.org/10.1017/dce.2020.21

Johannsen, C., Senger, D., & Kluss, T. (2021). A Digital Twin of the Social-Ecological System Urban Beekeeping. In *Advances and New Trends in Environmental Informatics*. https://doi.org/10.1007/978-3-030-61969-5_14

Jones, D., Snider, C., Nassehi, A., Yon, J., & Hicks, B. (2020). Characterising the Digital Twin: A systematic literature review. *CIRP Journal of Manufacturing Science and Technology, 29*, 36–52. https://doi.org/10.1016/j.cirpj.2020.02.002

Kampker, A., Stich, V., Jussen, P., Moser, B., & Kuntz, J. (2019). Business models for industrial smart services - the example of a digital twin for a product-service-system for potato harvesting. *Procedia CIRP, 83*, 534–540. https://doi.org/10.1016/j.procir.2019.04.114

Kim, S., & Heo, S. (2024). An agricultural digital twin for mandarins demonstrates the potential for individualized agriculture. *Nature Communications, 15*(1). https://doi.org/10.1038/s41467-024-45725-x

Kreuzer, T., Papapetrou, P., & Zdravkovic, J. (2024). Artificial intelligence in digital twins—A systematic literature review. *Data and Knowledge Engineering, 151*. https://doi.org/10.1016/j.datak.2024.102304

Li, W., Zhu, D., & Wang, Q. (2022). A single view leaf reconstruction method based on the fusion of ResNet and differentiable render in plant growth digital twin system. *Computers and Electronics in Agriculture, 193*. https://doi.org/10.1016/j.compag.2022.106712

Melesse, T. Y., Colace, F., Dembele, S. P., Lorusso, A., Santaniello, D., & Valentino, C. (2024). Digital Twin for Predictive Monitoring of Crops: State of the Art. *Lecture Notes in Networks and Systems, 695*, 1027–1036. https://doi.org/10.1007/978-981-99-3043-2_85

Mihai, S., Yaqoob, M., Hung, D. V., Davis, W., Towakel, P., Raza, M., Karamanoglu, M., Barn, B., Shetve, D., Prasad, R. V., Venkataraman, H., Trestian, R., & Nguyen, H. X. (2022). Digital twins: A survey on enabling technologies, challenges, trends and future prospects. *IEEE Communications Surveys and Tutorials, 24*(4), 2255–2291. https://doi.org/10.1109/COMST.2022.3208773

Nasirahmadi, A., & Hensel, O. (2022). Toward the next generation of digitalization in agriculture based on digital twin paradigm. In *Sensors* (Vol. 22, Issue 2). MDPI. https://doi.org/10.3390/s22020498

Neethirajan, S. (2022). Affective State Recognition in Livestock—Artificial Intelligence Approaches. In *Animals* (Vol. 12, Issue 6). MDPI. https://doi.org/10.3390/ani12060759

Neethirajan, S., & Kemp, B. (2021). Digital twins in livestock farming. *Animals, 11*(4). https://doi.org/10.3390/ani11041008

Nie, J., Wang, Y., Li, Y., & Chao, X. (2022). Artificial intelligence and digital twins in sustainable agriculture and forestry: a survey. *Turkish Journal of Agriculture and Forestry, 46*(5), 642–661. https://doi.org/10.55730/1300-011X.3033

Niggemann, O., Diedrich, A., Kuhnert, C., Pfannstiel, E., & Schraven, J. (2021). A generic DigitalTwin model for artificial intelligence applications. *Proceedings - 2021 4th IEEE International Conference on Industrial Cyber-Physical Systems, ICPS 2021*, 55–62. https://doi.org/10.1109/ICPS49255.2021.9468243

Peladarinos, N., Piromalis, D., Cheimaras, V., Tserepas, E., Munteanu, R. A., & Papageorgas, P. (2023). Enhancing smart agriculture by implementing digital twins: A comprehensive review. *Sensors, 23*(16). https://doi.org/10.3390/s23167128

Petropoulou, A. S., van Marrewijk, B., de Zwart, F., Elings, A., Bijlaard, M., van Daalen, T., Jansen, G., & Hemming, S. (2023). Lettuce production in intelligent greenhouses—3D imaging and computer vision for plant spacing decisions. *Sensors, 23*(6). https://doi.org/10.3390/s23062929

Pexyean, T., Saraubon, K., & Nilsook, P. (2022). IoT, AI and digital twin for smart campus. *Proceedings - 2022 Research, Invention, and Innovation Congress: Innovative Electricals and Electronics, RI2C 2022,* 160–164. https://doi.org/10.1109/RI2C56397.2022.9910286

Pylianidis, C., Osinga, S., & Athanasiadis, I. N. (2021). Introducing digital twins to agriculture. *Computers and Electronics in Agriculture, 184*. https://doi.org/10.1016/j.compag.2020.105942

Rahman, H., Shah, U. M., Riaz, S. M., Kifayat, K., Moqurrab, S. A., & Yoo, J. (2024). Digital twin framework for smart greenhouse management using next-gen mobile networks and machine learning. *Future Generation Computer Systems, 156,* 285–300. https://doi.org/10.1016/j.future.2024.03.023

Sharma, A., Kosasih, E., Zhang, J., Brintrup, A., & Calinescu, A. (2022). Digital twins: State of the art theory and practice, challenges, and open research questions. *Journal of Industrial Information Integration, 30*. https://doi.org/10.1016/j.jii.2022.100383

Smith, M. J. (2018). Getting value from artificial intelligence in agriculture, over the next 10+ years. *8th Australasian Dairy Science Symposium,* 1–7.

Symeonaki, E., Maraveas, C., & Arvanitis, K. G. (2024). Recent advances in digital twins for agriculture 5.0: Applications and open issues in livestock production systems. *Applied Sciences (Switzerland), 14*(2). https://doi.org/10.3390/app14020686

Tagarakis, A. C., Benos, L., Kyriakarakos, G., Pearson, S., Sørensen, C. G., & Bochtis, D. (2024). Digital twins in agriculture and forestry: A review. *Sensors, 24*(10). https://doi.org/10.3390/s24103117

Ubina, N. A., Lan, H. Y., Cheng, S. C., Chang, C. C., Lin, S. S., Zhang, K. X., Lu, H. Y., Cheng, C. Y., & Hsieh, Y. Z. (2023). Digital twin-based intelligent fish farming with Artificial Intelligence Internet of Things (AIoT). *Smart Agricultural Technology, 5*. https://doi.org/10.1016/j.atech.2023.100285

Verdouw, C., Tekinerdogan, B., Beulens, A., & Wolfert, S. (2021). Digital twins in smart farming. *Agricultural Systems, 189*. https://doi.org/10.1016/j.agsy.2020.103046

Wang, L. (2024). Digital twins in agriculture: A review of recent progress and open issues. *Electronics (Switzerland), 13*(11). https://doi.org/10.3390/electronics13112209

Zohdi, T. I. (2024). A machine-learning enabled digital-twin framework for next generation precision agriculture and forestry. *Computer Methods in Applied Mechanics and Engineering, 431*. https://doi.org/10.1016/j.cma.2024.117250

5

AI in Disaster Monitoring and Early Warning Systems

Yee Jian Chew, Shih Yin Ooi and Ying Han Pang

Introduction

Has there been a noticeable increase in both the number and the consequences of natural and man-made disasters over the past few decades? The recent increase is associated to the situation with global warming and climate change, the natural phenomena that have changed weather systems, caused a rise in disasters and complicated the prediction of even those occurrences. As such threats continue growing in coverage and in what they affect, the need to have efficient disaster monitoring and early warning systems in place has never been greater.

A great enhancement in relationship disaster-situated decision strategies brought out by disaster monitoring. Early warning systems management is aspirated to alleviate unnecessary loss related to impact bias. They allow for effective real-time assessment of impending risks, rapid intervention and prevention measures, which in the end contribute to lives, properties and the environment being safeguarded. With regards to these specificities, specially designed Computer-Aided Design (CAD) tools are warranted for these systems which approach considering most systems adopt a very centralised approach to problem management. And this is the point where all approaches tend to fail and artificial intelligence (AI) comes in.

The exponential growth in the development of AI and machine learning technologies has brought about revolutionary ideas in changing the approach with which disasters are managed. We can utilise the advantage of AI for analysing data better, faster, and bigger to broaden the scope of disaster comprehension and response. This chapter will analyse the value that AI adds to the sphere of disaster monitoring and early warning systems, specifically focusing on practical cases that prove the effectiveness of AI against global problems.

DOI: 10.1201/9781003509196-5

The Ernst & Young (EY) Data Science Challenge demonstrates the use of AI in solving feeding satellites even further – this is a competition that inspires people yearly to provide solutions with the help of AI to the problems of the world by using satellite imaging and other remote sensing methods. It started in 2021 and with different themes like wildfire detection and its management to extend to protecting biodiversity and strengthening coastal resiliency. This is how the challenge gives a practical picture of how AI can be used for disaster management through bringing together professionals from different industries and young people and the academia within the industry practising leaders at their level.

In this chapter, we intend to look at some case studies from the EY Data Science Challenge (2021, 2022) competitions in which our team actively participated. Not only were these experiences helpful in understanding the use of AI in monitoring disasters, it was also seen how new solutions can be applied to complex existing global challenges. Through these analyses, we want to show how the management of disasters could be transformed by the use of AI and the relevant issues that arise with it.

AI in Disaster Monitoring

The rapid growth of AI and machine learning has greatly changed many aspects of our daily lives. While these technologies have provided significant advantages to businesses, they have also sparked concerns, including ethical issues (Caglayan et al., 2024; Lin, 2023; Meyer et al., 2023), privacy challenges and potential biases. Nevertheless, AI has demonstrated considerable potential in disaster monitoring (Linardos et al., 2022), offering effective solutions to safeguard populations around the globe. Rather than concentrating solely on academic journals in this section, the focus will be on the EY Data Science Challenge, which aims to tackle global challenges using data, mainly satellite data and AI. This competition showcases the strength of collaboration between industries and universities in utilising AI and data science to address real-world issues.

Ernst & Young (EY) Data Science Challenge

Since 2021, EY has been hosting the Data Science Challenge (Ernst & Young, 2021b) in partnership with universities and industry leaders like NASA and Microsoft. This competition is designed to promote the use of AI and data to gain insights into global challenges and enhance quality of life. Through this initiative, EY aims to encourage the creation of data-driven solutions and informed decision-making to tackle issues related to global sustainability.

The challenge emphasises the use of satellite and remote sensing data, along with predictive modelling, to leverage participants' skills in data science and AI. Each year, the competition centres around a specific theme, inviting students and young professionals from across the globe to devise innovative solutions using AI and data analytics to confront urgent global issues. The themes, objectives and impacts of each year's challenge are outlined in Table 5.1.

In the following discussion, we will focus on the 2021 and 2022 challenges, as our team actively participated in these competitions – reaching the semifinals in 2021 and earning the runner-up position in 2022. These experiences were both insightful and rewarding. We hope this discussion will effectively convey the competition's context and demonstrate how AI can contribute to building a better world.

TABLE 5.1

Summary of EY Data Science Challenge Theme, Objective and Impact (2021–2025)

Year	Challenge Theme	Objective	Impact
2021	Wildfire Detection and Management	Develop automated methods for detecting wildfires using satellite imagery.	Enhanced decision-making during fire emergencies, leading to saved lives, protected property and preservation of natural habitats.
2022	Biodiversity Preservation	Predict the presence of nine frog species across multiple countries.	Supported conservation efforts to protect species critical to ecosystem health, reducing the risk of biodiversity loss.
2023	Combating World Hunger	Identify rice cultivation areas and forecast crop yields in Vietnam.	Improved agricultural productivity, leading to increased food security and potential to feed millions of people.
2024	Coastal Resilience	Detect storm damage using high-resolution satellite data.	Enhanced disaster response and recovery efforts in coastal communities, resulting in more effective support and quicker recovery after storms.
2025	Urban Heat Island Effect (upcoming)	Analyse urban heat islands to inform urban planning decisions.	Raised awareness of the impact of urban heat islands, leading to better-informed urban planning that improves societal well-being and resource use

EY Data Science Challenge 2021: Wildfire Detection and Management

The 2021 challenge focused on detecting and managing wildfires through automated fire edge detection using airborne and satellite imagery. The goal was to assist frontline responders in making critical decisions during fire emergencies, ultimately helping to save lives, protect property, and preserve natural habitats. Given the need for bushfire managers to have accurate information on active fire locations and the rate of fire spread, Challenge 1 provided participants with infrared linescan images captured by aircraft over active fire locations. These images were manually labelled by the Australia Country Fire Authority (CFA) before being shared with participants. The primary objective of this challenge was to automate the mapping of fire boundaries using machine learning and deep learning techniques. By exploiting linescan images, satellite data, and other remote sensing data, participants were expected to estimate the spread of wildfires effectively in the subsequent challenge.

Based on our findings and experiences from the first challenge, we proposed a U-Net model to automatically delineate fire boundaries from the infrared linescan data. Our model proved effective, and over the years, various image segmentation models (Ban et al., 2020; Hodges & Lattimer, 2019; Jiao et al., 2019; S. Wang et al., 2021; Y. Wang et al., 2019; G. Zhang et al., 2019; Q. Zhang et al., 2016) have been applied in the domain of forest fire detection. It is anticipated that with the advancement of AI and the increasing availability of data, these technologies can be further developed to mitigate the impact of forest fires more effectively. The overall concept and objectives of the challenge are illustrated in Figure 5.1. Figure 5.2 shows a sample output of the predicted fire boundary generated by our submitted U-Net model. To enhance the model's performance and prevent missed fire detections, morphological operations such as Opening, Dilation, and Closing were applied. Although the challenge information and submission pages are restricted to participants, the code from the GitHub repository remains publicly accessible (Ernst & Young, 2021a).

EY Data Science Challenge 2022: Preserving Biodiversity

The EY Data Science Challenge 2022 focused on preserving biodiversity by developing models to monitor frog populations at scale. Frogs are considered excellent bioindicators due to their permeable skin, which makes them highly sensitive to environmental changes and pollutants. Their dual life in both terrestrial and aquatic environments provides valuable insights into the health of these ecosystems. The presence or absence of frogs can reveal much about the overall health of an ecosystem; a thriving frog population typically signifies a healthy environment, whereas their decline or disappearance often indicates ecological distress.

This challenge highlighted the importance of using AI and data analytics to effectively monitor biodiversity, which is essential for guiding conservation

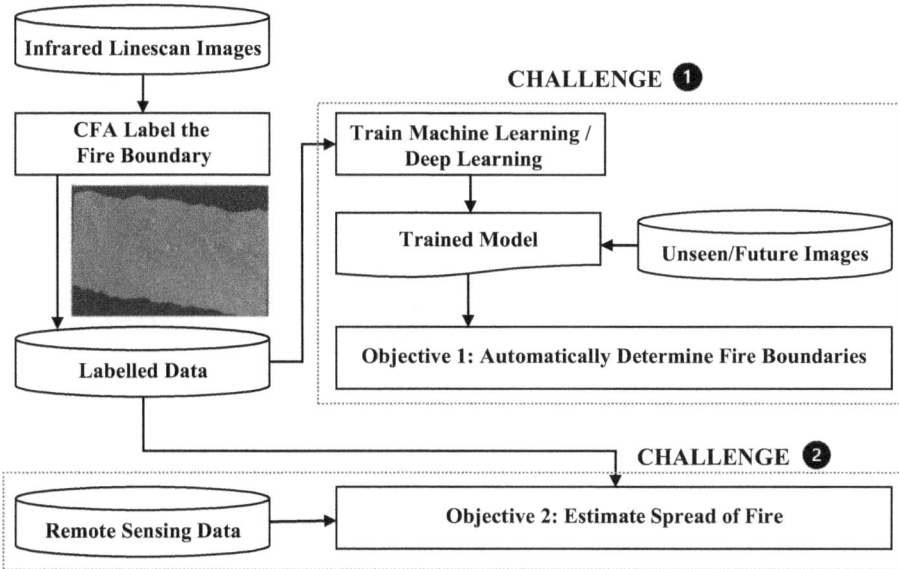

FIGURE 5.1
Overview of wildfire detection in the EY Data Science Challenge 2021.

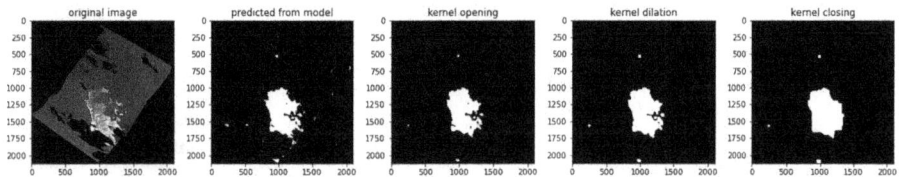

FIGURE 5.2
U-net model predictions with morphological operations: Opening, dilation and closing for fire boundary detection (sample).

actions aimed at protecting and restoring ecosystems. However, existing models have faced challenges in accurately representing frog species, many of which are highly localised with specific habitat requirements. The 2022 challenge sought to overcome these limitations by leveraging AI and data to improve the monitoring and protection efforts, thereby contributing to broader biodiversity conservation initiatives. The challenge's GitHub repository is available at Ernst & Young (2022). The overview of the challenges is illustrated in Figure 5.3, and the challenge was divided into three parts:

1. **Challenge 1**: Develop a local frog discovery tool for a single location using a single data source at a coarse spatial resolution, following the TerraClimate (Abatzoglou et al., 2018) data resolution of 4 km². TerraClimate provides global monthly meteorological data from

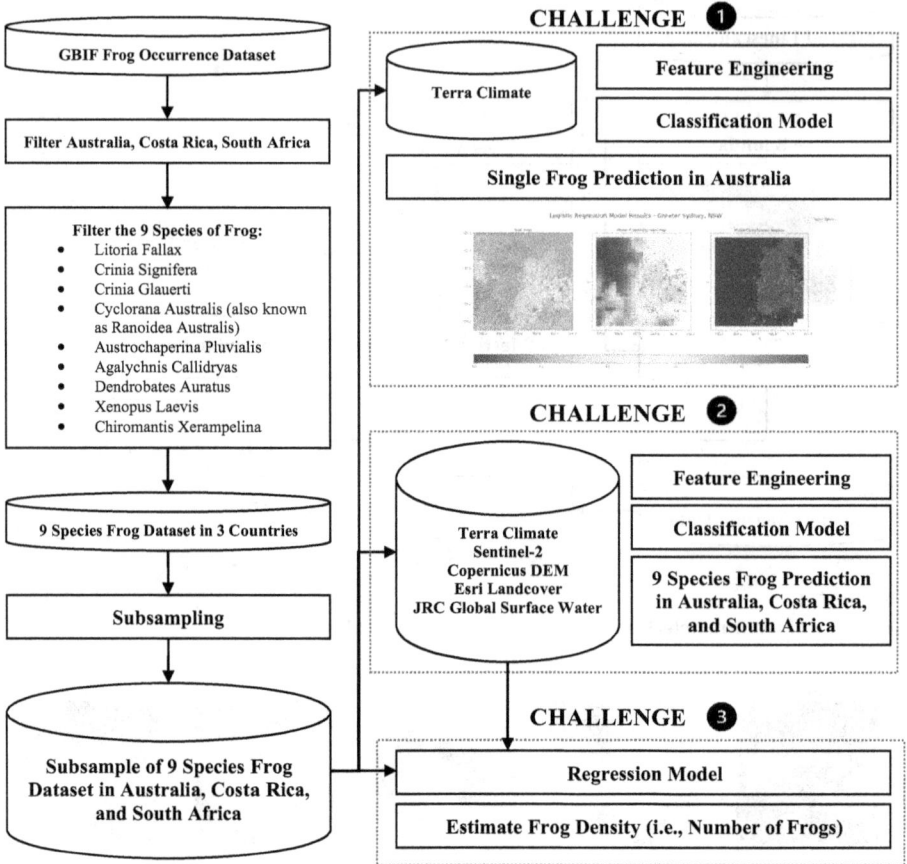

FIGURE 5.3
Overview of frog detection challenge in the EY Data Science Challenge 2022.

1958 to the present. From this dataset, a total of 14 attributes, including minimum temperature, maximum temperature, mean soil moisture and precipitation accumulation, were available for participants. Participants used a species distribution model for the frog species *Litoria Fallax*, incorporating TerraClimate variables to build a predictive model estimating its presence in Australia.

2. **Challenge 2**: Create a species distribution model for nine selected frog species across Australia, Costa Rica, and South Africa, utilising open-source geospatial data with a fine resolution of 10 km². Besides TerraClimate data, participants could utilise additional datasets, including satellite data such as Sentinel-2, Copernicus Digital Elevation Model (DEM), Esri Landcover, and JRC Global Surface

Water. The nine species were: *Litoria Fallax, Crinia Signifera, Crinia Glauerti, Cyclorana Australis (Ranoidea Australis), Austrochaperina Luvialis, Agalychnis Callidryas, Dendrobates Auratus, Xenopus Laevis,* and *Chiromantis Xerampelina.*

3. **Challenge 3**: Instead of focusing on species presence, participants were tasked with measuring frog density (count/number of frogs) in a given area using a regression model.

The frog dataset used in the challenge was derived from the Global Biodiversity Information Facility (GBIF) occurrence data, which integrates information from various sources, such as specimens from natural history museums, citizen science observations and automated environmental surveys. A significant portion of the Australian data comes from FrogID, a smartphone app developed by the Australian Museum (FrogID, 2020; Rowley et al., 2019). Figure 5.4 illustrates the distribution of frog species within the challenge locations.

While the competition provided access to a range of datasets, determining the most relevant factors for predicting frog presence can be challenging without domain expertise. Academic research serves as a crucial reference in this context. During the competition, we conducted a review of relevant research articles related to frogs and summarised the key findings in Table 5.2. These studies highlight several important variables that are essential for predicting frog presence. The identification of these factors requires understanding both the biological characteristics of frogs and the environmental conditions that influence their habitats. Overall, factors such as landcover, environmental variables affecting air quality and pollution (e.g., distance to roads), and meteorological variables influencing moisture and vegetation (e.g., soil moisture, humidity, temperature, and normalised difference vegetation index (NDVI)) are highly relevant to frog presence. The interplay of these variables not only reveals habitat suitability and potential risks for frogs but also guides us in selecting the most relevant factors from the wide range of open-source geospatial data. This aligns with the earlier discussion in the challenge description, which highlights that frogs are particularly vulnerable to changes in their environment and exposure to pollutants.

While the challenges were primarily focused on predicting frog species distribution and density, the developed models can also be valuable for detecting changes in frog presence over time. The trained model can be used to monitor biodiversity changes by comparing frog distribution maps across different time periods. For example, as illustrated in Figure 5.5, the model can predict frog distribution for a region using environmental data from before 2022. The same model can then be used to predict the distribution for the same region using data from 2022. By comparing these maps, we can assess whether frogs remain in the same locations, have relocated, or have

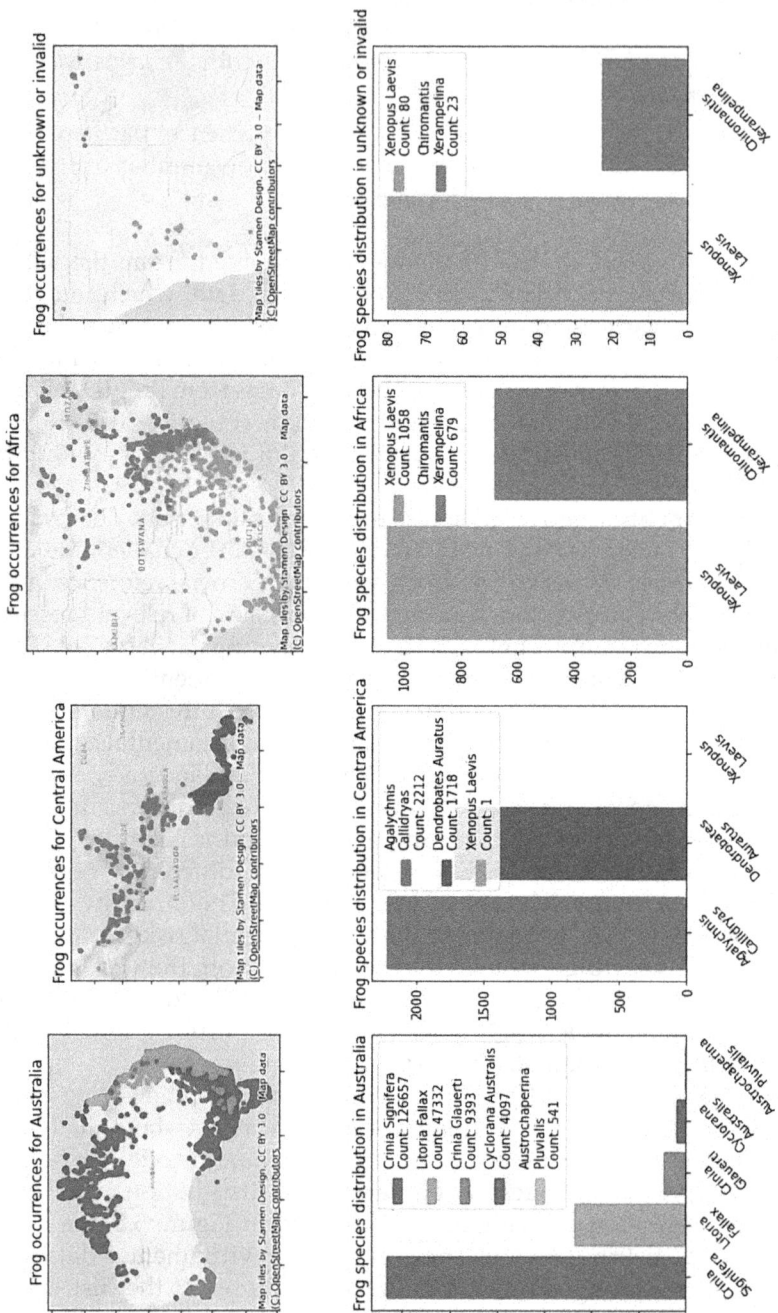

FIGURE 5.4
Distribution of Nine Frog Species in Australia, Central America and Africa (Adapted from (Ernst & Young, 2022)).

TABLE 5.2

Summary of Factors Affecting Frog Presence Based on Several Academic Literature

Reference	Factors affecting Frog Presence
Cree (1989)	Vegetation, Relative Humidity, Rainfall, Wetness of Vegetation, Vapor Pressure, Air Temperature, Wind Strength, Temperatures
Knutson et al. (1999)	Landcover (e.g., Urban Lands, Upland, Wetland Forests, Emergent Wetlands), Landscape Metrics (e.g., Edges, Patch Diversity, Edge Length Between Wetland and Forest, Forest Area, Agricultural Area), Water Quality, Vegetation Information
Hazell et al. (2001)	Area of Native Forest Canopy Cover, Annual Mean Temperature, Vegetation Cover at Water Edge
Chan-McLeod (2003)	Temperature, Humidity, Regional Weather Patterns
Westgate et al. (2018)	Modis Active Fire Hotspots, Burn Area
Aryal et al. (2020)	Soil Moisture, Distance to Road
Green et al. (2021)	Presence of Fish, Water Depth

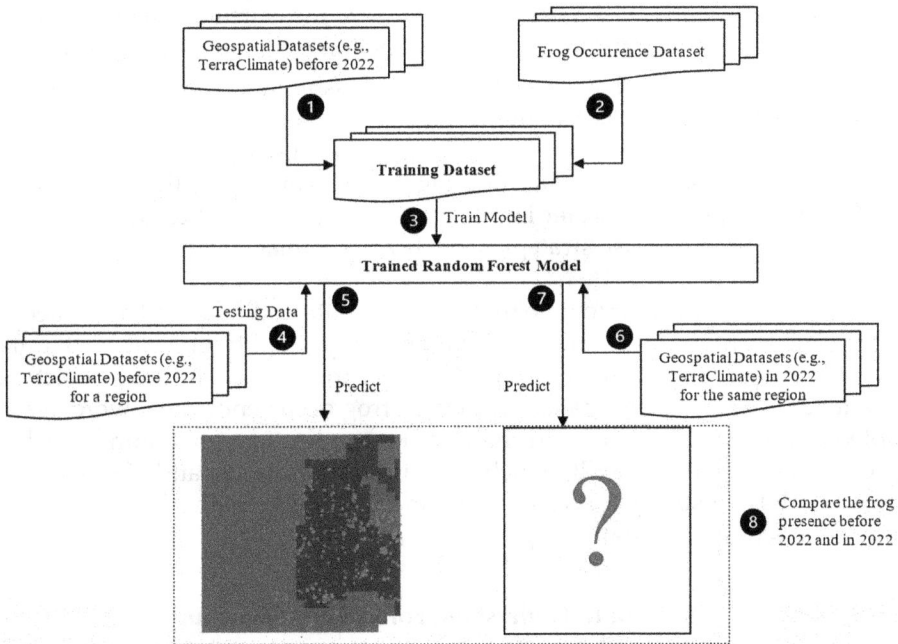

FIGURE 5.5

Monitoring changes in frog distribution using environmental data and a trained model.

disappeared. If relocation or disappearance is detected, further studies can be conducted to investigate possible causes, such as urbanisation or pollution.

It is noteworthy that the random forest (Breiman, 2001) model shown in Figure 5.5 achieved the best performance in Challenge 2, based on our submission, outperforming nine other notable classifiers, including Logistic Regression, XGBoost, Decision Tree, K-Nearest Neighbors, Naïve Bayes, Linear Support Vector Machine (SVM), RBF SVM, AdaBoost, and Artificial Neural Network (ANN). The random forest model attained an F1-Score of 0.9 on the competition's private test set.

With the success of using satellite data and AI (machine learning) for frog detection, numerous opportunities arise to leverage AI and data analytics in addressing various global challenges:

1. **Preventing Animal and Plant Extinction through Early Detection**: By analysing satellite data and environmental variables, AI can identify patterns and predict the likelihood of species decline or habitat degradation for both animals and plants. This enables early intervention strategies to protect at-risk populations and conserve critical habitats. For plants, AI can monitor changes in vegetation cover, detect the spread of invasive species, and identify areas affected by disease or climate change. Such proactive measures can help maintain biodiversity and prevent the extinction of vulnerable species.

2. **Disaster Monitoring and Damage Assessment**: AI models can be applied to real-time satellite imagery and remote sensing data to monitor natural disasters such as wildfires, floods, hurricanes and earthquakes. Machine learning algorithms can assess the extent of damage, predict disaster impact and assist in efficient resource allocation and response strategies for disaster management.

However, it is important to note that while satellite and AI-based approaches offer significant potential, the availability of high-quality ground truth data for model validation remains a challenge. In the case of the frog detection challenge, ground-based datasets, such as frog occurrence data, were available to validate the models. In many other applications, obtaining reliable ground data can be difficult, which may limit the accuracy and effectiveness of AI models. Ensuring robust datasets and validation methods is crucial for the success of such initiatives.

Leveraging Satellite Data to Understand Forest Fire Behaviour

Inspired by the EY Data Science Challenge, we expanded our focus to understanding forest fire behaviour in Peninsular Malaysia using satellite data. Beyond the previously mentioned opportunities, our goal is to analyse forest fires and identify the key factors that drive them. The methodology for creating a forest fire inventory dataset is outlined in Figure 5.6, with additional details provided in our published work (Chew et al., 2024). Due to the lack of available fire perimeter data and limited existing literature on the use of open-source geospatial data in the area of interest, several validation

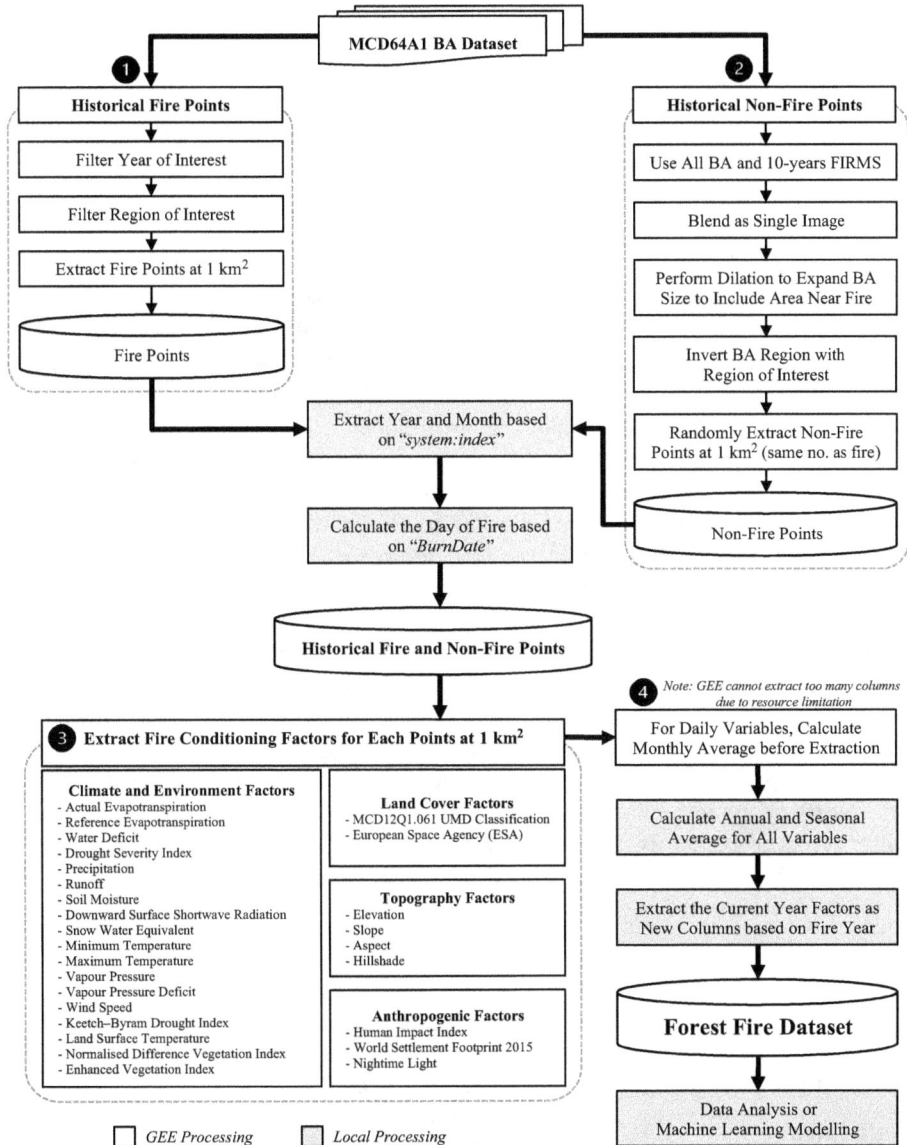

FIGURE 5.6
General methodology to build a forest fire inventory dataset (Replicated from (Chew et al., 2024)).

studies were conducted. These include hotspot trend analysis, burnt area validation and meteorological assessments. The details of each study are as follows:

1. **Hotspots Trend Analysis** (Chew et al., 2022): This study utilised MODIS Active Fire Hotspots data to assess the presence, location and timing of fire incidents. The primary objective was to evaluate whether the hotspots accurately represent the temporal and spatial patterns of fire activity in the country.

2. **Burnt Area Assessments** (Chew, Ooi, & Pang, 2023b): Due to the absence of burnt area data from the government and agencies, this study was crucial to validate the detected burnt areas. It compared the MCD64A1 burnt area dataset with surface reflectance data from Sentinel-2 and Landsat-8. Additionally, the detected burnt areas were validated using a burn severity map generated by the differenced normalised burn ratio (dNBR) algorithm (Nations, 2014).

3. **Meteorological Assessments** (Chew, Ooi, Pang, et al., 2023a): This study aimed to verify the relevance of the global TerraClimate data for forest fires in Malaysia. It examined the relationship between climatic variables and fire occurrences by analysing monthly changes in these variables over the six months leading up to the fire outbreak in March 2021, with a particular focus on the fire in Pahang state, Malaysia. The three variables selected for assessment were temperature, precipitation and wind speed.

These validations are crucial for ensuring the reliability of the dataset before adopting the framework to build a forest fire inventory dataset. This framework allows us to extract and identify the primary factors contributing to forest fires in the study area. Additionally, it supports the use of machine learning models for prediction and forecasting, aiding in early prevention and warning systems. We postulate that this methodology can be adapted to other types of disasters, allowing for the analysis of historical events, identification of influencing factors and forecasting of future occurrences through machine learning for early detection and prevention.

Ethical Considerations in AI Deployment

Data Privacy

Disaster monitoring and early warning systems that integrate data with AI require a huge volume of data and information processing including personal information. Such information is obtained from satellite images, social media sites and sensor networks and can disclose the whereabouts, activities and health status of individuals. The main concern is how to provide this kind of information because it is essential for the efficient organisation of disaster management and at the same time respect the privacy of people.

In Malaysia, the Personal Data Protection Act 2010 (PDPA) provides guidelines for the handling of personal data in the course of doing business transactions in order to prevent violations of people's rights. Disaster management related AI systems should also comply with the provisions of PDPA by applying appropriate measures that will enhance privacy safeguards in the processes. This entails the adoption of aggressive encryption strategies, anonymisation of information where applicable, and adherence to data protection policies in all stages of data acquisition, storage and utilisation. Furthermore, transparency regarding what information is collected, how it will be used, and how it will be stored is also very important in creating the trust of the public. Also, organisations operating in disaster management should take into account that the political ramifications of collected data should be addressed and that the data should not be used for any other purposes which are not emergency related.

Algorithmic Bias

There are established ways to place restrictions on the development and deployment of AI that are responsible, although given the sample of these algorithms from some data, there exist potential problems. They can also affect the outcome of an AI-governed activity if certain populations or users were historically underserved or disregarded for specific reasons, thus, creating imbalanced data to be used within the system. These issues include discrimination against certain groups or individuals in disaster management systems or solutions that help in the prediction of these disasters.

Others involve an AI model using mostly city or metropolitan data attempts to forecast calamities in a rural or marginalised area, hence failing terribly. Social media data biases can also lead to minority groups' lack of inclusion in disaster recovery actions. Thus, when making models for AI, one must take care to utilise a variety of different and representative datasets in order to avoid these risks. It should be a routine practice to test AI systems for Bias, and wherein there is evidence of Bias, it should be rectified through changes to the AI model, more representative datasets and retraining, or adjustments of metrics in the AI decisions.

Equitable Access to AI Technology

The full potential of AI in disaster management can only be realised if it is available to all communities, primarily the most vulnerable ones. However, the digital divide may preclude certain communities from equitable access to AI tools and technologies. In some regions, infrastructure, resources, or technical capacity to leverage AI-driven disaster management systems may be more limited – rural areas, low-income communities and even developing countries.

This warrants efforts toward making AI technologies more inclusive and accessible. It means building inexpensive, accessible AI tools meant to serve the needs of elected communities and providing funding for their accompanying infrastructures. Training programmes and knowledge-sharing platforms on AI will help localities exercise their role in using the technology according to the nation or local disaster prevention and management plan. We can also encourage these stakeholders to work closely together, through supporting strong collaboration between governments and industry or NGOs in the development of a global AI accord that seeks equitable distribution.

Future Directions

Emerging AI Technologies in Disaster Management

Advancing artificial intelligence has made these new frontiers possible at a faster pace than ever in disaster management. With global disasters like the recent wildfires in Texas and the sinkhole incident in Kuala Lumpur, Malaysia, having access to next-generation AI truly has the capacity for improving disaster monitoring, prediction and response. These technologies include the following:

- **AI-Driven Predictive Modelling**: By integrating AI with enhanced predictive models, we can more accurately identify disasters such as wildfires, floods and landslides. With access to vast data sets, AI algorithms can detect patterns and anomalies before these events occur.

- **Autonomous Systems and Drones**: AI-equipped drones and autonomous robotic systems can facilitate real-time monitoring in hazardous or inaccessible areas, conducting assessments while playing a vital role. They gather essential information during and after a disaster, enhancing search and rescue operations and performing damage evaluations.

- **Resilience with AI**: Leveraging AI technologies to model the effects of climate change on disaster trends can help design more resilient infrastructure and communities. AI can identify vulnerabilities across various climate scenarios, aiding in more effective long-term planning and mitigation strategies.

- **Integration of AI with Internet-of-Things (IoT) and Big Data**: The powerful combination of AI, IoT, and big data analytics has the potential to revolutionise disaster management. AI can process live data from IoT sensors and satellite imagery to deliver real-time updates during a disaster, generating dynamic insights that support quicker and more informed decision-making.

While AI is still a long way off from delivering on its promises, there are plenty of opportunities for further research. AI-powered tools and platforms offer the promise of faster, more proactive responses to disasters. This is ultimately translating into lives saved and less economic loss.

Interdisciplinary Collaboration

Using AI for disaster management is never at the mercy of one discipline. The integration of AI tools with disaster-specific technology will require new partnerships between the scientific community, those working in emergency management and public health policy to provide effective use of such technologies.

- **National Collaborative Research Infrastructure**: Cooperation between academia, industry, and the government can help develop advanced AI systems in addressing specific disaster circumstances. The EY Data Science Challenge is an example of the collaborative efforts that such a diverse group can make. It is also encouraging everyone to address global challenges using AI and data science.
- **Community Engagement**: Engaging local communities is essential to ensure the continued relevance and effectiveness of AI-driven disaster management systems. By incorporating community input, the system can be more tailored to meet the unique needs of individuals in different regions. Additionally, it is crucial to equip data stakeholders with robust AI technology where it is most needed.
- **Policy Development**: Policymakers have a vital role in fostering an environment that encourages the use of AI in disaster management. This involves creating regulations that facilitate data sharing, safeguard privacy and guarantee fair access to AI technologies. Engaging in collaborative policy development with AI specialists, disaster management officials and community members can lead to frameworks that promote the ethical and effective application of AI in this field.

There have already been notable advancements in disaster management through successful interdisciplinary collaboration, and ongoing efforts in this area will be essential to unlock the full potential of AI technologies. By joining forces, stakeholders can leverage AI to create safer, more resilient communities in response to growing global challenges.

Conclusions

This chapter has explored the essential role of AI in enhancing disaster monitoring and early warning systems, especially given the increasing challenges posed by global warming and climate change. By leveraging AI's capability to analyse vast and complex datasets (i.e., social media updates, satellite imagery, etc.), it is able to improve disaster response.

The discussion has also highlighted real-world instances, such as the EY Data Science Challenge, demonstrating the concrete impact of AI on addressing global issues like wildfire detection and biodiversity conservation.

The transformative potential of AI in disaster management is substantial. As AI technologies evolve, they offer the chance to build more resilient societies that can respond more effectively to both natural and human-made disasters. With innovations such as AI-driven predictive modelling, autonomous systems, and the integration of AI with the IoT, we can imagine a future where disaster management is not only more efficient but also more proactive.

However, the application of AI in disaster management raises important ethical and practical challenges. Issues related to data privacy, algorithmic bias and equitable access to AI technologies must be carefully considered to ensure that the benefits of AI are distributed fairly across all communities. Additionally, interdisciplinary collaboration will be vital in addressing these challenges and maximising AI's potential.

In conclusion, while AI offers powerful tools for disaster management, its implementation should be approached with a balanced perspective that considers both its opportunities and its limitations. By fostering collaboration, tackling ethical concerns and continuing to innovate, we can leverage AI to build safer, more resilient communities in the face of escalating global challenges.

References

Abatzoglou, J. T., Dobrowski, S. Z., Parks, S. A., & Hegewisch, K. C. (2018). TerraClimate, a High-resolution Global Dataset of Monthly Climate and Climatic Water Balance from 1958-2015. *Scientific Data, 5*(170191), 1–12. https://doi.org/10.1038/sdata.2017.191

Aryal, P. C., Aryal, C., Neupane, S., Sharma, B., Dhamala, M. K., Khadka, D., Kharel, S. C., Rajbanshi, P., & Neupane, D. (2020). Soil Moisture & Roads Influence the Occurrence of Frogs in Kathmandu Valley, Nepal. *Global Ecology and Conservation, 23*, e01197. https://doi.org/10.1016/j.gecco.2020.e01197

Ban, Y., Zhang, P., Nascetti, A., Bevington, A. R., & Wulder, M. A. (2020). Near Real-Time Wildfire Progression Monitoring with Sentinel-1 SAR Time Series and Deep Learning. *Scientific Reports*, *10*(1), 1322. https://doi.org/10.1038/s41598-019-56967-x

Breiman, L. (2001). Random Forests. *Machine Learning*, *45*(1), 5–32.

Caglayan, A., Slusarczyk, W., Rabbani, R. D., Ghose, A., Papadopoulos, V., & Boussios, S. (2024). Large Language Models in Oncology: Revolution or Cause for Concern? *Current Oncology*, *31*(4), 1817–1830. https://doi.org/10.3390/curroncol31040137

Chan-McLeod, A. C. A. (2003). Factors Affecting the Permeability of Clearcuts to Red-Legged Frogs. *The Journal of Wildlife Management*, *67*(4), 663. https://doi.org/10.2307/3802673

Chew, Y. J., Ooi, S. Y., & Pang, Y. H. (2023b). MCD64A1 Burnt Area Dataset Assessment using Sentinel-2 and Landsat-8 on Google Earth Engine: A Case Study in Rompin, Pahang in Malaysia. *2023 IEEE 13th Symposium on Computer Applications & Industrial Electronics (ISCAIE)*, 38–43. https://doi.org/10.1109/ISCAIE57739.2023.10165382

Chew, Y. J., Ooi, S. Y., Pang, Y. H., & Lim, Z. Y. (2023a). Investigating the Relationship between the Influencing Fire Factors and Forest Fire Occurrence in the Districts of Rompin, Pekan, and Kuantan in the State of Pahang, Malaysia, Using Google Earth Engine. *International Journal on Advanced Science, Engineering and Information Technology*, *13*(5), 1733–1741. https://doi.org/10.18517/ijaseit.13.5.19026

Chew, Y. J., Ooi, S. Y., Pang, Y. H., & Lim, Z. Y. (2024). Framework to Create Inventory Dataset for Disaster Behavior Analysis Using Google Earth Engine: A Case Study in Peninsular Malaysia for Historical Forest Fire Behavior Analysis. *In Forests* (Vol. 15, Issue 6). https://doi.org/10.3390/f15060923

Chew, Y. J., Ooi, S. Y., Pang, Y. H., & Wong, K. S. (2022). Trend Analysis of Forest Fire in Pahang, Malaysia from 2001-2021 with Google Earth Engine Platform. *Journal of Logistics, Informatics and Service Science*, *9*(4), 15–26. https://doi.org/10.33168/LISS.2022.0402

Cree, A. (1989). Relationship between Environmental Conditions and Nocturnal Activity of the Terrestrial Frog, Leiopelma Archeyi. *23, Journal of Herpetology*, 61–68.

Ernst & Young. (2021a). 2021 Better Working World Data Challenge. *GitHub*. https://github.com/EY-Data-Science-Program/2021-Better-Working-World-Data-Challenge

Ernst & Young. (2021b). EY Open Science AI & Data Program. https://challenge.ey.com/

Ernst & Young. (2022). 2022 Better Working World Data Challenge. *GitHub*. https://github.com/EY-Data-Science-Program/2022-Better-Working-World-Data-Challenge

Frog, I.D. (2020). *FrogID*. Australian Museum, Sydney. http://www.frogid.net.au

Green, J., Govindarajulu, P., & Higgs, E. (2021). Multiscale Determinants of Pacific Chorus Frog Occurrence in a Developed Landscape. *Urban Ecosystems*, *24*(3), 587–600. https://doi.org/10.1007/s11252-020-01057-4

Hazell, D., Cunnningham, R., Lindenmayer, D., Mackey, B., & Osborne, W. (2001). Use of Farm Dams As Frog Habitat In An Australian Agricultural Landscape: Factors Affecting Species Richness and Distribution. *Biological Conservation*, *102*(2), 155–169. https://doi.org/10.1016/S0006-3207(01)00096-9

Hodges, J. L., & Lattimer, B. Y. (2019). Wildland Fire Spread Modeling Using Convolutional Neural Networks. *Fire Technology*, *55*(6), 2115–2142. https://doi.org/10.1007/s10694-019-00846-4

Jiao, Z., Zhang, Y., Xin, J., Mu, L., Yi, Y., Liu, H., & Liu, D. (2019). A Deep Learning Based Forest Fire Detection Approach Using UAV and YOLOv3. *2019 1st International Conference on Industrial Artificial Intelligence (IAI)*, 1–5. https://doi.org/10.1109/ICIAI.2019.8850815

Knutson, M. G., Sauer, J. R., Olsen, D. A., Mossman, M. J., Hemesath, L. M., & Lannoo, M. J. (1999). Effects of Landscape Composition and Wetland Fragmentation on Frog and Toad Abundance and Species Richness in Iowa and Wisconsin, U.S.A. *Conservation Biology*, *13*(6), 1437–1446. https://doi.org/10.1046/j.1523-1739.1999.98445.x

Lin, Z. (2023). Why and How to Embrace AI Such as ChatGPT in Your Academic Life. *Royal Society Open Science*, *10*(8). https://doi.org/10.1098/rsos.230658

Linardos, V., Drakaki, M., Tzionas, P., & Karnavas, Y. L. (2022). Machine Learning in Disaster Management: Recent Developments in Methods and Applications. *Machine Learning and Knowledge Extraction*, *4*(2), 446–473. https://doi.org/10.3390/make4020020

Meyer, J. G., Urbanowicz, R. J., Martin, P. C. N., O'Connor, K., Li, R., Peng, P. C., Bright, T. J., Tatonetti, N., Won, K. J., Gonzalez-Hernandez, G., & Moore, J. H. (2023). ChatGPT and Large Language Models in Academia: Opportunities and Challenges. *BioData Mining*, *16*(20), 1–11. https://doi.org/10.1186/s13040-023-00339-9

Nations, U. (2014). Recommended Practice: Burn Severity Mapping. https://un-spider.org/advisory-support/recommended-practices/recommended-practice-burn-severity-mapping

Rowley, J. J. L., Callaghan, C. T., Cutajar, T., Portway, C., Potter, K., Mahony, S., Trembath, D. F., Flemons, P., & Woods, A. (2019). FrogID: Citizen Scientists Provide Validated Biodiversity Data on Frogs of Australia. *Herpetological Conservation and Biology*, *14*(1), 155–170.

Wang, S., Zhao, J., Ta, N., Zhao, X., Xiao, M., & Wei, H. (2021). A Real-time Deep Learning Forest Fire Monitoring Algorithm Based on An Improved Pruned + KD Model. *Journal of Real-Time Image Processing*, *18*(6), 2319–2329. https://doi.org/10.1007/s11554-021-01124-9

Wang, Y., Dang, L., & Ren, J. (2019). Forest Fire Image Recognition Based on Convolutional Neural Network. *Journal of Algorithms & Computational Technology*, *13*. https://doi.org/10.1177/1748302619887689

Westgate, M. J., MacGregor, C., Scheele, B. C., Driscoll, D. A., & Lindenmayer, D. B. (2018). Effects of Time Since Fire on Frog Occurrence Are Altered By Isolation, Vegetation and Fire Frequency Gradients. *Diversity and Distributions*, *24*(1), 82–91. https://doi.org/10.1111/ddi.12659

Zhang, G., Wang, M., & Liu, K. (2019). Forest Fire Susceptibility Modeling Using a Convolutional Neural Network for Yunnan Province of China. *International Journal of Disaster Risk Science*, *10*(3), 386–403. https://doi.org/10.1007/s13753-019-00233-1

Zhang, Q., Xu, J., Xu, L., & Guo, H. (2016). Deep convolutional neural networks for forest fire detection. *Proceedings of the 2016 International Forum on Management, Education and Information Technology Application*. Atlantis Press.

6

Economic Inequality Analysis and Machine Learning

En Lee and Yvonne Lee

Economic Inequality

The concept of economic inequality has evolved significantly over the course of history, moving beyond just discourses that focus on income and wealth to also include narratives regarding inequalities in consumption and living conditions. Traditionally, economic inequality in economic literature refers to the uneven distribution of economic resources, such as income and wealth, among individuals or groups within a society, or between different societies (Sen, 1997). Today, economic inequality encompasses more than just the uneven distribution of income and wealth; it also includes disparities in consumption, living standards, and other dimensions of wellbeing across different groups in society (Fitoussi et al., 2011). However, economic inequality is not solely about the uneven distribution of resources; it also reflects the factors that lead to such disparities (Lefranc et al., 2008). These factors – income, wealth, consumption and living standards – primarily reflect inequality of outcomes and focus on material differences experienced by individuals. To fully understand economic inequality, one must also consider the inequality of opportunities, which examines the unequal access to resources that can shape these outcomes. This brings us to the distinction between inequality of outcomes and inequality of opportunities. In addition to the inequality of outcomes, which concerns disparities in resource allocation, inequality of opportunities emphasises that economic equality must also include equal access to opportunities, such as opportunities to education and employment, regardless of one's background or circumstances at birth (Stiglitz, 2012).

Income and Consumption Inequality

Although economic inequality comprises a variety of inequalities, income and consumption inequalities are always the focal points in economic research (Fisher et al., 2014). The emphasis on income and consumption inequalities is not arbitrary. These measures are often considered reliable indicators of economic wellbeing (Attanasio et al., 2010; Citro and Michael, 1995; Meyer & Sullivan, 2017).

Income data is relatively easier to access by government authorities these days as well. For instance, wages and salaries are typically reported through periodic data collection, where government agencies access this information through surveys, tax records and employment reports. Moreover, most salaries are directly deposited into bank accounts these days, unlike the payment of wages in cash form previously. These factors make income data easier to be tracked and organised, making it a practical choice for researchers and policymakers to utilise it in analysing economic inequality.

In contrast, consumption data is said to be rare and costly, as it is usually obtained through detailed surveys conducted on the entire economy. Consumption data, or more specifically household expenditure consumption, refer to the amount of final consumption expenditure made by resident households to meet their everyday needs, such as for food, clothing, housing (rent), energy, transport, durable goods (notably cars), health costs, leisure and miscellaneous services (OECD, 2013). Collecting such wide-ranging data on the entire economy's spending information often requires costly and detailed surveys. Even with such efforts, obtaining accurate depictions of household spending behaviour remains challenging due to various factors. Firstly, cash remains a common medium of exchange for certain kinds of transactions, especially in informal sectors, or for purchasing of items in small quantities, making it difficult to track and accurately record these expenditures. Second, respondents might underreport or misreport their expenditures due to recall bias. Not everyone will remember every single item they have purchased in the past months and years. They might modify their responses to fit normative expectations or, worse, provide responses based on convenience or personal bias. This can lead to discrepancies between reported and actual spending patterns. If transactions are electronically recorded, like how employee salary is reported and stored, the use of inauthentic and weak spending data can be minimised. Thus, household consumption expenditure data is harder to be collected and tabulated accurately, to attain the level of reliability similar to other data sources for economic inequality study such as income data. However, consumption data, while sometimes more challenging to collect, provide insights into actual living standards as it captures the aspects of economic wellbeing that income measures might miss, such as access to credit or informal economic activities (Aguiar & Bils, 2015). Consumption data is now recognised as a critical indicator of economic inequality, and sometimes it is used in conjunction with income data to provide a more holistic understanding of economic inequality (Attanasio & Pistaferri, 2016).

In terms of economic inequality, income and consumption are two distinct concepts. Income inequality typically focuses on disparities in earnings before taxes and transfers, while consumption inequality reflects differences in spending patterns (Blundell & Preston, 1998). Income inequality is often measured using various metrics that compare the earnings of individuals or households across percentiles of the distributed population. One common approach is to examine the income share ratios between top and bottom earners. For instance, the T10/B50 ratio compares the total income of the top 10% earners of the population to that of the bottom 50% earners. The World Inequality Database (WID) often reports income and wealth inequality using such measures ("World Inequality Report 2022", 2022). Other frequently used comparisons include the P90/P10 ratio, which measures the income gap between the 90th percentile and 10th percentile, and the P90/P50 ratio, which compares the 90th percentile to the median income. These metrics are often employed by organisations such as the Organisation for Economic Co-operation and Development (OECD) in their inequality reports (OECD, 2015). Researchers typically choose these metrices based on the specific context of their study, the availability of data, and the particular aspects of inequality that they aim to highlight (for example, a research may have the objective of highlighting the income gap between the richest (90%) and the poorest (10%)).

Two widely accepted measures for quantifying income inequality are the Gini index and the Theil index. The Gini coefficient, ranging from 0 (perfect equality) to 1 (maximum inequality), represents the income distribution of a nation's residents. It's extensively used by the World Bank and the United Nations Development Programme (UNDP) for international comparisons (Haddad et al., 2024). The Theil index, which belongs to a member of the generalised entropy index family, is particularly useful for decomposing economic inequality into within-group and between-group components, making it valuable for analysing economic inequality across different demographic or geographic subgroups (Conceicao & Ferreira, 2000). There are also several other relevant economic inequality and measures in addition to the Gini and Theil indices, as well as the percentile ratios discussed above, such as the Ahluwalia–Chenery Welfare Index.

Recently, income inequality has been observed to decrease between countries and increase within countries. Referring to Figure 6.1, within individual countries, income inequality emerges as a serious issue as the statistic is almost doubled (from 8.5 times to 15 times) using the T10/B50 ratio. It is worth mentioning here that although the database recorded the decline in income inequality between countries, the average income of the global top 10% is 38 times higher than the average income of the bottom 50% in

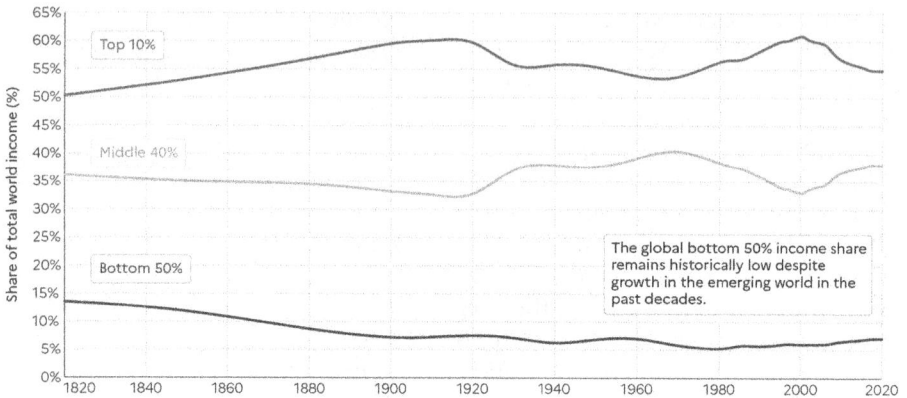

Interpretation: *The share of global income going to top 10% highest incomes at the world level has fluctuated around 50-60% between 1820 and 2020 (50% in 1820, 60% in 1910, 56% in 1980, 61% in 2000, 55% in 2020), while the share going to the bottom 50% lowest incomes has generally been around or below 10% (14% in 1820, 7% in 1910, 5% in 1980, 6% in 2000, 7% in 2020). Global inequality has always been very large. It rose between 1820 and 1910 and shows little long-run trend between 1910 and 2020.* **Sources and series:** *see wir2022.wid.world/methodology and Chancel and Piketty (2021).*

FIGURE 6.1
A line chart showing global income inequality during 1820–2020. The top 10% income share fluctuates between 50 and 60% and the middle fluctuates 30–40%, while the bottom 50%'s income share falls from 14% to 7%, highlighting the persistent inequality ("World Inequality Report 2022", 2022).

2020 ("World Inequality Report 2022", 2022). This unhealthy overall change in global income inequality is believed to be led by income increases experienced by the top income percentiles (Atkinson et al., 2011).

Consumption inequality is said to be more stable over time compared to income inequality as households utilise credit markets and savings to smooth consumption despite fluctuations in their income (Fisher et al., 2013; Krueger & Perri, 2006). Therefore, it is still vital that consumption inequality is measured and analysed, as changes of the above-mentioned economic factors have real implications on consumption patterns.

Macroeconomic View of Inequalities

Macroeconomics is a branch of economics that views the performance of an economy as a whole in order to understand the distribution of income and wealth within a society. Concepts such as economic growth, poverty, inequality, access to education and healthcare, technological advancement, and government policy are always at the forefront of discourses on economic performance. There are several aggregate indicators to measure the

determinants/dimensions introduced above such as GDP, Gini indices, poverty headcount ratio, human development index (HDI) and unemployment
rate. It is important to recognise that these dimensions are not necessarily uni-
directional in their relationships; some of them are interconnected through a
bidirectional relationship where each can influence and be influenced by the
other variables. For instance, higher economic growth can exacerbate income
inequality as gains or returns from growth are primarily channelled to the
top layers within businesses, such as company directors and executives,
while the labour force at the bottom of hierarchy often experiences minimal
increases or worse, no change at all in their wages. The resultant income
inequality, if remains unsolved, will in turn stifle economic growth.

One of the significant challenges that macroeconomic policies seek to
address is economic inequality. Inequality, especially income and consumption inequality, has profound implications for economic stability and growth.
Understanding the macroeconomic causes and consequences of inequality is
essential for designing policies that promote more equitable economic outcomes and sustainable growth. This section mainly discusses the income and
consumption inequalities from the macroeconomic perspective, but other
related inequalities are included as well.

Economic growth and economic inequality are deeply intertwined.
Generally, economic growth is not uniformly distributed, resulting in
income disparities where top earners pursue and receive significantly larger
increases in their earnings compared to those at the bottom of the income
distribution. This phenomenon contributes to rising consumption inequality too. Notably, income inequality tends to increase rapidly, particularly
during the early stages of development when specific sectors or regions
experience faster growth than others. China and the United States, being
the world's two largest economies, provide valuable insights in illustrating
changing income inequality levels in rapidly growing economies, especially
when facing challenges that arise when that growth is unevenly distributed.
In China, during the initial phases of rapid economic growth in the late
1970s and 1980s, rising profits and low wages in the industrial sector led to
increased income inequality. This inequality, fuelled by an increasing divide
between profits and wages, ultimately hampered economic growth in the
mid-2000s through decreased savings rates and intensified inflationary pressures, which in turn reduced investment. (Garnaut, 2010). The United States
has experienced similar patterns, where past economic growth strategies
that emphasised low wages and reduced investment in human capital led to
increasing inequality. Eventually, income inequality slowed down economic
growth by fostering political paralysis and reducing consumer confidence,
which led to underinvestment in critical areas like education and infrastructure (Wilensky, 2012). Interestingly, this pattern contradicts Simon Kuznets'
suggestion in his study on the relationship between economic growth and
income inequality, from which the well-known Kuznets Curve is derived as

shown in Figure 6.2 (Kuznets, 2019). According to the Kuznets Curve Theory, income inequality tends to increase in the early stages of economic growth as a country starts to industrialise, and then decreases as gains from the growth spread more evenly across the population. That is to say, if economic growth is sustained over a sufficiently long period of time, the negative impact of increasing income inequality could be reduced or improved over time. This is highly possible, as inferred by Tsounta et al. (2015) from their investigation of the income share ratios among emerging markets and developing countries (EMDCs). They found that the income shares of the bottom 20 percent are associated with higher GDP growth over the medium term of economic development.

Education, as a key indicator of human capital development, became especially valuable during the late 20th century when knowledge-based industries such as Information and Communication Technology (ICT) and research and development in science, technology, engineering and mathematics (STEM) fields began to expand. Educational attainment is increasingly critical for economic success, as populations with higher educational attainment levels tend to be more productive and innovative, which enhances overall economic performance (Hanushek & Woessmann, 2012). However, disparities in access to quality education contribute to widening income inequality, as those with higher education levels tend to be positioned in higher-paying jobs and thus accumulate wealth. This creates a cycle where economic gains are increasingly concentrated among the educated elite, exacerbating income inequality at the national level (OECD, 2015). Such unhealthy income inequality is also driven by the fact that low-education individuals often rely on labour income, which is significantly lower compared to income earned

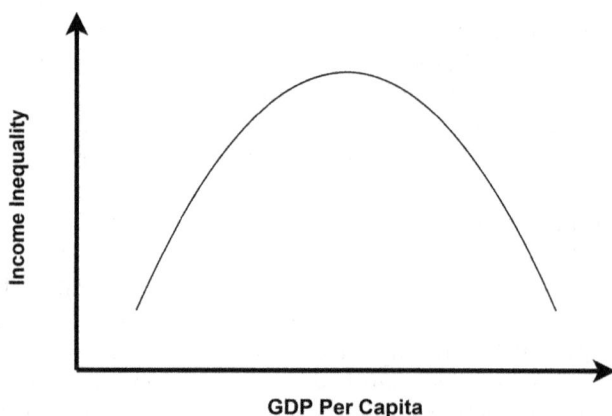

FIGURE 6.2
The Kuznets Curve, illustrating that income inequality initially rises and then declines as GDP per capita grows.

by knowledge workers and other highly educated elites. While high salaries for knowledge workers are inevitable and reasonable, this does not jus-
tify the reality that the lower wages being paid to less-educated workers are
significantly lower than that required to ensure a decent level of wellbeing.
In a study of eighteen OECD countries, strong labour market institutions
such as coordinated wage bargaining, and high union density actively help
to reduce income gap between the educated (elite) workers and the low-
education workers (Hope & Martelli, 2019). Besides ensuring fair wages are
being paid by profitable corporations through minimum wage and collective bargaining legislations, government policies aimed at reducing education inequality are crucial for promoting more equitable economic outcomes,
especially for people from low-income and disadvantaged backgrounds who
cannot afford the same quality education as those from wealthier families.
A cross-country data analysis study shows that higher educational attainment, along with a fairer distribution of education resource and government
social expenditure contributed to smaller income inequality (De Gregorio
& Lee, 2002). Public investment in education, particularly in underserved
regions, is essential for ensuring that society has a broader access to economic opportunities (UNESCO, 2020). By addressing education disparities,
policymakers can foster a more inclusive economy, reduce income inequality and support sustainable economic growth. Thus, education is not only a
fundamental human right but also a critical component of macroeconomic
stability and prosperity. The association between education attainment and
consumption inequalities is more complex. Cheng (2021) suggests that education plays a significant role in the nuances of consumption behaviour and
contributes to consumption inequality among urban migrants after China's
reform period that began in 1978.

Income and consumption inequalities are factors included in the ongoing
discussion on disparities in healthcare access and outcomes as well. These
inequalities can exacerbate differences in health status, create barriers to
healthcare services and lead to unequal distribution of healthcare resources.
Hence, unhealthy people are generally associated with poor income. In such
situations, children might be forced to leave school to take low-wage jobs,
such as manual labour, to support their sick parents who need expensive
healthcare and are unable to work full-time. This situation creates a vicious
cycle that continuously harms disadvantaged households. Income inequality
directly affects an individual's ability to access healthcare services. Higher
incomes allow individuals to afford better healthcare, including preventative care, timely medical interventions and access to specialised services. In
contrast, those with lower incomes often are unable to afford necessary care,
leading to delayed treatment and poorer health outcomes as a result. Pickett
and Wilkinson (2015) reviewed several studies from various countries to
investigate the relationship between income inequality and health outcomes.
Validating the existing literatures through epidemiological framework,

income inequality is found to be causally linked to health outcomes, and three out of the eight of causal criteria are met, which are temporality (inequality preceding health outcomes), biological plausibility (stress-related health effects), and consistency (similar findings across studies). Most of the reviewed studies found that large disparities in income negatively impact both health and social outcomes. This scenario is also observed in the relationship between consumption inequalities and healthcare services consumed. Lower consumption levels lead to poorer living conditions and nutrition among low-income groups, which can negatively impact this group's health. Studies have shown that consumption patterns are closely linked to health outcomes. For instance, Darmon and Drewnowski (2015) found that people with higher socioeconomic status spend more on healthier diets that cost more, than those from low socioeconomic status. Moreover, Alagiyawanna et al. (2015) found that the proper use of taxes and subsidies on food consumption and health services potentially improve citizens' health through changing the consumption patterns in some high-income countries.

The government plays a crucial role in shaping income and consumption inequalities through various monetary policies. These include monetary and fiscal policies, legislation and social programmes. While governments often aim to promote economic growth and stability, their policies may have unintended consequences which can further worsen the income inequality and consumption expenditure power of lower income groups. One key area where this impact is clearly seen, is in the implementation of monetary policies, especially contractionary ones. Contractionary monetary policies such as raising interest rates can disproportionately benefit wealthier households while harming lower-income households. Mankiw (2019) points out that this is mainly because those living in the bottom echelons of society are more prone to experiencing job losses or wage stagnation, due to economic slowdown and lower production during this period. In fact, the consequence of rising interest rates in the USA during the period of 1980–2008 is that wealthier households received a higher return through investments in financial assets like stocks and bonds, enabling them to maintain or even increase their consumption levels. In contrast, researchers observed that lower-income households, who rely more on labour income, faced a reduced ability to spend (Coibion et al., 2012). Similar findings were observed in South Korea during the aftermath of the Asian Financial Crisis from 1998 to 2015, where businesses faced higher borrowing rates and caused job losses and wage stagnation, with the outcome of widening of income inequality (Park, 2021). On the other hand, fiscal policy is a powerful tool that governments can use to address income and consumption inequalities. Studies have shown that progressive taxation and targeted social spending can effectively reduce inequalities. For instance, Woo et al. (2013) found that countries that implement progressive tax systems usually have higher social welfare expenditures and tend to exhibit lower income inequalities. However, the impact of fiscal policy is not always straightforward. Ball et al. (2013) demonstrated that fiscal consolidations, especially those focused on spending cuts rather than tax increases, often lead to increased inequalities. This highlights the complex nature of fiscal policy's effects on income distribution, and the importance of carefully designed interventions to achieve the desired outcomes of reduced inequalities.

Technological advancements have significant impact on income and consumption inequality in recent decades. Undeniably, technology has created new business opportunities and improved wellbeing, but it has also led to skill-biased technological changes, where the demand for high-skilled workers increases proportionately higher when compared to the demand for low-skilled workers. This in turn causes the widening of income disparities. Additionally, technology has transformed consumption patterns, potentially widening the gap between those who can access and afford new technologies and those who cannot. Technology has made transportation easier, cheaper and available to mostly everyone, facilitating communication among regions. This has created new markets, which in turn led to urban development and the migration of rural residents to these urban regions as the labour source for urban economic activities. As a result, millions of people have escaped poverty. However, inequality has also risen, which might be attributed to the fact that today's new jobs require special or specific technical skills, thus exacerbating technology advancement-led inequalities (Tsounta et al., 2015). In the early stages of new technology adoption, well-educated people are often favoured, and thus they receive better wages compared to unskilled labourers working in urban areas. A study by Acemoglu and Autor (2011) further supports this view, demonstrating how technological change can lead to job polarisation. They found that middle-skill jobs have declined relative to both high-skill and low-skill jobs, contributing to increased wage inequality. This is due to tasks that were previously handled by middle-skilled workers have been replaced by technology automating these routine tasks. Thus, technology complemented the mental dexterity required for high-skill, non-routine cognitive tasks. Such technological shifts not only affect income distribution but also influence consumption patterns, as different income groups have varying abilities to access and benefit from new technologies.

Microeconomic View of Inequalities

While macroeconomic determinants play a significant role in these disparities, a microeconomic perspective offers crucial insights into the individual-level determinants of these inequalities. This view emphasises on personal characteristics, choices and circumstances, and how they contribute to differences in income and consumption patterns across individuals and households. As Atkinson and Bourguignon (2000) argue in their seminal work on income distribution, an understanding of these micro-level factors is essential towards developing effective policies to address income inequality. The microeconomic approach examines various determinants such as education, health status, employment characteristics and personal financial decisions, each of which can significantly impact an individual's economic outcomes. For instance, Piketty and Saez (2003) demonstrate how changes in individual labour market outcomes, particularly at the top levels of income distribution, have contributed to rising income inequality in recent decades. This bottom-up microeconomic approach complements the top-down macroeconomic perspective discussed previously, providing an alternative view of inequality by examining the socioeconomic and demographic factors at individual or household levels. We explain some common factors below together with their impact on income and consumption inequalities.

Firstly, the basis of education's impact on one's income lies in human capital theory. Becker (1994) believes that education is a type of investment in human capital. An individual's productivity and earning potential/income strongly correlate with the amount of time and resource allocated by the individual for education. The concept of "returns to education" quantifies this relationship with an increase in earnings being observed to be associated with each subsequent year of schooling that an individual undergoes. Researchers consistently found a positive impact on personal earnings from the number of years of education attained. For instance, Card (2001) estimates that, on average, every single year of schooling increases earnings by about 10% in the United States. However, these returns are not uniform across all levels of education or for all individuals. Psacharopoulos and Patrinos (2018) conducted a global review on the returns to education. Their findings show that, while returns are generally positive, they vary across countries and education levels, with higher returns typically observed in developing countries and at higher levels of education. The impact of education on income inevitably affects consumption patterns, thus contributing to consumption inequalities. Individuals with higher levels of education tend to have higher income and thus a higher level of consumption. However, the positive relationship between education and consumption is not consistent across different categories of consumption. In other words, an increase in education does not always lead to a corresponding increase in consumption, especially when considering the complexity of different consumption types. Attanasio and Kaufmann (2014) found that more educated individuals tend to have different consumption preferences, often prioritising spending and investing in healthcare, education for their children and cultural goods. This shows that education not only affects the level of consumption but also the composition of consumption that could lead to the intergenerational transmission of both educational and health attainments that varies across different socio-economic groups.

Secondly, the link between health and productivity forms the foundation of health's impact on income. Healthier individuals are generally more productive, so they are paid a higher wage. Bloom and Canning (2000) argue that health improvements lead to a rise in productivity through several ways as those in good health conditions see improvement in their physical and cognitive function, have reduced absenteeism and have longer productive years in the job market. Another interesting finding is the relationship between adult height (as an indicator to measure for childhood nutrition and health) and wages. Schultz (2002) found that for every centimetre of increase in adult height, a 4–6% increase in wages was observed in Ghana and Brazil. People who experience prolonged unhealthy diets and limited healthcare access are more vulnerable to disease. This happens usually in lower-income families. A health crisis by a member of a low-income family could have a severe negative shock on the family's financials. The affected individual and the entire household's income potentially face drastic reductions due to the health crisis, especially if the affected individual is the family's sole income earner. Smith (1999) demonstrated that once a family member suffers from severe illness, this will lead to a substantial reduction in their accumulated wealth, particularly among older individuals who will dig into their savings to pay for the sick family member's medical expenses. Subsequently, healthy family members may be forced to reduce work hours, change to lower-paying jobs or exit the labour force entirely to care for family members requiring long-term care due to the illness. Therefore, a health crisis leads to both immediate and long-term income losses for the affected family. As such, healthy and higher income-earning individuals tend to earn more, while the bottom-level earners potentially face a large decline in wealth and income if a health crisis occurs, thus resulting in an even larger income gap. One of the ways to minimise the destructive impacts of serious illnesses is public health insurance. Finkelstein et al. (2012) studied the Oregon Health Insurance Experiment and confirmed that Medicaid coverage helped to reduce out-of-pocket medical expenditures. This study demonstrates that public health insurance for vulnerable groups tempers the severity of impacts on individual or household consumption patterns from health crises. Without health insurance, poor health status potentially widens the consumption gap between the lower and higher income groups, through impacting on consumption patterns, as health problems will require patients to spend more on out-of-pocket medical expenses. This in turn forces them to spend less on other forms of consumption, particularly on discretionary items and wants, such as shopping for clothing, dining out or engaging in leisure activities. According to Xu et al. (2003), around 150 million people worldwide encounter catastrophic health expenditures each year, and as a result, many of them fall into poverty. Access to health insurance can play a crucial role in mitigating the impact of health on income and consumption inequalities. Through its impact on productivity, earning potential and necessary health-related expenditures, we can see how health shapes not only an individual's income but also alters their consumption patterns.

Now, we look at how individual financial decisions relate to income, wealth and consumption inequalities. Financial decisions can range from savings and investment choices to borrowing behaviours. An individual's investment or consumption decisions are strongly correlated with that individual's income level. Lee et al. (2024) found that lower-income families (with "family" being defined as households where three or more individuals live together) tend to spend more on discretionary expenses compared to higher-income families. This is related to Dynan et al.'s (2004) findings that higher-income households usually save a larger amount of their income compared to lower-income households. This difference in savings rate contributes to wealth inequality over time. Moreover, the approach to investing is important. Wealthy individuals are more likely to invest in a diverse portfolio of assets, particularly assets that require high initial capital, such as land, which typically offer higher returns. This contrasts with normal savings accounts, which are more commonly targeted at less-wealthy individuals. On the other hand, poorly educated individuals with low levels of income and wealth often make wrong choices in their investment decisions due to their lack of knowledge about sophisticated financial products, thus further worsening wealth inequality between the two groups (Campbell, 2006). The channelling effect of income inequality discussed is very clear, where higher income inequality results in financial investment decision differences. High-income households are able to make investments in high-return and low-risk assets, thus increasing the wealth accumulation among these households and widening the wealth gap among the top and bottom earners. Similarly, borrowing decisions affect short-term consumption. In Spain, an empirical study showed that household borrowing helped to maintain a lower consumption inequality compared to income inequality during the period between 2000 and 2008 (Pardo & Sánchez Santos, 2014). Krueger and Perri (2006) found that the expansion of credit helps households to maintain their consumption levels in dealing with income shocks, but this somehow increases their vulnerability to financial stress due to accumulated debts.

Lastly, we investigate other demographic factors' role on income and consumption inequalities. Age is a critical demographic factor affecting income and consumption. The life-cycle hypothesis, pioneered by Modigliani (1955), suggests that while individuals tend to smoothen their consumption over their lifetime, incomes typically follow an inverted U-shape pattern. This shows that age-related income differences are a natural part of the economic lifecycle. Researchers have further decomposed consumption patterns and observe variations in consumption patterns across different age groups. Aguiar and Hurst (2013) report a U-shape pattern too; but in terms of the consumption of non-durables and services, where a hump-shaped profile is observed along an individual's life cycle and with consumption of non-durables and services peaking in the middle age. This variation in consumption patterns across different age groups contributes to observed consumption inequalities. Gender is another frequently highlighted factor in discussions of income inequality. Despite numerous efforts done on narrowing the gender income gap, a persistent gender wage gap still exists (Kunze, 2017). Among the factors contributing to a high gender wage gap includes a higher female share in lower-paying industries, number of children (particularly in developing countries), and labour force participation rates (Terada-Hagiwara et al., 2018). Another slightly delicate issue is racial inequality, which is challenging to address because it is deeply rooted in human behaviour and attitudes. According to Kuhn et al. (2020), the median wealth accumulated among white households in the United States is about ten times more than the median for black households.

Next Steps

Upon reviewing recent studies of inequalities in macroeconomic and microeconomic perspectives, it is essential to explore both microeconomic and macroeconomic factors to fully understand income and consumption inequalities. At the macroeconomic level, we examined how broad economic forces such as education systems, healthcare infrastructure, and overall economic growth contribute to income, consumption, and other forms of inequalities directly or indirectly. These factors create the overarching environment in which individual economic decisions and outcomes occur. For instance, the quality and accessibility of an education system directly influences human capital formation, which in turn indirectly determines productivity and economic growth. During the exploration of income and consumption inequalities from the microeconomic view, these microeconomic variables are found to interact with each other towards explaining inequalities, similar to observations for macroeconomic variables. Personal educational attainment, health status, financial decisions, and demographic factors such as age, gender and race, all play significant roles in affecting an individual's economic outcomes. Understanding these relationships is crucial, as pinpointing the causal links among these factors will further enhance the development of effective policies to tackle increasing inequalities. As Neckerman and Torche (2007) argue, integrating diverse micro and macro factors into comprehensive economic models is essential for fully understanding the nuanced dynamics of income and consumption inequalities. While integrating micro and macro perspectives offers a comprehensive view of these inequalities, studying micro- and macroeconomic aspects separately remain valuable, necessary and often relatively straightforward.

Thus, integrating these factors in an economic model to further uncover their interrelationship is the necessary step towards understanding the overall inequality (Heshmati, 2004). Additionally, interpreting these relationships from the economic model is crucial, as pinpointing the causal links among these dimensions will further enhance the development of effective policies in the future to unearth the roots of income and consumption inequalities. In the following sections, we move on to introduce Machine Learning and how it offers a novel approach in modelling compared to traditional economic models in studying income and consumption inequalities.

Introduction to Machine Learning

Machine Learning (ML) is a branch of artificial intelligence that uses data and/or answers as inputs to build a statistical model that encapsulates an algorithm (rule) inside it. Unlike traditional programming, which requires both data and explicit rule as inputs to produce the output, Machine Learning learns patterns directly from the input data or training data to make predictions. It typically requires a vast amount of data so that the built model is not under-fitted, which is where model cannot predict the unseen data/testing data well. Conversely, overfitting occurs when a model's learning from the training data is too detailed and results in it capturing noise rather than the true signal. The model becomes too complex as although it scores well based on training data, it performs poorly on testing data. The art of machine learning lies in finding the sweet spot between these two terms, ensuring that the model generalises well to testing data while still accurately reflecting the patterns learned from the training data.

Machine Learning is typically categorised into two main types of learning:

1. **Supervised Learning**: The algorithm is trained with labelled dataset, where both input data and the corresponding correct outputs (answers) are provided. The goal is for the algorithm to learn a function that maps inputs to outputs, which can then be used to make predictions on new, unseen data.

2. **Unsupervised Learning**: Here, the algorithm is given input data without labelled responses. The goal is to recognise the patterns or structures within the data. The aim is to group similar data points together or reduce the complexity of the data while maintaining its characteristics.

Next, Machine Learning tasks are often categorised into three main types:

1. **Classification**: Supervised Learning. This involves predicting a categorical label for a given input. For example, determining whether an email is spam or not spam.

2. **Regression**: Supervised Learning. This involves predicting a continuous numerical value for a given input. For example, predicting house prices based on various housing features.

3. **Clustering**: Unsupervised Learning. This involves grouping similar data points together. For example, segmenting customers based on their purchasing behaviour.

Finally, the process of developing a machine learning model (Figure 6.3):

1. **Data Preparation and Preprocessing**: This includes data collection, cleaning, and preprocessing to make it suitable for analysis.

2. **Feature Engineering**: Selecting or creating the most relevant features (input variables) for the model.

3. **Model Selection and Training**: Choosing an appropriate algorithm and using training data to train the model.

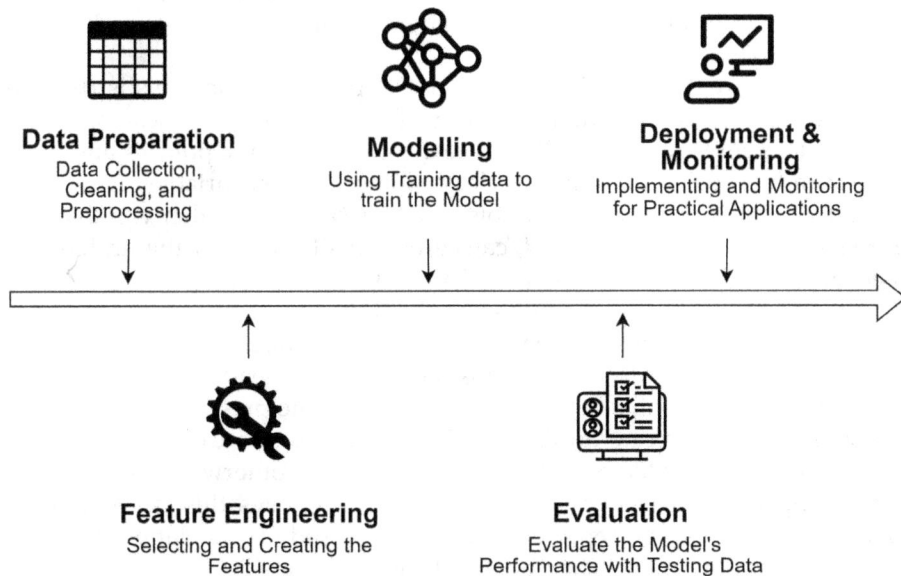

Data Preparation
Data Collection,
Cleaning, and
Preprocessing

Modelling
Using Training data to
train the Model

**Deployment &
Monitoring**
Implementing and Monitoring
for Practical Applications

Feature Engineering
Selecting and Creating the
Features

Evaluation
Evaluate the Model's
Performance with Testing Data

FIGURE 6.3
A typical Machine Learning model development process. It includes: 1) data preparation and preprocessing phase, 2) feature engineering, 3) model selection and training , 4) model evaluation and 5) model deployment and monitoring.

4. **Model Evaluation**: Evaluate the model's performance with testing data with several metrices such as accuracy (classification), silhouette coefficient (clustering) and R^2 (regression).

5. **Model Deployment and Monitoring**: Implementing the final model for real-world use.

Machine Learning as a Causal Inference Approach

Causal inference is a fundamental concept in economics that aims to identify and quantify cause-and-effect relationships between variables. In Machine Learning, during experiment, researchers often check variable correlations but not causal inference. However, since most Machine Learning projects are primarily focussed on enhancing their predicting performance, neither correlation nor causation is important. In economic research, causal inference allows economists to move beyond correlations and understand the underlying mechanisms that drive economic phenomena, including income and consumption inequalities. The Nobel winner, James Heckman emphasises that causal inference is the key of understanding economic relationships and developing effective policies. Without a clear understanding of causality, policymakers can fall into risk of implementing ineffective or even harmful polices (Heckman, 2000).

We often hear that correlation does not imply causation. This is particularly relevant and important in the study of economic inequalities, especially when research results are applied to real-world economic policies and decisions. While correlation identifies relationships between variables, it does not indicate that a change in one variable, say X, is causing another variable, say Y, to change. On the other hand, causation aims to uncover the underlying mechanisms driving these relationships. If the causation holds, we are confident to say that, "X directly influences Y". Causal inference is the methodological framework used to isolate specific effects while controlling for other influencing other factors. Correlations can sometimes lead to the inference of inauthentic relationships between two factors, as the presence of confounding variables may create an illusion that implies that a direct relationship exists between these factors although fact indicates otherwise. By explicitly accounting for confounders, causal inference mitigates this issue, thereby ensuring a more precise representation of cause-and-effect relationships.

In the economic field, methods such as Randomised Controlled Trials (RCTs), Instrumental Variables (IV), Difference-in-Differences (DiD) and Regression Discontinuity Design (RDD) have long been employed to understand causal inference. These methods help researchers navigate the intricacies of confounding variables and endogeneity, ensuring that observed relationships truly reflect the cause-and-effect relationships between two interested variables. On the other hand, Machine Learning is designed as a means to predict, so they prioritise recognising and learning patterns in data to optimise their predicting accuracy over uncovering causal relationships. Recently, some advanced Machine Learning models, like causal trees or causal inference algorithms, offer causal reasoning as part of their predictive models. By combining the predictive power of Machine Learning and causality checks of traditional econometrics, researchers can develop models that not only predict outcomes but also explain the underlying causes. In this way, a more robust economic analysis is achieved, where both correlation and causation are considered.

Machine Learning's Role in Measuring Income and Consumption Inequalities

One of the ways Machine learning can outperform traditional economic models, which are mostly linear based, is its tendency on capturing nonlinear relationships between variables. Traditional models often rely on linear assumptions, which unavoidably oversimplify complex economic phenomena, for example the U-shaped Kuznets Curve. In this section, we explore three key ML tasks that was explained earlier (regression, clustering, classification) and provide recent studies of Machine Learning that achieved notable results in the field of income and consumption inequalities.

Regression

Regression analysis is used to predict continuous outcomes, such as income distribution. In term of inequality measure, regression analysis is a core method in both traditional econometrics and machine learning, making it a common ground where these two approaches often intersect and be compared. This section discusses some recent studies that use of Machine Learning in measuring income distribution and inequality.

Athey and Imbens (2019) proposed Generalised Random Forest (GRF) algorithm to estimate heterogeneous treatment effects. The proposed model allows for the detection of causal nonlinear relationships between variables. It reveals how different factors, such as education, occupation and regional characteristics, affect income in ways that vary across different subpopulations. Escanciano and Terschuur (2022) employed Machine Learning techniques to measure Inequality of Opportunity (IOp) through outcomes such as income inequality and inequality indices such as the Gini coefficient. Based on data from 29 European countries in 2019, the study indicates that parental education and occupation are the most significant factors in explaining income inequality, with Romania and Bulgaria showing the highest levels of IOp. Wójcik & Andruszek (2021) use Open Street Map (OSM) data to study the usability of nonlinear model in predicting the wellbeing index. They demonstrated that nonlinear machine learning algorithms performed better than linear models in estimating an intra-urban wellbeing index. Additionally, they visually show the relationships between three selected dimensions of wellbeing and predictors through explainable artificial intelligence (XAI). One of the obvious nonlinear relationships is the U-shaped relationship between the wellbeing index and green areas.

Clustering

Clustering algorithms are useful in identifying the clusters that require assistance and intervention based on their common characteristics, such as income and consumption. While clustering may not directly measure inequality as what regression techniques normally do, it indirectly informs researchers about inequalities that exist between clusters. By segmenting populations into different socioeconomic groups, inequalities in terms of income and consumption can be known and analysed by comparing average income distribution and consumption patterns differences of these clusters. Hu (2022) used clustering to identify distinct groups based on income and spending patterns observed from U.S. Consumer Expenditure Survey. Result reveals that after-tax income, wage/salary income and the quarterly expenditure on food, housing are the five most important variables that differentiate each household into distinct clusters. Moradi et al. (2023) employ fuzzy clustering, one of the soft clustering methods, to classify Iranian households based on income and consumption patterns from 2011 to 2021. The authors observed a widening income inequality gap over time between top and bottom earners in Iran that is associated with their purchasing power as well as energy consumption.

Classification

Classification tasks in Machine Learning are typically designed for predicting categorical outcomes like poverty status. However, they are not well suited to measure economic inequality, which is generally continuous in nature. However, in certain cases, income or consumption can be used as target variables to help indirectly capture various aspects of the inequality. In this section, we discuss some of the studies of using income or consumption as categorical target output. Chakrabarty and Biswas (2018) utilise a Gradient Boosting Classifier to predict income levels of individuals in West Bengal, India. The study considers various attributes like age, education, and occupation. The results show that age and final weight are the most influential variables in explaining income inequality. Maruejols et al. (2022) applied several machine learning algorithms to classify subjective poverty using socioeconomic variables in China rural area. The target variable is subjective poverty, defined by authors as whether a household's income falls below the self-reported minimum income. The key predictors identified are income, consumption-related factors like medical and gift expenditures. In this study, the random forest classification model outperforms the rest, achieving 85.29% accuracy.

Machine Learning as Compared to Traditional Econometric Models

Recently, Machine Learning has dominated across various fields, including economics, primarily due to its ability to process vast structured and unstructured data. Another important point is its ability to handle nonlinear relationships that traditional methods often strictly assumed as linear. With advanced algorithms, Machine Learning guarantees higher accuracy in decision-making processes within economic contexts. Below, we explore some capabilities of Machine Learning that traditional economic models cannot effectively achieve.

First and foremost, the predictive power of Machine Learning models often surpasses that of traditional econometric approaches (Athey & Imbens, 2019). There are several factors that make Machine Learning particularly effective in prediction. Firstly, Machine Learning accepts nonlinear relationships between variables without the need for explicit specification in the initial setting. Economic research usually focuses on traditional linear models that often ignore or oversimplify the variance in data that is not fit to how their trends/structures appear in nature. Therefore, utilising nonlinear Machine Learning models will account for this missing variance, making them true representations of the underlying economic relationships. Second, some of the Machine Learning are ensemble models. These types of models combine multiple same or different kinds of models and processes for the prediction estimation using averaging or majority voting to obtain a more reliable prediction output than those from a single model. The most common type of ensemble model is Random Forest. Furthermore, Machine Learning models have self-learning capability algorithms. They automatically update their pattern-recognising rules as they receive new data, allowing them to adapt to changing economic conditions and trends. This adaptability feature makes machine learning particularly well-suited for measuring economic inequality, where the impact of socioeconomic factors can shift rapidly.

While the field of economics cares more about the process of interpreting results from economic models to facilitate decision-making later, it is crucial to emphasise highly accurate models too. Achieving precise predictions ensures that the subsequent interpretations and policy recommendations are reliable. Therefore, interpretability and predictive accuracy are two key advantages that Machine Learning models can offer. In the next section, we will delve into these advantages of Machine Learning models that are under-explored by researchers from economic and Machine Learning fields.

Secondly, Machine Learning algorithms excel at identifying intricate patterns in data that might be overlooked by traditional linear regression models. The algorithms detect nonlinear relationships and interactions between variables without the need for explicit specification. Recent studies show that nonlinear models are essential as they enhance the accuracy and efficiency of nonlinear economic modelling by handling complex, high-dimensional data and improving forecasting capability. Korobilis (2018) reviewed and discussed how machine learning algorithms are applied in high-dimensional macroeconomic models to extend the use to time-varying parameter models and vector autoregressions, specifically in a situation where the number of parameters is more than observations. Wang et al. (2022) studied the role of automated machine learning (AutoML). They emphasise the significant advantage of AutoML in simplifying the modelling process while ensuring the efficiency of nonlinear economic models. Li and Malin (2009) proposed the Back Propagation (BP) Neural Network algorithm to capture the time-varying characteristics of economic systems, which consequently aids in the prediction of complex economic behaviours.

Thirdly, Machine Learning is adaptable to various kinds of data, while traditional economic modelling requires well-structured data. In the instance of spatial data for example, traditional economic model is only able to process well-structured spatial data after several data preprocessing stages. On the other hand, Machine Learning can learn spatial information directly from the spatial data in the original form such as satellite images (granted, some preprocessing steps is still necessary for these images). Another reason that Machine Learning is superior to traditional economic models is that its own rules learn from data, without constraints imposed by humans. While traditional economic models can incorporate pre-processed satellite data, these older models rely on humans to identify and extract relevant features based on their own experience. In contrast, Machine Learning models, particularly Deep Learning architectures, can learn to recognise subtle patterns and features in raw imagery that humans might miss or find difficult to quantify, or may even inadvertently dismiss as irrelevant (Russakovsky et al., 2015).

The following steps show how Machine Learning processes satellite imagery: 1) Obtaining high-resolution satellite imagery of the area of interest from public available sources such as OpenStreetMap, 2) Enhancing image quality and standardising the data, 3) Using advanced models such as Convolutional

Neural Networks to identify relevant features such as buildings, roads, and land use patterns, 4) Developing indices based on the pixels' colour such as grey (building space coverage), blue (water space coverage) and green (green space coverage), 5) Combining these indices with traditional economic data or utilising them alone to derive measures of local economic conditions and inequality. Following are some studies that utilise satellite imagery to measure poverty. Jean et al. (2016) proposed a Convolutional Neural Network to process satellite imagery and socioeconomic survey data to predict the poverty rate. This model successfully explained up to 75% of the variation in wealth and consumption patterns at a local level, thus proving the reliability of these models in tracking economic outcomes, which could potentially stand in as a cost-effective tool to measure income distribution. Similarly, Abitbol and Karsai (2020) used deep learning models with French cities' satellite imagery to predict the local socioeconomic status (SES). Results show that high-density residential areas and proximity to infrastructure correlate with lower SES, while natural spaces and low-density areas are linked to higher SES. These findings emphasise how urban topology can shape socioeconomic inequalities. The availability of advanced Machine Learning model is useful for poor countries like African countries where traditional data collection methods like survey and census are often considered a burden due to their costs. As public satellite imagery repositories such as OpenStreetMap data become more accessible, these poor countries can find out their economic conditions and inequality patterns by utilising these images together with Machine Learning models. In addition, as these images are updated more frequently than the regularity of traditional economic surveys, this method of analysing inequality patterns is useful for both poor and rich countries.

Interpreting the Machine Learning Model

We have seen how well Machine Learning models perform in predicting and handling complex relationships in previous sections of this chapter. However, this remarkable capability comes at the cost of increased complexity compared to traditional econometric models. One of the primary concerns of machine learning is its "black box" nature. The lack of transparency makes it difficult for the researchers to understand how Machine Learning models arrive at their predictions. This limitation is then informed to policymakers and the public to ensure that no ethical problems arise from the analysis methodology. The "black box" characteristic is a serious issue because correlation or causal inference is core in the field of economics. Traditional econometric models remain dominant because they do not face the same issue (Mullainathan & Spiess, 2017). In econometric models, the relationship between variables is explicitly specified. The coefficients in these models convey clear economic meanings, allowing researchers to quantify the impact of specific factors on the outcome. Moreover, econometric models like linear regression have well-established standards used for interpretation and inference. Coefficients, standard errors and p-values provide a common language through which economists can actively and efficiently communicate, discuss and obtain feedback for their findings. In contrast, Machine Learning models often lack such standardised metrics that are consistent across different algorithms (Rudin, 2019). Last but most importantly, when talking about policy recommendations, economic models have well-developed procedures for hypothesis testing and constructing confidence intervals. Although numerous efforts are being made to put Machine Learning models on par with similar econometric frameworks, they have yet to achieve the same level of acceptability by the policymaking communities (Chy & Buadi, 2024).

Therefore, it is essential to explore recent advancements in explainable AI field that make the Machine Learning model more transparent to researchers and policymakers. Interpretability tools such as SHAP (SHapley Additive exPlanations) values and LIME (Local Interpretable Model-agnostic Explanations) have been widely adopted to interpret black-box Machine Learning model analysis (Bai et al., 2023; Herrera et al., 2023; Lee et al., 2024). Additionally, certain Machine Learning algorithms like causal forests are specifically designed to directly examine data, bridging the gap between prediction and interpretability. An important distinction between analysis tools and causal Machine Learning is that neither SHAP nor LIME are directly utilising causal inference, they only show the processes for getting the predictions. If the experiment's settings do not account for causal inference, then the usage of tools like SHAP and LIME can do nothing in terms of implying causation instead of just spurious correlations. Assisting the researchers to understand how different features contribute to the prediction outcome is these tools' primary purpose.

Following this, we explore various methods and approaches that enhance the interpretability of Machine Learning models making them more suitable for examining causal relationships between variables. It is important to note that Machine Learning is not intended to replace traditional econometric models. Instead, it is a powerful supporting tool augmenting the current econometric framework, and providing a deeper understanding toward the complex and dynamic economic phenomena like income and consumption inequality.

SHAP – SHapley Additive Explanations

SHAP is grounded in the concept of Shapley values, a game theory introduced by Lloyd Shapley in 1953. Originally developed in the context of cooperative game theory, Shapley values fairly distribute both the gains and costs among several actors working in a coalition. In game theory, there could be more than two players involved, who will corporate together to achieve an equitable payout. Fairness is guaranteed in this game, where the Shapley value helps to determine the amount of payoff for each of the players based on their contribution. In terms of economic and Machine Learning models, "players" refer to features and "payouts" are the list of predictions done.

Each feature has its own Shapley value, which is the average expected marginal contribution after considering all possible combinations. Specifically, the Shapley value of a feature is calculated by comparing the prediction outcome with and without that feature in the maximum combinations made. Since features interact in a multivariate situation, the considering of all possible feature combinations is necessary. This repeats until all possible subsets of features are considered to ensure that the resulting gain has been evaluated in different contexts.

SHAP is an application that inherits the Shapley values' working principle in the realm of Machine Learning, providing a framework for black-box model interpretation (Lundberg & Lee, 2017). Similar to Shapley value, features are "players" and a model's prediction is the "payoff". SHAP has its own "Shapley value", named SHAP values, which has similar calculation principles to the former. Next, we move on to look at what functions it provides to interpret the Machine Learning models.

Visualisation is how SHAP tells the story of what happened inside the model. There are a variety of insightful visualisation plots. These plots can be categorised into two types: global and local explanations. In simple terms, since there are numerous rows of variables and labels in a dataset, local explanation covers the SHAP values for a single row while global explanation covers the SHAP values across the entire dataset. The following are the commonly used visualisation plots.

1. **Summary Plot**: This plot provides a global explanation of the features. It displays and ranks them by their overall impact on the model's output. Each point on the plot represents a SHAP value for a feature and an instance. Its colour indicates whether the feature value is high (red) or low (blue). Meanwhile, these plots also indirectly tell the relationship amongst the points by observing the direction of colour change along the x-axis, the SHAP value scale.

   Dependence Plot: This plot provides a global explanation for one or two features and is best for visualising relationships. The x-axis represents the feature value, and the y-axis shows the contribution of the feature, which is the SHAP value. It comes with the option for users to integrate a second feature and show the two features' interaction effects through colour coding, forming a three-dimensional dependence plot. Figure 6.4 shows an example of the association

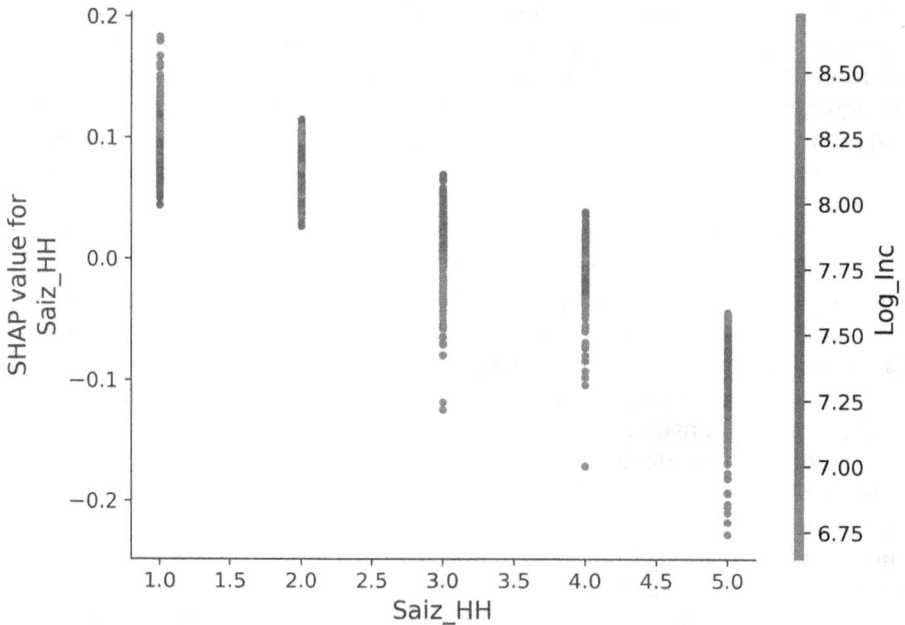

FIGURE 6.4

A scatter plot showing the relationship between household size (*Saiz_HH*, x-axis), SHAP value for per capita consumption expenditure (*Log_Inc*, y-axis), and income (colour scale). The plot indicates that as household size increases, consumption expenditure tends to decrease. Household heads living alone spend as much as they earn on basic needs and wants, while those living with families exhibit an opposite pattern, earning more but spending less on basic needs and wants. (Lee et al., 2024).

between consumption (y-axis), household size (x-axis) and income (colour) (Lee et al., 2024).

2. **Force Plots**: This plot provides a local explanation for a single row or prediction. A detailed breakdown of feature contributions toward the prediction is quantified and denoted by direction. The arrows show how each feature pushes the prediction higher or lower from the base prediction value. Red arrows indicate that the feature contributes positively toward prediction, while blue arrows indicate that feature contributes negatively towards prediction. The magnitude or the strength of a feature contribution is represented by the length of its arrow.

3. **Waterfall Plots**: This plot provides a local explanation like force plots but presents the feature contributions in a vertical layout to make for easier reading by the users, especially in cases where there are a lot of features. Starting from the base prediction value, the feature's

contributions is vertically added until they sum up to the final prediction value.

To demonstrate how these SHAP visualisation techniques are applied in economic research, particularly in understanding inequality, we can examine two recent studies that effectively utilised SHAP for analysing socioeconomic patterns.

Herrera et al. (2023) compared nonlinear machine learning models with traditional linear models on how ICT and socioeconomic determinants affected the household income distribution in Brazil. Using SHAP dependence plots, the relationship between education and income followed an exponential rather than linear pattern. This finding was validated by higher accuracy scores obtained in the nonlinear machine learning models. Similarly, Bai et al. (2023) investigated income distribution patterns in New York City using a combination of SHAP analysis and Gaussian Process Machine Learning model. Using several SHAP plots, the key reasons for income inequality are educational attainment, race and sex, which is approximately three times more significant than spatial variables.

LIME (Local Interpretable Model-agnostic Explanations)

LIME (Local Interpretable Model-agnostic Explanations) is another well-known interpreting tool to uncover the mask of complex machine learning models and aims to explain the predictions made by classification and regressor Machine Learning models (Ribeiro et al., 2016). Unlike SHAP, LIME is a local interpretable tool, which is a so-called local surrogate model. The core idea behind the training of a LIME model is to approximate a prediction made by a complex model until we get a simpler and interpretable LIME model. The ultimate goal is to understand the individual predictions produced by a Machine Learning model.

A LIME model is trained by perturbing the input data and then observing the magnitude of change in the predictions. It then learns a local linear model by approximating the complex model's behaviour from the surroundings of the instance being explained. This process can be described in the following steps:

1. Select the instance of interest.
2. Perturb the dataset and get the black box predictions for these new points.
3. Weight the new samples according to their proximity to the instance of interest.
4. Train a weighted, interpretable model with different variations.
5. Interpret the local model and explain the prediction.

LIME offers several visualisation options to present its explanations:

1. **Bar plots**: This plot shows the features' importance and direction of the contribution made to an individual prediction.
2. **Text highlights**: Use for text-based models. This plot shows which words or phrases are the main contributors to a prediction.
3. **Image superpixels**: Use for image recognition tasks. This plot shows the regions from a given image sample and informs on the pixels' contribution towards the classification prediction done.

Compared to SHAP, the strength of the LIME is its local interpretable nature, making it highly applicable if researchers attempt to interpret a simple model. However, LIME's drawback is that, by being a local surrogate model effective at explaining individual predictions, it lacks the comprehensiveness desired for explaining in terms of the global perspective.

Causal Forest

The SHAP and LIME models discussed above are analysis tools designed to uncover the relationships between variables in a Machine Learning model. However, it is important to note that they do not guarantee that causal relationships are identified. While SHAP and LIME improve the model interpretability, they do not enhance the model itself. Causation or correlation observations ultimately depend on the experiment setting and model used. Here, we introduce a Machine Learning model which is explicitly designed to estimate causal effects, named Casual Forest.

Causal Forest (a combination of several Causal Tree models, similar to the structure of Random Forest) is a Machine Learning model belonging to an extension of Random Forest algorithms that was developed purposely for the explainable AI field (Athey & Imbens, 2016). In a Random Forest model, the data is repeatedly split into several subsets and fed into trees inside the model to minimise the prediction error of an outcome variable. Causal forests work in a similar way except that it aims to maximise the difference across splits in the relationship between outcome variable and a "treatment" variable.

Causal Forest is used to study heterogeneous treatment effects by estimating the impact of a treatment across different subpopulations. Causal Forest aim to estimate the conditional average treatment effects (CATE) for each individual of a population non-parametrically (Wager & Athey, 2018). Causal forests are designed to uncover causal relationships, so the result obtained through this model is statistically valid and applicable to economics. Traditional methods consider average treatment effects across an entire population, while causal forests further decompose the treatment effect into individual or subgroup levels so that the researcher can find out any distinct differences between individual or subgroups from treatment placed.

Following are the key properties of interpretability of Causal Forest:

- In Random Forest, variable importance informs on the covariates' contribution towards prediction. In Causal Forest, variable importance informs on the covariates' contribution towards treatment effects. Researchers gain insight from the key factors of the estimated heterogeneous treatment effects.
- Causal Forest predict the treatment effects for each individual in the dataset, which can be visualised and analysed to uncover patterns and subgroups.
- Causal Forest quantified the uncertainty for the prediction made using honest confidence intervals.

To illustrate the practical application of Causal Forest in real-world research, consider a recent study by Chowdhury et al. (2023) that investigated BRAC's Ultra-Poor Graduation (UPG) model. The researchers employed Honest Causal Forest (HCF) to examine how the productive assets sponsored by the programme causally affected participants' wealth and expenditure levels. Their findings revealed the following heterogeneous treatment effects across different subgroups:

- Age-based differences: Older participants who were more dependent on wage income showed higher gains in asset outcomes
- Employment-based variations: Participants with higher baseline self-employment income experienced greater consumption gains.

Future Studies of Machine Learning in Economic Inequalities Field

The integration of Machine Learning into the field of economic inequality analysis showcases the alternative approach of measuring inequalities that traditional economic models may lack. However, there remain areas for further exploration in future research. In the following section, we explore some future directions, including algorithmic advancements and the integration of policy simulations, to better inform policymakers and improve the effectiveness of government interventions aimed at reducing poverty and inequality.

We have discussed several times about the potential of Causal Machine Learning methods such as Causal Forest in bridging the two unrelated fields of Machine Learning and economics. Causal Machine Learning field seeks to integrate the superiority of accuracy from Machine Learning and causation from economics. The critical issue here is that Causal Machine Learning is still young. It required more attention and effort towards making this analytics method strong and reliable enough, so that economists are interested and willing to use them. An example of a future study that can be done is the development of new algorithms that can further enhance the interpretability of the economic inequality outcome. These algorithms might incorporate techniques for handling high-dimensional data with complex interactions, methods for estimating long-term causal effects, and approaches for dealing with time-varying treatments and outcomes. The goal is to provide policymakers trustworthy evidence grounded on studies that incorporate causal inference, to ensure that the targeted interventions work on reducing economic inequality.

Another interesting point is the possibility of predicting the policy outcomes using Machine Learning. The trend right now is to focus on understanding the relationships between various socioeconomic factors and inequality outcomes first, followed by presenting the results for policymakers to undertake as part of their policy brainstorming session. Hence, one may try to use Machine Learning to simulate how will a policy impact on society based on data gathered from past policies' implementation. If the potential impacts from the simulation study are known, the undesired and harmful interventions can be avoided or minimised before they are implemented. These trained Machine Learning models could simulate the impacts of proposed policies by assessing them on their potential effects over various economic inequality metrics, such as income and consumption distribution, wealth or education attainment (Einav & Levin, 2014).

Furthermore, researchers may look for expert views regarding economic theories learnt from experience to validate the results obtained from historical data. It is beneficial to integrate expert views as qualitative data with statistical outputs and historical data as quantitative data, for a robust analysis. A Bayesian approach offers the possibility for this data source's merging. It allows the incorporation of prior economic knowledge as initial beliefs into Machine Learning models. For instance, Machine Learning models could be informed by economic theories like the Kuznets Curve, helping to discern the nonlinear relationships between economic inequality and development. This could provide a probabilistic interpretation of the drivers of economic inequality, capturing uncertainty and allowing economists to test hypotheses derived from theory. As Machine Learning continues to evolve and get more popular, researchers have to make sure their results align with economic principles that have long been proven true and valid, to ensure the statistical significance of their results. Through combining these two data sources via the Bayesian approach, the accuracy and reliability of economic inequality studies can be assured.

In conclusion, future research on utilising Machine Learning as an alternative method to analyse economic inequality shows great potential. By improving Causal Machine Learning methods and exploring new ideas like predicting policy outcomes, Machine Learning will become more popular in economics as it is capable of providing stronger and more practical results. Besides that, it is important to keep refining these methods to align with the existing economic theories. Moreover, incorporating expert knowledge as prior knowledge through Bayesian approaches will also increase the reliability and value of Machine Learning models in inequality studies, giving policymakers reliable insights that can be considering in developing better interventions for social benefits.

Acknowledgement

The work was supported by the Telekom Malaysia Research and Development Grant (Grant No: RDTC/241111).

References

Abitbol, J. L., & Karsai, M. (2020). Interpretable socioeconomic status inference from aerial imagery through urban patterns. *Nature Machine Intelligence*, 2(11), 684–692. https://doi.org/10.1038/s42256-020-00243-5

Acemoglu, D., & Autor, D. (2011). Skills, tasks and technologies: Implications for employment and earnings. In O. Ashenfelter & D. Card (Eds.), *Handbook of labor economics* (Vol. 4B, pp. 1043–1171). Elsevier. https://doi.org/10.1016/s0169-7218(11)02410-5

Aguiar, M., & Bils, M. (2015). Has consumption inequality mirrored income inequality? *American Economic Review*, 105(9), 2725–2726.

Aguiar, M., & Hurst, E. (2013). Deconstructing life cycle expenditure. *Journal of Political Economy*, 121(3), 437–492. https://doi.org/10.1086/670740

Alagiyawanna, A., Townsend, N., Mytton, O., Scarborough, P., Roberts, N., & Rayner, M. (2015). Studying the consumption and health outcomes of fiscal interventions (taxes and subsidies) on food and beverages in countries of different income classifications; a systematic review. *BMC public health*, 15, 887. https://doi.org/10.1186/s12889-015-2201-8

Athey, S., & Imbens, G. (2016). Recursive partitioning for heterogeneous causal effects. *Proceedings of the National Academy of Sciences*, 113(27), 7353–7360. https://doi.org/10.1073/pnas.1510489113

Athey, S., & Imbens, G. W. (2019). Machine learning methods that economists should know about. *Annual Review of Economics*, 11(1), 685–725. https://doi.org/10.1146/annurev-economics-080217-053433

Attanasio, O. P., & Kaufmann, K. M. (2014). Education choices and returns to schooling: Mothers' and youths' subjective expectations and their role by gender. *Journal of Development Economics*, 109, 203–216.

Attanasio, O. P., & Pistaferri, L. (2016). Consumption inequality. https://pubs.aeaweb.org/doi/pdf/10.1257/jep.30.2.3

Attanasio, O., Battistin, E., & Padula, M. (2010). Inequality in living standards since 1980. *Books*. https://www.aei.org/wp-content/uploads/2018/06/Inequality-in-Living-Standards-Since-1980.pdf

Atkinson, A., & Bourguignon, F. (2000). Introduction: Income distribution and economics. *In Handbook of income distribution* (pp. 1–58). https://doi.org/10.1016/s1574-0056(00)80003-2

Atkinson, A. B., Piketty, T., & Saez, E. (2011). Top incomes in the long run of history. *Journal of Economic Literature*, 49(1), 3–71. https://doi.org/10.1257/jel.49.1.3

Bai, R., Lam, J. C. K., & Li, V. O. K. (2023). What dictates income in New York City? SHAP analysis of income estimation based on Socio-economic and Spatial Information Gaussian Processes (SSIG). *Humanities and Social Sciences Communications*, 10(1). https://doi.org/10.1057/s41599-023-01548-7

Ball, L. M., Furceri, D., Leigh, D., & Loungani, P. (2013). The distributional effects of fiscal consolidation. *IMF Working Paper*, 13(151), 1. https://doi.org/10.5089/9781475551945.001

Becker, G. S. (1994, January 1). *Human capital: A theoretical and empirical analysis with special reference to education*, Third Edition. NBER. https://www.nber.org/books-and-chapters/human-capital-theoretical-and-empirical-analysis-special-reference-education-third-edition

Blundell, R., & Preston, I. (1998). Consumption Inequality and Income Uncertainty. *The Quarterly Journal of Economics*, 113(2), 603–640.

Bloom, D. E., & Canning, D. (2000). The health and wealth of nations. *Science*, 287(5456), 1207–1209. https://doi.org/10.1126/science.287.5456.1207

Campbell, J. Y. (2006). Household finance. *The Journal of Finance*, 61(4), 1553–1604.

Card, D. (2001). Estimating the return to schooling: Progress on some persistent econometric problems. *Econometrica*, 69(5), 1127–1160. https://doi.org/10.1111/1468-0262.00237

Chakrabarty, N., & Biswas, S. (2018). A Statistical approach to adult Census income level Prediction. *2018 International Conference on Advances in Computing, Communication Control and Networking (ICACCCN)*. https://doi.org/10.1109/icacccn.2018.8748528

Cheng, Z. (2021). Education and consumption: Evidence from migrants in Chinese cities. *Journal of Business Research*, 127, 206–215. https://doi.org/10.1016/j.jbusres.2021.01.018

Chowdhury, R. A., Ceballos-Sierra, F., & Sulaiman, M. (2023). Grow the pie, or have it? Using machine learning to impact heterogeneity in the Ultra-poor graduation model. *Journal of Development Effectiveness*, 1–20. https://doi.org/10.1080/19439342.2023.2276928

Chy, M. K. H., & Buadi, O. N. (2024). Role of machine learning in policy making and evaluation. *International Journal of Innovative Science and Research Technology (IJISRT)*, 456–463. https://doi.org/10.38124/ijisrt/ijisrt24oct687

Citro, C. F., Michael, R. T., Poverty, P. O., & Assistance, F. (1995). Measuring Poverty: a new approach. http://ci.nii.ac.jp/ncid/BA25059481

Coibion, O., Gorodnichenko, Y., Kueng, L., & Silvia, J. (2012). Innocent bystanders? monetary policy and inequality in the U.S. https://doi.org/10.3386/w18170

Conceicao, P., & Ferreira, P. (2000). The Young Person's guide to the THEIl Index: suggesting intuitive interpretations and exploring analytical applications. *SSRN Electronic Journal*. https://doi.org/10.2139/ssrn.228703

Darmon, N., & Drewnowski, A. (2015). Contribution of food prices and diet cost to socioeconomic disparities in diet quality and health: a systematic review and analysis. *Nutrition Reviews*, 73, 643–660.

De Gregorio, J., & Lee, J. (2002). Education and income inequality: New evidence from Cross-Country data. *Review of Income and Wealth*, 48(3), 395–416. https://doi.org/10.1111/1475-4991.00060

Dynan, K. E., Skinner, J., & Zeldes, S. P. (2004). Do the Rich Save More? *Journal of Political Economy*, 112(2), 397–444. https://doi.org/10.1086/381475

Einav, L., & Levin, J. (2014). The Data Revolution and economic analysis. *In Innovation Policy and the Economy* (Vol. 14, pp. 1–24). https://doi.org/10.1086/674019

Escanciano, J. C., & Terschuur, J. R. (2022). Machine learning inference on inequality of opportunity. *arXiv (Cornell University)*. https://doi.org/10.48550/arxiv.2206.05235

Finkelstein, A., Taubman, S., Wright, B., Bernstein, M., Gruber, J., Newhouse, J. P., Allen, H., & Baicker, K. (2012). The Oregon Health Insurance Experiment: Evidence from the first year. *The Quarterly Journal of Economics*, 127(3), 1057–1106. https://doi.org/10.1093/qje/qjs020

Fisher, J., Johnson, D., & Smeeding, T. (2013). Measuring the trends in inequality of individuals and families: Income and consumption. *American Economic Review*, 103(3), 184–188.

Fisher, J., Johnson, D. S., & Smeeding, T. M. (2014). Inequality of Income and Consumption in the U.S.: Measuring the Trends in Inequality from 1984 to 2011 for the Same Individuals. *Review of Income and Wealth*, 61(4), 630–650. https://doi.org/10.1111/roiw.12129

Fitoussi, J., Sen, A., & Stiglitz, J. E. (2011). Report by the commission on the measurement of economic performance and social progress. http://aaps.org.ar/pdf/area_politicassociales/Stiglitz.pdf

Garnaut, R. (2010). Macro-economic implications of the turning point. *China Economic Journal*, 3(2), 181–190. https://doi.org/10.1080/17538963.2010.511916

Haddad, C. N., Mahler, D. G., Diaz-Bonilla, C., Hill, R., Lakner, C., & Ibarra, G. L. (2024). *The World Bank's New Inequality Indicator: The Number of Countries with High Inequality*. In Washington, DC: World Bank eBooks. https://doi.org/10.1596/41687

Hanushek, E. A., & Woessmann, L. (2012). Do better schools lead to more growth? Cognitive skills, economic outcomes, and causation. *Journal of Economic Growth*, 17(4), 267–321. https://doi.org/10.1007/s10887-012-9081-x

Herrera, G. P., Constantino, M., Su, J., & Naranpanawa, A. (2023). The use of ICTs and income distribution in Brazil: A machine learning explanation using SHAP values. *Telecommunications Policy*, 47(8), 102598. https://doi.org/10.1016/j.telpol.2023.102598

Heshmati, A. (2004). Inequalities and their measurement. *SSRN Electronic Journal*. https://doi.org/10.2139/ssrn.571662

Heckman, J. J. (2000). Causal parameters and policy analysis in economics: A twentieth century retrospective. *The Quarterly Journal of Economics*, 115(1), 45–97.

Hope, D., & Martelli, A. (2019). The Transition to the Knowledge Economy, Labor Market Institutions, and Income Inequality in Advanced Democracies. *World Politics*, 71(2), 236–288. https://doi.org/10.1017/S0043887118000333

Hu, M. (2022). Multivariate understanding of income and expenditure in United States households with statistical learning. *Computational Statistics*, 37(5), 2129–2160. https://doi.org/10.1007/s00180-022-01251-2

Jean, N., Burke, M., Xie, M., Davis, W. M., Lobell, D. B., & Ermon, S. (2016). Combining satellite imagery and machine learning to predict poverty. *Science*, 353(6301), 790–794. https://doi.org/10.1126/science.aaf7894

Korobilis, D. (2018). Machine Learning Macroeconometrics: a primer. *SSRN Electronic Journal*. https://doi.org/10.2139/ssrn.3246473

Krueger, D., & Perri, F. (2006). Does income inequality lead to consumption inequality? Evidence and theory. *The Review of Economic Studies*, 73(1), 163–193.

Kuhn, M., Schularick, M., & Steins, U. I. (2020). Income and Wealth Inequality in America, 1949–2016. *Journal of Political Economy*, 128(9), 3469–3519. https://doi.org/10.1086/708815

Kunze, A. (2017). The gender wage gap in developed countries. In S. L. Averett, L. M. Argys, & S. D. Hoffman (Eds.), *The Oxford handbook of women and the economy* (pp. 368–394). Oxford University Press. https://doi.org/10.1093/oxfordhb/9780190628963.013.11

Kuznets, S. (2019). Economic growth and income inequality. In *The gap between rich and poor* (pp. 25–37). Routledge.

Lee, E., Ong, T. S., & Lee, Y. (2024). Evaluating Household Consumption Patterns: Comparative Analysis Using Ordinary Least Squares and Random Forest Regression Models. *HighTech and Innovation Journal*, 5(2), 489–507. https://doi.org/10.28991/hij-2024-05-02-019

Lefranc, A., Pistolesi, N., & Trannoy, A. (2008). Inequality of opportunities vs. Inequality of outcomes: Are western societies all alike? *Review of Income and Wealth*, 54(4), 513–546. https://doi.org/10.1111/j.1475-4991.2008.00289.x

Li, Y., & Malin, S. (2009). Research on BP neural network for nonlinear economic modeling and its realization based on Matlab. *2009 Third International Symposium on Intelligent Information Technology Application*. https://doi.org/10.1109/iita.2009.352

Lundberg, S.M., & Lee, S. (2017). A unified approach to interpreting model predictions. *Neural Information Processing Systems*. https://doi.org/10.48550/arxiv.1705.07874

Maruejols, L., Wang, H., Zhao, Q., Bai, Y., & Zhang, L. (2022). Comparison of machine learning predictions of subjective poverty in rural China. *China Agricultural Economic Review*, 15(2), 379–399. https://doi.org/10.1108/caer-03-2022-0051

Mankiw, N. G. (2019). *Macroeconomics* (Tenth edition). Worth.

Meyer, B. D., & Sullivan, J. X. (2017). Consumption and income inequality in the U.S. since the 1960s. *SSRN Electronic Journal*. https://doi.org/10.2139/ssrn.3037000

Modigliani, F. (1955). Utility analysis and the consumption function: An interpretation of cross-section data. *Post-Keynesian economics*. https://www.econbiz.de/Record/utility-analysis-and-the-consumption-function-an-interpretation-of-cross-section-data-modigliani-franco/1000250284

Moradi, A., Mansouri, M., Faramarzi, A., & Kiani, K. (2023). Investigating the effect of inflation on the consumption pattern of Iranian households. *Statistical Journal of the IAOS*, 39(3), 605–616. https://doi.org/10.3233/sji-230009

Mullainathan, S., & Spiess, J. (2017). Machine Learning: An Applied Econometric approach. *The Journal of Economic Perspectives*, 31(2), 87–106. https://doi.org/10.1257/jep.31.2.87

Neckerman, K. M., & Torche, F. (2007). Inequality: Causes and consequences. *Annual Review of Sociology*, 33, 335–357.

OECD. (2013). Household consumption. *National Accounts at a Glance 2013 | OECD iLibrary*. https://doi.org/10.1787/na_glance-2013-12-en

OECD. (2015). In it together: Why less inequality benefits all. *In OECD eBooks*. https://doi.org/10.1787/9789264235120-en

Park, J. (2021). Monetary policy and income inequality in Korea. *Journal of the Asia Pacific Economy*, 26(4), 766–793. https://doi.org/10.1080/13547860.2020.1870794

Pardo, G.P., & Santos, J.M. (2014). Household debt and consumption inequality: The Spanish Case. *Economies*, 2, 147–170.

Pickett, K. E., & Wilkinson, R. G. (2015). Income inequality and health: A causal review. *Social Science & Medicine (1982)*, 128, 316–326. https://doi.org/10.1016/j.socscimed.2014.12.031

Piketty, T., & Saez, E. (2003). Income inequality in the United States, 1913-1998. *The Quarterly Journal of Economics*, 118(1), 1–41. https://doi.org/10.1162/00335530360535135

Psacharopoulos, G., & Patrinos, H. A. (2018). Returns to investment in education: A decennial review of the global literature. *Education Economics*, 26(5), 445–458.

Ribeiro, M., Singh, S., & Guestrin, C. (2016). "Why Should I Trust You?": Explaining the Predictions of Any Classifier. *Proceedings of the 22nd ACM SIGKDD International Conference on Knowledge Discovery and Data Mining*. https://doi.org/10.1145/2939672.2939778

Rudin, C. (2019). Stop explaining black box machine learning models for high stakes decisions and use interpretable models instead. *Nature Machine Intelligence*, 1(5), 206–215. https://doi.org/10.1038/s42256-019-0048-x

Russakovsky, O., Deng, J., Su, H., Krause, J., Satheesh, S., Ma, S., Huang, Z., Karpathy, A., Khosla, A., Bernstein, M., Berg, A. C., & Fei-Fei, L. (2015). ImageNet Large Scale Visual Recognition Challenge. *International Journal of Computer Vision*, 115(3), 211–252. https://doi.org/10.1007/s11263-015-0816-y

Schultz, T. P. (2002). Wage Gains Associated with Height as a Form of Health Human Capital. *American Economic Review*, 92(2), 349–353. https://doi.org/10.1257/000282802320191598

Sen, A. K. (1997). From income inequality to economic inequality. *Southern Economic Journal*, 64(2), 384–401. https://doi.org/10.1002/j.2325-8012.1997.tb00063.x

Smith, J. P. (1999). Healthy bodies and thick wallets: the dual relation between health and economic status. *The Journal of Economic Perspectives*, 13(2), 145–166. https://doi.org/10.1257/jep.13.2.145

Stiglitz, J. E. (2012). The price of inequality: How today's divided society endangers our future. http://www.casinapioiv.va/content/dam/accademia/pdf/es41/es41-stiglitz.pdf

Terada-Hagiwara, A., Camingue, S., & Zveglich, J.E. (2018). *Gender Pay Gap: A Macro Perspective*. Asian Development Bank Institute Research Paper Series.

Tsounta, E., Suphaphiphat, N., Ricka, F., Dabla-Norris, E., & Kochhar, K. (2015). Causes and consequences of income inequality. *IMF Staff Discussion Note*, 2015(013), 1. https://doi.org/10.5089/9781513555188.006

Global Education Monitoring Report 2020: Inclusion and education: All means all. *Paris*. (2020). In *UNESCO eBooks*. https://doi.org/10.54676/jjnk6989

Wager, S., & Athey, S. (2018). Estimation and inference of heterogeneous treatment effects using random forests. *Journal of the American Statistical Association*, 113(523), 1228–1242. https://doi.org/10.1080/01621459.2017.1319839

Wang, W., Xu, W., Yao, X., & Wang, H. (2022). Application of data-driven method for automatic machine learning in economic research. *2022 21st International Symposium on Distributed Computing and Applications for Business Engineering and Science (DCABES)*, 42–45. https://doi.org/10.1109/dcabes57229.2022.00019

Wilensky, H. L. (2012). Policy implications for the United States: How to get off the low road. In *American Political Economy in Global Perspective* (pp. 191–270). chapter, Cambridge: Cambridge University Press.

Wójcik, P., & Andruszek, K. (2021). Predicting intra-urban well-being from space with nonlinear machine learning. *Regional Science Policy & Practice*, 14(4), 891–913. https://doi.org/10.1111/rsp3.12478

Woo, J., Bova, E., Kinda, T., & Zhang, Y. S. (2013). Distributional consequences of fiscal consolidation and the role of fiscal policy: What do the data say? *SSRN Electronic Journal*. https://doi.org/10.2139/ssrn.2338387

World Inequality Report 2022. (2022). In Harvard University Press eBooks. https://doi.org/10.4159/9780674276598

Xu, K., Evans, D. B., Kawabata, K., Zeramdini, R., Klavus, J., & Murray, C. J. (2003). Household catastrophic health expenditure: A multicountry analysis. *The Lancet*, 362(9378), 111–117. https://doi.org/10.1016/s0140-6736(03)13861-5

7

AI for Healthcare: Revolutionising Public Wellness in Smart Cities

Yee-Fan Tan and Pei-Sze Tan

Introduction

Over the last decade, the confluence of big data, advanced algorithms and increased computational power has led to an explosion of Artificial Intelligence (AI)-driven innovations across various industries (Secinaro et al. 2021). The integration of AI into the healthcare sector represents one of the most transformative advancements in the history of medicine. From diagnostic imaging to personalised treatment plans, AI is reshaping the landscape of healthcare by enhancing precision, efficiency and accessibility.

The proliferation of medical data in volume and variety – including electronic health records (EHRs), medical imaging, genomic data and real-time monitoring from wearable devices – has created an unprecedented opportunity for AI to thrive. Machine Learning (ML) and Deep Learning (DL), two key subsets of AI, have been at the forefront of this revolution, offering innovative solutions across various domains of healthcare (Ahmad et al. 2021). These technologies, with their ability to process and learn from large-scale data, enable healthcare providers to extract meaningful patterns that can inform better decision-making. Figure 7.1 illustrates how AI model is being employed for decision-making.

Studies are developing sophisticated models that can diagnose diseases (Mei et al. 2020), plan treatments (McIntosh et al. 2021), assist in surgical procedures (Varghese et al. 2024) and analyse medical images (Cui et al. 2022) with a level of accuracy that often surpasses human capabilities. These systems can identify patterns and anomalies that may be imperceptible to the human eye, leading to earlier and more precise diagnoses. This capability is especially valuable in detecting conditions like cancer, where early diagnosis significantly increases the chances of successful treatment. AI algorithms can analyse diverse data points to predict how different patients will respond to various treatments, allowing for the development of personalised treatment

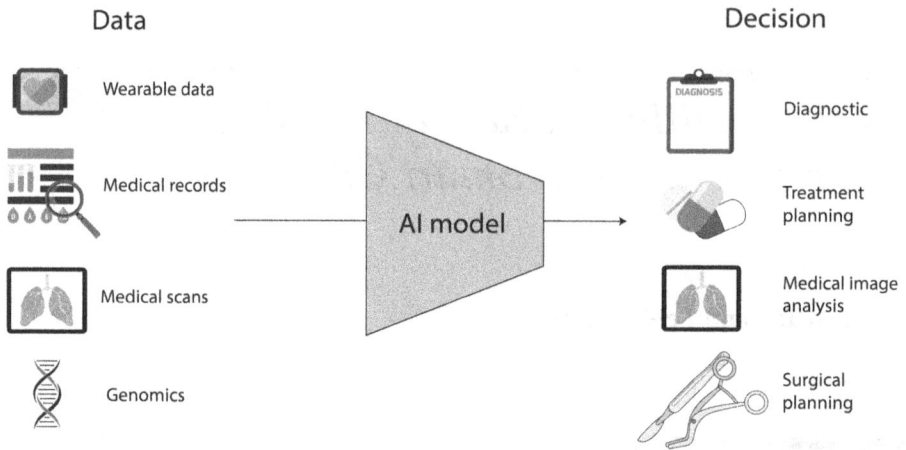

FIGURE 7.1
Overview of the AI model applications in the healthcare sector.

plans that are more effective and have fewer side effects. This approach not only improves patient outcomes but also reduces healthcare costs by avoiding ineffective treatments and minimising adverse reactions.

In medical image analysis, AI is pushing the boundaries of what is possible. Traditionally, the interpretation of medical images – such as X-rays, MRIs and CT scans – has relied heavily on the expertise of radiologists. However, AI models, particularly those utilising convolutional neural networks (CNNs) (LeCun, Bengio, and Hinton 2015), have demonstrated the ability to analyse images with a level of accuracy that rivals, and in some cases exceeds, human experts. These AI-driven systems can assist in a range of tasks, from detecting tumours to assessing the severity of fractures and predicting the likelihood of disease progression. Moreover, AI can enhance images, improve resolution and assist in the segmentation of complex anatomical structures, providing invaluable support in both diagnostics and surgical planning.

However, the integration of AI in healthcare is not without its challenges (Nasr et al. 2021). The adoption of AI technologies raises critical issues around accountability and transparency. AI systems, especially those based on complex machine learning models like deep learning, often operate as black box, making decisions based on processes that are not easily understood. This lack of transparency can be a significant barrier to trust, particularly in a field as sensitive as healthcare, where the consequences of decisions can be life altering.

Trustworthiness is another crucial factor in the adoption of AI in healthcare. For AI systems to be widely accepted and integrated into healthcare practices, they must not only be accurate but also reliable and consistent.

This requires rigorous testing and validation of AI models, as well as the establishment of standards and guidelines for their use. Moreover, AI systems must be designed to respect patient privacy and data security, adhering to ethical standards that protect patients' rights and maintain the confidentiality of their medical information.

In this chapter, we will examine the diverse applications of AI in healthcare, focusing on how it is revolutionising diagnostics, treatment planning, medical image analysis and surgical operations. Additionally, we will delve into advancements in medical image analysis, highlighting how AI models are surpassing traditional methods in accuracy and efficiency. The chapter will also discuss the significant challenges associated with AI integration, including issues of accountability, transparency and trustworthiness. We will explore the importance of explainability in AI models, the need for rigorous validation and reliability, and the ethical considerations related to patient privacy and data security. Finally, we will consider the future directions of AI in healthcare, outlining potential technological advancements and the steps needed to overcome current obstacles.

Applications of AI for Healthcare

AI's versatility enables its integration across various facets of healthcare, including diagnosis, treatment planning, medical image analysis and surgical operations. Each of these applications harnesses AI's capabilities, particularly through machine learning (ML) and deep learning (DL) techniques, to analyse vast datasets, identify patterns and generate predictive insights. By doing so, AI introduces innovative approaches that enhance and streamline existing healthcare workflows. In the following sections, we will explore how AI is applied in diagnosis, treatment planning, medical image analysis and surgical operations, illustrating its transformative impact on these critical areas.

Diagnosis

One of the most impactful and widely researched applications of AI in healthcare is in the field of diagnosis (Mei et al. 2020; S. Kaur et al. 2020; Dilsizian and Siegel 2014). AI techniques, particularly those leveraging machine learning (ML) and deep learning (DL) models, have demonstrated significant accuracy in the classification of various diseases and the prediction of disease progression. These models learn from vast datasets that include diverse types of medical information such as genomic data, demographic details and radiological scans, such as magnetic resonance imaging (MRI). By analysing these datasets, AI models can identify patterns and anomalies that may be too subtle for human clinicians to detect, thereby enhancing the diagnostic process.

AI has been applied to a broad range of medical conditions, demonstrating its versatility and effectiveness. For instance, studies have explored AI applications in diagnosing pneumonia (Vidhya et al. 2022), mental disorders (Liu et al. 2018), various types of cancer (S. Huang et al. 2020), and even in managing public health crises like the COVID-19 pandemic (Mei et al. 2020). In oncology, AI models have been particularly successful in analysing histopathological images to distinguish between benign and malignant tumours with high accuracy. These models are often capable of detecting cancerous changes at earlier stages than traditional diagnostic methods, which can lead to earlier interventions and improved patient outcomes.

Furthermore, AI is not just limited to disease classification. It can also predict the likelihood of disease development based on a patient's genetic makeup, lifestyle, and other risk factors. This predictive capability enables healthcare providers to implement preventive measures before the disease manifests, which can significantly reduce the incidence and severity of the condition.

AI models have been widely adopted across various medical fields, including neurology, oncology and cardiology, among others. Given sufficient and high-quality medical data, AI models can be trained to provide reliable and actionable insights. These models can be integrated into existing healthcare systems to support clinicians by offering a "second opinion", which can help reduce diagnostic errors and improve the overall quality of care. By augmenting the capabilities of healthcare providers, AI has the potential to significantly enhance patient outcomes and contribute to better quality of life.

Treatment Planning

Other than diagnostic, AI models are playing an increasingly critical role in treatment planning across various medical fields, particularly in oncology (Netherton et al. 2021), radiology (Jones et al. 2024; Zheng et al. 2019) and personalised medicine (Schork 2019).

For instance, in oncology, AI models are utilised to optimise radiation therapy and chemotherapy. For radiation therapy, AI can create more accurate dose distribution plans (Wang et al. 2019) by predicting tumour response and minimising radiation exposure to surrounding healthy tissues. These models can be used to predict the best radiation angles, doses, and patient positioning. These models, trained on imaging data, clinical outcomes and other relevant parameters, tailor treatments to the specific characteristics of the tumour and the patient. In chemotherapy, AI can predict patient response to different drug combinations (Shi et al. 2014), helping select the most effective and least toxic treatment regimen.

AI-driven treatment planning is also central to personalised medicine, where the goal is to tailor therapies to the individual characteristics of each patient. AI models analyse vast amounts of data, including genomic, proteomic and metabolic profiles, alongside clinical data, to predict how a patient will respond to different treatments. For example, in cancer treatment, AI can identify specific genetic mutations that might render a tumour susceptible to certain targeted therapies, allowing for the selection of the most appropriate drugs. Similarly, AI helps understand a patient's risk of adverse reactions to specific treatments, enabling more informed decision-making and reducing the likelihood of complications.

Medical Image Analysis

Data enhancement is a critical component of AI in medical image analysis. It refers to techniques used to improve the quality and utility of medical images. Given the diversity and variability of medical imaging data, AI models can be used to improve the image's quality in helping healthcare worker's decisions, including noise reduction, contrast improvements and segmentation.

For instance, noise reduction algorithms help in eliminating unwanted artifacts from medical images, which can obscure important details. By enhancing the clarity of these images, healthcare professionals can make more accurate assessments. Similarly, contrast enhancement techniques, like histogram equalisation, improve the visibility of specific structures within an image. This is particularly important in scenarios where subtle differences in tissue density or structure need to be identified, such as in tumour detection or vascular imaging. These tasks can also be achieved using trained ML model (De Cecco, Carlo, Van Assen, and Leiner 2022).

Apart from image enhancements, generative models, such as Generative Adversarial Networks (GANs) (Goodfellow et al. 2020) and Variational Autoencoders (VAEs) (Cinelli et al. 2021), have introduced groundbreaking possibilities in medical image analysis. In the healthcare sector, these models are increasingly being used to generate high-quality synthetic medical images and to fill in missing data, thereby directly benefiting healthcare workers. For example, in situations where certain medical images are incomplete or where specific scans are unavailable, generative models can be used to reconstruct or simulate the missing parts of the data (Pan et al. 2018; Emami et al. 2021). Figure 7.2 illustrates an example of utilising generative models in reconstructing high-quality MR images (Wu et al. 2020). This capability is invaluable in clinical settings where time is of the essence, and obtaining a new scan might not be immediately feasible. Additionally, generative models can create synthetic images that mimic the properties of real medical images, allowing healthcare professionals to explore different scenarios, plan surgeries, or practice on realistic, yet simulated, data.

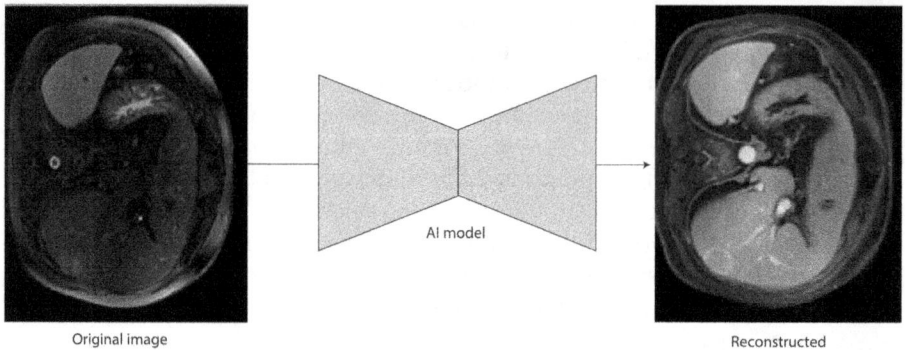

Original image   Reconstructed

FIGURE 7.2
Sample reconstructed MR images using a trained AI model (Wu et al. 2020).

Surgical Operations

From preoperative planning to real-time intraoperative assistance and postoperative care, AI is revolutionising traditional surgical operations to enhance a patient's outcome.

For preoperative phase (Birkhoff et al. 2021), with ML algorithms capable of analysing patient data, including medical history, imaging scans, and lab results, to predict potential risks and complications. This predictive capability allows surgeons to tailor their approach to each patient, reducing the likelihood of unexpected events during surgery. In addition, AI-powered imaging technologies, such as 3D reconstruction and advanced visualisation tools, enable surgeons to explore a patient's anatomy in unprecedented detail. For instance, AI can create highly accurate 3D models from MRI or CT scans, which surgeons can use to plan the best approach for complex procedures (Chen et al. 2021). Figure 7.3 shows an example using AI models for segmentation and interactive 3D lung model creation as surgery-assisted display (Sadeghi et al. 2024).

During surgery (Varghese et al. 2024; Zhou et al. 2020), AI systems provide real-time assistance to surgeons, enhancing their capabilities and reducing the margin of error. One of the most significant advancements in this area is the development of AI-driven robotic surgery systems. These systems, such as the da Vinci Surgical System, are equipped with AI algorithms that assist in controlling robotic arms with high precision, allowing for minimally invasive procedures that are less traumatic for the patient.

Finally, AI systems can analyse patient data to predict potential complications after surgical operations (Prete, Corsello, and Salvatori 2017), such as infections or blood clots, before they become critical. This proactive approach allows for timely interventions, improving patient recovery times and reducing the length of hospital stays.

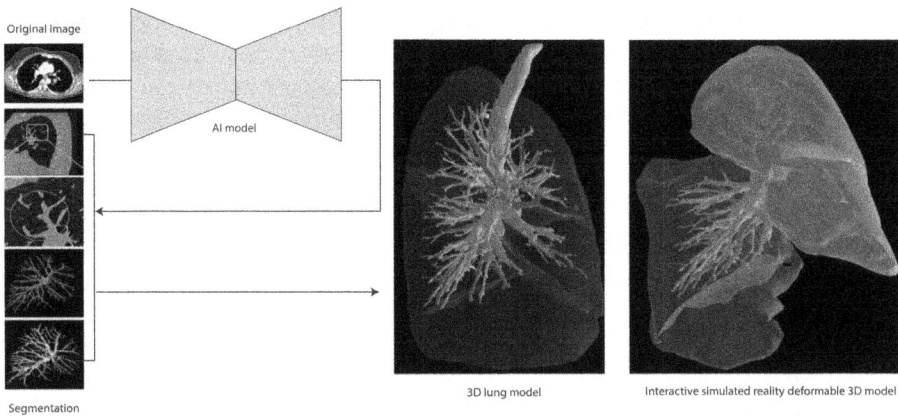

FIGURE 7.3
Sample of lung segmentation and 3D model creation (Sadeghi et al. 2024).

AI for healthcare: Challenges and Opportunities

Integrating AI into Healthcare Systems

AI in healthcare has been foretokened as a revolution, shown promising to enhance diagnostic healthcare and improve patient outcomes. However, this integration has its challenges. The healthcare sector, traditionally conservative in adopting new technologies, now faces the dual challenge of embracing AI's potential while managing the complexities it brings (Ahmad et al. 2021).

One of the most significant challenges is the need for substantial investments in advanced equipment and the training of healthcare professionals. AI technologies often require cutting-edge hardware, such as powerful graphics processing units for deep learning applications and specialised software that may not be compatible with existing healthcare infrastructure (Gibson et al. 2018). This necessitates significant capital investment, which can be a barrier for many healthcare institutions, particularly in developing countries.

Furthermore, the effective use of AI in healthcare demands a highly skilled workforce. Healthcare professionals must be trained to use AI tools and understand their underlying principles and limitations. This requires continuous learning and upskilling, as the pace of technological advancement in AI is rapid. For example, a radiologist might need to learn how to interpret AI-generated image analyses and understand both the strengths and weaknesses of these analyses to make informed decisions. The learning curve can be steep, and the demands on healthcare professionals' time are already substantial.

The rapid pace of technological change in AI also presents a challenge in maintaining the relevance of training. Healthcare professionals must stay abreast of new developments, which can be resource-intensive and challenging to maintain. This can lead to a situation where the technology outpaces the ability of the workforce to effectively utilise it, creating a gap between the potential of AI and its real-world application.

Moreover, utilising AI in healthcare systems must be carefully managed to avoid disrupting existing workflows (Singh et al. 2020). AI systems are often designed with efficiency in mind, but they can inadvertently introduce complexities if they are not seamlessly integrated into clinical workflows. For instance, an AI tool that flags potential issues in medical images must do so in a way that complements, rather than hinders, the radiologist's existing processes. The balance between leveraging AI for its benefits and managing the demands of integration is a critical issue that healthcare systems worldwide must navigate.

Accountability and Transparency

As AI becomes more embedded in healthcare decision-making (Lysaght et al. 2019; Bertl, Ross, and Draheim 2023), the question of accountability becomes increasingly pressing. AI systems now make or influence clinical decisions, sometimes with life-or-death implications. In this context, determining who is responsible for these decisions is complex. Is it the developers who designed the AI algorithms? The healthcare providers who use the systems? Or the institutions that implement them?

This question of accountability is further complicated by the "black box" nature of many AI algorithms (Figure 7.4). These algorithms, especially those based on deep learning, often operate in ways that humans do not fully understand. They can process vast amounts of data and identify patterns that are not immediately apparent to human observers, but the rationale behind their decisions can be opaque. This lack of transparency poses a significant challenge to accountability. If an AI system makes a wrong decision, it can be difficult to understand why, let alone assign responsibility.

The issue of transparency is critical in building trust in AI-driven healthcare. Patients and healthcare providers need to be confident that the decisions made by AI systems are based on sound reasoning. This is where the concept of explainable artificial intelligence (XAI) comes into play. XAI seeks to make AI decision-making processes more transparent and understandable. For example, instead of simply providing a diagnosis, an XAI system might also provide a rationale for the diagnosis, highlighting the specific factors or data points that influenced the decision.

Several XAI methods have been developed to enhance the transparency of AI models:

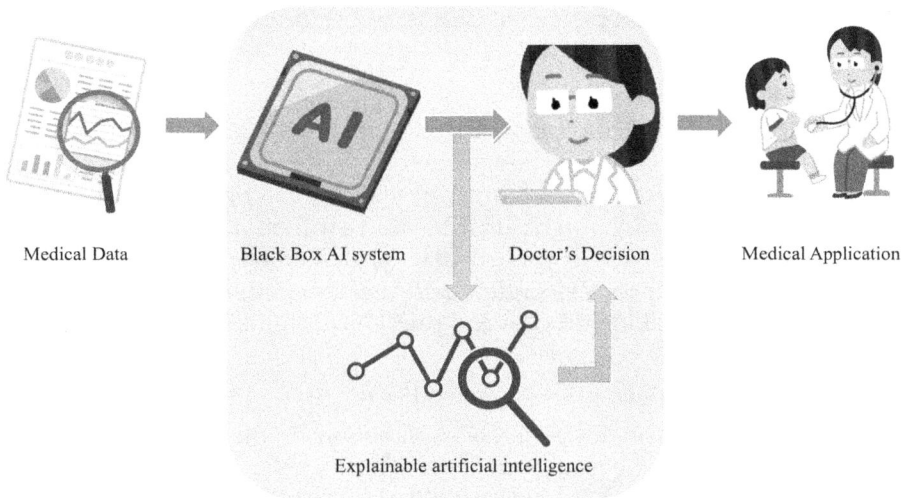

FIGURE 7.4
Flowchart illustrating the integration of XAI in healthcare.

1. LIME (Local Interpretable Model-Agnostic Explanations):
   - LIME (Ribeiro, Singh, and Guestrin 2016) is a popular XAI technique that approximates complex models with simpler, interpretable models locally around the prediction. It works by perturbing the input data and observing how the projections change, helping to identify which features most influence the model's decision in a specific instance. This method is beneficial for understanding individual predictions in complex models.

2. SHAP (SHapley Additive exPlanations):
   - SHAP (Lundberg and Lee 2017) values are derived from cooperative game theory and provide a measure of unified feature importance. By assigning an importance value to each feature for a particular prediction, SHAP allows a consistent interpretation of how each feature contributes to the model's output. SHAP is widely used because it provides global and local explanations, helping to demystify complex models by showing how each feature impacts predictions.

3. Saliency Maps (Arun et al. 2020):
   - In the context of neural networks, especially in image recognition tasks, saliency maps are visual explanations highlighting the regions of an input image that most influenced the model's decision. For instance, in a medical image analysis scenario, a saliency map might indicate the specific areas of an X-ray or MRI

scan that the AI system considered most indicative of a particular diagnosis.

4. Counterfactual Explanations:

- Counterfactual explanations (Wachter, Mittelstadt, and Russell 2017) focus on what changes to the input would alter the AI system's decision. For example, in a clinical setting, a counterfactual explanation might illustrate that a different diagnosis would have been made if a particular lab result were different. This method helps users understand the boundaries of the model's decision-making process and provides insights into how specific factors drive outcomes.

5. Rule-Based Explanations (Clancey 1983):

- Some XAI systems generate explanations in the form of decision rules or logic-based statements. These explanations are easy to understand and can be particularly useful in medical decision support systems, where clinicians might prefer to see a rule-based reasoning process that aligns with their own clinical logic.

The adoption of XAI in healthcare enhances transparency and aligns with ethical standards, ensuring that AI-driven decisions are made with a clear, interpretable rationale. By providing explanations that are understandable to clinicians and patients alike, XAI can help bridge the gap between complex AI models and the practical needs of healthcare providers, ultimately fostering greater trust in AI systems.

However, developing explainable AI models is challenging. There is often a trade-off between the accuracy of an AI model and its interpretability. More complex models like deep neural networks, tend to be more accurate but less interpretable. Conversely, simpler models, like decision trees, are easier to understand but may not be as accurate. Balancing these trade-offs is a key challenge in developing AI systems that are both effective and transparent.

Another aspect of transparency involves the data used to train AI models. Biases in training data can lead to biased AI systems, exacerbating existing health disparities. For example, if an AI system is trained primarily on data from a specific demographic group, it may not perform as well for other groups. Ensuring that AI systems are trained on diverse and representative datasets is essential to avoid these issues and build trust in AI-driven healthcare.

Trustworthiness

Trust is the cornerstone of any healthcare system, and this also extends to AI-driven healthcare. For AI systems to be successfully integrated into healthcare, they must be trustworthy. This means that they must be reliable, accurate and safe (Figure 7.5).

Ensuring the trustworthiness of AI systems involves rigorous testing and validation (D. Kaur et al. 2023). AI models should be tested in various clinical scenarios to perform consistently under different conditions. This testing should go beyond the initial development phase and continue throughout the AI system's lifecycle to maintain the model's robustness and generalisation. Continuous monitoring is essential to identify and address any issues that may arise as the system is used in the real world.

Moreover, trust in AI systems can be enhanced through the involvement of healthcare professionals in their development and implementation. Healthcare professionals bring invaluable insights and expertise that can guide the creation of AI systems that are not only innovative but also practical and aligned with the needs of medical practice (Alowais et al. 2023). For example, a clinician might provide feedback on how an AI tool's user interface could be improved to fit into existing workflows, making the tool more user-friendly and increasing the likelihood of adoption.

Building trust also involves ensuring that AI systems are transparent and explainable, as discussed earlier. When healthcare providers and patients understand how an AI system works and why it makes certain decisions, they are more likely to trust its outputs (Asan, Bayrak, and Choudhury 2020).

Furthermore, trustworthiness in AI is closely tied to the ethical considerations surrounding its use. AI systems must be designed and implemented to prioritise patient safety and privacy. This means protecting sensitive patient data and ensuring that AI systems are free from biases that could harm patients (Albahri et al. 2023). For example, an AI system used to

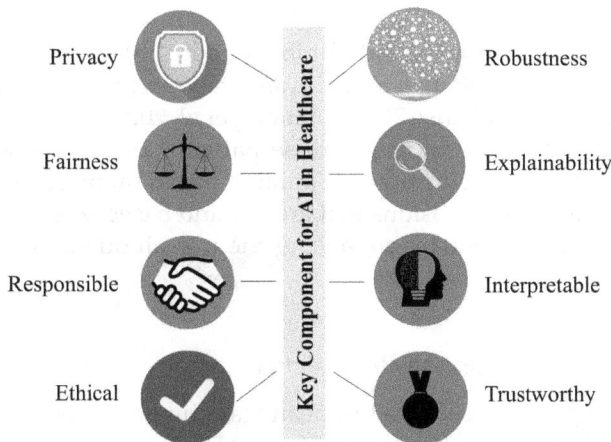

FIGURE 7.5
Key characteristics of machine learning models for clinical application (Rasheed et al. 2022).

prioritise patients for treatment should not inadvertently favour one group over another based on biased training data.

Bias mitigation is a critical component in achieving this goal. AI models are only as good as the data they are trained on, and if this data is biased, the AI system will likely replicate and even exacerbate these biases (Mehrabi et al. 2022). Potential biases in data can stem from various sources, including:

1. Historical Bias: This occurs when the data reflects past prejudices or inequalities. For example, if historically certain demographic groups have had less access to healthcare, the data will likely show poorer outcomes for these groups, leading the AI system to under-prioritise them in future treatment decisions.

2. Sampling Bias: This happens when the data used to train the AI model does not represent the entire population. For instance, if the training data predominantly includes patients from a particular age group, gender or ethnicity, the AI system may not perform well for individuals outside those groups.

3. Measurement Bias: This arises when data collection or measurement introduces systematic errors. For example, different healthcare providers might document patient symptoms differently, leading to inconsistencies in the data that can skew AI predictions.

4. Label Bias: This bias occurs when subjective judgments or flawed criteria influence the labels used for training the AI model. In healthcare, diagnostic labels might vary depending on the clinician's expertise or diagnostic approach, which could lead to biases in the AI's predictions.

By proactively addressing potential biases and implementing robust mitigation strategies, AI systems can be more trustworthy and equitable (Van Giffen, Herhausen, and Fahse 2022; J. Huang et al. 2022; Cary et al. 2024). For instance, an AI system used to prioritise patients for treatment should not inadvertently favour one group over another based on biased training data. Instead, it should make decisions that are fair and based solely on the clinical needs of the patients, thereby enhancing the overall quality and fairness of care provided.

Ethical Innovation and Responsible Practices

The successful deployment of AI in healthcare hinges on ethical innovation and responsible practices (Leslie 2019). As AI systems become more prevalent in healthcare, it is crucial to ensure that they are developed and used in ways that prioritise fairness and protect patient privacy.

Patient privacy is a fundamental concern in healthcare, extending to AI systems. AI systems often rely on large amounts of data, including sensitive patient information, to function effectively (Rajpurkar et al. 2022). Protecting this data is paramount. Healthcare institutions must implement robust data security measures to ensure patient information is not compromised. This includes securing the data and ensuring access to AI systems is tightly controlled and monitored (Shahid et al. 2022).

Beyond privacy, ethical considerations also involve ensuring that AI systems are used in ways that promote fairness and equity. AI can potentially worsen existing health disparities if it is not carefully managed. For example, if an AI system is trained on data that is not representative of the entire population, it may not perform as well for certain groups. This could lead to unequal treatment and worsen health outcomes for those already at a disadvantage.

To address these issues, engaging in continuous ethical review and involving diverse stakeholders in the development and deployment of AI systems is essential. This includes healthcare professionals, AI developers, patients and representatives from marginalised communities. By involving a broad range of perspectives, it is possible to identify and address potential ethical issues before they arise.

Ethical innovation also involves a commitment to responsible innovation. This means advancing technology and ensuring that these advancements benefit all population segments equitably. For example, efforts should be made to ensure that AI technologies are accessible to underserved communities in terms of availability and affordability. This might involve developing AI tools that can be used in low-resource settings or ensuring that AI-driven healthcare costs are not prohibitive for patients.

In conclusion, while AI holds great promise for transforming healthcare, its successful integration requires careful consideration of the challenges and ethical implications. By addressing the issues of technological advancement, accountability, trustworthiness and ethical innovation, it is possible to harness the power of AI to improve healthcare outcomes while ensuring that these advancements are implemented in a way that is fair, transparent and respectful of patient privacy.

Conclusions

The integration of AI into healthcare marks a transformative era, characterised by significant advancements in diagnostics, treatment planning, medical image analysis and surgical operations. As AI continues to evolve, it offers unparalleled precision, efficiency and personalised care, making it an indispensable tool for healthcare providers. However, the journey toward widespread AI adoption is accompanied by challenges, including the need for transparency, accountability and trustworthiness. Addressing these issues is crucial to ensuring that AI systems are not only effective but also reliable and ethically sound. By overcoming these challenges, AI has the potential to redefine the future of healthcare, improving patient outcomes and shaping a more advanced, efficient and equitable healthcare system.

References

Ahmad, Zubair, Shabina Rahim, Maha Zubair, and Jamshid Abdul-Ghafar. 2021. "Artificial Intelligence (AI) in Medicine, Current Applications and Future Role with Special Emphasis on Its Potential and Promise in Pathology: Present and Future Impact, Obstacles Including Costs and Acceptance among Pathologists, Practical and Philosophical Considerations. A Comprehensive Review." *Diagnostic Pathology* 16 (1): 24. https://doi.org/10.1186/s13000-021-01085-4

Albahri, A.S., Ali M. Duhaim, Mohammed A. Fadhel, Alhamzah Alnoor, Noor S. Baqer, Laith Alzubaidi, O.S. Albahri, et al. 2023. "A Systematic Review of Trustworthy and Explainable Artificial Intelligence in Healthcare: Assessment of Quality, Bias Risk, and Data Fusion." *Information Fusion* 96 (August):156–91. https://doi.org/10.1016/j.inffus.2023.03.008

Alowais, Shuroug A., Sahar S. Alghamdi, Nada Alsuhebany, Tariq Alqahtani, Abdulrahman I. Alshaya, Sumaya N. Almohareb, Atheer Aldairem, et al. 2023. "Revolutionizing Healthcare: The Role of Artificial Intelligence in Clinical Practice." *BMC Medical Education* 23 (1): 689. https://doi.org/10.1186/s12909-023-04698-z

Arun, Nishanth, Nathan Gaw, Praveer Singh, Ken Chang, Mehak Aggarwal, Bryan Chen, Katharina Hoebel, et al. 2020. "Assessing the (Un)Trustworthiness of Saliency Maps for Localizing Abnormalities in Medical Imaging." *Radiology: Artificial Intelligence* 3 (6), e200267. https://doi.org/10.1101/2020.07.28.20163899

Asan, Onur, Alparslan Emrah Bayrak, and Avishek Choudhury. 2020. "Artificial Intelligence and Human Trust in Healthcare: Focus on Clinicians." *Journal of Medical Internet Research* 22 (6): e15154. https://doi.org/10.2196/15154

Bertl, Markus, Peeter Ross, and Dirk Draheim. 2023. "Systematic AI Support for Decision-Making in the Healthcare Sector: Obstacles and Success Factors." *Health Policy and Technology* 12 (3): 100748. https://doi.org/10.1016/j.hlpt.2023.100748

Birkhoff, David C., H.M. Anne Sophie, Van Dalen, and Marlies P. Schijven. 2021. "A Review on the Current Applications of Artificial Intelligence in the Operating Room." *Surgical Innovation* 28 (5): 611–19. https://doi.org/10.1177/1553350621996961

Cary, Michael P., Sophia Bessias, Jonathan McCall, Michael J. Pencina, Siobahn D. Grady, Kay Lytle, and Nicoleta J. Economou-Zavlanos. 2024. "Empowering Nurses to Champion Health Equity & BE FAIR: Bias Elimination for Fair and

Responsible AI in Healthcare." *Journal of Nursing Scholarship*, July, jnu.13007. https://doi.org/10.1111/jnu.13007

Chen, Zhuxing, Yudong Zhang, Zeping Yan, Junguo Dong, Weipeng Cai, Yongfu Ma, Jipeng Jiang, Keyao Dai, Hengrui Liang, and Jianxing He. 2021. "Artificial Intelligence Assisted Display in Thoracic Surgery: Development and Possibilities." *Journal of Thoracic Disease* 13 (12): 6994–7005. https://doi.org/10.21037/jtd-21-1240

Cinelli, Lucas Pinheiro, Matheus Araújo Marins, Eduardo Antônio Barros Da Silva, and Sérgio Lima Netto. 2021. *Variational Methods for Machine Learning with Applications to Deep Networks*. Cham: Springer International Publishing. https://doi.org/10.1007/978-3-030-70679-1

Clancey, William J. 1983. "The Epistemology of a Rule-Based Expert System —A Framework for Explanation." *Artificial Intelligence* 20 (3): 215–51. https://doi.org/10.1016/0004-3702(83)90008-5

Cui, Zhiming, Yu Fang, Lanzhuju Mei, Bojun Zhang, Bo Yu, Jiameng Liu, Caiwen Jiang, et al. 2022. "A Fully Automatic AI System for Tooth and Alveolar Bone Segmentation from Cone-Beam CT Images." *Nature Communications* 13 (1): 2096. https://doi.org/10.1038/s41467-022-29637-2

De Cecco, Carlo N., Marly Van Assen, and Tim Leiner, eds. 2022. Artificial Intelligence in Cardiothoracic Imaging. *Contemporary Medical Imaging*. Cham: Springer International Publishing. https://doi.org/10.1007/978-3-030-92087-6

Dilsizian, Steven E., and Eliot L. Siegel. 2014. "Artificial Intelligence in Medicine and Cardiac Imaging: Harnessing Big Data and Advanced Computing to Provide Personalised Medical Diagnosis and Treatment." *Current Cardiology Reports* 16 (1): 441. https://doi.org/10.1007/s11886-013-0441-8

Emami, Hajar, Ming Dong, Siamak Nejad-Davarani, and Carri Glide-Hurst. 2021. "SA-GAN: Structure-Aware GAN for Organ-Preserving Synthetic CT Generation." arXiv. http://arxiv.org/abs/2105.07044

Gibson, Eli, Wenqi Li, Carole Sudre, Lucas Fidon, Dzhoshkun I. Shakir, Guotai Wang, Zach Eaton-Rosen, et al. 2018. "NiftyNet: A Deep-Learning Platform for Medical Imaging." *Computer Methods and Programs in Biomedicine* 158 (May):113–22. https://doi.org/10.1016/j.cmpb.2018.01.025

Goodfellow, Ian, Jean Pouget-Abadie, Mehdi Mirza, Bing Xu, David Warde-Farley, Sherjil Ozair, Aaron Courville, and Yoshua Bengio. 2020. "Generative Adversarial Networks." *Communications of the ACM* 63 (11): 139–44. https://doi.org/10.1145/3422622

Huang, Jonathan, Galal Galal, Mozziyar Etemadi, and Mahesh Vaidyanathan. 2022. "Evaluation and Mitigation of Racial Bias in Clinical Machine Learning Models: Scoping Review." *JMIR Medical Informatics* 10 (5): e36388. https://doi.org/10.2196/36388

Huang, Shigao, Jie Yang, Simon Fong, and Qi Zhao. 2020. "Artificial Intelligence in Cancer Diagnosis and Prognosis: Opportunities and Challenges." *Cancer Letters* 471 (February):61–71. https://doi.org/10.1016/j.canlet.2019.12.007

Jones, Scott, Kenton Thompson, Brian Porter, Meegan Shepherd, Daniel Sapkaroski, Alexandra Grimshaw, and Catriona Hargrave. 2024. "Automation and Artificial Intelligence in Radiation Therapy Treatment Planning." *Journal of Medical Radiation Sciences* 71 (2): 290–98. https://doi.org/10.1002/jmrs.729

Kaur, Davinder, Suleyman Uslu, Kaley J. Rittichier, and Arjan Durresi. 2023. "Trustworthy Artificial Intelligence: A Review." *ACM Computing Surveys* 55 (2): 1–38. https://doi.org/10.1145/3491209

Kaur, Simarjeet, Jimmy Singla, Lewis Nkenyereye, Sudan Jha, Deepak Prashar, Gyanendra Prasad Joshi, Shaker El-Sappagh, M. Saiful Islam, and S. M. Riazul Islam. 2020. "Medical Diagnostic Systems Using Artificial Intelligence (AI) Algorithms: Principles and Perspectives." *IEEE Access* 8:228049–69. https://doi.org/10.1109/ACCESS.2020.3042273

LeCun, Yann, Yoshua Bengio, and Geoffrey Hinton. 2015. "Deep Learning." *Nature* 521 (7553): 436–44. https://doi.org/10.1038/nature14539

Leslie, David. 2019. "Understanding Artificial Intelligence Ethics and Safety: A Guide for the Responsible Design and Implementation of AI Systems in the Public Sector." *Zenodo.* https://doi.org/10.5281/ZENODO.3240529

Liu, Xiaonan, Kewei Chen, Teresa Wu, David Weidman, Fleming Lure, and Jing Li. 2018. "Use of Multimodality Imaging and Artificial Intelligence for Diagnosis and Prognosis of Early Stages of Alzheimer's Disease." *Translational Research* 194 (April):56–67. https://doi.org/10.1016/j.trsl.2018.01.001

Lundberg, Scott M, and Su-In Lee. 2017. "A Unified Approach to Interpreting Model Predictions."

Lysaght, Tamra, Hannah Yeefen Lim, Vicki Xafis, and Kee Yuan Ngiam. 2019. "AI-Assisted Decision-Making in Healthcare: The Application of an Ethics Framework for Big Data in Health and Research." *Asian Bioethics Review* 11 (3): 299–314. https://doi.org/10.1007/s41649-019-00096-0

McIntosh, Chris, Leigh Conroy, Michael C. Tjong, Tim Craig, Andrew Bayley, Charles Catton, Mary Gospodarowicz, et al. 2021. "Clinical Integration of Machine Learning for Curative-Intent Radiation Treatment of Patients with Prostate Cancer." *Nature Medicine* 27 (6): 999–1005. https://doi.org/10.1038/s41591-021-01359-w

Mehrabi, Ninareh, Fred Morstatter, Nripsuta Saxena, Kristina Lerman, and Aram Galstyan. 2022. "A Survey on Bias and Fairness in Machine Learning." *ACM Computing Surveys* 54 (6): 1–35. https://doi.org/10.1145/3457607

Mei, Xueyan, Hao-Chih Lee, Kai-yue Diao, Mingqian Huang, Bin Lin, Chenyu Liu, Zongyu Xie, et al. 2020. "Artificial Intelligence–Enabled Rapid Diagnosis of Patients with COVID-19." *Nature Medicine* 26 (8): 1224–28. https://doi.org/10.1038/s41591-020-0931-3

Nasr, Mahmoud, M. Milon Islam, Shady Shehata, Fakhri Karray, and Yuri Quintana. 2021. "Smart Healthcare in the Age of AI: Recent Advances, Challenges, and Future Prospects." *IEEE Access* 9:145248–70. https://doi.org/10.1109/ACCESS.2021.3118960

Netherton, Tucker J., Carlos E. Cardenas, Dong Joo Rhee, Laurence E. Court, and Beth M. Beadle. 2021. "The Emergence of Artificial Intelligence within Radiation Oncology Treatment Planning." *Oncology* 99 (2): 124–34. https://doi.org/10.1159/000512172

Pan, Yongsheng, Mingxia Liu, Chunfeng Lian, Tao Zhou, Yong Xia, and Dinggang Shen. 2018. "Synthesizing Missing PET from MRI with Cycle-Consistent Generative Adversarial Networks for Alzheimer's Disease Diagnosis." In *Medical Image Computing and Computer Assisted Intervention – MICCAI 2018,* edited by Alejandro F. Frangi, Julia A. Schnabel, Christos Davatzikos, Carlos Alberola-López, and Gabor Fichtinger, 11072:455–63. Lecture Notes in Computer Science. Cham: Springer International Publishing. https://doi.org/10.1007/978-3-030-00931-1_52

Prete, Alessandro, Salvatore Maria Corsello, and Roberto Salvatori. 2017. "Current Best Practice in the Management of Patients after Pituitary Surgery." *Therapeutic Advances in Endocrinology and Metabolism* 8 (3): 33–48. https://doi.org/10.1177/2042018816687240

Rajpurkar, Pranav, Emma Chen, Oishi Banerjee, and Eric J. Topol. 2022. "AI in Health and Medicine." *Nature Medicine* 28 (1): 31–38. https://doi.org/10.1038/s41591-021-01614-0

Rasheed, Khansa, Adnan Qayyum, Mohammed Ghaly, Ala Al-Fuqaha, Adeel Razi, and Junaid Qadir. 2022. "Explainable, Trustworthy, and Ethical Machine Learning for Healthcare: A Survey." *Computers in Biology and Medicine* 149 (October):106043. https://doi.org/10.1016/j.compbiomed.2022.106043

Ribeiro, Marco Tulio, Sameer Singh, and Carlos Guestrin. 2016. "'Why Should I Trust You?': Explaining the Predictions of Any Classifier." In *Proceedings of the 22nd ACM SIGKDD International Conference on Knowledge Discovery and Data Mining*, 1135–44. San Francisco California USA: ACM. https://doi.org/10.1145/2939672.2939778

Sadeghi, Amir H., Quinten Mank, Alper S. Tuzcu, Jasper Hofman, Sabrina Siregar, Alexander Maat, Alexandre Mottrie, Jolanda Kluin, and Pieter De Backer. 2024. "Artificial Intelligence–Assisted Augmented Reality Robotic Lung Surgery: Navigating the Future of Thoracic Surgery." *JTCVS Techniques* 26 (August):121–25. https://doi.org/10.1016/j.xjtc.2024.04.011

Schork, Nicholas J. 2019. "Artificial Intelligence and Personalised Medicine." In *Precision Medicine in Cancer Therapy*, edited by Daniel D. Von Hoff and Haiyong Han, 178:265–83. Cancer Treatment and Research. Cham: Springer International Publishing. https://doi.org/10.1007/978-3-030-16391-4_11

Secinaro, Silvana, Davide Calandra, Aurelio Secinaro, Vivek Muthurangu, and Paolo Biancone. 2021. "The Role of Artificial Intelligence in Healthcare: A Structured Literature Review." *BMC Medical Informatics and Decision Making* 21 (1): 125. https://doi.org/10.1186/s12911-021-01488-9

Shahid, Jahanzeb, Rizwan Ahmad, Adnan K. Kiani, Tahir Ahmad, Saqib Saeed, and Abdullah M. Almuhaideb. 2022. "Data Protection and Privacy of the Internet of Healthcare Things (IoHTs)." *Applied Sciences* 12 (4): 1927. https://doi.org/10.3390/app12041927

Shi, Jinghua, Oguzhan Alagoz, Fatih Safa Erenay, and Qiang Su. 2014. "A Survey of Optimization Models on Cancer Chemotherapy Treatment Planning." *Annals of Operations Research* 221 (1): 331–56. https://doi.org/10.1007/s10479-011-0869-4

Singh, Rishi P., Grant L. Hom, Michael D. Abramoff, J. Peter Campbell, Michael F. Chiang, and on behalf of the AAO Task Force on Artificial Intelligence. 2020. "Current Challenges and Barriers to Real-World Artificial Intelligence Adoption for the Healthcare System, Provider, and the Patient." *Translational Vision Science & Technology* 9 (2): 45. https://doi.org/10.1167/tvst.9.2.45

Van Giffen, Benjamin, Dennis Herhausen, and Tobias Fahse. 2022. "Overcoming the Pitfalls and Perils of Algorithms: A Classification of Machine Learning Biases and Mitigation Methods." *Journal of Business Research* 144 (May):93–106. https://doi.org/10.1016/j.jbusres.2022.01.076

Varghese, Chris, Ewen M. Harrison, Greg O'Grady, and Eric J. Topol. 2024. "Artificial Intelligence in Surgery." *Nature Medicine* 30 (5): 1257–68. https://doi.org/10.1038/s41591-024-02970-3

Vidhya, B., M. Nikhil Madhav, M. Suresh Kumar, and S. Kalanandini. 2022. "AI Based Diagnosis of Pneumonia." *Wireless Personal Communications* 126 (4): 3677–92. https://doi.org/10.1007/s11277-022-09885-7

Wachter, Sandra, Brent Mittelstadt, and Chris Russell. 2017. "Counterfactual Explanations Without Opening the Black Box: Automated Decisions and the GDPR." *SSRN Electronic Journal.* https://doi.org/10.2139/ssrn.3063289

Wang, Chunhao, Xiaofeng Zhu, Julian C. Hong, and Dandan Zheng. 2019. "Artificial Intelligence in Radiotherapy Treatment Planning: Present and Future." *Technology in Cancer Research & Treatment* 18 (January):153303381987392. https://doi.org/10.1177/1533033819873922

Wu, Kun, Yan Qiang, Kai Song, Xueting Ren, WenKai Yang, Wanjun Zhang, Akbar Hussain, and Yanfen Cui. 2020. "Image Synthesis in Contrast MRI Based on Super Resolution Reconstruction with Multi-Refinement Cycle-Consistent Generative Adversarial Networks." *Journal of Intelligent Manufacturing* 31 (5): 1215–28. https://doi.org/10.1007/s10845-019-01507-7

Zheng, Dandan, Julian C. Hong, Chunhao Wang, and Xiaofeng Zhu. 2019. "Radiotherapy Treatment Planning in the Age of AI: Are We Ready Yet?" *Technology in Cancer Research & Treatment* 18 (January):153303381989457. https://doi.org/10.1177/1533033819894577

Zhou, Xiao-Yun, Yao Guo, Mali Shen, and Guang-Zhong Yang. 2020. "Application of Artificial Intelligence in Surgery." *Frontiers of Medicine* 14 (4): 417–30. https://doi.org/10.1007/s11684-020-0770-0

8

Biometrics and Authentication

Min-Er Teo, Lee-Ying Chong and Siew-Chin Chong

Introduction

Nowadays, we live in a digital world where all of a person's data has been digitised, including sensitive information such as medical records, personal information, etc. Various strategies have been developed and implemented to protect sensitive information. Traditional methods of protecting information include PINs, smart cards and passwords to prove an individual's authentication. However, these traditional methods have some disadvantages, such as the theft of smart cards and fragile passwords or PINs. Therefore, biometric recognition technology appears as a new solution to protect information from unauthorised access.

Due to the rapid growth and development of technology, biometric recognition technologies are continually evolving and are gradually being deployed and used around the world. Biometrics is the biological measurement and statistical analysis of a person's unique physical and behavioural characteristics. The main purpose of this technology is to identify and provide access control for the authorised person of the system. It can be briefly divided into three types: physiological (physical) biometrics, behavioural biometrics and multimodal biometrics. Many biometric recognition systems are used in our daily life, such as the fingerprint recognition system at airports, the facial recognition system when unlocking smartphones, signature recognition when accessing sensitive information, and more. Therefore, user authentication is becoming increasingly important due to the application of technologies such as mobile devices and the exchange of confidential information.

Biometric authentication has gained popularity in recent years as the demand for reliable and simple identification methods has increased across a wide range of applications. Biometric technologies have become an essential part of modern security solutions due to their improved security, resilience and ease of use achieved through rapid technological development compared to traditional methods using passwords or PINs. Although biometrics bring the benefits mentioned above, they also come with some challenges,

DOI: 10.1201/9781003509196-8

such as privacy concerns, cyber-attack issues and system performance issues. Therefore, a comprehensive understanding of biometric features, their use in user identification and the variables that influence the effectiveness of the system is important to address the above issues and ensure the continued effectiveness and reliability of biometric systems.

This article aims to provide a comprehensive survey of the recent biometric technology with the following main contributions:

- This article discusses the different types of biometric modalities, such as physical, behavioural and multimodal biometrics.
- The dissimilarities among the three types of biometric authentication, such as biometrics identification, verification and authentication are examined.
- The internal process of biometric authentication and the latest technology (machine learning and deep learning) used in biometric authentication are described.

The remaining sections of this article are organised as follows: Section "Biometrics Modalities" provides a brief overview of the types of biometric modalities, categorised into three groups: physiological (physical) biometrics, behavioural biometrics and multimodal biometrics. Section "Type of Biometric Authentication" introduces three types of biometric processes: identification, authentication and verification. In Section "Process of Biometric Authentication", an overview of the biometric authentication framework/process, which includes the enrolment and authentication phases, is presented. Section "Biometric Applications" contrasts and discusses various popular biometric applications used in the real world. Moreover, Section "Latest Technology" introduces several recent technologies used in biometrics, such as machine learning and deep learning. Finally, the conclusion is presented in Section "Conclusion".

Biometrics Modalities

Biometrics modalities can be briefly divided into three categories: physiological (physical) biometrics, behavioural biometrics and multimodal biometrics. Some examples of physiological (physical) biometrics are the face, eyes, ears and fingerprints, that is, the parts of the human body that are unique to each person. In addition, voice, gait and signature patterns are examples of behavioural biometrics that represent a person's unique way of acting. Furthermore, multimodal biometrics combine numerous unique characteristics of a person such as fingerprints, face, voice or gait for authentication

TABLE 8.1

Two Types of Biometrics Modalities

Physiological (Physical) Biometrics	Behavioural Biometrics
Face recognition	Voice recognition
Fingerprint recognition	Signature recognition
Iris recognition	Gait recognition
Retina recognition	Handwriting recognition
Ear recognition	Hand Gesture

to produce more accurate and trustworthy results than techniques that use only one characteristic. Table 8.1 lists examples of physiological (physical) and behavioural biometric characteristics.

Physiological (Physical) Biometrics

The physical characteristics of the human body, such as its structure, size and shape, are directly related to user authentication. Physiology-based methods generally retrieve discrete, compact characteristics to perform user authentication. Face recognition, fingerprint recognition, iris recognition, retina recognition and ear recognition are some of the most commonly used techniques. A detailed analysis of the mentioned physical biometrics is discussed in the following section.

Face Recognition

Face recognition technology exists as a type of biometric security that uses biometric data and characteristics of the face to confirm a person's identity. This technology can be used to identify people in photos, videos and ultimately in real-time. Face recognition has attracted the interest of researchers because it enables non-intrusive recognition and provides proof of a person's identity without their consent or cooperation (Teo et al., 2024). Face recognition is divided into three types: 2D, 2.5D and 3D. 2D face recognition is a facial recognition strategy that utilises the two-dimensional structure of the human face. It is more accepted by the public and requires a less expensive image-capture device. 3D face recognition requires a 3D scanner to capture a person's facial characteristics across the entire head. The geometric details in the 3D feature improve the recognition rate in difficult situations. 2.5D face recognition appears like a 2D format but consists of a 3D facial structure. The 2.5D face data provides the additional z-coordinate, a depth value, which is the essential element of a 3D structure that solves illumination changes and facial expression problems (Teo et al., 2024). Table 8.2 shows the comparison between three types of face recognition systems.

TABLE 8.2

Differences between Three Types of Face Recognition (Teo et al., 2024)

Face Recognition Technology	2D	2.5D	3D
Image Format	Texture-based image	Depth image	3D facial model
Pre-processing Element	Easy	Middle	Hard
Cost of Gadget	Cheap	Middle	Expensive
Coordinates Involved	Coordinates x, y	Coordinates x, y, z	Coordinates x, y, z
Limitations	Posture, facial expression, lighting	Posture, facial expression	Posture, facial expression

Fingerprint Recognition

Fingerprint recognition is a biometric process that can be used to identify people based on the characteristic patterns of their fingerprints. Fingerprints are distinctive patterns of loops, ridges and swirls found on a person's fingertips. These patterns, which are formed during foetal development and remain unchanged throughout a person's life, can be used to uniquely identify individuals (Innovatrics, 2024a). This technology enables secure access to devices, facilities and confidential information by capturing and analysing a person's characteristic fingerprints. It provides a reliable and practical means of biometric authentication by using advanced algorithms and cameras to recognise and match fingerprints. Fingerprint recognition is widely used because it is easy to capture compared to other biometric technologies, has a proven track record and is accepted by the public. Examples of applications that use fingerprint recognition include attendance systems, airports, civil identification and others (Innovatrics, 2024a).

Iris Recognition

Iris recognition refers to an autonomous biometric recognition technology that recognises characteristic patterns within a ring-shaped area around the pupil of each eye. The iris is a round, pigmented muscle in front of the human eye that controls the diameter of the pupil and the amount of light entering the eye to ensure the best possible vision. To recognise unique features such as the structure of the rings, furrows and crypts, the system uses high-resolution images of the iris taken with special cameras or scanners. A digital template created from these features is then stored in a database and used for matching during authentication. When an authentication request is made, a new image of a person's iris is taken and compared with the stored templates using pattern-matching techniques. Iris identification technology is known for its accuracy and reliability, as the iris patterns are very unique and consistent over time. Security and access control in the government sector, healthcare sector, financial services and many more are examples of applications that utilise iris recognition systems (Innovatrics, 2024b).

Retina Recognition

Retina recognition is a system that uses low-intensity light to map the individual patterns of the retina. This technique evaluates the structure of the blood vessels of the retina, as the blood vessels at the back of the eye have a specific pattern that is different for each person. As the retina cannot be seen directly, it must be illuminated with an efficient infrared light source. The blood vessels of the retina absorb the infrared radiation quickly compared to the surrounding tissue. An analysis of the image of the retinal blood vessels is then performed (Elvir & Uran, 2022). The entire process of the retinal detection method requires a person to take off their glasses, hold their eye close to the scanning device, look at a specific spot, remain still and focus on a specific area for about ten to fifteen seconds while the image is captured. A retina scan is unable to be falsified since it is currently impractical to manufacture a human retina. Retina recognition is mainly utilised in situations that demand exceptionally high degrees of confidentiality. For instance, this technology is primarily employed at military sites, nuclear facilities and top-tier laboratories.

Ear Recognition

Human ears have a number of distinct and unique features that allow for individual identification, just like faces, irises and fingerprints. Human ears are born with a specific visual shape. Besides, the human ear does not change as a person grows or ages (Elvir & Uran, 2022). Since the human ear does not rely on the cooperation of the person to be identified and retains its original shape over time, it is an ideal feature for passive person recognition. Since human ears are clearly visible even in situations where a mask is worn, capturing a person's ear image is very easy. The ear recognition system could be used in conjunction with other biometric systems in an automatic person recognition system to provide proof of identity in situations where information from other systems is missing or inaccurate (Ahila Priyadharshini et al., 2021).

Behavioural Biometrics

Behavioural biometrics proves a person's identity based on certain patterns that emerge when interacting with a system. It identifies a person's identity by analysing the person's behaviour and body movements or structures. The following section presents a comprehensive study of the behavioural biometric methods mentioned above.

Voice Recognition

Voice recognition is a behavioural biometric system that uses a person's voice to identify, recognise and authorise a person's identity. This technique examines the specific characteristics of each person's voice, such as natural accent, pitch and frequency. Voice recognition serves as a contactless, software-based technique and is one of the most practical and widely accepted forms of biometrics. It also enables users to interact with technology simply by speaking, allowing for hands-free inquiries, notifications, and other convenient activities. To enhance security, it is often used in conjunction with facial recognition for greater protection. Voice recognition has proven to be a useful tool in law enforcement investigations, as it allows suspects to be recognised from a sound recording even when no other identifying characteristics are present (Alexander, 2024).

Signature Recognition

Signature recognition is a biometric method that verifies a person's identity using their unique signature. The process involves capturing a person's signature with a digital device, such as a smartphone or tablet, and then analysing it with complex algorithms to identify distinctive characteristics, including size, shape, speed and pressure. There are two types of techniques employed in signature recognition: static and dynamic. Static signature recognition involves converting a person's handwritten signature into an image, which is then compared against previously stored signatures. Conversely, dynamic signature recognition is a more advanced system that records various dynamic characteristics of a person's signature as they sign on a touch-sensitive surface of an electronic device, including structure, pressure, direction, timing and stroke (Soelistio et al., 2021). Signature recognition is useful in various scenarios, including access control, document authorisation and banking transactions. It is widely used in financial institutions to verify the identity of customers who sign checks, authorise withdrawals of funds, or perform other financial transactions (Octatco, 2022).

Gait Recognition

Gait recognition is a behavioural biometric technique that detects and analyses the distinct walking patterns of individuals. Each person has a unique gait that is difficult to imitate. One of the main advantages of gait recognition is that it does not require active participation from the individual to be recognised. The distinctiveness of gait patterns makes them a powerful biometric indicator, capable of distinguishing between different individuals based on their gait and motion characteristics. This approach involves analysing gait form and dynamics, including step width, step length, speed, and cycle time, as well as kinematic parameters such as thigh, knee and ankle movements (Aratek, 2022). Gait recognition can be used in law enforcement and surveillance systems for monitoring and tracking individuals as they move through a specific area. Additionally, gait recognition can be utilised in physical access control to verify individuals as they enter or exit an authorised location.

Handwriting Recognition

Handwriting recognition refers to a method used to identify the writer of a particular text based on handwriting patterns. It falls under the category of behavioural biometric systems since it relies on the skill and writing patterns that an individual has learned. From a researcher's perspective, handwriting serves as a synthetic representation of an individual's behavioural traits and the postnatal learning process. The writing process varies among individuals, so researchers are working to identify these differences as indicators of personal identity. Furthermore, the handwriting recognition technique involves formatting, character segmentation and language model training to learn how to structure meaningful words and phrases. The input data for this technique can be of two types: online and offline. For example, a person's handwriting pattern on a digital device, such as a tablet or smartphone, is an example of online handwriting recognition. In contrast, handwriting scanned from paper, books, or images serves as an example of offline handwriting recognition (Pragati, 2022).

Hand Gesture

Hand gestures are a form of non-verbal communication typically expressed through the position of the palm, the placement of the fingers and the shape formed by the hand. There are two categories of hand gestures: static and dynamic. A static gesture is defined by a fixed hand position, while a dynamic gesture involves a sequence of hand movements, such as waving. Hand gestures can vary widely; for instance, a handshake differs depending on the individual, location and timing (Oudah et al., 2020). Hand gesture recognition converts sign language hand movements into text or audio output. It can generally be divided into two categories based on how the technique records sign language hand gestures: vision-based systems, which use one or more cameras to record the gestures, and device-based systems, which utilise direct-measure devices, such as specially designed electronic gloves with sensors, to connect the individual with the system (Mohamed et al., 2021).

Differences between Biometrics Modalities

Table 8.3 shows the differences between biometric modalities in terms of modality type, accuracy, cost, user acceptance and ease of use.

Multimodal Biometrics

Multimodal biometrics refers to the use of several biometric recognition identifiers to verify an individual's identity. This technique integrates multiple biometric recognition results to enhance the performance of the authentication system, preventing unauthorised users from authenticating and lowering the false acceptance rate. Compared to the unimodal biometrics system that utilises only one type of biometric to obtain authentication, multimodal biometrics systems which employ several types of biometrics gain a higher performance and provide stronger security. For instance, the face and fingerprint of a person can be used in the multimodal biometric system for authentication purposes. Applications for multimodal biometric systems include smart cards, passports, visas, e-commerce, law enforcement and more (Parkavi et al., 2017).

Multimodal biometrics can be divided into two categories, which are pre-matching fusion and post-matching fusion. Pre-matching fusion refers to the merging of data just before the matching stage. It involves the integration of different biometric features to build a composite feature for classification. This feature fusion phase, which consists of the combination of different unique traits of biometrics contains more rich information that can improve the performance of the system. For example, the merging of the face and voice features can enhance the system's performance than only using a sole feature (Modak & Jha, 2019).

Moreover, post-matching fusion represents the merging of data after the matching stage. Compared to the pre-matching fusion that performs feature fusion before the classification, post-matching fusion performs fusion after the classification by adding the result of each biometrics trait together and producing a final result. This type of fusion is preferable due to its simplicity. For instance, match score fusion, rank fusion and decision fusion are examples of post-matching fusion (Modak & Jha, 2019).

Type of Biometric Authentication

Biometric Identification

Biometric identification is the procedure of confirming an individual's identification through the comparison of their biometric data with a database of previously recorded biometric data. The method employs a one-to-many

TABLE 8.3

Differences Among Biometric Modalities

Biometrics Modalities	Modalities type	Accuracy	Cost	User acceptance	Ease of use
Face	Physiological (Physical)	High	Medium	High	High
Fingerprints	Physiological (Physical)	High	Medium	Medium	High
Iris	Physiological (Physical)	Very high	High	Medium-Low	Medium
Retina	Physiological (Physical)	Very high	High	Low	Low
Ear	Physiological (Physical)	Medium	Low	Medium	High
Voice	Behavioural	Medium	Medium	High	High
Signature	Behavioural	Low	Medium	High	Medium
Handwriting	Behavioural	Low	Medium	High	Medium
Gait	Behavioural	Medium	Medium	Low	Medium
Hand Gesture	Behavioural	Medium	Low	High	Medium

(1:N) matching technique to determine a match between the biometric sample with several entries in the database. Moreover, it is widely used in law enforcement and border control. For example, it is normally used in border control when travelling to other countries by using fingerprint or face recognition to confirm one's identity.

Biometric Verification

Biometric verification represents the procedure of verifying a person's claimed identity by matching their biometric sample with a previously recorded biometric template. This approach employs a one-to-one (1:1) matching process, in which the biometric sample is contrasted with a sole recorded biometric template to confirm the stated identity. In addition, it is widely employed in access control and financial transactions activities. For instance, the bank sector may implement a fingerprint recognition system to verify one's identity as an extra layer of security when performing high-value transactions.

Biometric Authentication

Biometric authentication examines a person's authenticity as a way of proving their authorisation for accessing a system and sensitive data. It entails building confidence in authenticity, verifying an individual's identity, and offering an authenticator. Furthermore, this procedure also utilising a one-to-one (1:1) matching process, in which the biometric sample is contrasted with a sole recorded biometric template to confirm the stated identity. For example, an individual unlocks his/her smartphone by using a face or fingerprint recognition. In this case, the programme provides a secure way to verify the user's claimed identity, guaranteeing that only the authorised user has access to the device. Figure 8.1. illustrates the difference between biometric identification, biometric verification and biometric authentication.

Process of Biometric Authentication

Biometric recognition system can be divided into two phases, which are the enrolment and verification phases. Figure 8.2 shows the enrolment and verification phase in the biometric recognition system.

Enrolment Phase

The enrolment phase represents the procedure of registering a new user into a system based on capturing the user's biometric sample, retrieving its

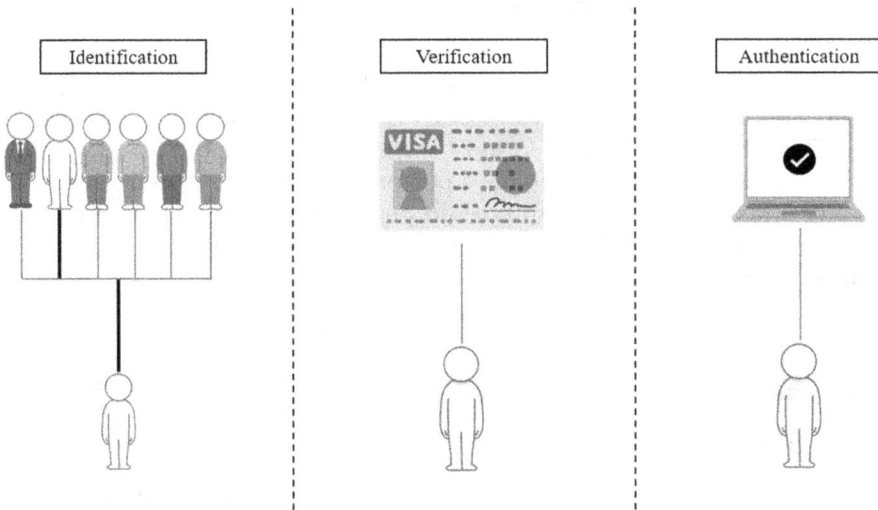

FIGURE 8.1
Comparison between biometric identification, verification and authentication.

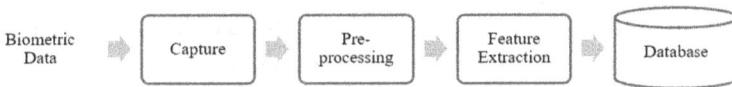

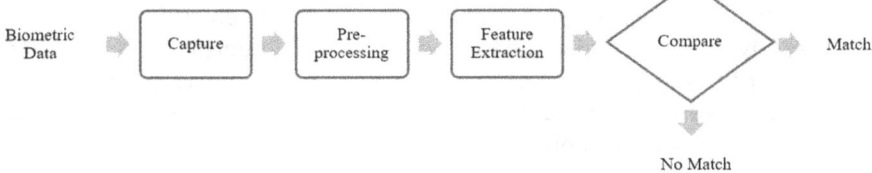

FIGURE 8.2
The enrolment and verification stage for the biometrics recognition system.

unique features, and transforming it as a biometric template in order to store it in the database of the system for future comparison. This stage acts as the fundamental structure for systems that use biometrics to perform authorisation purposes, including financial transactions, unlocking smartphones and voter verification during elections.

Authentication/Verification Phase

The authentication (verification) stage serves as a one-to-one (1:1) procedure that matches the biometric sample with the biometric template stored within the database to approve or deny a specific person as an authorised user. This phase represents the most important part of biometric recognition as it provides accessibility for a person to access the system. Failure to identify a fake person as an authorised person may result in the leaking of sensitive information. Thus, the verification process is an essential stage for biometric identification to confirm an individual's identity.

Biometric Applications

Due to the increasing popularity of biometrics recognition, there are plenty of biometrics applications have been presented, including:

- Airport biometrics: Biometrics recognition systems such as face recognition and fingerprint recognition are commonly used in airports to verify the identity of an individual. This technique acquires real-time physical biometric data like fingerprints or the face of an individual and compares it to the stored biometric template in the database. This authentication procedure confirms that the particular individual represents the authorised ticket holder.
- Biometric locks: The biometric locks serve as a locking mechanism that utilises biometric data, such as facial, fingerprint or voice recognition, to lock and open doors or cabinets. Fingerprint smart door locks, face door locks, fingerprint cabinet locks and so on are some of the examples of biometric locks that have been utilised in daily life by some organisations or companies. Biometric locks provide an additional level of security since only the authorised person can enter a particular place by scanning their biometrics like fingerprint, which are hard to fool.
- Physical and logical access: Face recognition, fingerprint recognition and iris recognition are some of the examples of biometric recognition systems that are widely used in the world. It can be easily found in companies and organisations where the employees can enter a room or pass through a place by scanning their fingerprints on the system. In addition, retina recognition is utilised in situations that demand exceptionally high degrees of confidentiality like military sites.
- Mobile biometrics: Mobile biometrics such as fingerprint recognition, iris recognition, face recognition and voice recognition are

commonly used nowadays in daily life. These systems are used to unlock the mobile devices and perform banking transactions. It brings convenient and advanced security for the user compared to traditional authentication systems which use passwords.

- Financial services: Biometrics recognition technologies like face and fingerprint recognition are rapidly being used during transaction activities such as in the bank sector in order to verify a specific transaction.
- Attendance system: Unlike the traditional attendance system, which takes attendance using manual signing, an attendance system with the use of biometrics is widely used nowadays. The attendance system that uses biometrics such as fingerprint, face and iris is employed to ensure that only the actual person is attending the class or workplace.

Latest Technology

With the rapid growth of technology, biometrics recognition systems nowadays also incorporate with latest technology such as machine learning and deep learning algorithms (Jadhav et al., 2023; Mehraj & Mir, 2020; Ortiz et al., 2018). Figure 8.3 shows an example of utilising biometric systems integrated with machine learning or deep learning techniques.

Machine Learning

Machine Learning (ML) represents a subset of Artificial Intelligence (AI) which believes systems are able to learn from data, find patterns, and make

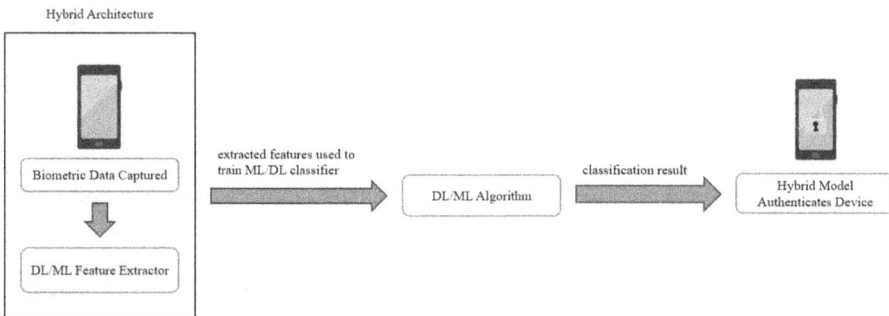

FIGURE 8.3
The process of biometric authentication incorporates machine learning or deep learning techniques.

choices without much interaction from humans. It comprises a machine performing a comprehensive investigation of scientific techniques which enables the system to mimic learning like a person without explicit programming. The implementation of ML in biometrics systems can help the system learn more details about the characteristics of the biometrics and increase the accuracy rate of the system.

For example, a toy named Hello Barbie leverages machine learning, natural language processing, and sophisticated analytics that listen to kids and then reply. Barbie can communicate with a kid since a microphone on her sends the words of what the kid says to the servers, which then is analysed and it sends back the proper replies in less than one second to Barbie. Answers to queries that might be utilised later in the conversation are saved (IDmission Team, 2020).

Deep Learning

Deep learning algorithms have lately acquired popularity in biometric recognition systems because of their potential to significantly boost the system's performance (Mekruksavanich & Jitpattanakul, 2021; Minaee et al., 2023; Sengar et al., 2020). Deep learning techniques that mimic a human brain, as opposed to traditional approaches, could "learn" more complicated and deeper traits. This method uses neural networks together with multiple hidden layers and a large amount of training data to retrieve low-level features in order to construct high-level key components of the system.

Convolutional Neural Network (CNN) serves as one of the most widely utilised deep learning algorithms in biometric recognition systems. For instance, the fingerprint recognition system with the use of CNN can increase the accuracy rate of the system as CNN can automatically learn unique features and characteristics of the fingerprint. Figure 8.4 shows the process of fingerprint recognition using CNN.

Conclusion

Biometrics recognition systems have gained popularity around the world nowadays due to the high performance and security of the system. Biometrics recognition brings more convenience and security to users by using biometrics which is unique for everyone rather than using traditional methods like passwords or pins. Biometrics modalities can roughly be classified into three groups, which are physiological (physical) biometrics, behavioural biometrics and multimodal biometrics. Different types of biometrics modalities

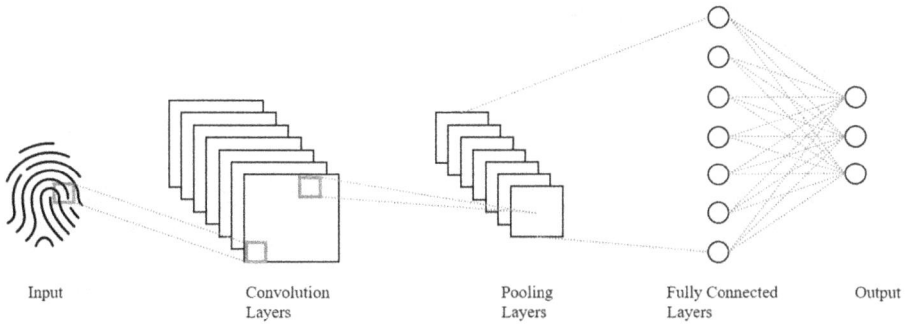

| Input | Convolution Layers | Pooling Layers | Fully Connected Layers | Output |

FIGURE 8.4
The process of fingerprint recognition utilises CNN.

have been discussed and compared in this paper. Furthermore, this paper also describes the differences among three types of biometrics authentication including biometric identification, authentication and verification. The process of biometrics authentication that involves enrolment and verification phases has been illustrated and discussed. In addition, this paper also describes several biometrics applications and further elaborates on the latest technology, such as machine learning and deep learning used in biometric authentication. Finally, although biometrics recognition has brought many benefits to the user, it is important to understand and utilise it wisely to prevent any incident from happening.

References

Ahila Priyadharshini, R., Arivazhagan, S., & Arun, M. (2021). A Deep Learning Approach for Person Identification Using Ear Biometrics. *Applied Intelligence, 51*(4), 2161–2172. https://doi.org/10.1007/s10489-020-01995-8

Alexander, S. G. (2024). What is Voice Recognition and How Does It Work? https://www.techtarget.com/searchcustomerexperience/definition/voice-recognition-speaker-recognition#:~:text=Voice%20or%20speaker%20recognition%20is,Amazon's%20Alexa%20and%20Apple's%20Siri

Aratek. (2022). Stepping Up: Gait Recognition Biometrics Gain Attention. https://www.aratek.co/news/gait-recognition-biometrics-gain-attention

Elvir, M., & Uran, L. (2022). Biometric Authentication. 7. https://www.researchgate.net/publication/371567274_Biometric_Authentication

I Dmission Team. (2020). How Machine Learning and Biometric Technology Work Together. https://www.idmission.com/en/blog/how-machine-learning-and-biometric-technology-work-together

Innovatrics. (2024a). Fingerprint Technology—Innovatrics—How it Works. https://www.innovatrics.com/fingerprint-technology/#:~:text=Fingerprint%20recognition%20is%20the%20process,series%20of%20ridges%20and%20grooves

Innovatrics. (2024b). Iris Recognition Technology—Innovatrics—How it Works. https://www.innovatrics.com/iris-recognition-technology/

Jadhav, D. B., Chavan, G. S., Bagal, V. C., & Manza, R. R. (2023). Review on Multimodal Biometric Recognition System Using Machine Learning. *Artificial Intelligence and Applications.* https://doi.org/10.47852/bonviewAIA3202593

Mehraj, H., & Mir, A. (2020). A Survey of Biometric Recognition Using Deep Learning. *EAI Endorsed Transactions on Energy Web*, 166775. https://doi.org/10.4108/eai.27-10-2020.166775

Mekruksavanich, S., & Jitpattanakul, A. (2021). Biometric User Identification Based on Human Activity Recognition Using Wearable Sensors: An Experiment Using Deep Learning Models. *Electronics*, *10*(3), 308. https://doi.org/10.3390/electronics10030308

Minaee, S., Abdolrashidi, A., Su, H., Bennamoun, M., & Zhang, D. (2023). Biometrics Recognition Using Deep Learning: A Survey. *Artificial Intelligence Review*, *56*(8), 8647–8695. https://doi.org/10.1007/s10462-022-10237-x

Modak, S. K. S., & Jha, V. K. (2019). Multibiometric Fusion Strategy and Its Applications: A Review. *Information Fusion*, *49*, 174–204. https://doi.org/10.1016/j.inffus.2018.11.018

Mohamed, N., Mustafa, M. B., & Jomhari, N. (2021). A Review of the Hand Gesture Recognition System: Current Progress and Future Directions. *IEEE Access*, *9*, 157422–157436. https://doi.org/10.1109/ACCESS.2021.3129650

Octatco. (2022). What is Signature recognition? https://octatco.com/bloge=19

Ortiz, N., Hernandez, R. D., Jimenez, R., Mauledeoux, M., & Aviles, O. (2018). Survey of Biometric Pattern Recognition via Machine Learning Techniques. *Contemporary Engineering Sciences*, *11*(34), 1677–1694. https://doi.org/10.12988/ces.2018.84166

Oudah, M., Al-Naji, A., & Chahl, J. (2020). Hand Gesture Recognition Based on Computer Vision: A Review of Techniques. *Journal of Imaging*, *6*(8), 73. https://doi.org/10.3390/jimaging6080073

Parkavi, R., Chandeesh Babu, K. R., & Kumar, J. A. (2017). Multimodal Biometrics for user authentication. *2017 11th International Conference on Intelligent Systems and Control (ISCO)*, 501–505. i

Pragati, B. (2022). Handwriting Recognition: Definition, Techniques & Uses. https://www.v7labs.com/blog/handwriting-recognition-guide#what-is-handwriting-recognition

Sengar, S. S., Hariharan, U., & Rajkumar, K. (2020). Multimodal Biometric Authentication System using Deep Learning Method. *2020 International Conference on Emerging Smart Computing and Informatics (ESCI)*, 309–312. https://doi.org/10.1109/ESCI48226.2020.9167512

Soelistio, E. A., Hananto Kusumo, R. E., Martan, Z. V., & Irwansyah, E. (2021). A Review of Signature Recognition Using Machine Learning. *2021 1st International Conference on Computer Science and Artificial Intelligence (ICCSAI)*, 219–223. https://doi.org/10.1109/ICCSAI53272.2021.9609732

Teo, M.-E., Chong, L.-Y., & Chong, S.-C. (2024). Fusion-Based 2.5D Face Recognition System. *Journal of Telecommunications and the Digital Economy*, *12*(1), 19–38. https://doi.org/10.18080/jtde.v12n1.770

9

Artificial Intelligence in Digital Marketing Analytics

Lee-Yeng Ong and Meng-Chew Leow

Introduction

E-commerce has experienced explosive growth in the last decade since the internet transformation in the early 2000s. Smartphones become a primary tool for online shopping, contributing massive amounts of data in digital marketing. Major advancements in technology, such as AI and machine learning, have enhanced personalised shopping experiences and customer service through new smart inventions like chatbots and recommendation engines (Ziakis & Vlachopoulou, 2023). Additionally, the proliferation of social media platforms has given rise to social commerce, where users can shop directly through social media apps. The COVID-19 pandemic further accelerated e-commerce adoption, as lockdowns and social distancing measures led to a significant increase in online shopping.

AI is the simulation of human intelligence in machines. It is designed to perform tasks such as learning, reasoning and self-correction. Digital Marketing Analytics involves collecting, measuring, analysing and reporting data from digital marketing channels to understand campaign effectiveness and make data-driven decisions in areas like website analytics, social media analytics, email marketing analytics and SEO analytics (Cioppi et al., 2023). Collectively, they help businesses to optimise strategies and improve customer experiences. The integration of AI into digital marketing analytics revolutionises how businesses understand and engage with their audience by automating data collection, analysis and interpretation. AI-powered tools can process vast amounts of data in real time, identify patterns, predict consumer behaviours and personalise marketing efforts. This leads to more accurate targeting, improved customer experiences and higher return of investment. For instance, AI can optimise ad placements, recommend content and even generate insights from social media interactions, making digital marketing more efficient and effective (Hicham et al., 2023).

DOI: 10.1201/9781003509196-9

Initially, the role of AI in marketing was limited to basic data analysis and customer segmentation due to slower hardware processing capabilities. As technology advances, AI-powered tools like recommendation engines and programmatic advertising become more prevalent and promising, leading to the development of chatbots and advanced analytics tools, allowing for more personalised and efficient marketing strategies. As digital marketing advances, the focus shifted towards understanding consumer behaviours and optimising marketing strategies. The development of advanced analytics tools and the integration of AI and machine learning in the 2010s allowed marketers to gain deeper insights, predict trends and personalise customer experiences. The introduction of generative AI tools like ChatGPT and Google Bard in the early 2020s further revolutionised the field by enabling hyper-personalised content creation and predictive analytics. Today, digital marketing analytics becomes an essential component of any marketing strategy, providing real-time data and actionable insights to drive business growth. The journey of AI in digital marketing has been marked by continuous innovation and transformation.

Today, AI is an integral part of marketing strategies in driving customer experience, growth and productivity. Businesses leverage AI in automating repetitive tasks, optimising ad placements and enhancing customer engagement through personalising recommendations and better campaign targeting. The adoption of AI in different parts of the marketing operations is diversified:

- Predictive Analytics: Using historical data to predict future outcomes.
- Computer Vision: Analysing visual content for marketing insights.
- Enhanced Data Analysis: AI can process vast amounts of data quickly and accurately.
- Automation: Streamlining repetitive tasks, such as email marketing and social media posting.
- Personalisation: Tailoring marketing messages to individual customer preferences.
- Customer Segmentation: Identifying distinct customer groups for targeted marketing.
- Content Creation: Generating personalised content based on customer data.
- Customer Service: AI-powered chatbots and virtual assistants.
- Campaign Optimisation: Real-time adjustments to marketing campaigns based on AI insights.
- Improved Decision-Making: Data-driven marketing strategies and planning.

Customer Segmentation in Digital Marketing Analytics

Customer segmentation in digital marketing involves dividing a customer base into distinct groups to uniquely tailor marketing efforts more effectively (Das & Nayak, 2022; Rosário & Raimundo, 2021). Table 9.1 summarises the commonly available types of customer segmentation practices. Notably, technographic segmentation focuses on technology usage behavioural patterns, while firmographic segmentation is used in the context of B2B transactions by clustering the companies or organisations based on their shared attributes. Needs-based segmentation addresses specific customer needs, and social media segmentation looks at social media behaviours such as customer purchasing patterns, engagement patterns and online behaviours. These strategies help businesses create highly personalised marketing campaigns, enhancing customer satisfaction and driving better sales.

AI significantly enhances customer segmentation process by utilising sophisticated algorithms and machine learning techniques to analyse massive datasets with remarkable speed and precision. Traditional segmentation methods often rely on manual data analysis, which is time-consuming and susceptible to human error. In contrast, AI can process and interpret data from multiple sources, such as purchasing history, browsing behaviour, social media interactions, and demographic information, to create highly detailed and accurate customer profiles.

TABLE 9.1

Types of Customer Segmentation Applied for Digital Marketing

Type of Segmentation	Description	Examples
Demographic	Groups customers based on demographic factors.	Age, Gender, Income, Education
Geographic	Segments customers by their geographical location.	Country, Region, City, Climate
Behavioural	Focuses on customer behaviours and patterns.	Purchase History, Brand Loyalty
Psychographic	Delves into psychological aspects of customers.	Lifestyle, Values, Interests
Technographic	Groups customers based on their technology usage and preferences.	Devices Used, Software Preferences
Firmographic	Used in B2B marketing to segment businesses.	Industry, Company Size, Revenue
Needs-Based	Focuses on specific needs and pain points of customers.	Unique Customer Needs, Pain Points
Social Media	Segments customers based on their social media behaviour.	Platforms Used, Engagement Levels

One of the key advantages of AI in performing customer segmentation is its ability to identify complex patterns and correlations in various granularity that might be overlooked by human analysts. The wider contextual window of the data analysed by the AI transcends the typical cognitive capability of a normal human being. For instance, AI can detect subtle behavioural trends and preferences that indicate customer likelihood of purchasing a particular product or responding to a specific marketing campaign. This minute level of insights allows businesses to tailor their marketing strategies very precisely, ensuring that the right message reaches the right audience at the right time.

Moreover, AI-driven customer segmentation is dynamic and adaptive, realistically reflecting the changes in customer behaviours. Traditional segmentation methods often result in static customer groups that may not reflect changes in customer behaviour over time. AI, however, continuously learns and updates its models based on new data, allowing for real-time adjustments to segmentation strategies. This adaptability ensures that businesses can respond promptly to shifts in customer preferences and market conditions, maintaining the relevance and effectiveness of their marketing efforts.

AI also enables hyper-personalisation, which goes beyond traditional segmentation by creating individualised marketing experiences for each customer. By analysing data at a granular level, AI can generate personalised recommendations, offers, and content that resonate better with individual customers. This level of personalisation not only enhances customer experience and satisfaction, but also drives higher conversion rates and revenue.

In summary, AI revolutionises customer segmentation by providing actionable and transformative insights, real-time adaptability, hyper-personalisation and automation. These capabilities enable businesses to create more effective targeted marketing strategies, ultimately leading to improved customer engagement, satisfaction and business performance. As AI technology continues to evolve, its role in customer segmentation is likely to become even more integral, offering new opportunities for progressive and disruptive growth in digital marketing.

AI-based Customer Segmentation Framework

User experience is defined as the creation and synchronisation of aspects that affect users' experience with a particular organisation, shaping their perceptions and behaviour towards the organisation. The aspects include what users can perceive with their five senses while interacting with it. User experience is designed to understand the feelings and emotions that the customers experienced when using the service. Hence, user experience should be carefully crafted for effective advertising in digital marketing website for active user engagement (Lim et al., 2021a; Lim et al., 2021b). To obtain insights on useful activities of the users, customer segmentation is performed on the input data from different types of customer segmentation process, as listed in Table 9.1.

AI-based customer segmentation framework aims to extract and discover the user navigational patterns while the users are interacting with the digital marketing website. AI can automate the segmentation process, reducing the need for manual intervention and freeing up valuable resources for other strategic initiatives. Automation also ensures consistency and accuracy in segmentation, minimising the risk of errors and biases that frequently occur in the manual methods. It also allows businesses to gracefully scale their segmentation efforts, handling large volumes of data and complex segmentation criteria with ease.

Figure 9.1 illustrates the structured flow involved in the AI-based customer segmentation framework. There are four main stages of Input Data, Data Preprocessing, Pattern Discovery and Pattern Analysis (Lim et al., 2021a). The process begins with collecting various types of data, providing a rich foundation for subsequent analysis. Following that, the Data Preprocessing stage prepares the raw data for pattern discovery through steps like data cleaning, transformation, feature engineering, dimensionality reduction, data encoding, and data balancing. These steps ensure the data is accurate, consistent and suitable for pattern discovery. The Pattern Discovery stage then employs various techniques, including clustering, classification, anomaly detection, statistical pattern analysis and time-series analysis, to uncover meaningful patterns within the data. Finally, the Pattern Analysis stage interprets these patterns to gain insights into user characteristics, engagement, journeys, and to forecast future trends. This structured flow ensures that data is systematically processed and analysed, producing actionable insights that can inform decision-making and strategic planning.

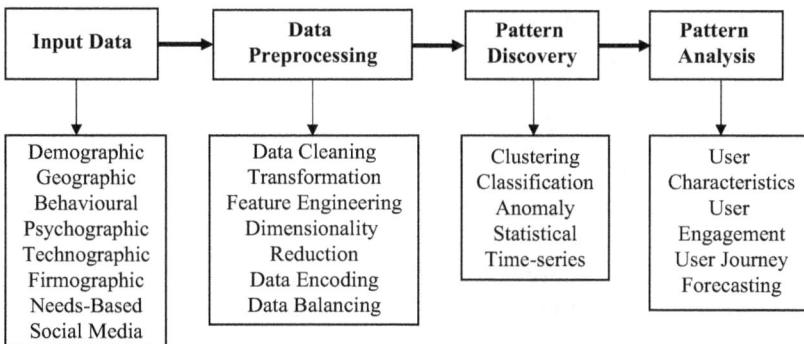

FIGURE 9.1
Customer segmentation framework.

Data Preprocessing

Data preprocessing is a crucial step in converting raw data into a clean and usable format. It is a fundamental step in extracting meaningful insight from data. This process begins with data cleaning, which involves handling missing values, removing duplicates and correcting errors. Missing values can be addressed by imputation methods, such as filling in with the mean, median, or using more sophisticated techniques like k-nearest neighbours and Kalman filter estimation. Removing duplicates ensures that the dataset is free from redundant information while correcting errors involves identifying and fixing inaccuracies in the data.

Next, data transformation is performed to convert the data into a suitable format for analysis. This includes normalisation and standardisation, which scale the data to a uniform range, making it easier to compare different features (Mallikharjuna et al., 2023). Normalisation typically scales the data to a range of 0 to 1, while standardisation transforms the data to have a mean of 0 and a standard deviation of 1. Normalisation is particularly useful when the data features have different scales, ensuring that no single feature dominates the analysis due to its scale. For example, if one feature ranges from 1 to 1000 and another from 0 to 1, normalisation brings them to a comparable scale. Unlike normalisation, standardisation is useful when the data follows a Gaussian or normal distribution. Standardisation helps in stabilising the variance and making the data more comparable across different features. It is particularly beneficial for algorithms that assume normally distributed data, such as linear regression and logistic regression.

Subsequently, feature engineering is carried out to create new features from existing data, leveraging domain knowledge to enhance the predictive power of the dataset. This step can involve creating interaction terms, polynomial features, or aggregating data at different levels. For example, if you have a dataset with date and time information, you can create new features like day of the week, month or hour of the day. These new features can help the model capture patterns that are not immediately obvious from the raw data. Additionally, it is recommended to use suitable behavioural modelling techniques related to the context of the domain knowledge to create new features that express customer behaviours.

Finally, dimensionality reduction and data encoding are applied to simplify the dataset and make it more manageable. By reducing the number of features while retaining the most important or significant information, dimensionality reduction helps in mitigating the curse of dimensionality, leading to better model performance and generalisation. Fewer features mean less computational power and time requirement for training the models, making the process more efficient. This process is essential in handling high-dimensional data, which can be computationally expensive and prone to overfitting for machine learning. Furthermore, dimensionality reduction techniques, such as PCA and t-SNE enhance the visualisation of high-dimensional data in two or three dimensions, making it easier to identify patterns and insights (Charalampidis, 2023).

Since many machine learning algorithms require numerical input, data encoding is the essential process for converting categorical variables into numerical format. Proper encoding helps models learn better by providing meaningful numerical representations of categorical data. Techniques like binary encoding and frequency encoding can help reduce the dimensionality of the dataset, making it more manageable and efficient to process. Common data encoding types include one-hot encoding, label encoding, binary encoding, frequency encoding and target encoding. Table 9.2 describes each of these encoding methods. Each method has its advantages and is chosen based on the specific requirements of the dataset and the machine learning model being used.

Data balancing is a crucial technique to deal with imbalanced datasets where one class significantly outnumbers the others. This imbalance can lead to biased models that perform well on the majority class but poorly on the minority class. Balancing the dataset helps in training models that are not biased towards the majority class, leading to better overall performance and more accurate predictions for the minority class. Metrics such as precision, recall, and F1-score are more reliable when the dataset is balanced, providing a clearer picture of model performance. Models trained on balanced datasets are more likely to be generalized to new, unseen data, as they learn to recognise patterns in both majority and minority classes.

Common data balancing methods include oversampling and undersampling. Oversampling increases the number of instances in the minority class through techniques like SMOTE (Synthetic Minority Over-sampling Technique). Undersampling reduces the number of instances in the majority class to balance the dataset. Hybrid methods combine both oversampling and undersampling to optimise balance. Additionally, cost-sensitive learning adjusts the learning algorithm to give more importance to the minority class. Ensemble methods like Balanced Random Forests and Easy Ensemble use multiple models to improve performance on imbalanced data. These

TABLE 9.2

Types of Encoding Methods

Encoding Type	Encoding Method
One-hot encoding	Creates binary vectors for each category
Label encoding	Assigns unique integers to categories
Binary encoding	Converts categories to binary code
Frequency encoding	Replaces categories with their frequency in the dataset
Target encoding	Uses the mean of the target variable for each category

techniques help create fairer and more accurate models by ensuring that all classes are adequately represented. Together, these preprocessing steps ensure that the data is clean, well-structured and ready for pattern discovery and analysis.

Pattern Discovery

Pattern discovery aims at identifying meaningful patterns, trends and structures within large datasets. This process involves various techniques and algorithms that uncover hidden relationships and insights. One common method in pattern discovery is clustering, which groups similar data points together based on their characteristics or attributes. Clustering algorithms, such as K-means, hierarchical clustering and DBSCAN, are used to identify natural groupings within the data. This can be particularly useful in customer segmentation, where businesses can tailor their marketing efforts to different customer groups based on common behavioural patterns and preferences through unsupervised learning.

Unlike clustering, classification is a supervised learning algorithm. Classification is used when the goal is to predict a predefined categorical outcome based on input features. It is ideal for scenarios where the data can be divided into distinct classes or categories, such as spam detection in emails (spam or not spam), medical diagnosis (disease or no disease) and customer segmentation (high-value or low-value customers). Classification algorithms, like decision trees, support vector machines and neural networks, are employed to learn from labelled training data to make accurate predictions on new, unseen data.

Anomaly pattern represents the rare or unusual data points that differ significantly from the majority of the data. Anomaly pattern detection is widely used in predictive maintenance, fraud detection, network security, and fault detection in industrial systems. By identifying anomalies without the need of labelled data, making them suitable for large-scale server environments where manual monitoring is impractical (Lee et al., 2023). By pinpointing anomalies, organizations can take proactive measures to address potential issues, such as fraudulent transactions or system failures more effectively.

On the other hand, statistical patterns are identified using methods like hypothesis testing, p-value calculation and confidence intervals for validating the significant patterns within data. Statistical pattern is particularly useful in fields like medical research, where identifying statistically significant patterns can lead to new insights and advancements in treatment. For example, hypothesis testing can determine whether a new treatment is more effective than a placebo in clinical trials.

Time-series pattern is extremely useful in discovering the frequent sequences in data, such as trends, seasonal effects and cyclical patterns in customer purchase behaviour over time. This is essential in forecasting and planning, predicting future values based on historical data. Techniques like ARIMA (Auto-Regressive Integrated Moving Average), Generalized Autoregressive Conditional Heteroscedasticity (GARCH), Hidden Markov Model (HMM), Random Forest (RF) and Support Vector Machine (SVM) are commonly used to model and forecast time-series data (Tan et al., 2021). This approach is valuable in various domains like finance, weather forecasting and inventory management, where understanding temporal patterns is key to making informed decisions. Overall, data pattern discovery provides valuable insights that can drive decision-making, optimise operations and enhance strategic planning across various domains.

Pattern Analysis

Pattern analysis is the last stage in customer segmentation framework that involves examining and interpreting patterns discovered within datasets for meaningful insights. Based on the recurring structures, trends or anomalies from pattern discovery, pattern analysis provides a deeper and valuable information on the underlying processes or behaviours related to the domain knowledge. Pattern analysis can interpret the customer segmentation outcomes particularly on interesting user characteristics, user engagement, user journey and by forecasting future purchasing trends or seasonal behaviours.

Another important aspect of pattern analysis is the visualisation process. It helps in interpreting and communicating the patterns comprehensively. Tools like scatter plots, heatmaps and network graphs can illustrate complex relationships and trends in an intuitive manner. Visualisation not only aids in understanding the data but also in presenting findings to stakeholders in a clear and impactful manner. By combining visualisation with pattern analysis, this stage provides a comprehensive approach to uncovering and leveraging insights from data, ultimately supporting informed decision-making and strategic planning.

Understanding user characteristics is fundamental in pattern analysis as it provides detailed insights into the attributes and behaviours of different user segments. By analysing demographic data (such as age, gender, and location), psychographic data (like lifestyle and interests), and behavioural data (including purchase history and website interactions), businesses can identify distinct user groups. This segmentation enables more personalised marketing strategies, product recommendations and customer service, enhancing user satisfaction and loyalty.

User engagement metrics, such as click-through rates, time spent on a site, and interaction frequency, are essential for understanding how users interact with a product or service. For example, user interest and engagement with social media posts are measured by website actions like clicking, viewing, liking, commenting and sharing. These actions reflect the impressions of social media users towards the advertisement posts. Analysing these patterns helps identify content or features most appealing to users, informing decisions on better content creation, feature development and user interface design. High engagement levels often correlate with greater user satisfaction and retention, making it a key area for enhancing overall user satisfaction. Understanding audience behavioural patterns provides businesses with valuable insights, enabling them to design and implement more effective marketing strategies to boost sales (Sakas & Reklitis, 2021).

User journey analysis helps businesses understand customers' experiences throughout the decision-making process by examining the various stages and touchpoints a user goes through (Pantouvakis & Gerou, 2022). This process identifies areas for improvement, optimises the customer experience, and guides effective marketing strategies. In product design, this is known as a "User Journey Map", which documents user interactions and touchpoints with a specific product. In marketing and service design, it is referred to as a "Customer Journey Map", presenting a visual narrative of customer interactions and touchpoints with a brand. Despite the different terms, both approaches are fundamentally similar, emphasising the stages and touchpoints in the customer's interaction with products or services and illustrating the user experience from beginning to end.

Forecasting for customer segmentation involves predicting future customer behaviours and trends by dividing customers into distinct groups based on distinct characteristics. For instance, a clothing retailer might segment customers into young professionals, families and seniors to forecast demand for different styles and sizes, ensuring they stock the right inventory for the season. Similarly, a technology-based company could segment customers into small businesses, large enterprises, and individual consumers to anticipate the unique need for various products and services, allowing them to tailor customised sales packages for their clients. By understanding the unique needs and behaviours of each segment, businesses can make more accurate predictions, optimise inventory, and tailor marketing strategies effectively, ensuring the businesses remain agile and responsive to market changes, driving sustainable growth and competitiveness.

Case Studies and Examples

AI-driven customer segmentation frameworks revolutionise digital marketing analytics by enabling marketers to efficiently identify website engagement patterns from large datasets to enhance traditional marketing models. AI can segment customers based on their online behaviours, such as page views, click-through rates, and time spent on site, allowing marketers to tailor content and offers to specific user groups, effectively increasing engagement and conversion rates. Additionally, AI can work with traditional marketing models to better understand the customer decision-making process across different stages of the customer journey, from awareness to purchase. This integration helps marketers understand and predict customer needs and preferences at each stage, producing more personalised and effective marketing strategies. This section includes real-world case studies that customised the AI-driven customer segmentation framework based on several specific domain knowledges in digital marketing.

Measuring User Engagement of Digital Marketing Websites

User engagement is the part of user experience that measures how attracted the users are to using a certain product or service. The level of user attention while navigating a website is a key factor in determining their engagement level. The involvement level of the users correlates with the interest level and the relevance of the website. This case study customised the AI-driven customer segmentation framework into what is called the Cluster-N-Engage Framework. It measures user engagement based on the clusters of user navigational behaviours on digital marketing websites (Lim et al., 2023b). An attention score is formulated to describe the intensity of user attention on a specific session cluster towards the website based on the user navigational patterns.

The Cluster-N-Engage Framework (Lim et al., 2023b) provides a robust alternative to traditional methods of measuring user engagement. Conventional methods such as questionnaires and interviews are highly subjective because they rely heavily on users' provided opinions, which can be heavily coloured by their interpretations and feelings at the moment, thus affecting data reliability. To address this problem of subjectivity, another conventional method requires physiological measurement devices like cameras and eye trackers to monitor users' movements, these are invasive to the customers because they are being consciously observed in the process. The Cluster-N-Engage Framework overcomes these limitations by offering a more objective and less intrusive way to measure user engagement.

This framework is particularly useful for exploring and recognising the session clusters that capture high user attention in the digital marketing website. User attention is measured by how active and frequent users visit the website. Consequently, users who visit a website actively and frequently are investing more attention on it, leading to good engagement score. This framework is shown to be able to gain customer segmentation insights from the user navigational behaviours on two different types of digital marketing weblogs, demonstrating the pragmatic value of systematic data analytics approach. The key difference between these two weblogs lies in their primary objectives, which affect the patterns of their user interactions. The online roadshow website focuses on engaging users through interactive games and marketing activities, while the e-commerce website is mainly intending to boost product purchases, providing a platform for product recommendations and reviews. The online roadshow requires users to complete marketing tasks to redeem rewards, whereas the e-commerce site is a straightforward purchasing experience.

The online roadshow website (Leow et al., 2023) is a virtual marketing event designed to promote products or services. The primary goal of this website is to engage users through interactive games. These games are embedded with product-specific advertising elements to enhance user engagement with the brand and products. New users must create an account when joining the campaign, and then access a dashboard with six games. Completing all six games allows users to redeem vouchers that they can use to redeem products towards the end of the session. In contrast, the second weblog is an e-commerce website (Chodak et al., 2020). This website is designed to facilitate the purchase of products or services online. Users must register for an account to use the website, after which they can search for products using a list or a search bar. When users decide to purchase a product, they add it to their shopping cart, place an order and make a payment. Additionally, users can recommend products to others and leave reviews after completing their purchases.

During the preprocessing stage, both weblogs are initially cleaned to remove irrelevant entries and to perform necessary data type conversions. Although the data cleaning processes for each weblog differ, they share common steps of removing unnecessary columns and pages before converting them into standard data types. Subsequently, user identification is performed to determine the unique user identity for the entries. For the online roadshow weblog, users are identified using the user ID field, while the IP ID and user agent fields are used in the e-commerce weblog. A web session includes all actions performed by a user from the entry into the website till they exit. Session identification splits user page access into separate sessions using a 30-minute timeout flag. A new session starts if a user: (1) accesses a page for over 30 minutes, (2) accesses the last recorded page, or (3) accesses a logout page. Each web session represents a sequence of navigational paths taken by the user. The pages visited within the same session are compiled into a list, forming a navigational path sequence. To handle the multidimensional nature of the feature set, three-dimensionality reduction techniques – PCA, TSNE and UMAP – are applied to the web session matrices before web session clustering to improve the clustering quality.

To conduct pattern discovery, web session clustering is performed on preprocessed data. The optimal number of clusters is first determined using the Elbow Method with Sum of Squared Error (SSE). Four clustering techniques, such as k-means, k-medoids, bisecting k-means and fuzzy c-means are applied, using Euclidean distance as the similarity measure. The clustering results are evaluated using the Silhouette Index (SI), Davies–Bouldin Index (DBI) and Calinski–Harabasz Index (CHI).

In pattern analysis, four user engagement (UE) metrics of the clusters, namely hourly activeness, hourly traffic, daily activeness and daily traffic are derived from the two commonly used user engagement metrics of the number of clicks and the number of sessions. Based on the UE metrics, the user navigational behaviours can be comprehensively described for every session cluster. Each UE metric provides a different perspective on engagement levels using the quartile formula, offering a clearer understanding of the user interaction patterns for each website. For example, high engagement across all metrics indicates active and frequent website navigation by users in that cluster. Based on these metrics, an Attention Score is introduced to describe the intensity of the user attention of a specific session cluster toward the website. Instead of showing the overall engagement of the website, the Cluster-N-Engage Framework highlights the user attention levels of various session clusters. The framework is adaptable to different website types to measure user engagement accurately.

The Attention Score indicates the user attention level for each session cluster, helping to identify navigational behaviours that contribute to good website engagement. By analysing these scores, organisations can understand how navigational behaviours influences user attention, allowing organisations to pinpoint high-attention behaviours. As capturing user attention is crucial in making a good impression for effective advertising, high attention scores indicate the success of digital marketing website in achieving its goals.

The main objective of the online roadshow is to attract users to engage in playing games to better expose to brand and product information. Product-specific advertising elements are embedded in the games to engage users on the website. Hence, organisations expect high attention scores in session clusters involving games to be successful. In this specific case study, clusters with high attention scores indicated that the online roadshow website was effective in achieving its main objective. In contrast, the e-commerce website aims to attract users who want to find and purchase products. Organisations expect high attention scores in session clusters involving pages with product descriptions and purchasing processes to be successful. Therefore, in this specific case study, the medium to low attention scores on the product purchase page indicated that the website was less effective in achieving its objective. Therefore, the suggested recommendation was for the business owner to enhance the user experience of the various product pages of their e-commerce website to improve their UE metrics.

These case studies demonstrate the customisation of an AI-based customer segmentation framework to measure user engagement across various digital marketing websites. While each stage of the framework follows a similar structure, the specific steps within each stage are tailored to meet the unique requirements of the unique weblog studied.

Leveraging of Traditional Marketing Models

Traditional marketing models like RFM (Recency, Frequency, Monetary) and AIDA (Attention, Interest, Desire, Action) have a long-standing history of being essential tools for understanding user behaviours and mapping the user journey. The RFM Model segments customers based on how recently they made a purchase, how often they make purchases, and how much they spent (Lim et al., 2023a). This segmentation model helps businesses identify their most valuable customers to tailor marketing strategies accordingly. For instance, customers with high recency, frequency and monetary value are considered the best customers and should receive special offers and personalised communication to maintain their loyalty. On the other hand, customers with high recency but low frequency and monetary value might be new and need more encouragement to make repeat purchases.

The AIDA Model outlines the four stages (Attention, Interest, Desire, Action) a consumer goes through before making a purchase (Ikhsana et al., 2022). This model helps marketers design campaigns that guide potential customers through each stage of the buying process. For example, marketers can use eye-catching advertisements to grab attention, provide detailed information to build interest, use testimonials to create desire, and offer clear calls to action to prompt purchase. By integrating the understanding of user behaviours from RFM and the user journey from the AIDA Model into the AI-driven customer segmentation framework, businesses can create highly targeted marketing strategies that move customers through the buying journey effectively, ensuring a more efficient and impactful marketing approach.

Other than using weblog to investigate user behaviours, Wi-Fi advertising has a profound impact on digital marketing by offering a unique and highly targeted approach of getting more intimate with the consumers. When users connect to a Wi-Fi network, businesses can deliver ads based on the user current location and behaviour. Captive portals, which are the login pages users see when they first connecting to a Wi-Fi network, can be used to display interactive ads, promotions, or surveys. This not only captures the user attention but also provides an opportunity for immediate interaction. For instance, in a shopping mall, different ads can be displayed to the users based on their location within different stores or areas. A user in a bookstore might receive ads for upcoming book signings or special promotions on bestsellers. This level of personalisation can enhance the user experience by ensuring that the ads pushed are relevant to the user's immediate context, increasing the likelihood of engagement and higher chances of conversion to sales. Wi-Fi advertising also enhances user engagement. For example, a restaurant might offer a discount code in exchange for completing a short survey. This type of engagement can lead to higher conversion rates when promoting loyalty programmes or special offers, encouraging repeat visits and fostering long-term customer relationships.

The remaining subsections explore the potential of integrating AI with traditional marketing models to better comprehend the customer decision-making process across different stages in the customer journey analysis for Wi-Fi advertising. Leveraging the customer segmentation approach, marketers can assess the engagement levels of customers throughout their journey, offering a comprehensive perspective for measuring campaign effectiveness.

Creating a New Engagement Model – RFI

The RFM Model is a widely used method of behavioural analysis across various industries such as e-commerce, banking and insurance. This model ranks customers based on three quantifiable factors: recency (how recently a customer made a purchase), frequency (how often a customer makes a purchase) and monetary value (how much money a customer spent). By analysing these factors, businesses can segment customers into homogeneous groups and tailor their marketing strategies accordingly. The recency component measures the time since the customer's last interaction or transaction, with a shorter gap indicating a higher likelihood of responding to future promotions. The frequency component of the RFM Model is determined by the total number of transactions a customer has made or the average time between transactions. A higher frequency score indicates greater customer loyalty and stronger product demand, leading to increased repurchases. First-time customers are considered potential targets for follow-up marketing efforts for conversion into regular customers. The monetary component can be assessed in two ways: the average transaction amount over a specified period or the total accumulated transaction amount. The former approach is commonly preferred to reduce collinearity effect between the frequency and monetary components. This component helps businesses to identify whether a customer is a light or heavy spender, influencing their likelihood to respond to new deals and becoming repeat customers.

However, the RFM Model is not suitable for interpreting customer behaviours without monetary involvement, for instance in the context of Wi-Fi advertising. Majority of customer purchasing decisions are influenced by subconscious impressions of advertising. Wi-Fi advertising aims to implant brand and product information into the subconscious mind of the public rather than directly promoting purchases. To leverage the interaction data from the Wi-Fi advertising, the RFM Model is adapted into the RFI (Recency, Frequency, Interest) Model to better reflect the audience engagement behaviours (Lim et al., 2023a). This model aims to discover patterns in audience behaviours in reaction to the advertisements, focusing more on the engagement experience rather than monetary transactions. In the RFI Model, recency is redefined as the duration since the audience was last impressed by an advertisement, with a shorter interval indicating a stronger impression. Frequency measures how often the audience is exposed to the advertisement, and interest represents the level of attraction and impression the audience has towards the advertisement.

The RFI-based framework (Lim et al., 2023a) is particularly useful for segmenting the audience based on their behaviours, providing better insights into their recency, frequency and interest attitude towards the advertisement. More active campaigns generate larger volumes of data, offering a richer dataset for analysis. With a rich dataset, various patterns can be explored, providing insights into audience behaviours that influence the success or failure of a campaign. In this particular case study, the two most active advertising campaigns were selected to investigate audience behavioural patterns.

In the preprocessing stage, data cleaning is first performed by removing unnecessary data columns, dealing with missing values and converting the data type into a suitable format. Next, data transformation is performed by converting raw data into meaningful data based on the RFI Model. The recency, frequency and interest metrics are computed based on individual audience engagement behaviours towards the two most active advertisement campaigns. The recency metric is defined as the time interval between when the audience returns to the Wi-Fi advertising system, with shorter intervals indicating stronger impressions. The frequency metric is defined as the total number of advertisement count recorded for a specific audience in a campaign, with higher occurrences leading to stronger subconscious impressions. Finally, audience clicks on the advertisement webpages indicate interest, and the total view duration is correlated to the overall number of clicks, signifying their interest in the advertisement.

In the pattern discovery stage, clustering is applied to group similar data points together based on their common characteristics or attributes. Clustering algorithms such as K-means, agglomerative hierarchical, and Gaussian Mixture Model are used to identify natural groupings within the data. To identify the best-performing clustering algorithm, performance evaluation metrics like the silhouette score, CH Index and Dunn Index are used for comparison.

During pattern analysis, the RFI Model was used to analyse audience behaviour in response to advertising. To provide a comprehensive view of the audience behaviour, a dynamic range is introduced by dividing the RFI values into five quartiles. This dynamic nature of measurement infers that the actual ranges vary depending on the RFI values of different campaigns. The strongly engaged behavioural group consists of individuals who exhibit the shortest time gap since their last engagement and the highest frequency of engagement, indicating a strong interest in the advertisement. This group is more likely to revisit the Wi-Fi advertisement service within a short period of about 3 days, resulting in a more lasting impression of the content and greater enjoyment watching the advertisements. Conversely, the weakly engaged behavioural group includes one-time users who watched the advertisement only once. This behaviour is characterised by the longest time gap since their last engagement and a low-frequency engagement. This group exhibits minimal to no interest in the advertisement, with engagement time of 0 to half a second.

Using clustering and the dynamic characteristic range table, audience behavioural patterns were successfully interpreted. Consequently, it can be inferred that the new RFI Model can be broadly applied to different Wi-Fi advertising attributes, demonstrating varying advertising effectiveness in terms of audience engagement. Furthermore, the RFI values of each segmented audience group were translated into meaningful characteristics using the dynamic characteristic range table. Therefore, it can be concluded that the dynamic characteristic range table offers a viable approach for audience behavioural segmentation based on their respective RFI values. With insights into audience behavioural patterns, businesses can better understand their customer engagement to leverage these characteristics to design and implement more effective marketing strategies for boosting sales.

Analysing User Journey with AIDA Model

User journey analysis and the AIDA Model serve different but complementary purposes in understanding and optimising customer experiences (Wong et al., 2024). User journey analysis focuses on examining the process in which a user typically goes through when interacting with a product or service. This includes all stages and touchpoints, from initial awareness of the brand, product or service to post-purchase behaviours. The goal is to identify areas for improvement, to optimise the engagement experience, and to customise highly personalised marketing strategies for every unique user. It provides a detailed, holistic view of the customer's interactions and experiences, allowing businesses to pinpoint specific pain points and opportunities for enhancement.

On the other hand, the AIDA Model, which was introduced in 1898, is a communication theory that breaks down the customer decision-making process into four separate stages: Attention, Interest, Desire and Action. It is primarily used to evaluate the effectiveness of marketing communications to better formulate strategies that facilitate customers through these stages. The AIDA Model focuses on the cognitive and emotional journey of the customers, explaining how they move from being unaware of a product to ultimately making a purchase decision.

User journey analysis and the AIDA Model can work together effectively. The AIDA Model provides a structured framework for understanding the psychological and behavioural stages customers go through, which can be mapped onto the broader user journey. By integrating the AIDA stages into user journey analysis, businesses can gain deeper insights into how marketing efforts influence customer behaviours at each touchpoint. This combined approach allows for a more comprehensive understanding of the customer experience, enabling businesses to tailor their strategies to better meet customer needs to more effectively drive conversions.

In this case study, the AIDA-based framework (Wong et al., 2024) highlights the benefits of using an AIDA-based segmentation approach to understand the user journeys within a Wi-Fi advertising system. This approach resembles an AI-driven customer segmentation framework that is customised into four key elements. The Data Pre-processing involves preparing the data for analysis using AIDA modelling, where data is structured according to the AIDA stages (Attention, Interest, Desire, Action). This helps in organising the data in a way that reflects the different stages of the customer journey. In Pattern Discovery with Clustering, clustering techniques are used to identify patterns within the data. By grouping users based on similar behaviours and characteristics, businesses can uncover distinct segments within the user base. Once patterns are discovered, the Pattern Analysis with User Journey Mapping interprets these patterns in the context of the user journey. This involves mapping out the user journeys for each segment identified in the clustering process. In doing so, businesses can gain insights into the specific paths users take, the touchpoints they interact with, and the stages they go through from initial product awareness to the final purchasing action. By integrating these elements, the AIDA-based framework provides a comprehensive approach to understanding how different groups of users interact with the Wi-Fi advertising system.

The first step in analysing the Wi-Fi advertising dataset involves data preprocessing, which includes three primary tasks: data cleaning, data transformation and data modelling. Data cleaning removes redundant columns, handles missing values, and renames columns. Data transformation converts data types, while data anonymisation techniques ensure privacy by masking confidential information. This process safeguards sensitive information while performing meaningful analysis. Data modelling calculates metrics specific to Attention, Interest, Desire and Action stages by assessing user behaviours in relation to each advertising campaign.

The AIDA Model begins with the Attention Stage, where users first encounter the campaign while attempting to connect to the Wi-Fi network. A higher number of views indicates greater attention, as users are initially presented with the campaign, capturing their focus and creating awareness about the brand or product. This initial exposure helps establish the brand or product in the users' consciousness, reflecting the Attention Stage of the AIDA Model. Next is the Interest Stage, where users show curiosity by watching the advertisement beyond the mandatory watch time. This interest metric reflects users who are drawn to the campaign and invest additional time beyond the required viewing period. By extending their view duration, users demonstrate a willingness to explore the content further, indicating a growing interest in the campaign's offerings.

This is followed by the Desire Stage, where users are convinced that the product or service will fulfil their needs, leading to a strong motivation and desire to acquire it. This stage demonstrates the users transforming interest into desire, as users may repeatedly watch the campaign beyond the mandatory view time, indicating a stronger motivation and desire for the advertised product or service. A higher ratio signifies a greater level of motivation and desire. Finally, the Action Stage is where users take concrete steps towards acquiring the product or service, such as visiting the advertisement website. A higher count of visits suggests a substantial level of action, showing the campaign's effectiveness in motivating users to take the final step. This stage aligns with the objective of advertising in the campaigns, demonstrating the campaign's success in driving user actions.

In this case study, instead of analysing the user journey across all advertisement campaigns collectively, clustering algorithms such as K-Means, BIRCH and Gaussian Mixture Model were applied to explore distinct patterns within each specific campaign. Specifically, the clustering process was conducted after generating the AIDA scores. Using transformed data ensured that it was appropriately prepared and structured, allowing the clustering algorithms to capture relevant patterns and user behaviours from the Wi-Fi advertising system. This approach provides more granular insights into how different user segments responded to each campaign.

Once the dataset was clustered, various evaluation methods like the Elbow Method, Silhouette Score, CH Index and Dunn Index were used to assess the effectiveness of each clustering algorithm. These methods help identify the optimal number of clusters and the best algorithm for different datasets. The Elbow Method finds the point where adding more clusters does not significantly improve the model, while the Silhouette Score measures how well an object fits within its cluster compared to others. The CH Index and Dunn Index further evaluate clustering quality. Different algorithms often produce varying results on the same dataset due to their unique approaches, highlighting the need for multiple evaluation methods. The optimal number of clusters for each algorithm was determined by their scores and frequency of occurrence, ensuring accurate and meaningful data segmentation.

The AIDA Model was employed to understand the user journey of each segment and identify how users navigate through each campaign. A dynamic characteristic quartiles table was created to provide a clearer understanding of user behaviours. This table divides the AIDA scores into four quartiles for each campaign, with five characteristics defined according to different quartiles. The upper limit of each quartile is determined by 25%, 50% and 75%, with initial characteristics set at zero and subsequent segments represented as low, moderate, high and highest. By using the dynamic quartiles table, the actual range may vary between campaigns due to differences in data distribution within the AIDA stages. The characteristics of each user segment in both campaigns are interpreted to highlight the values of the least favourable and most favourable clusters. Multiple user journey maps are provided in Rosário & Raimundo (2021) to demonstrate various behaviours from user groups extracted based on practical applications in real-world Wi-Fi advertising systems.

The implications of these findings for businesses or marketers are significant. They offer better insights into how different user segments interact with campaigns and how marketing strategies can be refined to meet the needs and behaviours of each segment. For example, weakly engaged user groups show low engagement across all AIDA stages. Marketers can increase engagement by redesigning campaigns to be more visually appealing, especially at the entry point. Another example shows user groups with moderate Attention, highest Interest and Desire, but low Action. Marketers can enhance conversion rates by highlighting exclusive offers or additional content to motivate user's action. These user journeys provide deeper insights into each user group, allowing marketers to design and implement more effective strategies to boost campaign performance.

Overall, the customer segmentation framework provides a powerful tool for digital marketers to reach and engage with their audience in a highly targeted and personalised manner. By leveraging the data collected through Wi-Fi networks, businesses can create more effective marketing campaigns that resonate with users and drive impactful results.

Conclusion

The integration of AI with digital marketing analytics has significantly transformed the landscape of consumer behaviour understanding and marketing strategy optimisation. By leveraging AI-driven insights, marketers can now engage customers more effectively and enhance campaign performance. This chapter has demonstrated the profound impact of AI on digital marketing through three customised AI-driven customer segmentation frameworks. The first framework highlights the importance of customer segmentation in digital marketing analytics, showcasing how AI can identify website engagement patterns from different digital marketing websites, thereby enabling marketers to tailor their strategies more precisely. The second and third frameworks explored the integration of AI with traditional marketing models to better understand the customer engagement level and decision-making process across different stages of the customer journey. This comprehensive approach allows marketers to assess customer engagement levels throughout their journey, providing valuable insights for measuring campaign effectiveness.

The rapid growth of the Web has led to increased interactions between Internet users and various digital marketing websites. User experience, which encompasses the creation and synchronisation of elements that influence users' perceptions and behaviours, plays a crucial role in shaping these interactions. By understanding the feelings and emotions customers experience while using a service, marketers can design more effective advertising strategies that foster active user engagement. The structured flow of AI-based customer segmentation frameworks automates the segmentation process, ensuring the understanding the feelings and emotions of customers experience. These frameworks involve four main stages: Input Data, Data Preprocessing, Pattern Discovery, and Pattern Analysis. This systematic approach begins with collecting diverse data types to provide a comprehensive view of the subject under study. The Data Preprocessing Stage prepares the raw data for pattern discovery through various steps, ensuring its accuracy and consistency. The Pattern Discovery Stage employs techniques such as clustering, classification, anomaly detection and time-series analysis to uncover meaningful patterns within the data. Finally, the Pattern Analysis Stage interprets these patterns to gain insights into user characteristics, engagement, journeys and future trends. This structured process ensures that data is thoroughly analysed, leading to actionable insights that inform decision-making and strategic planning.

In conclusion, AI-driven customer segmentation frameworks have revolutionised digital marketing analytics by enabling marketers to efficiently identify website engagement patterns and enhance traditional marketing models. By segmenting customers based on their online behaviours, marketers can tailor content and offers to specific user groups, thereby increasing engagement and conversion rates. Additionally, integrating AI with traditional marketing models allows for a deeper understanding of the customer decision-making process across different stages of the customer journey. This integration helps marketers predict customer needs and preferences, leading to more personalised and effective marketing strategies. The real-world case studies presented in this chapter demonstrate the transformative potential of AI-driven customer segmentation frameworks in various digital marketing domains, highlighting their ability to drive significant improvements in customer engagement and campaign effectiveness.

References

Charalampidis, D. (2023). Visualizing population structures by multidimensional scaling of smoothed PCA-transformed data. *IEEE Access*, *11*, 13594–13604. http://doi.org/10.1109/ACCESS.2023.3243573

Chodak, G., Suchacka, G., & Chawla, Y. (2020). HTTP-level e-commerce data based on server access logs for an online store. *Computer networks*, *183*, 107589. http://doi.org/10.1016/j.comnet.2020.107589

Cioppi, M., Curina, I., Francioni, B., & Savelli, E. (2023). Digital transformation and marketing: a systematic and thematic literature review. *Italian Journal of Marketing*, 2023(2), 207–288. http://doi.org/10.1007/s43039-023-00067-2

Das, S., & Nayak, J. (2022). Customer segmentation via data mining techniques: state-of-the-art review. *Computational Intelligence in Data Mining: Proceedings of ICCIDM 2021*, 489–507. http://doi.org/10.1007/978-981-16-9447-9_38

Hicham, N., Nassera, H., & Karim, S. (2023). Strategic framework for leveraging artificial intelligence in future marketing decision-making. *Journal of Intelligent Management Decision*, 2(3), 139–150. http://doi.org/10.56578/jimd020304

Ikhsana, M. C., Astutib, V. S., Wijayac, A. A., Finuliyahd, F., & Qulube, A. M. (2022). Does paid promote influences user frequency to purchase? An analysis using aida dimension. *Airlangga Journal of Innovation Management*, 3(2), 114–122. https://doi.org/10.20473/ajim.v3i2.20460

Lee, T. W., Ong, L. Y., & Leow, M. C. (2023). Experimental study using unsupervised anomaly detection on server resources monitoring. In *2023 11th International Conference on Information and Communication Technology (ICoICT)* (pp. 517–522). IEEE. http://doi.org/10.1109/ICoICT58202.2023.10262795

Leow, K. R., Leow, M. C., & Ong, L. Y. (2023). A new big data processing framework for the online roadshow. *Big Data and Cognitive Computing*, 7(3), 123. http://doi.org/10.3390/bdcc7030123

Lim, S. T., Ong, L. Y., & Leow, M. C. (2023a). New RFI model for behavioral audience segmentation in Wi-Fi advertising system. *Future Internet*, 15(11), 351. http://doi.org/10.3390/fi15110351

Lim, Z. Y., Ong, L. Y., & Leow, M. C. (2021a). A review on clustering techniques: Creating better user experience for online roadshow. *Future Internet*, 13(9), 233. http://doi.org/10.3390/fi13090233

Lim, Z. Y., Ong, L. Y., & Leow, M. C. (2021b). Experimental study on predictive modeling in the gamification marketing application. In *Advances and Trends in Artificial Intelligence. From Theory to Practice: 34th International Conference on Industrial, Engineering and Other Applications of Applied Intelligent Systems, IEA/AIE 2021, Kuala Lumpur, Malaysia, July 26–29, 2021, Proceedings, Part II 34* (pp. 379–390). Springer International Publishing. http://doi.org/10.1007/978-3-030-79463-7_32

Lim, Z. Y., Ong, L. Y., & Leow, M. C. (2023b). Cluster-n-engage: A new framework for measuring user engagement of website with user navigational behavior. *IEEE Access*. http://doi.org/10.1109/ACCESS.2023.3322958

Mallikharjuna Rao, K., Saikrishna, G., & Supriya, K. (2023). Data preprocessing techniques: emergence and selection towards machine learning models-a practical review using HPA dataset. *Multimedia Tools and Applications*, 82(24), 37177–37196. http://doi.org/10.1007/s11042-023-15087-5

Pantouvakis, A., & Gerou, A. (2022). The theoretical and practical evolution of customer journey and its significance in services sustainability. *Sustainability*, 14(15), 9610. http://doi.org/10.3390/su14159610

Rosário, A., & Raimundo, R. (2021). Consumer marketing strategy and E-commerce in the last decade: a literature review. *Journal of theoretical and applied electronic commerce research*, 16(7), 3003–3024. http://doi.org/10.3390/jtaer16070164

Sakas, D. P., & Reklitis, D. P. (2021). The impact of organic traffic of crowdsourcing platforms on airlines' website traffic and user engagement. *Sustainability*, 13(16), 8850. http://doi.org/10.3390/su13168850

Tan, Y. F., Ong, L. Y., Leow, M. C., & Goh, Y. X. (2021). Exploring time-series forecasting models for dynamic pricing in digital signage advertising. *Future Internet*, *13*(10), 241. http://doi.org/10.3390/fi13100241

Wong, S. Y., Ong, L. Y., & Leow, M. C. (2024). AIDA-based customer segmentation with user journey analysis for Wi-Fi advertising system. *IEEE Access*. http://doi.org/10.1109/ACCESS.2024.3424833

Ziakis, C., & Vlachopoulou, M. (2023). Artificial intelligence in digital marketing: Insights from a comprehensive review. *Information*, *14*(12), 664. http://doi.org/10.3390/info14120664

10

Churn Prediction Using Machine Learning in Telecommunication Industry

Lim Jing Yee

Introduction

In recent years, the telecommunications (telco or telecom) industry has become more competitive, and customer churn is one of the most important areas of focus as it represents a potential revenue loss, customer loyalty, and also reflects on business growth. Thus, they are continuously striving to understand the reasons why their customers leave and how they can be convinced to continue their subscriptions. The action of retaining an existing customer is not only more cost-effective than acquiring a new one, but it also really helps in raising long-term customer loyalty and maintaining their brand image over the year. The retention of existing customers has become more difficult as customers in this fast-paced, developed era have a wide range of choices and can easily switch their subscriptions to another company whenever they feel dissatisfied with current services. Therefore, focusing on churn prediction becomes a key for a company to avoid or prevent losing customers, as they can alert when there is a customer with a higher potential risk of churn.

An effective churn prediction model is able to help companies build and implement successful retention strategies; it is not just a powerful tool for predicting customer behaviour. This model can directly aid companies in decreasing their customers' turnover rate and boosting their business growth. In the past, churn prediction models were widely developed using traditional machine learning (ML) techniques, and they have also shown their effectiveness in predicting churn. The main logic behind these models is quite straightforward. By examining a set of historical data, such as how frequently a customer subscribed to their services, their payment or transaction history, and any previous interactions with the company, these models will then try to find a pattern through the datasets that alerts the company that there is a customer likely to end their subscriptions with the company.

DOI: 10.1201/9781003509196-10

However, as customer interaction data increases over time, the explosion of data directly increases the complexity of the dataset. Traditional models are then facing challenges in handling complex data and also struggling to capture the intrinsic patterns within these data. This may lead to a decrease in the efficiency and accuracy of using traditional models in churn prediction. At this moment, the rise of deep learning (DL) techniques has become a game changer in this field, which can overcome most of the limitations of traditional approaches. Deep learning techniques are able to process large amounts of complex data and capture sequential and temporal patterns from a bunch of customers' interactions, then make higher accuracy predictions on churn according to their learning.

Therefore, it is never an easy task to develop an effective yet efficient churn prediction model; most researchers have spent years of effort on this task. Starting by researching all the existing churn prediction models, techniques and approaches, they choose the best dataset for their experiment. The selected dataset needs to go through stages of data preprocessing to make sure models are able to digest the data well, followed by all the stages of developing a stable prediction model. The main contribution of this study is that it provides a comprehensive review of the concept of customer churn and churn prediction, deep learning technique and its approaches to churn prediction and some comparisons with machine learning models. The research gaps and future directions throughout the studies will be discussed. Furthermore, the overall flow of churn prediction using deep learning model, most selected Telco dataset for churn prediction and the performance metrics will also be reviewed in this study.

What is Customer Churn and Churn Prediction?

Customer churn, commonly known as customer attrition, is a condition when a customer cancels subscribing to a service from a company over some time. This makes it a significant metric for industries especially in highly competitive markets as it will negatively impact the company's overall growth. It is not only customers who cancel their subscriptions or close their accounts will be categorised as churners, those who significantly minimise their engagement or spending with a company's service can also be counted as churners.

Churn can be categorised into two types:

a. Voluntary Churn

Voluntary churn happens when customers decide to end their relationship with a company, usually caused by dissatisfaction with the service provided by the company. This leads customers to find better options from another company that can offer them better quality products or more suitable features. For some special cases, customers might choose to churn just because they are no longer using the service, for example when their requirement to a specific service offer has been changed or they choose another service provided by another competitor which offers them with better packages. There are few other factors that might lead to voluntary churn such as company providing poor customer services, new product with less innovation or their competitor offering lower price options for the same services. In short, business should consistently improve their products to reach customer's expectations in order to retain their loyalty because voluntary churn directly reflects the will of customers selection between competitive markets.

b. Involuntary Churn

Involuntary churn typically occurs due to external factors such as credit card expiration, payment issues or failed transactions which are beyond customer's control or intention. These external factors may cause the cancellation of the service subscription. Besides, technical issues such as the deactivation of customer accounts or the failure to renew on time could be the reason for involuntary churn. For these special cases, customers might still be interested in continuing their subscription but they are unable to resume it because of technical issues. Hence, company can take preventive measures to manage involuntary churn by handling these technical issues such as by providing reminders or alerts before the expiration of service subscriptions or payment methods.

Churn prediction is an approach that applies data analysis and modelling techniques to forecast which customers are the high-risk churners in the near future. Churn prediction model can capture the pattern that represents a high likelihood of churn by analysing historical customer data such as interaction history, payment method, demographics and other relevant features. These insights can help businesses to identify potential churners and to focus on applying target strategies on them.

In a highly competitive industry, retaining customers becomes an essential topic for sustainable growth for every business, and this makes customer churn a critical issue for them. Churn prediction enables companies to prevent losing customers by taking proactive measures and implementing targeted retention strategies when they are identified as at-risk customers. In short, businesses can significantly reduce customer churn rates through churn prediction model.

Importance of Churn Prediction

- Valuable Customers Retention

  Retaining existing valuable customers is important for a business' sustainability, because acquiring new customers usually has a higher cost than retaining the existing ones. By applying churn prediction, businesses are able to identify customers with higher potential to leave which allows them to put efforts on keeping the high-value customers who contribute more to long-term profitability. Companies can reduce churn and also build customer loyalty by using targeted strategies such as enhancing customer services and providing special promotions and personalised offers. These methods can significantly increase customer satisfaction towards the products or services they are currently subscribing, and this directly helps the company to retain their revenue. Customer satisfaction can lead to long-term engagement with companies and reduce the cost of acquiring new customers.

- Marketing and Sales Efforts Optimisation

  Churn prediction enables companies to optimise the allocation of their marketing and sales resources through identifying high-risk churners. This allows companies to spend their marketing budgets efficiently by focusing on the potential churners who need more attention to stay engaged with companies. With churn prediction, businesses can reduce extra spending on customers who are unlikely to churn and directly increase the effectiveness of their campaigns. Besides, by optimising the resources, overall return on investment can be boosted and it also allows companies to engage more with the customers who need more focus. This can directly improve conversion rates and also customer retention.

- Improve Customer Experience

  Churn prediction model can provide useful insights into the issues that are causing a customer to be dissatisfied with the companies, such as lack of product features, poor customer service and unmet requirements. Businesses can identify these issues in the early stage and handle them with proactive measures which helps them to improve overall customer experience, for example, they can redefine their customer service processes or train their sales team on servicing customers. This step not only helps the company to prevent customer churn but also builds stronger relationships with their customer, directly increasing their satisfaction and loyalty towards the company.

- Driving Services and Products Improvements

  Insights from churn prediction can highlight aspects of a company's product that cause customer churn. It enables businesses to prioritise improvements to the product's features that align with their customer expectations. By focusing on enhancing products, companies can retain existing customers and attract new customers from competitors due to the product's innovation. This continuous improvement cycle can help companies to reduce churn and increase customer satisfaction while staying competitive in the market.

- Financial Planning and Forecasting Enhancement

  As a high churn rate can have a huge impact on company profitability and affect the cash flow, managing churn becomes essential to every company. Companies can predict their future revenue trends more precisely by understanding the factors that cause churn and making financial decisions accordingly. Company can improve their financial forecast, maintain consistent revenue growth and also allocate their resources more accurately by stabilising customer retention. Therefore, good churn management can help a company create a more predictable and stable financial environment which can ensure better long-term planning and resource optimisation.

Overview of Deep Learning

Deep learning (DL) is a specialised subset of machine learning which consists of a structure that mimics human brains through deep neural networks (DNNs). It is composed of interconnected layers of neurons, and these networks automatically learn and extract features from raw data in the datasets. The advantages of this structure are that it can eliminate the need for manual feature selection or feature engineering like traditional machine learning methods. It has changed the field of Artificial Intelligence with its ability to learn through complex data and then make precise predictions or decisions based on them. Deep learning model can identify the underlying patterns in a huge dataset by adjusting its neuron connections through backpropagation and gradient descent. Through these functions, deep learning models can achieve highly accurate prediction results. Its complex architectures like Convolutional Neural Networks (CNNs), Transformer models and Recurrent Neural Networks (RNNs) have revolutionised various fields such as natural language processing and computer vision. With these architectures, tasks such as image recognition, object detection and speech recognition have gained huge advancements, especially in industries like healthcare, finance and autonomous systems. However, deep learning also faces challenges, such as requiring high computational costs, need for large datasets for training and the difficulties in model interpretability, despite its scalability due to advancements in computational power.

In the below section, each key component in deep learning will be introduced and explained.

i. Neural Networks

It is inspired by the structure and function of human brain which consists of a large number of interconnected processing units that work together to solve problems. The aim of neural networks is to replicate how humans learn by adjusting the hyper-parameters and processing the input data to maximise the prediction results. Each neuron inside neural networks will receive an input signal and then process it with an activation function. After finishing processing, it will then send an output to the next layer. Neurons are organised in neural networks layer in a sequence of: an input layer, one or more hidden layers and then followed by an output layer. In between the connection of neurons, there are weights that are tuned during the training phase. For better learning and fitting of the model to the complex data, biases will be responsible for shifting the activation function.

ii. Layers in Neural Networks

The first layer in neural networks is called input layer, which receives the raw input data, such as, in a churn prediction scenario, customer attributes such as age, subscription plan and transaction history will be sent into the input layer as raw data. The raw data will then be processed in the hidden layers, which are the layers located in between the input and output layers and where the majority of the computations will occur. In these layers, each hidden layer will capture different patterns in the data allowing the network to learn the complex representation from the dataset. There are three types of hidden layers: Fully Connected Layer (Dense), Convolutional Layer and Recurrent Layer. The last layer will be the output layer, where the network's output is produced.

iii. Activation Functions

Activation functions enable a network to learn complex data by introducing non-linearity into the network through the neuron's outputs. Neural networks can only learn linear mappings if the activation function is not applied to it. There are three most commonly used activation functions, such as ReLU (Rectified Linear Unit), Sigmoid and Tanh. ReLU can mitigate the gradient vanishing problem and help networks train faster, while Sigmoid is commonly used in binary classification problems. Tanh offers better gradient flow than Sigmoid but still suffers from saturation issues.

iv. Backpropagation

Backpropagation operates by calculating the gradient of the loss function with respect to each weight in the networks, and this process allows the model to learn and iteratively adjust its weights. This minimises the error between the predicted and actual outputs. There are two key phases in backpropagation:

1. Forward Pass: In this phase, input data will pass through each layer of the network to compute the predicted output. The weight and bias remain unchanged as it processes the input.

2. Backward Pass: Backward pass will then compute the gradients by propagating the error from the output layer to the input layer after calculating the prediction. The weights are updated based on these gradients through an optimisation algorithm to reduce error.

This process will repeat iteratively until the model reaches a satisfactory level of accuracy or when the loss function starts to converge. The aim is to optimise the performance of the network by minimising the differences between the true value and the predicted results.

v. Optimisation Algorithms

This function is applied to minimise the loss function which is used to measure how well the model's predicted value matches with the actual value. Examples of the optimisation algorithms are Stochastic Gradient Descent (SGD) and Adam (Adaptive Moment Estimation) where SGD helps in faster convergence and Adam can adapt learning rates for each parameter.

vi. Loss Functions

Loss functions are used to calculate the difference between the actual targeted value and the predicted output. It is important to select a suitable loss function while training a neural network. The commonly used loss functions include Mean Squared Error (MSE) which measures the squared difference between predicted and actual values and Cross-Entropy Loss which is usually used for classification tasks in deep learning. For Cross-Entropy Loss function, it measures the difference between the actual probability and the predicted probability distribution.

vii. Regularisation Techniques

Regularisation techniques are used to prevent overfitting of the training model where the model can only perform well on training data. Examples of the regularisation techniques are dropout and L1/L2 regularisation. Dropout layer can randomly drop neurons during the training phase to prevent the network from being too reliant on specific paths while L1/L2 regularisation will add a penalty to the loss function based on the weights' magnitude.

viii. Batch normalisation

Batch normalisation is used to improve the speed, stability of neural networks and performance of the model as it can normalise the input data for each layer. This function helps in fastening the training process and makes the deep networks more stable.

ix. Learning Rate Schedulers

Learning rate schedulers are used to improve model convergence by adjusting the learning rate during training. A low learning rate can result in a long period training process while a high learning rate can miss the optimal point. Examples of learning rate schedulers are step decay which works to reduce the learning rate by a factor after a specific number of epochs and exponential decay which works to reduce the learning rate exponentially based on the epoch number.

Related Studies in Churn Prediction

In churn prediction for the telecommunication industry, there are two categories of methods that have been widely explored and investigated by researchers to capture the data patterns in customer behaviour in order to make an accurate prediction of the retention of customers, which are Machine Learning (ML) and Deep Learning (DL). In this section, several previous studies investigating ML and DL models in churn prediction by researchers will be discussed.

- Machine learning approaches

  In Bhuse et al. (2020), the author explored various ML techniques for telco customer churn prediction, including Random Forest (RF) and SVM method. By using an open-source telecom churn dataset, RF achieved 90.96% accuracy before optimisation and 91.26% after using grid search tuning. The author applied different hyperparameter optimisation techniques and attribute combinations in model enhancement stage. In another work, Agarwal et al. (2022) applied Support Vector Machine (SVM) and Naïve Bayes (NB) methods for churn prediction. NB performed better than the existing method – Logistic Regression (LR) and SVM, with an accuracy of 84.75% on imbalanced dataset and 91.95% on a balanced dataset. The author suggested combining other ML algorithms such as Light Gradient Boosting Machine (LGBM) with boosting techniques to improve overall accuracy.

For ensemble ML models, Yu and Weng. (2022) evaluated multiple ML models including LR, SVM, RF, LGBM and AdaBoost, Gradient Boosting Decision Tree (GBDT), XGBoost, and CatBoost. LGBM outperformed others with an AUC of 85% and 81% accuracy using the IBM Watson Dataset with 7043 instances and 21 features. The authors suggested applying grid search and Bayesian optimisation for model tuning. Patel and Kumar. (2023) proposed XGBoost which achieved 94% of accuracy. It is recommended for use in churn prediction because of its superior prediction performance.

For feature engineering and model optimisation, Patel and Kumar. (2023) reviewed several ML techniques such as SVM, ensemble methods, Genetic Algorithms and Generalised Additive Models (GAMs). The performance matrices used were Accuracy, Area Under the Curve (AUC), Sensitivity and Specificity which are often used in churn prediction research. In Qutub et al. (2021), the author explored various ML models and ensemble methods using IBM HR analytics datasets. Logistic regression achieved the best prediction result of 88.43% accuracy and 85.9% AUC-ROC. The authors provided complete insights into both customer churn prediction and employee attrition.

- Deep learning approaches

Deep learning architectures started to be involved in the investigation of researchers in the field of churn prediction. Throughout the studies, the DL models selected by researchers consist of four types, which are Convolutional Neural Networks, Artificial Neural Networks, Long Short-Term Memory, and also Transfer Learning. The proposed DL models achieved overall good performance in predicting potential churners and also overcame the problem of handling complex datasets in most of the Telco industry's datasets. Among the previous studies, the most applied DL model is the CNN model for churn prediction. In the work of Mishra and Reddy. (2017); Umayaparvathi and Iyakutti, n.d.; Saha et al. (2024); Khattak et al. (2023); De Caigny et al. (2020), researchers chose CNN as their DL churn prediction model and compared the performance of the model with other ML techniques. The authors of Mishra and Reddy. (2017) utilised a CNN on the CrowdAnalytix dataset, achieving an accuracy of 86.65%, precision of 91.08% and 93.08% of recall, while in the study of Umayaparvathi and Iyakutti, n.d., the author developed three deep neural networks for churn prediction modified from CNN using two Telco datasets, CrowdAnalytix and Cell2Cell. The experimental results showed the DL model performed as well as traditional models – RF and DT, without using any manual feature selection. The proposed models are LFNN, SFNN and CNN which achieved an accuracy of 93.1%, 91.24% and 71.66%, respectively.

Saha et al. (2024) proposed a ChurnNet model with CNN techniques and selected three public datasets in model evaluation. The best result achieved was an accuracy of 97.52% and F1-Score of 97.81% in Churn-data-UCI dataset. Data imbalance was tackled using different variations of the Synthetic Minority Oversampling Technique (SMOTE). Besides, in the work of Khattak et al. (2023), the author developed a composite DL model (Bi-Long Short Term Memory-CNN) on the IBM Watson dataset, achieving an accuracy of 81%, precision of 66% and recall of 64%, and noted the difficulties of model performance tuning in such complex data. Seymen et al. (2023) showed that by comparing DL methods with ML methods, DL models, specifically CNN and ANN, can achieve better prediction with an accuracy of 97.62% using CNN and 96% for ANN. In 2021, this author also proposed a churn prediction model using ANN (Seymen et al., 2021), performance achieved is 91% accuracy, 92.1% recall and 93.5% precision. De Caigny et al. (2020) proposed a novel DL approach using CNN which experts in data pattern extraction in unstructured data. The model achieved 6.868 Time-Dependent Loss (TDL) and an AUC of 89.87% using a real-life dataset provided by a European financial service provider.

For the studies of Transfer Learning (TL) as a DL churn model, Ahmed et al. (n.d.) employed TL with a Genetic Programming-Adaboost (GP-Adaboost) ensemble classifier which achieved 75.4% accuracy on CrowdAnalytix dataset, showcasing the ability of Transfer Learning in churn prediction when dealing with limited labelled data. In Khan et al. (2019), an ANN churn model was proposed to predict potential churn in a telco dataset from Pakistan, which achieved 59% of Accuracy in prediction performance. Gore et al. (2023) developed an ANN-based prediction model using a Multilayer Perceptron on the IBM Watson dataset and successfully achieved 94% accuracy compared to the Decision Tree model (92%). The author applied the SMOTE method to tackle the data imbalance problem during the experiment.

Limitation of ML and DL in Churn Prediction

Limitation of Machine Learning Techniques

Even though traditional machine learning techniques have been widely applied in churn prediction, there are several limitations in performing prediction of customer churn being pointed out in the previous studies. Each limitation will be listed in the following paragraphs:

- Handling Imbalanced Datasets in Churn Prediction

  One of the major challenges in applying ML models in churn prediction is the data imbalance problem in most real-world datasets. Usually in churn prediction, the number of customers that are classified as churn is lower than those classified as non-churn which causes churners becoming the minority class compared to non-churn. This can lead to poor performance of the model when predicting a minority class of churners (Gore et al. 2023). This results in machine learning models tending to achieve high overall accuracy but getting very low precision and recall when predicting potential churners, which is the main concern of telco companies. This scenario showed that the model is highly overfitted with majority class and cannot capture minority class' patterns.

  As Seymen et al. (2023) pointed out, this imbalance has significantly decreased the performance of ML models in predicting customer attrition. However, there are researchers applying extra techniques to solve the class imbalance problem in datasets such as the resampling method, which is either oversampling the minority class or undersampling the majority class but this method consists of other issues, for example, loss of valuable data or potential overfitting. In the work of Agarwal et al. (2022), the authors have explored several sampling strategies to tackle the imbalance problem but highlighted that applying these methods usually required very careful calibration to avoid bringing new bias into the prediction model.

- Limited feature engineering capabilities

  The reliance on data becomes one of the weaknesses of traditional ML models as this leads to a need for extensive manual feature engineering from the researcher or domain expertise. As noted in the work of Umayaparvathi and Iyakutti, n.d., this process is highly time-consuming and requires repetition for different datasets where the domain experts need to select and transform each relevant feature from raw data into meaningful inputs for the model. Not only that, it could also cause the model to incorrectly capture important patterns from the interaction between variables.

Furthermore, the work of Karanovic et al. (2018) also highlighted that without depending on human intervention in manually selecting insightful features, the model's ability to discover novel patterns or adapt to new datasets will not be restricted. For the reason, that manually capturing all relevant features can lead to suboptimal models, the work of Bhuse et al. (2020) introduced a method called automated feature engineering and selection; this method aims to ease experts in enhancing churn prediction models, especially in large datasets. Still, the cons of this method are that it requires a lot of computational resources and may still miss important features.

Limitations of Deep Learning Techniques

- Model Interpretability

  There is only one point being discussed in deep learning which is the lack of transparency in the complex architecture of DL models, which makes it low in model interpretability, also known as the "black box" nature. This problem brings a significant barrier to the application of DL model in business environment as it cannot be explained to stakeholders how these models make predictions. Unlike the simple architecture of the machine learning model, the architecture of DL models consists of multiple layers and various parameters, making it hard to trace the actual logic behind every prediction output. This problem may lead to a loss of trust among stakeholders due to the inability to understand the overall decision-making process of DL models. Therefore, being unable to explain in detail why the model predicts a churner can make it hard for companies to perform action with confidence (Kumar and D., 2016; Saha et al. 2023).

Strengths of Deep Learning Model in Churn Prediction

Deep learning, with its capabilities when dealing with huge datasets, is able to handle complex model patterns and also interactions between variables. It has been proven to deliver promising performance in detecting and making predictions. Below are the strengths of deep learning models stated in the previous studies with explanation:

- Handling complex data patterns

  Deep learning models are good at capturing complex and non-linear relationships in the input data by using their multi-layered architecture. For example, CNN and LSTM can automatically learn hierarchical representations and detect the intrinsic patterns in the data, which are often missed by traditional ML models. This is the main concern in churn prediction where customer behaviour presented in the datasets is affected by various interconnected factors. In the case study of Saha et al. (2024), the author introduced the ChurnNet model, which is a combination of CNNs with residual learning and attention mechanisms in order to enhance the model prediction accuracy. Therefore, the ability of the model to learn the patterns from the raw data is marked as a key strength of the deep learning model.

- Not requiring extensive feature engineering

  Deep Learning models have the ability to learn and extract useful features straight from the raw data in the datasets, which can directly reduce the reliance on the experts to do any manual intervention during feature selection stages. As everybody knows, the data volume and the complexity of the telco datasets can make feature engineering stage a big problem. Thus, this ability makes the process of developing a churn prediction model more efficient. In the work of Seymen et al. (2023), the author applied a DL model – CNNs on a retail dataset for churn prediction; CNN has successfully outperformed most of the ML models in handling the unstructured data, which cannot be done well in traditional models.

- Scalability and Flexibility

  Deep learning models are more scalable and adaptable to various kinds of data types and prediction tasks, and this enables it to do integrated analysis of the diverse data sources in industries such as telecommunication which leads to more accurate predictions. For example, whether it is dealing with time-series data, images or text, it can be customised to handle the particular requirement according to the needs of the data types. As in the work of Khattak et al. (2023), a BiLSTM-CNN model is developed which combined the strengths of both DL models to tackle different aspects of the data. The results also showed that it has been successful in applying the models to the datasets, showing the flexibility and adaptability of the model.

Research Gaps and Current Issues

There are several research gaps and issues in churn prediction identified from previous studies which still remain unsettled even with the advancement of ML and DL approaches. These challenges showed that there is still

TABLE 10.1

Comparison table for Machine Learning (ML) and Deep Learning (DL)

Criteria	Machine Learning	Deep Learning	Reason
Dataset Size	Small Telecom dataset	Large telecom dataset	ML models perform well with smaller datasets, while DL models benefit from large amounts of data to improve accuracy.
Data Imbalance	Suitable if using resampling methods (e.g., oversampling)	Suitable for highly imbalanced datasets but requires tuning to avoid overfitting	ML models handle resampled datasets, while DL models leverage large datasets even with class imbalance if tuned correctly.
Feature Engineering	When manual feature selection is feasible (e.g., analysing call duration, plan type)	When working with complex customer behaviour data (e.g., raw text logs or clickstream)	ML models often require manually created features; DL models automatically learn feature hierarchies from raw data.
Interpretability Requirement	When explaining churn predictions to stakeholders is critical	When the "black box" nature of DL is acceptable for prediction-only purposes	ML models are more transparent and easier to interpret, while DL models are complex, making stakeholder explanations challenging.
Data Complexity	When churn data has simpler patterns (e.g., demographic and basic usage)	For complex, multi-dimensional data (e.g., sequential transaction or behaviour data)	DL models capture complex behavioural patterns, common in churn data with rich temporal or multivariate information.
Computation Resources	Limited resources available, such as on-premises servers	When scalable resources are available (e.g., cloud GPUs)	ML models use fewer resources, while DL models require more computational power for training.
Scalability and Flexibility	When scalability is not critical, e.g., for small businesses	For large telecom dataset needs high flexibility	DL models are scalable and handle diverse data types (e.g., structured and unstructured data).
Prediction Accuracy Goal	When moderate accuracy is acceptable (e.g., identifying basic churn risk segments)	When highest prediction accuracy is critical to identifying complex churn patterns	DL models often achieve higher accuracy by learning complex data representations in customer behaviour.
Time Constraints	When fast deployment is needed (e.g., simple models for quick risk alerts)	When time is available for fine-tuning and iterative testing	ML models are quicker to deploy, while DL models require longer training and tuning times.

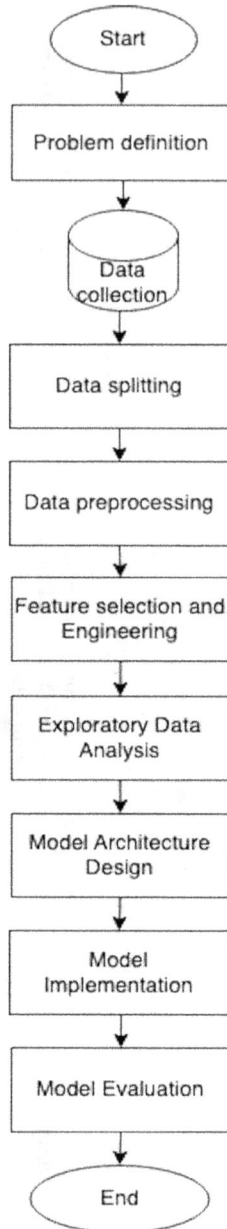

FIGURE 10.1
Overall flow of Churn Prediction.

space for further improvement in churn prediction in the telecommunication field. First is the problem of lacking real-time prediction ability in existing prediction model. This is because current models usually rely on historical data, which may not be able to immediately capture the most recent churner behaviours and alert companies on time to take preventive actions (Saha et al., 2023). Another gap is the lack of integration of other valuable data sources which causes the limited incorporation of diverse data sources in the research. This is because traditional datasets are often used in research, but incorporating additional data sources could provide a more comprehensive understanding of customer behaviour (Seymen et al., 2021). Next, heavy reliance on structured data becomes one of the existing gaps in getting a higher accuracy model as the potential of unstructured data such as customer reviews or customer feedback have high potentials in enhancing prediction accuracy on churners (De Caigny et al., 2020).

Moreover, the challenges of dealing with class imbalance and high dimensionality in most of the telecom datasets remain because existing methods have frequently struggled to handle these issues effectively (Ahmed et al., n.d.). Additionally, focusing solely on the accuracy metric as the only performance measurement tool might be one of the biggest gaps for current prediction models as this is not effective in aligning with business objectives such as customer lifetime value and profit maximisation (Kumar and D., 2016). Then, as data privacy concerns grow over time, the need to train models on decentralised data without affecting individual privacy grows. Thus, the exploration of federated learning approaches for decentralised data becomes an important gap (Saha et al., 2023). The integration of mixed data by combining structured, textual and image data into a single churn prediction model is still unexplored even though it has the potential to greatly improve the model's performance (De Caigny et al., 2020). Last but not least, there is still a huge need for creating more innovative algorithmic methods that are specially designed to solve existing problems in churn prediction rather than merely applying existing deep learning architectures to processed churn data (Gore et al., 2023).

Deep Learning for Churn Prediction

The process of developing a churn prediction model involves several stages, each contributing to building an efficient and robust predictive system for Telecom Churn. In Figure 10.1, an overall flow of developing a churn prediction model is shown. In this section, a detailed overview of each stage is provided, starting with data splitting, data preprocessing, feature selection for deep learning, followed by a discussion of popular Telecom churn datasets, model selection techniques and also commonly used performance metrics. The quality of dataset can directly affect the predictive performance of the churn model.

I. Problem Definition and Data Collection

The first step in creating a churn prediction model is to clearly define the problem for this field, by specifying the norms of customer churn – such as a customer discontinuing the service for more than a range of days or a sign of a significant drop in usage is shown in statistic. Thus, data collection is an important action that needs to be taken before the research.

Two Telecom Churn datasets commonly used in Churn prediction studies:

a) IBM Watson Telco Customer Churn Dataset (IBM Watson, 2019): This dataset is an open-source churn prediction dataset provided by IBM and consists of 7,043 instances with 21 features. These features include customer demographic information, account information, payment transactions and other service usage details. This dataset is popularly used in churn prediction model research and experiments because of its complete overview of the factors that contribute to customer churn in the telecommunication industry.

b) CrowdAnalytix Telco Churn Dataset/BigML Churn Dataset (CrowdAnalytix Community, 2012): This dataset is an open-source dataset provided by CrowdAnalytix, and it includes 3,333 instances with 20 attributes. It provides various features such as customer tenure, service usage and previous payment history. These features are very important for Churn model to understand and learn the dynamics of customer retention and to identify the potential churner.

II. Data splitting and Data preprocessing

It is always very critical to split the dataset into training, validation and testing before performing any of the data preprocessing because this can cause data leakage, where the information in the testing and validation dataset can unintentionally influence the training of the model. Therefore, it is important to split data before the preprocessing steps. After data splitting, preprocessing steps such as scaling, encoding and imputation should be applied to training dataset first. This is to ensure that the test data does not affect the training process and maintains the integrity of the model's evaluation. Preprocessing of test dataset will be applied after the training process is done. The commonly used splitting ratio used in the experiment is the ratio of 80:20 train test split.

After the splitting is done, the next process will be data preprocessing stages. A raw dataset will contain unclean data which includes missing data, categorical variables, different ranges of variables and also class imbalance problems. Therefore, some preprocessing techniques such as data imputation, data encoding, data normalisation and data sampling to tackle class imbalance problems. Missing values are usually handled using data imputation with mean or median values. Categorical data like customer payment methods will be converted into numerical form using one-hot encoding or target encoder. Then, data normalisation or scaling is done to ensure all variables are on a consistent scale for better model learning. Class imbalance in the dataset will be handled using methods such as SMOTE (Latheef and Vineetha, 2021), K-Means (Aravinda et al., 2024) or Tomek Links (Kimura, 2022) methods, but when using deep learning to train churn models, it is not necessary to apply, unless there is severe class imbalance.

III. Feature Selection and Engineering

The advantage of using DL in churn prediction is their capabilities to learn relevant features from data; it reduces the need for extensive manual feature selection and engineering. However, some feature selection is still necessary to make sure the irrelevant or redundant features do not have a bad impact on model performance. Therefore, it is important to remove those unused features such as the features that are not logically linked to churn behaviour. Thus, feature relevance and quality still remain significant for optimising DL model performance.

IV. Exploratory Data Analysis (EDA)

EDA is necessary for researchers to understand data's underlying structure, identify patterns, and then perform feature selection. It involves data distribution visualisation, correlation checking and also can be used to detect any outliers in data. For example, analysing the distribution of customer tenure can reveal specific periods at higher risk of churn. Besides, correlation matrices can help researchers to identify extra features that need to be removed. EDA provides very valuable insights necessary for dataset refining and performance improvement.

V. Model Architecture Design

The stage of designing model architecture involves the selection of appropriate DL models, such as a Recurrent Neural Network (RNN) (Hu et al., 2018) for sequential data or a CNN for structured data. Figure 10.2 shows the architecture of an RNN which includes an input layer, multiple recurrence hidden layers and an output layer.

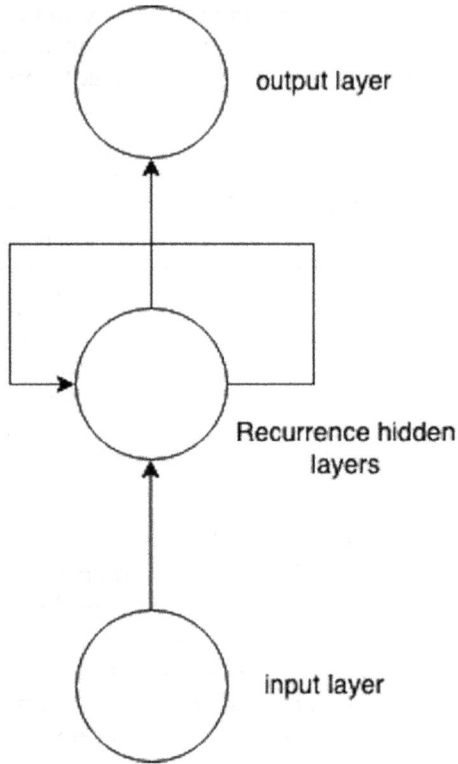

FIGURE 10.2
Model architecture of an RNN model.

For these DL models, researchers need to configure the layers, hyper-parameters and suitable activation functions. Number of layers and neurons in each layer will directly affect the prediction performance of the model. For example, Deep Neural Network (DNN) with multiple hidden layers might be applied to learn the complex patterns in customer behaviour. The section below provides examples of DL models that can be used in churn prediction:

a. Convolutional Neural Network (CNN)

A CNN is primarily used for spatial or sequential data, such as images or time series data. However, its ability to capture local dependencies in complex data makes it adaptable for non-sequential datasets and useful in identifying patterns in customer behaviour that happen over time. Several studies (e.g., Mishra and Reddy, 2017; Khattak et al., 2023) have successfully employed CNNs for churn prediction in the telecom industry, even with structured, non-sequential data. The architecture of a CNN might include several convolution layers, followed by pooling layers and fully connected layers. The convolution layers apply filters to input data in order to detect local patterns and features, then pooling layers reduce the spatial dimensions to prevent overfitting and improve computational efficiency. The extracted features are then passed through a flattening layer, which transforms two-dimensional feature maps into a one-dimensional vector for further processing. In the fully connected layer, these extracted features are aggregated to make accurate predictions. Finally, the output layer uses sigmoid activation function in binary classification tasks such as classifying class of churn and non-churn in order to produce probabilities for each class. For example, when applied to non-sequential data such as customer demographic information and payment method or account activity metrics, a 1D-CNN can take these structured datasets as a grid of input features, where each convolution filter extracts local features interactions relevant to churn prediction. The advantages of using CNNs are that they are highly effective in reducing the number of parameters which allows them to be efficient in capturing complex data and efficiently handling large customer datasets through learning hierarchical feature representations. Figure 10.3 illustrates the architecture of a CNN model for churn prediction, starting with raw customer data as input, then convolutional one-dimensional layers for feature extraction, followed by fully connected layers for decision-making, and output layers that provide the final prediction of churn probabilities using sigmoid function.

The convolution operation in a CNN can be represented mathematically in equation (10.1) below:

$$h_{i,j}^k = f\left(\sum_{m=0}^{M-1} \sum_{n=0}^{N-1} x_{i+m,j+n} w_{m,n}^k + b^k \right) \tag{10.1}$$

where:

$h_{i,j}^k$ is the output feature map.

$x_{i+m,j+n}$ is the input.

$w_{m,n}^k$ is the filter.

b^k is the bias.

f is the activation function, typically ReLU.

b. Long Short-Term Memory (LSTMs)

LSTMs are experts in handling sequential data, making them suitable for capturing temporal dependencies of customer behaviour data in Churn datasets such as customer usage patterns over time (Alboukaey et al., 2020). The architecture of an LSTM model consists of multiple LSTM layers, each containing cells that will control the

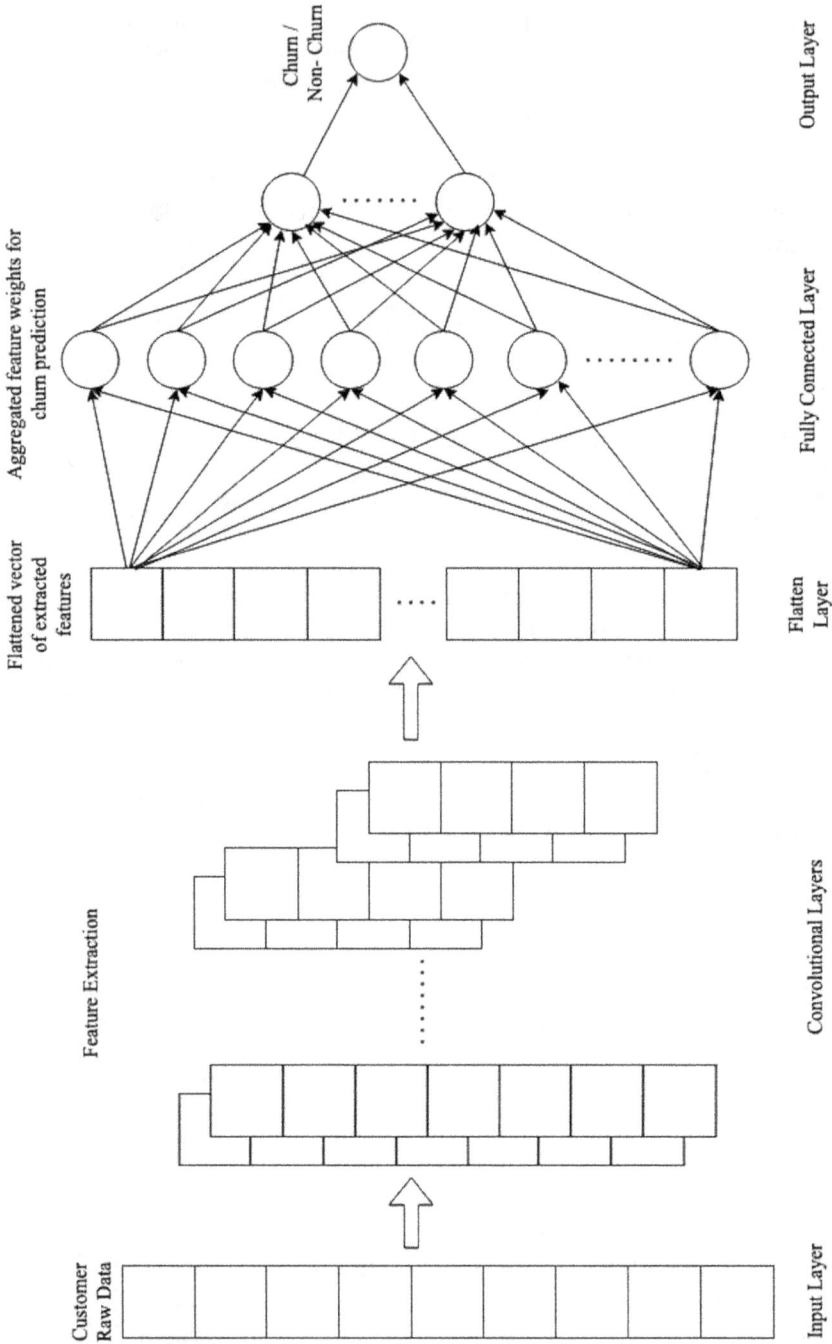

FIGURE 10.3

Architecture of CNN model for Churn Prediction.

flow of information through three gates – Forget gate, Input gate and Output gate.

- Forget Gate, f_t: Determines which information to discard from the cell state, as calculated in Equation (10.2):

$$f_t = \sigma\left(W_f \cdot [h_{t-1}, x_t] + b_f\right) \tag{10.2}$$

- Input Gate, i_t: Decides which new information to store in the cell state, as calculated in Equation (10.3):

$$i_t = \sigma\left(W_i \cdot [h_{t-1}, x_t] + b_i\right) \tag{10.3}$$

- Output Gate, o_t: Determines the next hidden state, as calculated in Equation (10.4):

$$o_t = \sigma\left(W_o \cdot [h_{t-1}, x_t] + b_o\right) \tag{10.4}$$

- Cell State Update: Cell state C_t updated using previous state C_{t-1} and the new candidate values $\tilde{C}_t$, calculated as Equation (10.5):

$$C_t = f_t * C_{t-1} + i_t * \tilde{C}_t \tag{10.5}$$

where:

σ is the sigmoid function,

W_f is the weight matrix,

h_{t-1} is the previous hidden state,

x_t is the input at time t, and b_f is the bias.

These gates are responsible for deciding which data needs to be retained or discarded from the sequences, helping the model maintain long-term dependencies, and improving the churn model's predictive performance based on historical behaviour. Figure 10.4 shows a block diagram of LSTMs, where each memory cell consists of three gates that can be observed in the figure.

The advantages of LSTMs are their effectiveness in learning data sequences with different lengths and their ability to handle the vanishing gradient problem better than traditional RNN models. This makes LSTM suited for analysing customer behaviour that happens over time. However, it requires more computational resources compared to traditional RNN models.

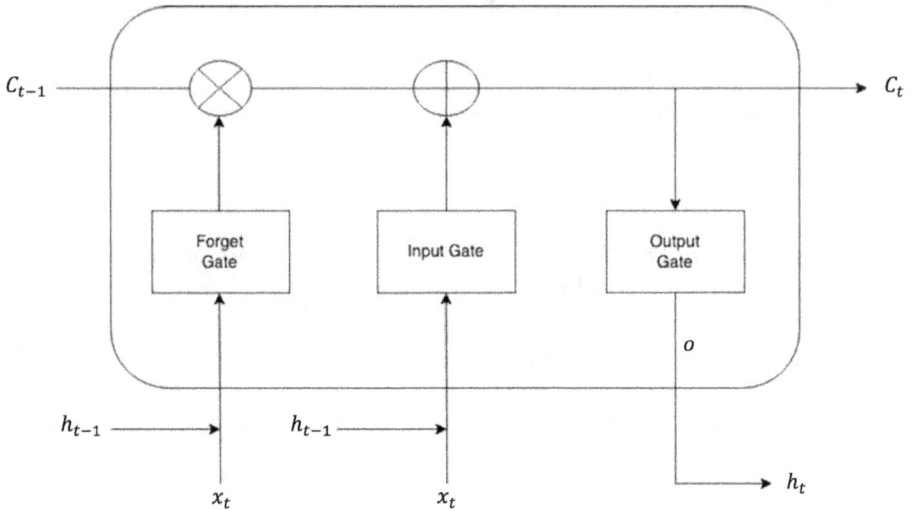

FIGURE 10.4
Architecture of an LSTM block.

VI. Model Implementation, Training and Enhancement

After designing the DL model architecture, the model needs to be implemented using deep learning frameworks such as TensorFlow or PyTorch. In this stage, an efficient data pipeline will be set up, loss function is defined, and an optimisation algorithm is selected. After the implementation of the model, the next step is the model training stage. Training stage involves iterative data feeding, loss calculation and weight updates. Then, hyperparameter tuning will be performed to enhance the performance of the model after observing the model prediction results. There are several hyperparameter tuning techniques that can be used, such as grid search (Koçoğlu and Özcan, 2022) and random search. It can also adjust the learning rate and batch size to optimise model's performance. Cross-validation techniques are often used to ensure that the selected hyperparameters can generalise well across the subsets of data, with early stopping applied to prevent overfitting. At the end of this stage, the model's performance and effectiveness in churn prediction will be maximised.

VII. Model Evaluation

In churn prediction, there are several performance metrics used to evaluate predictive performance, which are Accuracy, Precision, Recall, F1-Score and AUC-ROC. The equations of these key metrics will be discussed in the section below.

a. Accuracy: It measures overall correctness by calculating the ratio of correct churn predictions to overall total predictions. However, it can be misleading with imbalanced data.

$$\text{Accuracy} = \frac{\text{True Positives} + \text{True Negatives}}{\text{Total Predictions}} \tag{10.6}$$

b. Precision: It measures the proportion of true churners with those predicted to churn and it is an important reference to false positives minimisation.

$$\text{Precision} = \frac{\text{True Positives}}{\text{True Positives} + \text{False Positives}} \tag{10.7}$$

c. Recall: It measures how well the models capture the actual churners and high recall means the model can identify most of the actual churners.

$$\text{Recall} = \frac{\text{True Positives}}{\text{True Positives} + \text{False Negatives}} \tag{10.8}$$

d. F1-Score: It balances the precision and recall and is a useful metric to check the prediction performance of imbalanced data.

$$\text{F1} - \text{Score} = 2 \times \frac{\text{Precision} \times \text{Recall}}{\text{Precision} + \text{Recall}} \tag{10.9}$$

e. AUC-ROC: It is used to evaluate the effectiveness of churners classification. A higher AUC-ROC indicates the churn prediction model had a better predictive power of churn and non-churn classes.

$$\text{AUC} - \text{ROC} = \text{Area Under the ROC Curve} \tag{10.10}$$

Conclusion and Future Directions

To sum up, Deep Learning techniques as a specialised subset of machine learning offer a lot of advantages in handling complex data patterns in the datasets, reducing the need for extensive manual feature engineering and also providing scalability. However, to fully utilise the potential of DL models in churn prediction, several research gaps need to be addressed, such as data complexity and quality. In the future, churn prediction can focus on model performance enhancement through advanced techniques like hyperparameter optimisation, and federated learning, which can create a decentralised environment for the training of models (Saha et al., 2024). Exploring advanced deep learning techniques, such as the transformer models and attention mechanism can be a way to improve the accuracy and robustness of the prediction model (Saha et al., 2023). The researchers also suggest combining more different data sources and complex models to build Hybrid models such as multidimensional CNNs to address challenges like data imbalance or large datasets. In addition, to better handle unstructured data, researchers recommend refining DL models to improve prediction accuracy and interpretability.

Reference

Agarwal, V., Taware, S., Yadav, S.A., Gangodkar, D., Rao, A., Srivastav, V.K., 2022. Customer - Churn Prediction Using Machine Learning, in: *2022 2nd International Conference on Technological Advancements in Computational Sciences (ICTACS)*, IEEE, Tashkent, Uzbekistan, pp. 893–899. https://doi.org/10.1109/ICTACS56270.2022.9988187

Ahmed, U., Khan, A., Khan, S.H., Basit, A., Haq, I.U., Lee, Y.S., n.d. Transfer Learning and Meta Classification Based Deep Churn Prediction System for Telecom Industry.

Alboukaey, N., Joukhadar, A., Ghneim, N., 2020. Dynamic behavior based churn prediction in mobile telecom. *Expert Syst. Appl.* 162, 113779. https://doi.org/10.1016/j.eswa.2020.113779

Aravinda, N.L., Reddy, R.A., Dhandayuthapani V B., Nayak, J.P.R., Husseen, A., 2024. Customer Churn Prediction in the Telecom Sector with Machine Learning and Adaptive k-Means Cluster using Imbalance Data, in: *2024 International Conference on Distributed Computing and Optimization Techniques (ICDCOT)*, IEEE, Bengaluru, India, pp. 1–5. https://doi.org/10.1109/ICDCOT61034.2024.10515832

Bhuse, P., Gandhi, A., Meswani, P., Muni, R., Katre, N., 2020. Machine Learning Based Telecom-Customer Churn Prediction, in: *2020 3rd International Conference on Intelligent Sustainable Systems (ICISS)*, IEEE, Thoothukudi, India, pp. 1297–1301. https://doi.org/10.1109/ICISS49785.2020.9315951

CrowdAnalytix Community, 2012. CrowdAnalytix(BigML) Telco Churn Dataset. https://www.crowdanalytix.com/community

De Caigny, A., Coussement, K., De Bock, K.W., Lessmann, S., 2020. Incorporating textual information in customer churn prediction models based on a convolutional neural network. *Int. J. Forecast.* 36, 1563–1578. https://doi.org/10.1016/j.ijforecast.2019.03.029

Gore, S., Chibber, Y., Bhasin, M., Mehta, S., Suchitra, S., 2023. Customer Churn Prediction using Neural Networks and SMOTE-ENN for Data Sampling, in: *2023 3rd International Conference on Artificial Intelligence and Signal Processing (AISP)*, IEEE, VIJAYAWADA, India, pp. 1–5. https://doi.org/10.1109/AISP57993.2023.10134827

Hu, J., Zhuang, Y., Yang, J., Lei, L., Huang, M., Zhu, R., Dong, S., 2018. pRNN: A Recurrent Neural Network based Approach for Customer Churn Prediction in Telecommunication Sector, in: *2018 IEEE International Conference on Big Data (Big Data)*, IEEE, Seattle, WA, USA, pp. 4081–4085. https://doi.org/10.1109/BigData.2018.8622094

IBM Watson, 2019. IBM Watson Customer Churn Dataset. https://community.ibm.com/community/user/businessanalytics/blogs/steven-macko/2019/07/11/telco-customer-churn-1113

Karanovic, M., Popovac, M., Sladojevic, S., Arsenovic, M., Stefanovic, D., 2018. Telecommunication Services Churn Prediction - Deep Learning Approach, in: *2018 26th Telecommunications Forum (TELFOR)*. Presented at the 2018 26th Telecommunications Forum (TELFOR), IEEE, Belgrade, pp. 420–425. https://doi.org/10.1109/TELFOR.2018.8612067

Khan, Y., Shafiq, S., Naeem, A., Ahmed, S., Safwan, N., Hussain, S., 2019. Customers Churn Prediction using Artificial Neural Networks (ANN) in Telecom Industry. *Int. J. Adv. Comput. Sci. Appl.* 10. https://doi.org/10.14569/IJACSA.2019.0100918

Khattak, A., Mehak, Z., Ahmad, H., Asghar, M.U., Asghar, M.Z., Khan, A., 2023. Customer churn prediction using composite deep learning technique. *Sci. Rep.* 13, 17294. https://doi.org/10.1038/s41598-023-44396-w

Kimura, T., 2022. Customer churn prediction with hybrid resampling and ensemble learning 25.

Koçoğlu, F.Ö., Özcan, T., 2022. A grid search optimized extreme learning machine approach for customer churn prediction. *J. Eng. Res.* https://doi.org/10.36909/jer.16771

Kumar, S. D. C., 2016. A Survey on Customer Churn Prediction using Machine Learning Techniques. *Int. J. Comput. Appl.* 154, 13–16. https://doi.org/10.5120/ijca2016912237

Latheef, J., Vineetha, S., 2021. LSTM Model to Predict Customer Churn in Banking Sector with SMOTE Data Preprocessing, in: 2021 2nd International Conference on Advances in Computing, Communication, Embedded and Secure Systems (ACCESS), in: *2021 2nd International Conference on Advances in Computing, Communication, Embedded and Secure Systems (ACCESS)*, IEEE, Ernakulam, India, pp. 86–90. https://doi.org/10.1109/ACCESS51619.2021.9563347

Mishra, A., Reddy, U.S., 2017. A Novel Approach for Churn Prediction Using Deep Learning, in: 2017 IEEE International Conference on Computational Intelligence and Computing Research (ICCIC), in: *2017 IEEE International Conference on Computational Intelligence and Computing Research (ICCIC)*, IEEE, Coimbatore, pp. 1–4. https://doi.org/10.1109/ICCIC.2017.8524551

Patel, A., Kumar, A.G., 2023. Predicting Customer Churn In Telecom Industry: A Machine Learning Approach For Improving Customer Retention, in: *2023 IEEE 11th Region 10 Humanitarian Technology Conference (R10-HTC)*, IEEE, Rajkot, India, pp. 558–561. https://doi.org/10.1109/R10-HTC57504.2023.10461822

Qutub, A., Al-Mehmadi, A., Al-Hssan, M., Aljohani, R., Alghamdi, H.S., 2021. Prediction of Employee Attrition Using Machine Learning and Ensemble Methods. *Int. J. Mach. Learn. Comput.* 11, 110–114. https://doi.org/10.18178/ijmlc.2021.11.2.1022

Saha, L., Tripathy, H.K., Gaber, T., El-Gohary, H., El-Kenawy, E.-S.M., 2023. Deep Churn Prediction Method for Telecommunication Industry. *Sustainability* 15, 4543. https://doi.org/10.3390/su15054543

Saha, S., Haque, Md.M., Alam, Md.G.R., Talukder, A., 2024. ChurnNet: Deep Learning Enhanced Customer Churn Prediction in Telecommunication Industry. *IEEE Access* 12, 4471–4484. https://doi.org/10.1109/ACCESS.2024.3349950

Seymen, O.F., Dogan, O., Hiziroglu, A., 2021. Customer Churn Prediction Using Deep Learning, in: Abraham, A., Ohsawa, Y., Gandhi, N., Jabbar, M.A., Haqiq, A., McLoone, S., Issac, B. (Eds.), *Proceedings of the 12th International Conference on Soft Computing and Pattern Recognition (SoCPaR 2020), Advances in Intelligent Systems and Computing.* Springer International Publishing, Cham, pp. 520–529. https://doi.org/10.1007/978-3-030-73689-7_50

Seymen, O.F., Ölmez, E., Doğan, O., Er, O., Hiziroğlu, K., 2023. Customer Churn Prediction Using Ordinary Artificial Neural Network and Convolutional Neural Network Algorithms: A Comparative Performance Assessment. *Gazi Univ. J. Sci.* 36, 720–733. https://doi.org/10.35378/gujs.992738

Umayaparvathi, V., Iyakutti, K., n.d. Automated Feature Selection and Churn Prediction using Deep Learning Models 04.

Yu, W., Weng, W., 2022. Customer Churn Prediction Based on Machine Learning, in: 2022 4th International Conference on Artificial Intelligence and Advanced Manufacturing (AIAM). *Presented at the 2022 4th International Conference on Artificial Intelligence and Advanced Manufacturing (AIAM),* IEEE, Hamburg, Germany, pp. 870–878. https://doi.org/10.1109/AIAM57466.2022.00176

11

Artificial Intelligence in Bioinformatics and -omics

Joon Liang Tan and Li Wen Yow

Introduction

The roles of Bioinformatics have been increasingly prominent in recent decades. In contrast to other known fields, Bioinformatics integrates major distinct disciplines, that are life sciences, computational sciences and engineering (Sayood & Otu, 2022). The disciplines collaborated by transforming life sciences information into data, such as images and strings of characters, to be analysed and simulated in computer algorithms. On top of that, new algorithms were also developed to handle molecular-derived data in accordance with biological theories (Botlagunta et al., 2023; Mukherjee et al., 2017; Kosov et al., 2018).

Phylogenetics and comparative analyses are the common analyses in Bioinformatics. Historically, the aforementioned analyses and tools were developed with a focus on specific targets, such as *16S rRNA* gene of bacteria (Clarridge, 2004). The trend changed when -omics were introduced, that is targeting an entire collection of molecular types instead of specific regions. Many new discoveries and theories were formulated when the analyses were viewed beyond the single targeted site (Magro et al., 2024; Micheel et al., 2012; Min et al., 2021). The first whole genome sequencing was dated back in 1977 on bacteriophage ΦX174 (Sanger et al., 1977). The continuous ambitious research led capability of technology to yield the human genome (Lander et al., 2001; Ledford, 2007). The human reference genome was concluded with a size of 3.055×10^9 base pairs (Nurk et al., 2022).

The research on big data in biology, covering different molecules, such as genomes, transcriptomes, epigenomes, proteomes, are still the trend at present. This can be observed with the increasing amount of data in public databases, such as the National Centre for Biotechnology Information Whole Genome Shotgun (NCBI WGS) (Figure 11.1). As of June 2024, approximately

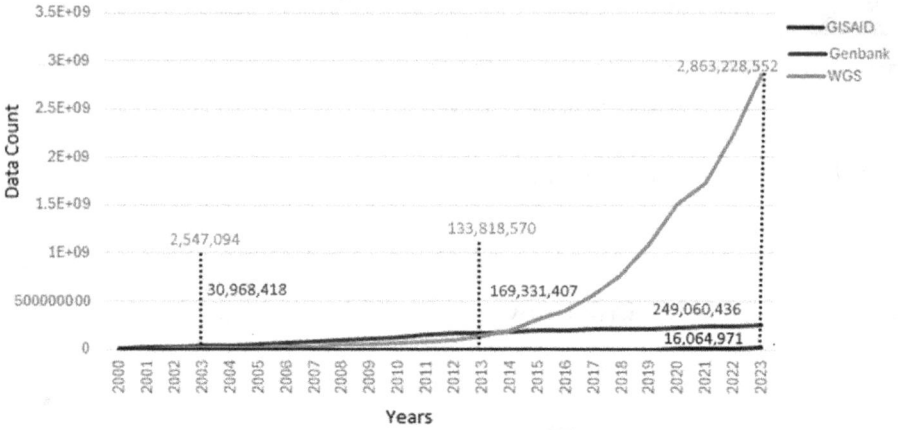

FIGURE 11.1
Growth of DNA Sequence Data in Major Genomic Databases from 2000 to 2023.

2.79×10^{13} characters, covering 3.3×10^9 organisms have been sequenced and deposited in the database. Even in the state of global public health emergency caused by COVID-19, researchers around the world were focused on -omics-based approaches with the aim of understanding the hitherto known SARS-CoV-2 in the Global Initiative on Sharing All Influenza Data (GISAID). This has enabled the change of analytical trends from individual omics to population-based omics research.

The complexity and dimensionality of omics data are pushing the need for proper techniques to process, simulate and classify in an automated and rapid manner. Artificial intelligence (hereafter referred to as AI) is known to have the capability to handle data with the aforementioned properties. AI has been integrated into a wide range of applications, ranging from transportation to household applications. In bioinformatics, multiple reports proved the predictive capability of AI on complex heterogeneous data. One of the examples of AI in bioinformatics research is the prediction of stem cell transformation by utilisation of noisy, high-dimensional data from public databases (Wytock & Motter, 2024). The impactful breakthrough from the AI-driven research indicated that progress in AI will have a direct positive influence on bioinformatics. Another support for the significance of AI in Bioinformatics is it was forecasted that AI in the Bioinformatics market will have a value of USD 217.38 million in 2030 from 2.53 million in 2022 (*AI In Bioinformatics Market Size, Demand & Industry Research By 2030*, n.d.). All these suggest the potential of more incoming AI-driven research and emerging AI-related algorithms. In this chapter, the current applications of AI in different omics research will be discussed.

AI in Genomics

A genome refers to the complete set of genetic material of an organism (Goldman & Landweber, 2016). It contains information and instructions needed to build and maintain cells. Genomics is the study of genetic information and aims to identify sequences and understand the functions and interaction of genes. It provides insights into the genetic basis for traits, diseases and evolutionary relationships of inter- and intra-populations. For example, genomics in personalised medicine enables tailored treatments based on individual genetic profiles. Individual-based diagnosis and prognosis can be determined by detection of genetic mutations associated with specific conditions (Lee, 2023; Wekesa & Kimwele, 2023) for more accurate medication prescriptions and dosages (Prins et al., 2021). In the agricultural sector, there were reports on the advantages of genomics in improving the quality and sustainability of agricultural production. The achievements were the results of genetically superior and disease-resistant crop varieties yielded from genomics analyses (Amas et al., 2023; Chachar et al., 2024).

Despite the progressions and breakthroughs in multiple areas contributed by genomics, the amount of raw data has challenged the traditional analyses and protocols (Figure 11.2). Traditional analyses mostly focused on targeted genes and with maximum sequence length of up to 700 bp. However, at least 30× sequencing coverage, equivalent to approximately 9.6×10^{10} bp nucleotides is needed for a human genome size of 3.2×10^9 bp. AI algorithms can identify genetic patterns, make predictions and classify genetic variations based on the training of large datasets (Talukder et al., 2020). Furthermore, AI enables researchers to discover sequence patterns and biological mechanisms that are difficult to be elucidated using conventional methods (J. Xie et al., 2020). For these reasons, AI has been increasingly used on genomic data. AI algorithms were employed in bioinformatics prediction tasks such as variant calling, genome annotation and phenotype-to-genotype mapping. These applications offer several advantages over traditional methods, including improving accuracy, increasing analysis efficiency, supporting identification of novel mutations and enhancing biomarker discovery (Dias & Torkamani, 2019). For example, AI makes cancer treatments more personalised and effective. AI algorithms have shown promising cancer detection by identification of genome-wide cancer-specific mutations. The approach allows earlier and more accurate diagnosis, which is crucial for effective treatments. Moreover, AI accelerates the analysis of large genomic datasets, a task that would be time-consuming and intensive for human manual labour. This rapid analysis can uncover new genetic markers and pathways involved in cancer progression, potentially leading to the discovery of new therapeutic targets (Bazarkin et al., 2024; H. Chen et al., 2023; S. Lee et al., 2018; Wang & Li, 2020).

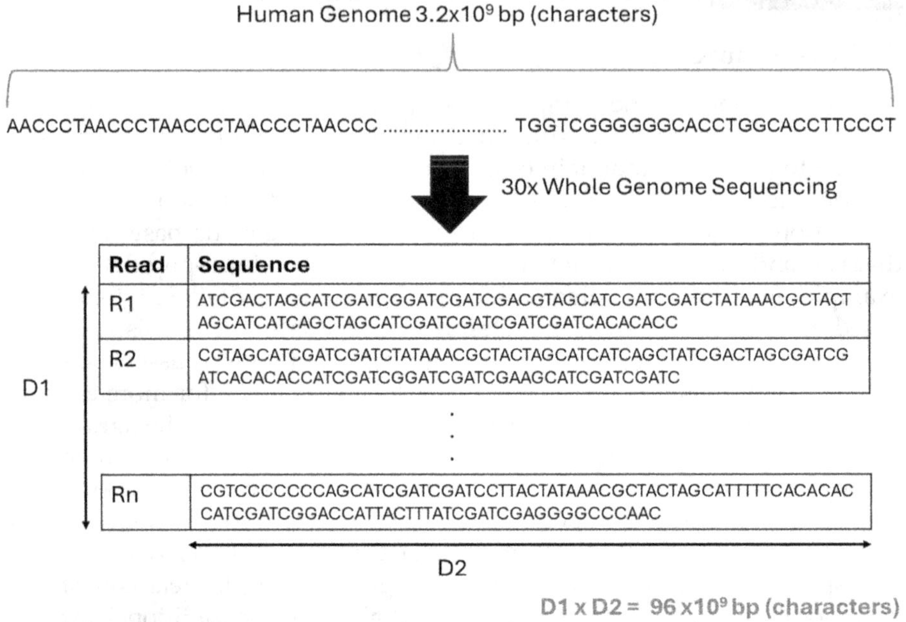

Human Genome 3.2x10⁹ bp (characters)

FIGURE 11.2
Whole Genome Sequencing: From Human Genome to Raw Data Generation.

The discoveries derived from genomic data were commonly focused on three main analyses, that are: variant calling, genome annotation and evolutionary analysis. In the subsequent sections, the roles of AI in the stated genomic analyses will be discussed.

Variant Calling

Variant calling in genomics involves identification of variants by comparing orthologous biological sequences. The variants are single nucleotide variants (SNVs), that is the changes of nucleotides at each sequence position and insertion/deletions(INDEL), representing addition or removal of nucleotides at the respective sequence positions of being compared. Variants can be predicted based on reference and *de novo* protocols. However, reference-based protocol is usually preferred over *de novo* approach. Pipelines of traditional reference-based variant calling typically require read mapping, quality filtering and statistical modelling. The two reference-based tools commonly used are SAMtools (H. Li et al., 2009) and the Genome Analysis Toolkit (GATK) (McKenna et al., 2010), which compare sequences against a known reference. Although the two tools have been the backbone in most variants' prediction research, the accuracy of predictions remains a main challenge, especially within complex genomic regions or in low-quality data. Research by Z. Li et al. notes that the Bayesian approach used by SAMtools may become confused when aligning reads to regions adjacent to candidate indels, indicating challenges in indel calling. In contrast, GATK-HC is known to be superior in predicting exonic INDELs, but it exhibits a high false positive rate for intronic INDELs. Previous studies indicate that GATK-HC predicts 52.22% false positive intronic INDELs with interval padding, significantly higher than other tools (Zanti et al., 2021). However, the assembly based approach used by GATK-HC has extremely high computational complexity and a large number of candidate haplotypes, which can lead to longer runtimes, especially for low-coverage data (Z. Li et al., 2018).

The complex genomic features and increased amount of sequencing data highlight the need for more advanced approaches in variant calling. In addition, different sequencing technologies (e.g., Illumina, PacBio, Oxford Nanopore) generate raw reads with varying characteristics (length, error profiles and coverage patterns), affecting the sensitivity of variant detection (Koboldt, 2020). These issues led to the exploration of AI to improve variant calling accuracy. AI-based tools such as DeepVariant (Poplin et al., 2018) and DNAscope (Freed et al., 2022) have shown promising outputs in variant calling predictions. DNAscope enhances variants prediction accuracy by combining traditional methods and machine learning. The algorithm works similarly to GATK-HC: detection of active regions, local assembly with de Bruijn graphs and likelihood calculation of read-haplotype through PairHMM. However, DNAscope improves these steps for greater sensitivity and robustness. DNAscope uses a Gradient Boosting Machine (GBM) model trained on the structured data from multiple samples. This model learns to differentiate systematic noise and true variants by identifying errors from library preparation, sequencing and alignment. DNAscope can effectively capture complex relationships between variant features and errors that are challenging for any traditional statistical methods to model (Freed et al., 2022).

DeepVariant is another common AI-based variants prediction tool. In contrast to DNAscope which integrates both modern and traditional methodologies, DeepVariant is fully designed in AI to accurately identify genetic variants from the NGS data. The algorithm works in three main steps: Firstly, it uses standard preprocessing techniques to find candidate variants with high sensitivity but with low specificity; secondly, it encodes reference and sequence read data around each candidate variant into a pileup image; finally, based on the Inception architecture, its Convolutional Neural Network (CNN) analyses the generated images to predict the probability of each possible diploid genotype. The CNN was trained on labelled true genotypes, learned to recognise patterns in the pileup images that represent different variants. This methodology allows DeepVariant to model complex relationships among reads without relying on explicit statistical models. The trained model can be applied to new samples and on different species and even data generated from different sequencing technologies. This functionality showcases AI versatility in handling data heterogeneity. By treating the variant calling as an image classification task, DeepVariant is able to achieve higher accuracy and consistency than other traditional tools. It is particularly effective at handling the complex errors commonly found in sequencing data (Poplin et al., 2018).

NanoCaller is another AI framework specifically designed for variant calling. It takes advantage of long reads data generated by the third-generation sequencing technologies. NanoCaller incorporates long-range haplotype information into its variants detection process. For SNVs calling, NanoCaller also uses CNN that inputs long-range heterozygous SNVs sites in pileup images. The sites can be hundreds or thousands of base pairs away from each candidate site. This method allows NanoCaller to fully utilise long reads feature, setting it apart from known techniques that focus on local regions. For INDELs calling, NanoCaller performs phasing on sequencing reads using predicted SNVs. It then performs local multiple sequence alignment around the candidate INDEL to create input features for another deep neural network (Ahsan et al., 2021). The algorithm improves the accuracy of variant calling in long read sequencing data.

AI-based tools have generally proven to be suitable for genomic data and outperform conventional methods in terms of prediction accuracy and computational efficiency, especially for long-read data (Abdelwahab et al., 2023). The algorithms have the potential to mine previously undetectable variants and further advance our understanding in variants–phenotypes relationships.

Genome Annotations

Genome annotation involves the identification of the gene sequences, positions, functions and other genomic features. Common genome annotation tools include Prokka, Maker and many others (Rainer et al., 2019; Seemann, 2014; Tatusova et al., 2016; Zhao & Zhang, 2015). All the tools are using different algorithms to annotate genomes. With the different annotation algorithms, BLAST (Basic Local Alignment Search Tool) is the most common search tool integrated in the genome annotation tools. It is frequently used to align sequences with known databases for annotation purposes (Jung et al., 2020). The outputs of current annotation tools can vary significantly, are often biased, and make it challenging to reach a single consensus, even with the development of various statistical models aimed at addressing these issues. Merging heterogeneous types of information from different sources remains a major challenge (Stanke et al., 2006). The study by Salzberg (2019) highlighted that the challenges and annotation accuracy have not been improved significantly. Automated procedures often lead to erroneous predictions, especially in large, fragmented draft genomes.

AI algorithms are increasingly used due to their ability to handle high dimensional data and to model nonlinear relationships among genome features (Lourenço et al., 2024). AI algorithms can be used to predict the functional elements from genome sequence data. For example, CNNs enhance sensitivity by detecting local features in gene sequences, resulting in higher accuracy for gene findings. The CNN architectures include convolutional layers that identify specific patterns in the DNA, pooling layers that condense and summarise these features, and fully connecting layers that perform final classifications. Additionally, methods like SVM-RSE (Random Subspace Ensemble) and XGBoost were also utilised to improve gene function prediction accuracy. SVM-RSE combines multiple SVM models trained on different subsets of feature space. On the other hand, XGBoost is an advanced gradient-boosting technique that builds a series of decision trees, where each tree corrects errors made by the previous tree.

Alongside AI, Combined Annotation-Dependent Depletion (CADD) is an advanced tool that estimates the potential impact of genetic variants. The tool was trained to distinguish 4.7 million high-frequency human-derived alleles and an equal number of simulated variants. The algorithm integrates 63 different annotations, including conservation metrics, regulatory information, transcript details and protein scores. It also includes a few interacting terms among the annotations. CADD scores all the 8.6 billion possible human single-nucleotide variants, assigning a C score to each variant using the previously trained model. To enhance its usability, these C scores are converted to a scaled score ranging from 1 to 99, reflecting their rank among all the possible substitutions in the human reference genome. This method provides a single, comprehensive measure of harmfulness that applies to both coding and non-coding variants. By combining diverse annotations and scoring every possible variant, CADD becomes a powerful resource for prioritising variants in genetic studies, offering insights into their potential impact (Kircher et al., 2014; Rentzsch et al., 2019).

The AI algorithms are not only proven to handle large datasets efficiently but have also improved runtime and memory requirements. As genomic data continue to grow in complexity, the role of AI in annotation is likely to become increasingly important, potentially leading to more accurate and comprehensive genomic analyses.

Evolutionary Analysis

Evolutionary analysis is a powerful analysis to understand the genetic relationships and populational history of organisms. It involves studying the relationship between organisms through the evaluation of genetic variations. The analysis typically involves two major key steps: sequence alignment and phylogenetic tree reconstruction. Sequence alignment consists of multiple sequence alignment (MSA) of multiple organisms to identify the conserved regions and their mutations. ClustalW, MUSCLE and MAFFT are the three most common tools used for performing MSA (Edgar, 2004; Katoh & Standley, 2013; Thompson et al., 2002). The current trend in phylogeny inference is based on phylogenomics, that is evolutionary analysis based on omic-wide data. One of the steps in phylogenomics is to perform MSA based on the whole-genome sequence or alignment of sequences based on genome sampling. The entire sequences from different organisms were aligned to identify the orthologous and accessories sequences. Whole genome alignment poses computational and biological challenges, such as execution time and memory usage (Saada et al., 2024).

In phylogenomic tree reconstructions, Maximum Likelihood and Bayesian inference represent evolutionary relationships among species were employed (Challa & Neelapu, 2019; Zou et al., 2024) and MEGA and BEAST are usually used for the purposes (Bouckaert et al., 2019). Maximum Likelihood and Bayesian inferences require complex model settings, increasing computational demands (Zou et al., 2024). Combining multiple data sources (e.g., genome sequences, fossil occurrences) into a single model is also conceptually and computationally challenging (Bouckaert et al., 2019). Different assumptions in different phylogenetic tree reconstruction methods can impact the accuracy of the phylogenetic trees. Moreover, the quality of sequence alignment can also significantly affect the resulting phylogenetic tree (Hall, 2013). All these issues serve as important factors in determining the accuracy of the inferred tree.

AI facilitates the identification of clustering patterns and inference of evolutionary relationships from genomic data. Model testing is capable to evaluate genetic variations and evolutionary pressures. It enhances the accuracy of constructing phylogenetic trees and tackles associate uncertainties by utilising AI and probabilistic approaches. For instance, ARTree is a deep autoregressive model that employs graph neural networks (GNNs) to generate phylogenetic tree topologies. The algorithm begins with a star-shaped structure of three nodes and adds new nodes sequentially. It determines the position to attach a new node by calculating learnable topological features of the current tree using the GNNs. This allows ARTree to create a conditional distribution over potential attachment edges. The model incorporates message passing networks, node hidden states, and edge decision networks within its GNN architecture. This innovative approach enables ARTree to provide distributions that fully cover the entire tree topology space. Unlike other methods that relied on pre-sampled topologies or heuristic features, ARTree offers more expressive tree distributions over tree topologies. Additionally, it supports a straightforward sampling and density estimation, making it an ideal tree topology density estimation and variational Bayesian phylogenetic inference tasks. Overall, ARTree enhances the accuracy and efficiency of modelling evolutionary relationships among species (T. Xie & Zhang, 2023). Another example of AI-based phylogenomics is exploration of generative adversarial networks (GANs) as potential algorithms in phylogenomics inference (Smith & Hahn, 2023). GANs enable heuristic searches of complex model spaces, allowing for the evaluation of new models at each iteration.

There are not many AI-based algorithm for evolutionary studies. However, collective evidence regarding the performance of current tools indicates that AI is suitable for phylogeny inference and will gain increasing significance in the context of phylogenomics.

AI in Metabolomics

Metabolism refers to the biochemical processes that occur within living organisms to sustain life (Astarita et al., 2023). During the processes, small molecules known as metabolites are produced. Metabolites can be categorised into primary and secondary metabolites. Primary metabolites are essential for growth, development, and reproduction. In contrast, secondary metabolites often serve ecological functions. Metabolomics is the study of the metabolites within a system under specific physiological or pathological conditions.

Metabolomics is primarily used for identification of biomarkers, especially in the context of disease predictions. Biomarkers are measurable indicators of biological states or conditions. Unique metabolic profiles are associated with various diseases. Changes in metabolites level provide valuable insights into disease aetiology, status and therapeutic response (Anwardeen et al., 2023). For example, ceramides emerged as biomarkers that can predict adverse cardiovascular events, highlighting metabolites that can portray both physiological and pathological states (Astarita et al., 2023). From a food health perspective, the metabolic signatures associated with food intake and individual responses to dietary changes can be observed. Metabolomics identify biomarkers that reflect metabolic health and responsiveness to specific diets, enabling precise and personalised dietary recommendations. Tailored dietary advice based on individual metabolic profiles is often more effective than a general guideline, promoting better health outcomes (Guasch-Ferré et al., 2018; Moniuk, 2024; Tebani & Bekri, 2019).

Apart from biomarker identification, metabolites are also useful in drug target discovery. Drug targets are molecules that can be modified through medications to achieve therapeutic effects. Flux analysis is one of the methods used in metabolomics to identify druggable metabolic enzymes and regulators. This approach measures the rate of conversion between metabolites, revealing activities of enzymes and metabolic pathways under different conditions. By studying the conversion rates, researchers evaluate drugs' efficacies and identify promising drug targets. Another approach,

Activity-Based Metabolic Profiling (ABMP), detects changes in metabolites level from enzymatic activities, leading to gene functional annotation and drug target discovery (Tounta et al., 2021).

Metabolomics has proven its importance in maintaining and promoting human health. However, there are several bottlenecks in metabolomic analysis: i) the data often contains a significant amount of missing information, complicating multivariate analysis and classification; ii) large volume of information generated which require advanced statistical techniques for meaningful analysis (Tounta et al., 2021); iii) lack of validation studies to confirm biomarkers effectiveness; iv) experimental variabilities leading to non-standardised outputs for a meaningful interpretation (Anwardeen et al., 2023; Moniuk, 2024).

There are an increasing number of publications that implement AI techniques to address the challenges in metabolomics. AI techniques such as neural networks and deep learning are effective in handling non-linear relationships, complex and high dimensionality of metabolomic data. Neural network consists of layered units called neurons. These neurons evaluate multiple inputs to produce a single output. The network learns to link inputs (metabolite concentrations) to a desired output (disease risk). The algorithms can identify the most relevant features and reduce noise from the high-dimensional nature of metabolomic data, which often consists of hundreds or thousands of metabolites. This enables researchers to extract meaningful insights from complex metabolic profiles, facilitating a deeper understanding of metabolic processes in healthy and sick hosts (Galal et al., 2022).

Metabolomics, coupled with AI, is becoming a powerful tool to understand biochemical changes in different health conditions. As AI continues to evolve, it promises to enhance the metabolomics field, leading to a more reliable and early disease diagnosis. It would be able to provide valuable insights into physiological states and prediction of potential biomarkers.

AI in Transcriptomics

A transcriptome refers to the complete collection of RNA transcripts available in an individual or a population. In contrast to targeted approaches, transcriptome analysis offers insights into the spatiotemporal conditions of genes and their possible interactions. The sequencing of transcriptomes from multiple species has resulted in the discovery of novel genes, variations associated with alternative splicing and gene interaction networks. These insights can enhance our understanding of processes related to cellular differentiation, cancer development and gene regulation (Dong & Chen, 2013; Lowe et al., 2017; Rajawat, 2018). In addition to the discovery of the aforementioned aspects, transcriptome was also analysed for the changes in spatiotemporal gene expressions (McLendon et al., 2008; Rajawat, 2018; Salemi et al., 2024). There are three common techniques used for transcriptomics, which are Expressed Sequence Tag (EST), microarray and RNA sequencing (RNA-Seq) (Cockrum et al., 2020; Lowe et al., 2017; Rajawat, 2018; Sun et al., 2018). The EST and microarray are able to quantitate gene expression but the outputs are limited to their yields and costs. Next-Generation Sequencing (NGS) however has revolutionised transcriptome analysis by allowing massively parallel sequencing. Deep sequencing generates millions to billions of sequences and sufficiently covers the transcriptome and improved sensitivity for detection of lowly expressed genes.

A proper bioinformatics approach is crucial in ensuring sequence quality, mapping of sequencing reads to the reference genomes, and identifying differentially expressed genes. Another major issue in transcriptome analysis is its requirement on computing resources and the large volumes of sequencing data (Lowe et al., 2017; You et al., 2024). Research by Partin et al. (2023) highlights that gene expression data plays a crucial role in drug response prediction (DRP) models. Approximately 90% of these models utilise gene expression data, either alone or in conjunction with other data types, such as mutation data and copy number variations (Figure 11.3). This reliance on gene expression comes from the 2014 NCI-DREAM challenge, which found that gene expression microarray data was better at predicting drug response than other data types (Costello et al., 2014). Consequently, it has been recognised as a valuable feature for developing effective DRP models. Building on these insights, the paper by Partin et al. (2023) discusses the application of various deep learning architectures to gene expression data. Models like dense neural networks, convolutional neural networks (CNNs), and graph neural networks (GNNs) have been employed in this context.

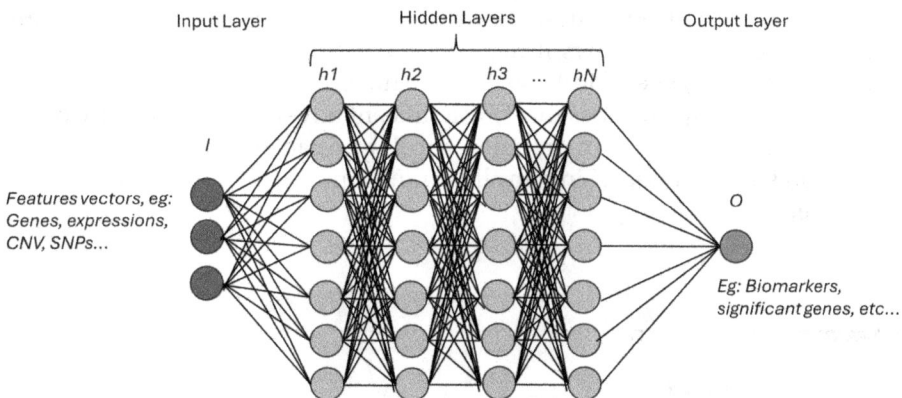

FIGURE 11.3
Deep Learning Neural Network for Transcriptomic Data Analysis.

Through multiple layers, these neural networks were able to identify more complex and informative representations from the gene expression profiles that could then be used to predict drug treatment outcomes.

Maurya et al. (2021) demonstrated AI can identify potential disease biomarkers, such as the *TMEM236* in colorectal cancer. To address the issue on class imbalance of the dataset, oversampling techniques were applied. Feature selection techniques such as LASSO (Least Absolute Shrinkage and Selection Operator) and Relief were applied to identify significant genes within the large datasets. The step was crucial for finding the most informative genes among the vast arrays of expression data. These methods reduced the initial 23,186 gene set to a smaller set, with LASSO identifying 64 key features. After feature selection, classification models such as Random Forest (RF), K-Nearest Neighbours (KNN) and Artificial Neural Networks (ANN) were used. Notably, the combination of classification model and feature selection managed to achieve up to 100% accuracy in classifying samples. The combinatorial approaches led to the discovery of potential new biomarkers, including TMEM236, which had not previously been linked to colorectal cancer.

In another study, Chawla et al. (2022) showed AI improved drug response prediction in cancer. A deep neural network (DNN) framework was used to process bulk RNA sequencing data from multiple cancer cell lines. The framework converts gene expression data into pathway enrichment scores. The scores along with numeric drug descriptors serve as the input features for the predictive models. The DNN architecture consists of features analysed in 2–6 hidden layers, which can be adjusted as a hyperparameter. The model was trained using high-throughput screening data from public resources such as the Cancer Cell Line Encyclopedia (CCLE), the Genomics of Drug Sensitivity in Cancer (GDSC) and the Cancer Therapeutics Response Portal v2 (CTRPv2). By integrating pathway activity estimates with drug descriptors, the framework achieved high accuracy in predicting drug sensitivity, often measured as IC50 values. The model's incorporation of pathway scores and drug descriptors allows it to make predictions for nearly any sample-drug combination, even for drugs that are not encountered during training.

The AI-driven approaches mark a significant advancement in many bioinformatics areas. Using AI in precision oncology as an example, it provides an insight on suitability of AI in handling transcriptomic data that are complex in nature.

AI in Proteomics

The application of AI in protein research can be dated back to 1993 (Rost & Sander, 1993). Proteomics is the study of the complete collection of proteins produced in an organism, specifically the chemical modifications, structures and interactions of proteins. The proteome holds functional information of genes. Unlike genome which is relatively fixed, the proteome is dynamic and in response to multiple signals and factors. Understanding proteome is essential for exploring gene function, though it is more complex than studying genes alone (Aslam et al., 2017). A major application of proteomics is functional proteomics. Functional proteomics explores the roles of proteins in biological processes and systems, a more direct approach to understanding gene function and regulation (Nadeau et al., 2021). Different amino acid sequences lead to various protein shapes and affect their functions. Tools like SWISS-MODEL and Modeller are used for the prediction of protein structures and 3D modelling.

The key technologies in proteome identification are mass spectrometry (MS), Matrix-Assisted Laser Desorption Ionisation Time of Flight (MALDI-TOF), and protein microarrays (Han et al., 2008; Greco et al., 2018; Darie-Ion et al., 2022). Samples will be sent in the form of mixtures such as blood, urine or tissue samples for protein abundance and structural modification information identification. Liquid Chromatography coupled with Tandem MS (LC-MS/MS) shows an advantage in sample preparation and data analysis, enhancing its clinical applications. On the other hand, protein microarrays allow high-throughput detection of proteins from small sample volumes, making them suitable for applications where only limited amounts of samples are available (Birhanu, 2023).

Complexity in capturing protein structures and protein-ligand docking are the main issues in proteomics. Techniques such as neural networks and graph convolutional networks (GCN) are commonly used for this purpose (Zheng et al., 2022). The AI algorithms analyse large biological datasets, learning hidden patterns and relationships that could not be predicted by traditional methods. For instance, X. Wang et al. (2021) proposed a three-tunnel deep neural network model to explore drug-target binding affinities. The model capitalises on neural networks' ability to discern intricate patterns from a large dataset, potentially enhancing the accuracy of drug-target interaction predictions. The innovative aspect of this model lies in its three-channel input system. It processes protein sequences, positive drug samples, and negative samples at the same time. The model utilises convolutional neural networks to extract protein features and multi-layer perceptron to analyse drug molecules. Additionally, it employs a triplet loss function to improve feature discrimination. Overall, this AI-driven approach outperforms previous methods, highlighting its potential to speed up drug discovery processes.

The use of GCN in the GADTI method, proposed by Liu et al. (2021), has shown significant advantages in the field of proteomics. This methodology begins by constructing a heterogeneous network that effectively integrates various data sources, including information about drugs, protein targets, diseases and side effects. By doing so, it enhances the analysis and understanding of complex biological interactions. GADTI operates on a graph autoencoder framework that consists of an encoder and a decoder.

The GCN learns to encode the complex relationships into lower-dimensional representations, useful for predicting new interactions. The encoder features a GCN that gathers local neighbourhood information, along with a Random Walk with Restart (RWR) component that spreads node influence throughout the network. This combination enables GADTI to effectively capture both local and global network structures. The decoder employs the DistMult matrix factorisation model to recreate the original network from the learned node representations. By transforming protein interaction data into a graph, GADTI demonstrates that graph-based deep learning techniques improve predictions of drug-target interactions.

AI can process large datasets, detect complex patterns, and make predictions faster and more accurately than traditional methods. AI models are trained on various atomic features, such as bond lengths and angles, compared to known protein crystal structures. The Critical Assessment of Structure Prediction (CASP) evaluates these methods biannually, showcasing the usability of tools such as the MULTICOM method and deep learning techniques in predicting protein contact distances. Research by Staples et al. (2019) examined different AI approaches that improve the accuracy of protein structure prediction. Neural networks, especially deep and convolutional neural networks (CNNs), are effective in extracting important features and identifying patterns in protein folding. A leading tool in proteomics is AlphaFold. AlphaFold can predict structural information without referring to any known protein structure database. AlphaFold uses a two-stage neural network, that is the Evoformer and the Structure Module. The Evoformer processes input data, including the protein's amino acid sequence and multiple sequence alignments of orthologous proteins. This stage employs a unique attention mechanism to understand evolutionary relationships and interactions between amino acids. Structure Module refines the 3D protein structure predictions through iterative processes. It uses "invariant point attention" to maintain 3D geometry. The model is trained end-to-end to predict 3D coordinates directly. The step also employs multi-task learning to predict structure, estimate accuracy, and reconstruct missing parts from the input sequences. AlphaFold enhances its learning through self-distillation techniques, using both labelled and unlabelled protein data. By training on large datasets of protein sequences and structures, AlphaFold has achieved remarkable accuracy, outperforming other methods in the CASP14 assessment. The latest version, AlphaFold3, improves upon its predecessor by predicting the joint structure of complexes, including proteins, nucleic acids and small molecules. This version uses a diffusion-based approach, enhancing accuracy for complex interactions, such as protein-ligand and antibody-antigen bindings (Jumper et al., 2021; Abramson et al., 2024).

In summary, proteomics is a powerful field that explores the complex world of proteins and their functions. Technologies and AI tools in this area enhance our understanding of biology and disease, leading to advancements in diagnostics and treatment strategies. Despite challenges, the integration of AI continues to propel proteomics into a promising future.

AI in Epigenomics

Epigenomics is the study of biochemical modifications to DNA and proteins that regulate gene expression without changing the DNA sequence (Z. Chen et al., 2017). DNA methylation and histone modification are significant in determining gene expression in different cell types and contexts. Various techniques were employed to study epigenomics, each targeting different elements of the epigenome. One of the commonly used methods is Assay for Transposase-Accessible Chromatin with high-throughput sequencing (ATAC-seq) (Buenrostro et al., 2015). This method identifies regions of open chromatin that are more accessible to transcription factors and other regulatory proteins. It provides a comprehensive view of chromatin accessibility and highlights the most active transcriptional regions of the genome.

Epigenomics has found valuable applications in many areas. In agriculture, scientists identify crop traits and stress responses through epigenomics of plants, providing an alternative to traditional genetic approaches. This is especially useful for crops with limited genetic diversity. By manipulating epigenetic variations, researchers can improve stress tolerance, yield, and adaptability in plants. Techniques such as epigenome editing can create desirable traits by altering how genes are expressed. The changes affect plant development and crop response to environmental factors (Agarwal et al., 2020). In medicine, epigenomics research identify biomarkers for diagnosis and prognosis. RNA-binding proteins serve as important biomarkers for diagnosing diseases, monitoring disease progression and predicting treatment responses. Targeting these proteins and their epigenetic changes offers new possibilities for innovative treatments (Dang et al., 2024). The approach in yielding epigenomic profiles serves as one of the components in personalised medicine.

The current methods for analysing whole genome DNA methylation are often expensive and time-consuming. Techniques like bisulfite genomic sequencing require specialised skills, making them inaccessible to many researchers. Additionally, obtaining comprehensive DNA methylation profiles from various cell types and tissues poses significant challenges (Sandoval et al., 2011). The epigenome is highly dynamic, even within a single tissue, and disentangling epigenetic effects among heterogeneous cell populations can be difficult (Fallet et al., 2023). Furthermore, epigenetic assays often require substantial amounts of cellular material, complicating their integration with large-scale genetic studies (Rubin et al., 2019). Previous methods are known to have limitations in throughput and sensitivity, hindering their ability to detect subtle but biologically significant differences in chromatin accessibility and gene expression (Ma et al., 2020). For these, AI has been used to predict DNA methylation patterns and classify genetic changes. One example of an advanced tool for epigenomics study is DeepCpG. It uses deep neural networks to predict DNA methylation in individual cells more accurately than previous known methods and tools. The core algorithm consists of three interconnected modules. The first module uses convolutional neural networks (CNNs) to extract features from a 1001 base pair window around each CpG site. The second module employs bidirectional gated recurrent units (GRUs) to model relationships between neighbouring CpG sites across different cells. The third module combines outputs from the first and second modules to predict methylation states for multiple cells at once. This architecture allows DeepCpG to automatically learn complex sequence patterns and capture long-range dependencies in the methylation process without the need for predefined genomic annotations. Its multi-task learning approach facilitates information sharing across cells, making it effective for sparse single-cell data. By leveraging deep learning techniques, DeepCpG can identify important features directly from raw data. It adapts well to different cell types and experimental protocols. This capability leads to superior accuracy in predicting methylation states, especially in low-coverage regions or areas with high variability (Angermueller et al., 2017).

Chang et al. (2018) have also demonstrated deep learning techniques, specifically CNNs, can be used to identify genetic mutations and epigenetic modifications (such as O(6)-methylguanine-DNA methyltransferase (MGMT) promoter methylation) in gliomas using non-invasive Magnetic Resonance Imaging (MRI) as an input data. This method marks a significant advance in brain tumour characterisation. It offers a new, non-invasive way to infer genetic and epigenetic information. The CNN enables researchers to extract complex patterns from MRI data that relate them to genetic and epigenetic changes. The accuracy rates are as high as 94% for Isocitrate Dehydrogenase 1 (IDH1) mutation, 92% for 1p/19q codeletion, and 83% for MGMT promoter methylation. This approach could reduce the need for invasive tissue sampling, allowing the study of genetic and epigenetic changes in larger groups of glioma patients. Additionally, this AI-driven method identifies specific imaging features linked to each genetic or epigenetic alteration, such as enhancement patterns and tumour locations.

The ability of AI in detecting patterns which are impossible to be achieved by human observation highlights the need for AI-driven bioinformatics tools. This could lead to new insights and potential discovery on epigenetic changes in affecting phenotypes of an individual, especially in healthcare.

The Future of Bioinformatics: Advancing Into
Multi-Omics Research through Artificial Intelligence

The Next Generation Sequencing and other technologies have led to a significant increase of biological data in public databases, such as NCBI, European Nucleotide Archive (ENA) and Ensembl. Consequently, life science research has shifted from hypothesis-driven to data-driven research, opening new avenues for discovery and analysis. The contributions of genomics, transcriptomics, proteomics, metabolomics and epigenetics have been discussed in many reports. However, the current approaches still do not utilise the omics data to its full potential.

Multi-omics or integrative omics merges data from independent omics into single component for analyses (Ballard et al., 2024). Multi-omics is a new modelling approach and is believed to be a changer in bioinformatics research. While it could provide a more precise result, the progression of multi-omics was challenged by several factors. The major issue is the augmentation of data complexity for analysis when the output yielded from individual omics was combined as a single vector. For this reason, the nature of AI is believed to be highly potential to cater to the complexity of the data in multi-omics.

The future of multi-omics research, especially when combined with AI, holds great promise (Figure 11.4) for developments in many life science

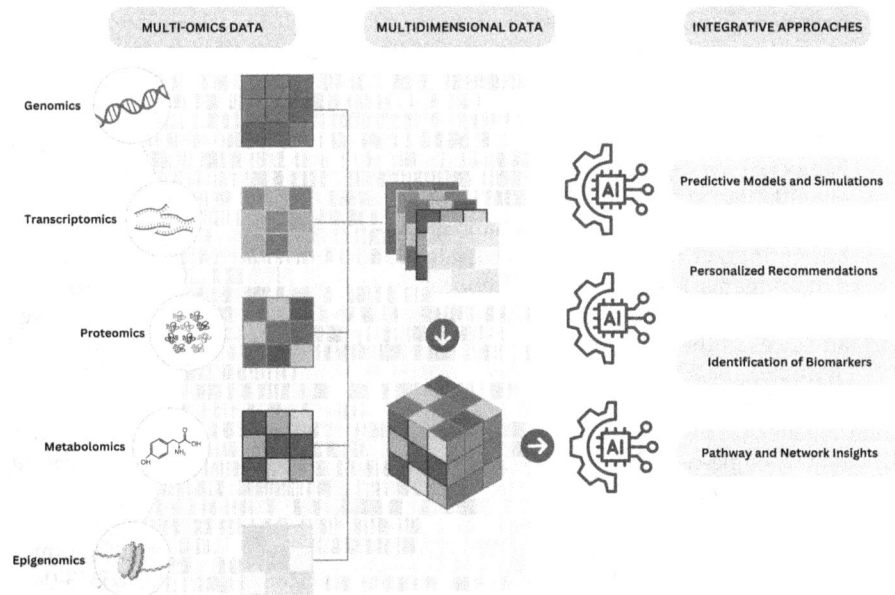

FIGURE 11.4
Integration of Multi-Omics Data with AI for Comprehensive Biological Insights.

areas. Although there were reports on AI applications in the multi-omics research (Gao et al., 2022; Wei et al., 2023; Ahmed et al., 2024), the "curse of dimensionality" will always persist due to variability of research design and data. Hence, future research will focus on AI modelling that can effectively combine data from multiple -omics layers, enabling a more comprehensive understanding of biological systems.

Reference

Abdelwahab, O., Belzile, F., & Torkamaneh, D. (2023). Performance analysis of conventional and AI-based variant callers using short and long reads. *BMC Bioinformatics, 24*(1), 472. https://doi.org/10.1186/s12859-023-05596-3

Abramson, J., Adler, J., Dunger, J., Evans, R., Green, T., Pritzel, A., Ronneberger, O., Willmore, L., Ballard, A. J., Bambrick, J., Bodenstein, S. W., Evans, D. A., Hung, C.-C., O'Neill, M., Reiman, D., Tunyasuvunakool, K., Wu, Z., Žemgulytė, A., Arvaniti, E., … Jumper, J. M. (2024). Accurate structure prediction of biomolecular interactions with AlphaFold 3. *Nature, 630*(8016), 493–500. https://doi.org/10.1038/s41586-024-07487-w

Agarwal, G., Kudapa, H., Ramalingam, A., Choudhary, D., Sinha, P., Garg, V., Singh, V. K., Patil, G. B., Pandey, M. K., Nguyen, H. T., Guo, B., Sunkar, R., Niederhuth, C. E., & Varshney, R. K. (2020). Epigenetics and epigenomics: Underlying mechanisms, relevance, and implications in crop improvement. *Functional & Integrative Genomics, 20*(6), 739–761. https://doi.org/10.1007/s10142-020-00756-7

Ahmed, Z., Wan, S., Zhang, F., & Zhong, W. (2024). Artificial intelligence for omics data analysis. *BMC Methods, 1*(1), 4. https://doi.org/10.1186/s44330-024-00004-5

Ahsan, M. U., Liu, Q., Fang, L., & Wang, K. (2021). NanoCaller for accurate detection of SNPs and indels in difficult-to-map regions from long-read sequencing by haplotype-aware deep neural networks. *Genome Biology, 22*(1), 261. https://doi.org/10.1186/s13059-021-02472-2

Ai In Bioinformatics Market Size, Demand & Industry Research By 2030. (n.d.). Data bridge market research. Retrieved falseAugust 30, 2024, from https://www.databridgemarketresearch.com/reports/global-ai-in-bioinformatics-market

Amas, J. C., Thomas, W. J. W., Zhang, Y., Edwards, D., & Batley, J. (2023). Key advances in the new era of genomics-assisted disease resistance improvement of *Brassica* Species. *Phytopathology®, 113*(5), 771–785. https://doi.org/10.1094/PHYTO-08-22-0289-FI

Angermueller, C., Lee, H. J., Reik, W., & Stegle, O. (2017). DeepCpG: Accurate prediction of single-cell DNA methylation states using deep learning. *Genome Biology, 18*(1), 67. https://doi.org/10.1186/s13059-017-1189-z

Anwardeen, N. R., Diboun, I., Mokrab, Y., Althani, A. A., & Elrayess, M. A. (2023). Statistical methods and resources for biomarker discovery using metabolomics. *BMC Bioinformatics, 24*(1), 250. https://doi.org/10.1186/s12859-023-05383-0

Aslam, B., Basit, M., Nisar, M. A., Khurshid, M., & Rasool, M. H. (2017). Proteomics: Technologies and their applications. *Journal of Chromatographic Science*, 55(2), 182–196. https://doi.org/10.1093/chromsci/bmw167

Astarita, G., Kelly, R. S., & Lasky-Su, J. (2023). Metabolomics and lipidomics strategies in modern drug discovery and development. *Drug Discovery Today*, 28(10), 103751. https://doi.org/10.1016/j.drudis.2023.103751

Ballard, J. L., Wang, Z., Li, W., Shen, L., & Long, Q. (2024). Deep learning-based approaches for multi-omics data integration and analysis. *BioData Mining*, 17(1), 38. https://doi.org/10.1186/s13040-024-00391-z

Bazarkin, A., Morozov, A., Androsov, A., Fajkovic, H., Rivas, J. G., Singla, N., Koroleva, S., Teoh, J. Y.-C., Zvyagin, A. V., Shariat, S. F., Somani, B., & Enikeev, D. (2024). Assessment of prostate and bladder cancer genomic biomarkers using artificial intelligence: A systematic review. *Current Urology Reports*, 25(1), 19–35. https://doi.org/10.1007/s11934-023-01193-2

Birhanu, A. G. (2023). Mass spectrometry-based proteomics as an emerging tool in clinical laboratories. *Clinical Proteomics*, 20(1), 32. https://doi.org/10.1186/s12014-023-09424-x

Botlagunta, M., Botlagunta, M. D., Myneni, M. B., Lakshmi, D., Nayyar, A., Gullapalli, J. S., & Shah, M. A. (2023). Classification and diagnostic prediction of breast cancer metastasis on clinical data using machine learning algorithms. *Scientific Reports*, 13(1), 485. https://doi.org/10.1038/s41598-023-27548-w

Bouckaert, R., Vaughan, T. G., Barido-Sottani, J., Duchêne, S., Fourment, M., Gavryushkina, A., Heled, J., Jones, G., Kühnert, D., De Maio, N., Matschiner, M., Mendes, F. K., Müller, N. F., Ogilvie, H. A., du Plessis, L., Popinga, A., Rambaut, A., Rasmussen, D., Siveroni, I., … Drummond, A. J. (2019). BEAST 2.5: An advanced software platform for Bayesian evolutionary analysis. *PLoS Computational Biology*, 15(4), e1006650. https://doi.org/10.1371/journal.pcbi.1006650

Buenrostro, J., Wu, B., Chang, H., & Greenleaf, W. (2015). ATAC-seq: A method for assaying chromatin accessibility genome-wide. *Current Protocols in Molecular Biology / Edited by Frederick M. Ausubel … [et Al.]*, 109, 21.29.1. https://doi.org/10.1002/0471142727.mb2129s109

Chachar, Z., Fan, L., Chachar, S., Ahmed, N., Narejo, M.-N., Ahmed, N., Lai, R., & Qi, Y. (2024). Genetic and genomic pathways to improved wheat (Triticum aestivum L.) yields: A review. *Agronomy*, 14(6), Article 6. https://doi.org/10.3390/agronomy14061201

Challa, S., & Neelapu, N. R. R. (2019). Phylogenetic trees: Applications, construction, and assessment. In K. R. Hakeem, N. A. Shaik, B. Banaganapalli, & R. Elango (Eds.), *Essentials of Bioinformatics, Volume III: In Silico Life Sciences: Agriculture* (pp. 167–192). Springer International Publishing. https://doi.org/10.1007/978-3-030-19318-8_10

Chang, P., Grinband, J., Weinberg, B. D., Bardis, M., Khy, M., Cadena, G., Su, M.-Y., Cha, S., Filippi, C. G., Bota, D., Baldi, P., Poisson, L. M., Jain, R., & Chow, D. (2018). Deep-learning convolutional neural networks accurately classify genetic mutations in gliomas. *AJNR: American Journal of Neuroradiology*, 39(7), 1201–1207. https://doi.org/10.3174/ajnr.A5667

Chawla, S., Rockstroh, A., Lehman, M., Ratther, E., Jain, A., Anand, A., Gupta, A., Bhattacharya, N., Poonia, S., Rai, P., Das, N., Majumdar, A., Jayadeva, Ahuja G.,

Hollier B. G., Nelson C. C., & Sengupta D. (2022). Gene expression based inference of cancer drug sensitivity. *Nature Communications, 13*(1), 5680. https://doi.org/10.1038/s41467-022-33291-z

Chen, H., Yang, W., & Ji, Z. (2023). Machine learning-based identification of tumor-infiltrating immune cell-associated model with appealing implications in improving prognosis and immunotherapy response in bladder cancer patients. *Frontiers in Immunology, 14*. https://doi.org/10.3389/fimmu.2023.1171420

Chen, Z., Li, S., Subramaniam, S., Shyy, J. Y.-J., & Chien, S. (2017). Epigenetic regulation: A new frontier for biomedical engineers. *Annual Review of Biomedical Engineering, 19*, 195–219. https://doi.org/10.1146/annurev-bioeng-071516-044720

Clarridge, J. E. (2004). Impact of 16S rRNA gene sequence analysis for identification of bacteria on clinical microbiology and infectious diseases. *Clinical Microbiology Reviews, 17*(4), 840–862, table of contents. https://doi.org/10.1128/CMR.17.4.840-862.2004

Cockrum, C., Kaneshiro, K. R., Rechtsteiner, A., Tabuchi, T. M., & Strome, S. (2020). A primer for generating and using transcriptome data and gene sets. *Development (Cambridge, England), 147*(24), dev193854. https://doi.org/10.1242/dev.193854

Costello, J. C., Heiser, L. M., Georgii, E., Gönen, M., Menden, M. P., Wang, N. J., Bansal, M., Ammad-Ud-Din, M., Hintsanen, P., Khan, S. A., Mpindi, J.-P., Kallioniemi, O., Honkela, A., Aittokallio, T., Wennerberg, K., Collins, J. J., Gallahan, D., Singer, D., Saez-Rodriguez, J., ... Stolovitzky, G. (2014). A community effort to assess and improve drug sensitivity prediction algorithms. *Nature Biotechnology, 32*(12), 1202–1212. https://doi.org/10.1038/nbt.2877

Dang, Y., Wang, W., Lyu, A., Wang, L., & Ji, G. (2024). Editorial: Application of genomics and epigenetics in disease and syndrome classification. *Frontiers in Genetics, 15*. https://doi.org/10.3389/fgene.2024.1421163

Darie-Ion, L., Whitham, D., Jayathirtha, M., Rai, Y., Neagu, A.-N., Darie, C. C., & Petre, B. A. (2022). Applications of MALDI-MS/MS-based proteomics in biomedical research. *Molecules, 27*(19), 6196. https://doi.org/10.3390/molecules27196196

Dias, R., & Torkamani, A. (2019). Artificial intelligence in clinical and genomic diagnostics. *Genome Medicine, 11*(1), 70. https://doi.org/10.1186/s13073-019-0689-8

Dong, Z., & Chen, Y. (2013). Transcriptomics: Advances and approaches. *Science China Life Sciences, 56*(10), 960–967. https://doi.org/10.1007/s11427-013-4557-2

Edgar, R. C. (2004). MUSCLE: Multiple sequence alignment with high accuracy and high throughput. *Nucleic Acids Research, 32*(5), 1792–1797. https://doi.org/10.1093/nar/gkh340

Fallet, M., Blanc, M., Di Criscio, M., Antczak, P., Engwall, M., Guerrero Bosagna, C., Rüegg, J., & Keiter, S. H. (2023). Present and future challenges for the investigation of transgenerational epigenetic inheritance. *Environment International, 172*, 107776. https://doi.org/10.1016/j.envint.2023.107776

Freed, D., Pan, R., Chen, H., Li, Z., Hu, J., & Aldana, R. (2022). *DNAscope: High accuracy small variant calling using machine learning* (p. 2022.05.20.492556). *bioRxiv*. https://doi.org/10.1101/2022.05.20.492556

Galal, A., Talal, M., & Moustafa, A. (2022). Applications of machine learning in metabolomics: Disease modeling and classification. *Frontiers in Genetics, 13*. https://doi.org/10.3389/fgene.2022.1017340

Gao, F., Huang, K., & Xing, Y. (2022). Artificial intelligence in omics. *Genomics, Proteomics & Bioinformatics, 20*(5), 811–813. https://doi.org/10.1016/j.gpb.2023.01.002

Goldman, A. D., & Landweber, L. F. (2016). What is a genome? *PLOS Genetics, 12*(7), e1006181. https://doi.org/10.1371/journal.pgen.1006181

Greco, V., Piras, C., Pieroni, L., Ronci, M., Putignani, L., Roncada, P., & Urbani, A. (2018). Applications of MALDI-TOF mass spectrometry in clinical proteomics. *Expert Review of Proteomics, 15*(8), 683–696. https://doi.org/10.1080/14789450.2018.1505510

Guasch-Ferré, M., Bhupathiraju, S. N., & Hu, F. B. (2018). Use of metabolomics in improving assessment of dietary intake. *Clinical Chemistry, 64*(1), 82–98. https://doi.org/10.1373/clinchem.2017.272344

Hall, B. G. (2013). Building phylogenetic trees from molecular data with MEGA. *Molecular Biology and Evolution, 30*(5), 1229–1235. https://doi.org/10.1093/molbev/mst012

Han, X., Aslanian, A., & Yates, J. R. (2008). Mass Spectrometry for Proteomics. *Current Opinion in Chemical Biology, 12*(5), 483–490. https://doi.org/10.1016/j.cbpa.2008.07.024

Jumper, J., Evans, R., Pritzel, A., Green, T., Figurnov, M., Ronneberger, O., Tunyasuvunakool, K., Bates, R., Žídek, A., Potapenko, A., Bridgland, A., Meyer, C., Kohl, S. A. A., Ballard, A. J., Cowie, A., Romera-Paredes, B., Nikolov, S., Jain, R., Adler, J., … Hassabis, D. (2021). Highly accurate protein structure prediction with AlphaFold. *Nature, 596*(7873), 583–589. https://doi.org/10.1038/s41586-021-03819-2

Jung, H., Ventura, T., Chung, J. S., Kim, W.-J., Nam, B.-H., Kong, H. J., Kim, Y.-O., Jeon, M.-S., & Eyun, S. (2020). Twelve quick steps for genome assembly and annotation in the classroom. *PLOS Computational Biology, 16*(11), e1008325. https://doi.org/10.1371/journal.pcbi.1008325

Katoh, K., & Standley, D. M. (2013). MAFFT multiple sequence alignment software version 7: Improvements in performance and usability. *Molecular Biology and Evolution, 30*(4), 772–780. https://doi.org/10.1093/molbev/mst010

Kircher, M., Witten, D. M., Jain, P., O'Roak, B. J., Cooper, G. M., & Shendure, J. (2014). A general framework for estimating the relative pathogenicity of human genetic variants. *Nature Genetics, 46*(3), 310–315. https://doi.org/10.1038/ng.2892

Koboldt, D. C. (2020). Best practices for variant calling in clinical sequencing. *Genome Medicine, 12*(1), 91. https://doi.org/10.1186/s13073-020-00791-w

Kosov, S., Shirahama, K., Li, C., & Grzegorzek, M. (2018). Environmental microorganism classification using conditional random fields and deep convolutional neural networks. *Pattern Recognition, 77*, 248–261. https://doi.org/10.1016/j.patcog.2017.12.021

Lander, E. S., Linton, L. M., Birren, B., Nusbaum, C., Zody, M. C., Baldwin, J., Devon, K., Dewar, K., Doyle, M., FitzHugh, W., Funke, R., Gage, D., Harris, K., Heaford, A., Howland, J., Kann, L., Lehoczky, J., LeVine, R., McEwan, P., … The Wellcome Trust (2001). Initial sequencing and analysis of the human genome. *Nature, 409*(6822), 860–921. https://doi.org/10.1038/35057062

Ledford, H. (2007). All about Craig: The first "full" genome sequence. *Nature, 449*(7158), 6–7. https://doi.org/10.1038/449006a

Lee, M. (2023). Deep Learning Techniques with Genomic Data in Cancer Prognosis: A Comprehensive Review of the 2021–2023 Literature. *Biology, 12*(7), Article 7. https://doi.org/10.3390/biology12070893

Lee, S., Kerns, S., Ostrer, H., Rosenstein, B., Deasy, J. O., & Oh, J. H. (2018). Machine learning on a genome-wide association study to predict late genitourinary toxicity after prostate radiation therapy. *International Journal of Radiation Oncology, Biology, Physics, 101*(1), 128–135. https://doi.org/10.1016/j.ijrobp.2018.01.054

Li, H., Handsaker, B., Wysoker, A., Fennell, T., Ruan, J., Homer, N., Marth, G., Abecasis, G., Durbin, R., & 1000 Genome Project Data Processing Subgroup. (2009). The Sequence Alignment/Map format and SAMtools. *Bioinformatics (Oxford, England), 25*(16), 2078–2079. https://doi.org/10.1093/bioinformatics/btp352

Li, Z., Wang, Y., & Wang, F. (2018). A study on fast calling variants from next-generation sequencing data using decision tree. *BMC Bioinformatics, 19*(1), 145. https://doi.org/10.1186/s12859-018-2147-9

Liu, Z., Chen, Q., Lan, W., Pan, H., Hao, X., & Pan, S. (2021). GADTI: Graph Autoencoder Approach for DTI Prediction From Heterogeneous Network. *Frontiers in Genetics, 12.* https://doi.org/10.3389/fgene.2021.650821

Lourenço, V. M., Ogutu, J. O., Rodrigues, R. A. P., Posekany, A., & Piepho, H.-P. (2024). Genomic prediction using machine learning: A comparison of the performance of regularized regression, ensemble, instance-based and deep learning methods on synthetic and empirical data. *BMC Genomics, 25*(1), 152. https://doi.org/10.1186/s12864-023-09933-x

Lowe, R., Shirley, N., Bleackley, M., Dolan, S., & Shafee, T. (2017). Transcriptomics technologies. *PLOS Computational Biology, 13*(5), e1005457. https://doi.org/10.1371/journal.pcbi.1005457

Ma, S., Zhang, B., LaFave, L. M., Earl, A. S., Chiang, Z., Hu, Y., Ding, J., Brack, A., Kartha, V. K., Tay, T., Law, T., Lareau, C., Hsu, Y.-C., Regev, A., & Buenrostro, J. D. (2020). Chromatin Potential Identified by shared single-cell profiling of RNA and Chromatin. *Cell, 183*(4), 1103–1116. https://doi.org/10.1016/j.cell.2020.09.056

Magro, D., Venezia, M., & Rita Balistreri, C. (2024). The omics technologies and liquid biopsies: Advantages, limitations, applications. *Medicine in Omics, 11,* 100039. https://doi.org/10.1016/j.meomic.2024.100039

Maurya, N. S., Kushwaha, S., Chawade, A., & Mani, A. (2021). Transcriptome profiling by combined machine learning and statistical R analysis identifies TMEM236 as a potential novel diagnostic biomarker for colorectal cancer. *Scientific Reports, 11*(1), 14304. https://doi.org/10.1038/s41598-021-92692-0

McKenna, A., Hanna, M., Banks, E., Sivachenko, A., Cibulskis, K., Kernytsky, A., Garimella, K., Altshuler, D., Gabriel, S., Daly, M., & DePristo, M. A. (2010). The genome analysis toolkit: A MapReduce framework for analyzing next-generation DNA sequencing data. *Genome Research, 20*(9), 1297–1303. https://doi.org/10.1101/gr.107524.110

McLendon, R., Friedman, A., Bigner, D., Van Meir, E. G., Brat, D. J. M., Mastrogianakis, G., Olson, J. J., Mikkelsen, T., Lehman, N., Aldape, K., Alfred Yung, W. K., Bogler, O., VandenBerg, S., Berger, M., Prados, M., Muzny, D., Morgan, M., Scherer, S., Sabo, A., … National Human Genome Research Institute. (2008). Comprehensive genomic characterization defines human glioblastoma genes and core pathways. *Nature, 455*(7216), 1061–1068. https://doi.org/10.1038/nature07385

Micheel, C. M., Nass, S. J., Omenn, G. S., Trials, C. (2012). Omics-based clinical discovery: Science, technology, and applications. In *Evolution of Translational Omics: Lessons Learned and the Path Forward*. National Academies Press (US). https://www.ncbi.nlm.nih.gov/books/NBK202165/

Min, E. K., Lee, A. N., Lee, J.-Y., Shim, I., Kim, P., Kim, T.-Y., Kim, K.-T., & Lee, S. (2021). Advantages of omics technology for evaluating cadmium toxicity in zebrafish. *Toxicological Research*, 37(4), 395–403. https://doi.org/10.1007/s43188-020-00082-x

Moniuk. (2024). Metabolomics in personalized nutrition: Identifying biomarkers for dietary interventions. *13*(3). https://doi.org/10.4172/2168-9652.1000465

Mukherjee, S., Kumar, P., Saini, R., Roy, P., Dogra, D. P., & Kim, B.-G. (2017). *Plant Disease Identification using Deep Neural Networks*. J. Multim. Inf. Syst. https://www.semanticscholar.org/paper/Plant-Disease-Identification-using-Deep-Neural-Mukherjee-Kumar/91713deff92c335342e12d7f750584b1537930d2

Nadeau, R., Byvsheva, A., & Lavallée-Adam, M. (2021). PIGNON: A protein–protein interaction-guided functional enrichment analysis for quantitative proteomics. *BMC Bioinformatics*, 22(1), 302. https://doi.org/10.1186/s12859-021-04042-6

Nurk, S., Koren, S., Rhie, A., Rautiainen, M., Bzikadze, A. V., Mikheenko, A., Vollger, M. R., Altemose, N., Uralsky, L., Gershman, A., Aganezov, S., Hoyt, S. J., Diekhans, M., Logsdon, G. A., Alonge, M., Antonarakis, S. E., Borchers, M., Bouffard, G. G., Brooks, S. Y., … Phillippy, A. M. (2022). The complete sequence of a human genome. *Science*, 376(6588), 44–53. https://doi.org/10.1126/science.abj6987

Partin, A., Brettin, T. S., Zhu, Y., Narykov, O., Clyde, A., Overbeek, J., & Stevens, R. L. (2023). Deep learning methods for drug response prediction in cancer: Predominant and emerging trends. *Frontiers in Medicine*, 10, 1086097. https://doi.org/10.3389/fmed.2023.1086097

Poplin, R., Chang, P.-C., Alexander, D., Schwartz, S., Colthurst, T., Ku, A., Newburger, D., Dijamco, J., Nguyen, N., Afshar, P. T., Gross, S. S., Dorfman, L., McLean, C. Y., & DePristo, M. A. (2018). A universal SNP and small-indel variant caller using deep neural networks. *Nature Biotechnology*, 36(10), 983–987. https://doi.org/10.1038/nbt.4235

Prins, B. P., Leitsalu, L., Pärna, K., Fischer, K., Metspalu, A., Haller, T., & Snieder, H. (2021). Advances in genomic discovery and implications for personalized prevention and medicine: Estonia as example. *Journal of Personalized Medicine*, 11(5), Article 5. https://doi.org/10.3390/jpm11050358

Rainer, J., Gatto, L., & Weichenberger, C. X. (2019). ensembldb: An R package to create and use Ensembl-based annotation resources. *Bioinformatics*, 35(17), 3151–3153. https://doi.org/10.1093/bioinformatics/btz031

Rajawat, J. (2018). Transcriptomics. In P. Arivaradarajan & G. Misra (Eds.), *Omics Approaches, Technologies And Applications: Integrative Approaches For Understanding OMICS Data* (pp. 39–56). Springer. https://doi.org/10.1007/978-981-13-2925-8_3

Rentzsch, P., Witten, D., Cooper, G. M., Shendure, J., & Kircher, M. (2019). CADD: Predicting the deleteriousness of variants throughout the human genome. *Nucleic Acids Research*, 47(D1), D886–D894. https://doi.org/10.1093/nar/gky1016

Rost, B., & Sander, C. (1993). Improved prediction of protein secondary structure by use of sequence profiles and neural networks. *Proceedings of the National Academy of Sciences of the United States of America, 90*(16), 7558–7562.

Rubin, A. J., Parker, K. R., Satpathy, A. T., Qi, Y., Wu, B., Ong, A. J., Mumbach, M. R., Ji, A. L., Kim, D. S., Cho, S. W., Zarnegar, B. J., Greenleaf, W. J., Chang, H. Y., & Khavari, P. A. (2019). Coupled single-cell CRISPR screening and epigenomic profiling reveals causal gene regulatory networks. *Cell, 176*(1), 361–376. https://doi.org/10.1016/j.cell.2018.11.022

Saada, B., Zhang, T., Siga, E., Zhang, J., & Magalhães Muniz, M. M. (2024). Whole-genome alignment: Methods, challenges, and future directions. *Applied Sciences, 14*(11), Article 11. https://doi.org/10.3390/app14114837

Salemi, M., Schillaci, F. A., Lanza, G., Marchese, G., Salluzzo, M. G., Cordella, A., Caniglia, S., Bruccheri, M. G., Truda, A., Greco, D., Ferri, R., & Romano, C. (2024). Transcriptome Study in Sicilian Patients with Autism Spectrum Disorder. *Biomedicines, 12*(7), Article 7. https://doi.org/10.3390/biomedicines12071402

Salzberg, S. L. (2019). Next-generation genome annotation: We still struggle to get it right. *Genome Biology, 20*(1), 92. https://doi.org/10.1186/s13059-019-1715-2

Sandoval, J., Heyn, H., Moran, S., Serra-Musach, J., Pujana, M. A., Bibikova, M., & Esteller, M. (2011). Validation of a DNA methylation microarray for 450,000 CpG sites in the human genome. *Epigenetics.* https://doi.org/10.4161/epi.6.6.16196

Sanger, F., Air, G. M., Barrell, B. G., Brown, N. L., Coulson, A. R., Fiddes, J. C., Hutchison, C. A., Slocombe, P. M., & Smith, M. (1977). Nucleotide sequence of bacteriophage φX174 DNA. *Nature, 265*(5596), 687–695. https://doi.org/10.1038/265687a0

Sayood, K., & Otu, H. H. (2022). Introduction. In K. Sayood & H. H. Otu (Eds.), *Bioinformatics: A One Semester Course* (pp. 1–9). Springer International Publishing. https://doi.org/10.1007/978-3-031-20017-5_1

Seemann, T. (2014). Prokka: Rapid prokaryotic genome annotation. *Bioinformatics (Oxford, England), 30*(14), 2068–2069. https://doi.org/10.1093/bioinformatics/btu153

Smith, M. L., & Hahn, M. W. (2023). Phylogenetic inference using generative adversarial networks. *Bioinformatics, 39*(9), btad543. https://doi.org/10.1093/bioinformatics/btad543

Stanke, M., Schöffmann, O., Morgenstern, B., & Waack, S. (2006). Gene prediction in eukaryotes with a generalized hidden Markov model that uses hints from external sources. *BMC Bioinformatics, 7*(1), 62. https://doi.org/10.1186/1471-2105-7-62

Staples, M., Chan, L., Si, D., Johnson, K., Whyte, C., & Cao, R. (2019). Artificial intelligence for bioinformatics: Applications in protein folding prediction. *2019 IEEE Technology & Engineering Management Conference (TEMSCON)*, 1–8. https://doi.org/10.1109/TEMSCON.2019.8813656

Sun, M., Shao, X., & Wang, Y. (2018). Microarray Data Analysis for Transcriptome Profiling. In Y. Wang & M. Sun (Eds.), *Transcriptome Data Analysis: Methods and Protocols* (pp. 17–33). Springer. https://doi.org/10.1007/978-1-4939-7710-9_2

Talukder, A., Barham, C., Li, X., & Hu, H. (2020). Interpretation of deep learning in genomics and epigenomics. *Briefings in Bioinformatics, 22*(3), bbaa177. https://doi.org/10.1093/bib/bbaa177

Tatusova, T., DiCuccio, M., Badretdin, A., Chetvernin, V., Nawrocki, E. P., Zaslavsky, L., Lomsadze, A., Pruitt, K. D., Borodovsky, M., & Ostell, J. (2016). NCBI prokaryotic genome annotation pipeline. *Nucleic Acids Research, 44*(14), 6614–6624. https://doi.org/10.1093/nar/gkw569

Tebani, A., & Bekri, S. (2019). Paving the Way to Precision Nutrition Through Metabolomics. *Frontiers in Nutrition, 6.* https://doi.org/10.3389/fnut.2019.00041

Thompson, J. D., Gibson, T. J., & Higgins, D. G. (2002). Multiple sequence alignment using ClustalW and ClustalX. *Current Protocols in Bioinformatics, Chapter 2*, Unit 2.3. https://doi.org/10.1002/0471250953.bi0203s00

Tounta, V., Liu, Y., Cheyne, A., & Larrouy-Maumus, G. (2021). Metabolomics in infectious diseases and drug discovery. *Molecular Omics, 17*(3), 376–393. https://doi.org/10.1039/D1MO00017A

Wang, C., & Li, J. (2020). A Deep Learning Framework Identifies Pathogenic Noncoding Somatic Mutations from Personal Prostate Cancer Genomes. *Cancer Research, 80*(21), 4644–4654. https://doi.org/10.1158/0008-5472.CAN-20-1791

Wang, X., Zhong, Y., & Ding, M. (2021). Repositioning Drugs to the Mitochondrial Fusion Protein 2 by Three-Tunnel Deep Neural Network for Alzheimer's Disease. *Frontiers in Genetics, 12.* https://doi.org/10.3389/fgene.2021.638330

Wei, L., Niraula, D., Gates, E. D. H., Fu, J., Luo, Y., Nyflot, M. J., Bowen, S. R., El Naqa, I. M., & Cui, S. (2023). Artificial intelligence (AI) and machine learning (ML) in precision oncology: A review on enhancing discoverability through multiomics integration. *British Journal of Radiology, 96*(1150), 20230211. https://doi.org/10.1259/bjr.20230211

Wekesa, J. S., & Kimwele, M. (2023). A review of multi-omics data integration through deep learning approaches for disease diagnosis, prognosis, and treatment. *Frontiers in Genetics, 14.* https://doi.org/10.3389/fgene.2023.1199087

Wytock, T. P., & Motter, A. E. (2024). Cell reprogramming design by transfer learning of functional transcriptional networks. *Proceedings of the National Academy of Sciences, 121*(11), e2312942121. https://doi.org/10.1073/pnas.2312942121

Xie, J., Zhang, L., & Xiao, M. (2020). A Review of Artificial Intelligence Applications in Bacterial Genomics. *2020 IEEE International Conference on Bioinformatics and Biomedicine (BIBM)*, 1870–1876. https://doi.org/10.1109/BIBM49941.2020.9313323

Xie, T., & Zhang, C. (2023). *ARTree: A Deep Autoregressive Model for Phylogenetic Inference* (arXiv:2310.09553). arXiv. http://arxiv.org/abs/2310.09553

You, Y., Fu, Y., Li, L., Zhang, Z., Jia, S., Lu, S., Ren, W., Liu, Y., Xu, Y., Liu, X., Jiang, F., Peng, G., Sampath Kumar, A., Ritchie, M. E., Liu, X., & Tian, L. (2024). Systematic comparison of sequencing-based spatial transcriptomic methods. *Nature Methods, 21*(9), 1743–1754. https://doi.org/10.1038/s41592-024-02325-3

Zanti, M., Michailidou, K., Loizidou, M. A., Machattou, C., Pirpa, P., Christodoulou, K., Spyrou, G. M., Kyriacou, K., & Hadjisavvas, A. (2021). Performance evaluation of pipelines for mapping, variant calling and interval padding, for the analysis of NGS germline panels. *BMC Bioinformatics, 22*(1), 218. https://doi.org/10.1186/s12859-021-04144-1

Zhao, S., & Zhang, B. (2015). A comprehensive evaluation of ensembl, RefSeq, and UCSC annotations in the context of RNA-seq read mapping and gene quantification. *BMC Genomics, 16*(1), 97. https://doi.org/10.1186/s12864-015-1308-8

Zheng, P., Wang, S., Wang, X., & Zeng, X. (2022). Editorial: Artificial Intelligence in Bioinformatics and Drug Repurposing: Methods and Applications. *Frontiers in Genetics, 13.* https://doi.org/10.3389/fgene.2022.870795

Zou, Y., Zhang, Z., Zeng, Y., Hu, H., Hao, Y., Huang, S., & Li, B. (2024). Common methods for phylogenetic tree construction and their implementation in R. *Bioengineering, 11*(5), Article 5. https://doi.org/10.3390/bioengineering11050480

12

Charting the Future of AI in the Next Decade: Emerging Trends and Conclusions

Umar Ali Bukar, Hamza Ibrahim and Bello Sani Yahaya

Introduction

Artificial Intelligence (AI) stands as among the most transformative technologies of the present era, shaping industries, economies and societies across the globe, which has propelled into virtually every aspect of human endeavour by revolutionising industries, driving innovation, and reshaping traditional paradigms. Innovations behind this technology include big data, robotics, and the Internet of Things (IoT). This has resulted in a surge of enterprise-scale businesses integrating AI into their operations, with many others considering its adoption. Generative AI, which includes techniques like Generative Adversarial Networks (GANs) or Generative Pre-trained Transformers (GPT), has showcased the potential of AI, allowing machines to create new content (e.g., text, images, and music) by learning based on existing data. Hence, comprehending the taxonomy of the AI landscape is vital for shaping AI policies and applications. Moreover, it is imperative to highlight the trajectory of AI development and forecast its future impact, fuelled by unprecedented computing power, vast data availability, and breakthroughs in machine learning (ML) algorithms.

The purpose of this chapter is to offer an inclusive roadmap for the future of AI, highlighting the taxonomy of various AI techniques and methods. In particular, the dominant AI techniques such as machine learning, deep learning (DL), computer vision and data analytics techniques are discussed. The major achievements of AI in the last decade are covered. In addition, the major trends of AI in the next decade such as explainable AI and Edge AI are discussed.

DOI: 10.1201/9781003509196-12

Landscape of AI and Taxonomy

AI has rapidly evolved into a transformative technology, driving significant shifts across numerous domains, and impacting industries, societies and daily life. This section explores the AI landscape through a structured taxonomy, outlining the key categories of AI, its dominant enablers, significant achievements, and the diverse range of services AI provides. By understanding this taxonomy, we can better appreciate AI's role in shaping the present and future of technology-driven environments.

AI Taxonomy

There are various areas of interest associated with AI. The work of Samoili et al. (2020), AI Watch, represents a captivating representation that is difficult to overlook, conducted by following a mixed methodology through natural language processing and qualitative analysis of several documents from three complementary perspectives. The AI field can be divided into core and transversal domains. Core domains focus on the fundamental objectives of AI, while transversal domains encompass broader issues that cut across multiple disciplines without being tied to a specific academic field. The proposed domains and subdomains are interconnected rather than distinct, and the taxonomy serves as a flexible framework representing AI from the perspectives of research, policy and industry.

Within the core domains, the reasoning subdomain includes knowledge representation, automated reasoning and common-sense reasoning, which deal with how machines transform data into knowledge or draw inferences. The planning domain involves subdomains like planning and scheduling, search, and optimisation, aiming to design and execute strategies, typically by intelligent agents, autonomous robots or unmanned vehicles. The learning subdomain encompasses machine learning (ML), which enables systems to learn, make decisions, predict, and adapt to changes without explicit programming. ML is a foundational element of AI, employing various learning methods such as reinforcement, supervised, semi-supervised, and unsupervised learning. Additionally, communication covers natural language processing (NLP) and large language models (LLMs), focusing on machines' ability to understand, process, and generate human language. Lastly, perception includes subdomains like computer vision and audio processing, referring to systems' ability to perceive their environment through vision, hearing and other sensory inputs, with vision and hearing being the most advanced areas in AI.

In the transversal domains, integration and interaction include subdomains such as multi-agent systems, robotics, and automation, as well as connected and automated vehicles (CAVs). This domain focuses on how AI systems integrate perception, reasoning, action, learning, and environmental interaction. Robotics and automation deal with the application and development of intelligent technologies to assist or replace human activities, while the CAVs subdomain addresses technologies for autonomous and connected vehicles, covering all levels of automation and communication (V2X). AI services encompass cloud-based infrastructure, software, and platforms that provide on-demand services, reducing the need for complex infrastructure management. Ethics and philosophy examine the ethical and philosophical challenges of AI, which are gaining attention as intelligent systems become more widespread, raising concerns among citizens and prompting policy discussions. The AI Watch taxonomy illustrating these domains is shown in Figure 12.1.

Dominant AI Enablers

The current landscape of AI is characterised by significant advancements in ML, NLP, robotics, and computer vision. Similarly, a significant trend in AI is the growing prominence of deep learning, a branch of machine learning that leverages neural networks to process intricate data (LeCun et al., 2015). Deep learning has allowed AI systems to reach cutting-edge performance in areas such as speech recognition, image recognition and natural language processing. Another trend is the increasing use of edge AI, which involves processing AI workloads on edge devices, such as smartphones and smart home devices, to reduce latency and improve real-time processing (Khan et al., 2019). AI has also made significant inroads in healthcare, with applications in medical imaging, disease diagnosis, and personalised medicine. Additionally, AI-powered virtual assistants and chatbots have become widespread in customer service, enhancing user experience and improving efficiency. However, despite these achievements, AI faces challenges related to explainability, bias, and job displacement. As AI systems grow more complex, understanding their decision-making processes becomes increasingly challenging, leading to concerns about accountability and trust (Doshi-Velez & Kim, 2017), an issue leading to a solution known as Explainable AI. For instance, AI systems have the potential to reinforce biases embedded in the datasets used for their training, which can lead to biased outcomes and discriminatory practices (Barocas & Selbst, 2016). This issue highlights a key ethical challenge in AI development, as unfair treatment of individuals or groups can occur if biases in data are not properly addressed. Additionally, a significant concern surrounding AI is job displacement. As AI technologies increasingly automate routine, repetitive tasks, many jobs, particularly those in sectors with tasks that are easily automated, may be at risk of elimination. However, while automation poses this threat, AI also opens up new job prospects in areas such as AI development, deployment, system maintenance and oversight. The rise of AI is thus a double-edged sword, presenting

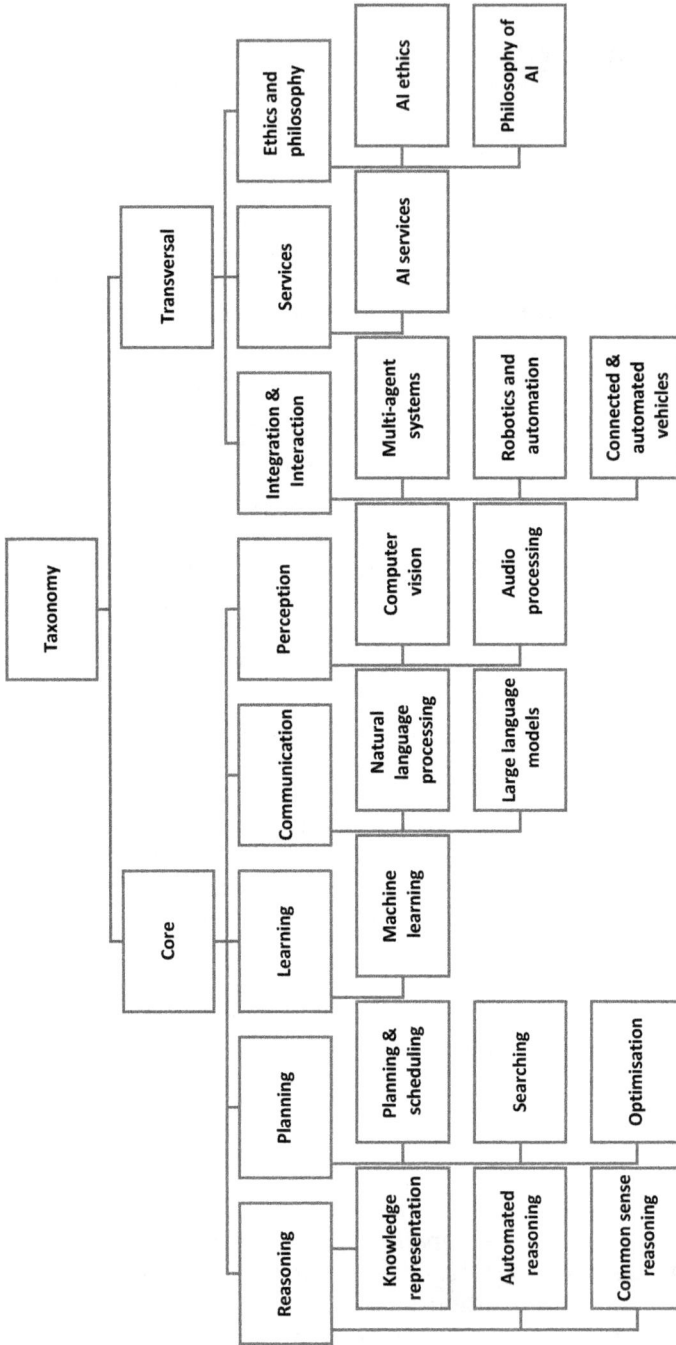

FIGURE 12.1
AI Taxonomy based on AI Watch.	Source: Samoili et al. (2020).

both risks to traditional employment and opportunities for growth in emerging fields. Accordingly, the prevailing AI techniques can be summarised and categorised as follows:

- Machine Learning Dominance: Machine learning, a branch of AI, has become the dominant method for creating intelligent systems, allowing computers to learn patterns and make decisions based on data without explicit programming (Jordan & Mitchell, 2015). ML has been applied successfully across a wide range of applications, such as image and speech recognition, natural language processing, and even in areas like game playing, making it a cornerstone of modern AI technologies.

- Advancements in Deep Learning: A specialised form of ML, deep learning, has seen extraordinary progress in areas like image and speech recognition, natural language processing, and game playing (LeCun et al., 2015). DL's ability to automatically learn and extract complex patterns from large datasets has led to significant advancements in fields like computer vision and natural language understanding, further pushing the boundaries of AI's capabilities.

- Increased Computing Power: The development and availability of specialised hardware, including Graphics Processing Units (GPUs) and Tensor Processing Units (TPUs), have dramatically enhanced the computational power required for AI tasks (Jouppi et al., 2017). This boost in processing capability has enabled the training of larger, more sophisticated models, leading to better performance and more refined AI systems capable of handling complex tasks.

- Data-Driven Decision-Making: AI systems rely heavily on large datasets to improve their learning and decision-making processes, emphasising the importance of data collection, storage and processing (Mayer-Schönberger, 2013). The growing availability of big data has fuelled AI's evolution, allowing these systems to continuously adapt, learn from experience and respond to novel situations with greater accuracy and effectiveness.

Major Achievements

The past decade has witnessed significant advancements and achievements in AI. From deep learning to explainable AI, AI has transformed numerous aspects of our lives. As AI continues to evolve, we can anticipate even more innovative applications and solutions to emerge. The following briefly discusses the major advancements and achievements of AI in the past decade.

- AlphaGo's Victory Over Human Go Champion (2016): In a ground-breaking achievement, Google DeepMind's AlphaGo defeated Lee Sedol, a world-renowned Go player, highlighting AI's potential to exceed human expertise in complex games (Silver et al., 2016). This event marked a significant milestone in AI research, illustrating the effectiveness of deep learning and reinforcement learning techniques in mastering intricate strategic tasks.

- Advancements in Natural Language Processing: AI models such as BERT (Kenton et al., 2019) and RoBERTa (Liu et al., 2019) have achieved state-of-the-art results in various language tasks, including understanding, translation and generation. These advancements have paved the way for applications like chatbots, language translation software and text summarisation tools, enhancing human-computer interaction and making language processing more efficient.

- Progress in Image Recognition and Computer Vision: AI has seen remarkable advancements in image recognition, object detection, and segmentation, enabling a wide range of applications, including self-driving cars, medical image analysis and facial recognition (Krizhevsky et al., 2012). These developments have been driven by the availability of extensive datasets and the creation of innovative algorithms, leading to improved accuracy and efficiency in visual tasks.

- The Rise of Explainable AI (XAI): As AI systems become more prevalent, there is an increasing demand to comprehend their decision-making processes, which has spurred the development of Explainable AI (XAI) techniques (Adamson, 2020). XAI seeks to enhance the transparency, accountability and trustworthiness of AI systems, allowing users to better understand and trust the decisions made by AI-driven technologies.

AI Services

Capturing the full scope of services provided by AI is a complex challenge. However, Dong et al. (2020) offer a detailed discussion of the services available in smart campuses. Given that AI is a crucial technology driving the intelligence, adaptability, and efficiency of these environments, this section explores the application of AI within smart campus services, examining both the general functions and specific AI-driven innovations that enhance the overall campus experience. Accordingly, in the context of AI applications in society, the provision of smart services is not limited to educational environments like smart campuses; these services can be equally valuable when applied to broader societal contexts. Therefore, the services that AI

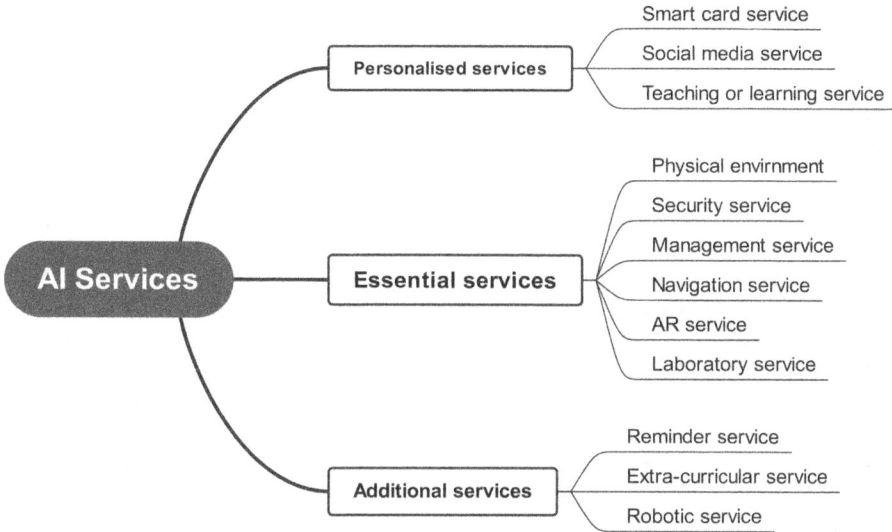

FIGURE 12.2
Important Category of AI Service.

can enable in various societal settings can similarly be categorised into three groups according to their significance, functionality and target users: essential services, personalised services and additional services (Dong et al., 2020). Each category offers solutions aimed at enhancing the well-being of communities and individuals, ensuring efficiency, and addressing both physical and digital challenges through AI technologies. Accordingly, this adaptation of smart campus services for society, as presented in Figure 12.2, highlights how AI can be leveraged to enhance public services, improve safety, streamline resource management and create personalised experiences across a wide range of societal applications. By integrating AI technologies, societies can enhance their adaptability, efficiency and responsiveness to the needs of their citizens.

Essential Services

Essential services are the foundational AI-powered functions that benefit society as a whole. These services focus on improving public safety, environmental conditions and resource management, making them vital for smart and sustainable living. Firstly, the physical environment in public and private spaces affects the well-being, cognition and productivity of individuals. AI-based physical environment services leverage IoT technologies to monitor and optimise key environmental factors like temperature, lighting and humidity, creating a comfortable and sustainable living environment. These services not only improve personal comfort but also contribute to broader societal goals such as reducing carbon emissions and promoting energy efficiency (Caţă, 2015). AI systems can automatically adjust these factors in real time, considering the conditions and activities of individuals, thus enhancing societal well-being.

Secondly, in both public and private sectors, AI-driven security services address physical and cyber threats. In physical security, AI systems analyse video footage from surveillance cameras in real time, tracking suspicious activities and identifying potential threats. This proactive approach reduces the likelihood of security incidents and eliminates human error, providing a safer environment for public spaces (Kwok, 2015) such as schools parks, shopping centres, and residential areas. Cybersecurity is another critical area where AI can protect society. With the increasing digitisation of public services, data security is paramount. AI-based cybersecurity services can detect and prevent cyber threats such as data breaches, denial-of-service attacks (Sánchez-Torres et al., 2018) and unauthorised access. By enhancing data protection through encryption and redundancy, these services ensure the safe transmission of sensitive information, which is essential for public trust in digital systems.

In addition, AI-based management services in society enable efficient allocation and use of resources such as energy, water and space. Through the collection of real-time data on usage patterns, AI systems can optimise resource distribution to reduce waste and improve efficiency. For example, AI can intelligently allocate space resources (Sutjarittham et al., 2019) and can manage public utilities by adjusting energy consumption in response to demand, ensuring that public resources are used sustainably and cost-effectively. Moreover, AI-enabled navigation services can provide real-time indoor and outdoor navigation for individuals in public spaces (Chen et al., 2018) like hospitals, airports, and shopping malls. By using facial recognition and tracking technologies, AI systems can offer personalised guidance, helping people find their way more easily and reducing the time spent searching for locations. These services contribute to the efficiency and convenience of daily life, especially for those with accessibility needs.

Furthermore, Augmented Reality (AR) services have the potential to transform how individuals interact with digital content in the real world. In society, AR can be used for educational and entertainment purposes, as well as for enhancing everyday experiences. For instance, AR could transform museums into interactive learning environments or turn outdoor locations into immersive, historical experiences. AR-based services can help bridge the gap between digital and physical realities, creating engaging and informative experiences that enrich daily life (Dong et al., 2020). In addition to industries that require hands-on training or experimentation, smart laboratories can be found in healthcare, engineering, and research sectors, which can automatically adjust equipment settings and offer personalised assistance based on user actions. Virtual laboratories (Jara et al., 2011) can also be employed in remote settings, making specialised training accessible to more people without the need for physical resources.

Personalised Services

AI can deliver personalised services that cater to individual needs in society, enhancing user experiences and fostering more efficient and tailored interactions with services. For example, smart card services, powered by AI, allow for the consolidation of multiple identification and access functions into a single card, making life more convenient for citizens. These cards can integrate identification, financial transactions, public transportation access, and healthcare management, streamlining everyday tasks for individuals and enhancing security (Priya et al., 2023). Moreover, AI-driven social media services can analyse user behaviour and preferences to deliver personalised content and improve user experience. In societal applications, this could mean better-targeted public service announcements, tailored community engagement programmes, or even real-time sentiment analysis during emergencies to help local authorities gauge public opinion and needs (Bukar et al., 2022). Such AI services foster a more connected and responsive society. Furthermore, AI systems can create personalised learning and development pathways for individuals in society, mapping out the most efficient routes for skill acquisition and career advancement. By analysing individual performance data, technologies such as AI systems can recommend relevant courses, materials and opportunities for personal and professional growth, ensuring that citizens remain competitive in an evolving job market (Erdt et al., 2015; Qu et al., 2018).

Additional Services

AI can also provide additional services that enhance the quality of life in society through personalised and context-aware support. For instance, AI-powered reminder services help individuals manage their daily schedules by sending adaptive notifications for upcoming appointments, health-related reminders, or important public events. These services can be tailored to individual preferences and health conditions, promoting well-being and productivity. Also, AI-based activity planning services can organise and tailor recreational activities for groups based on user preferences, availability, and location. This is especially useful in promoting social engagement, encouraging community participation, and fostering creativity in society. Moreover, robotics, as a physical manifestation of AI, has the potential to assist individuals with everyday tasks in society. Whether through robotic companions for the elderly, service robots in public spaces, or AI-powered personal assistants, robotics can improve the quality of life by providing continuous support and enabling greater independence for individuals in need (Lubold et al., 2016).

Major Trends in AI for the Next Decade

The next decade is expected to be transformative for AI, with emerging trends poised to revolutionise numerous aspects of society and humanity. In particular, Explainable AI and Edge AI are expected to shape AI research and development in the future. The sooner is used for transparent decision-making, enabling trust and accountability in AI systems, and the latter focuses on real-time processing, reducing latency and improving efficiency in IoT devices. These concepts are broadly explained in the proceeding sections.

Trend 1: Explainable AI (XAI)

XAI aims to create AI systems that offer clear and understandable explanations for their decisions and actions (Ribeiro et al., 2016a), as illustrated in Figure 12.3. This trend is driven by the need for trust, transparency, and accountability in AI decision-making processes. XAI aims to make AI more understandable and reliable, enabling users to trust AI-driven decisions. This trend has many potential impacts on society and industries such as XAI increasing trust in AI, improving accountability, and enabling more effective human-AI collaboration. Industries like healthcare, finance, and transportation will

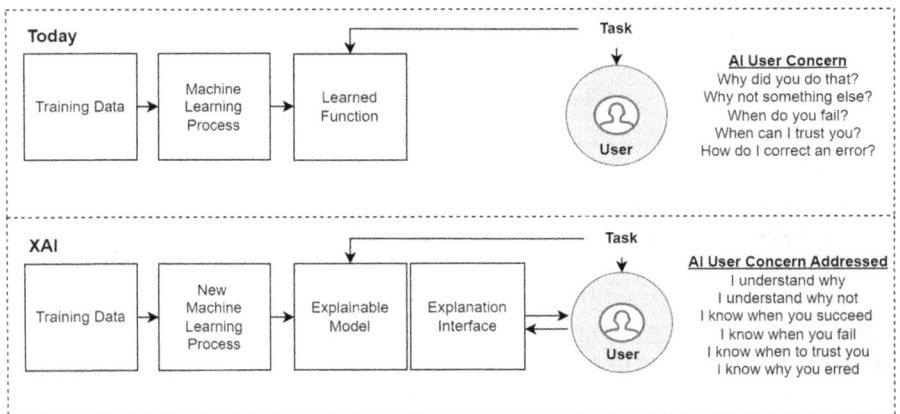

FIGURE 12.3
The concept of Explainable AI (XAI).

benefit from XAI, as it can help professionals understand and trust AI-driven decisions. XAI can also enhance AI safety and security, reducing the risk of errors and cyber-attacks. There are numerous examples or case studies already available for XAI, such as Google's Explainable AI initiative, DARPA's XAI program, and the development of explainable machine learning models like Local Interpretable Model-agnostic Explanations (LIME) (Ribeiro et al., 2016b). XAI has been utilised across multiple fields, such as natural language processing, computer vision and recommendation systems.

Several techniques have already been developed and proposed for XAI. These include feature attribution, model interpretability and explanation generation (Doshi-Velez & Kim, 2017). Feature attribution methods, such as saliency maps and feature importance, highlight the most relevant input features contributing to AI decisions. Model interpretability methods, such as model-agnostic explanations and transparent models, provide insights into AI decision-making processes. Explanation generation methods, such as text and visual explanations, communicate AI decisions to users. Accordingly, XAI faces issues like explainability-accuracy trade-offs, scalability, and evaluation metrics (Zhou et al., 2019). Explainability-accuracy trade-offs occur when increasing explainability reduces AI accuracy. Scalability issues arise when applying XAI to large, complex AI models. In addition, evaluation metrics for XAI are still being developed and refined.

Trend 2: Edge AI

The Edge AI involves processing AI workloads on devices like smartphones, smart home devices and autonomous vehicles, reducing reliance on cloud computing (Satyanarayanan, 2017), as illustrated in Figure 12.4. This trend is driven by the need for faster, more secure, and more efficient AI applications. Edge AI enables real-time processing, reduced latency, and improved user experience. Accordingly, the potential impact of Edge AI on society and industries includes its capability to enable faster, more secure, and more efficient AI applications, benefiting industries like healthcare, manufacturing and transportation. Edge AI enhances AI safety and security, reducing the risk of data breaches and cyber-attacks. Notable examples or case studies of Edge AI include Apple's Core ML, Google's TensorFlow Lite, and the development of edge AI-powered smart glasses and smart home devices. Edge AI has been implemented in a variety of fields, including natural language processing, computer vision and predictive maintenance.

The technical approaches for Edge AI include techniques such as model compression, knowledge distillation, and federated learning (Khan et al., 2019). Model compression reduces AI model size, enabling deployment on edge devices. Knowledge distillation transfers knowledge from large AI models to smaller edge AI models. Federated learning allows edge devices to work together in training AI models collaboratively. However, some of the

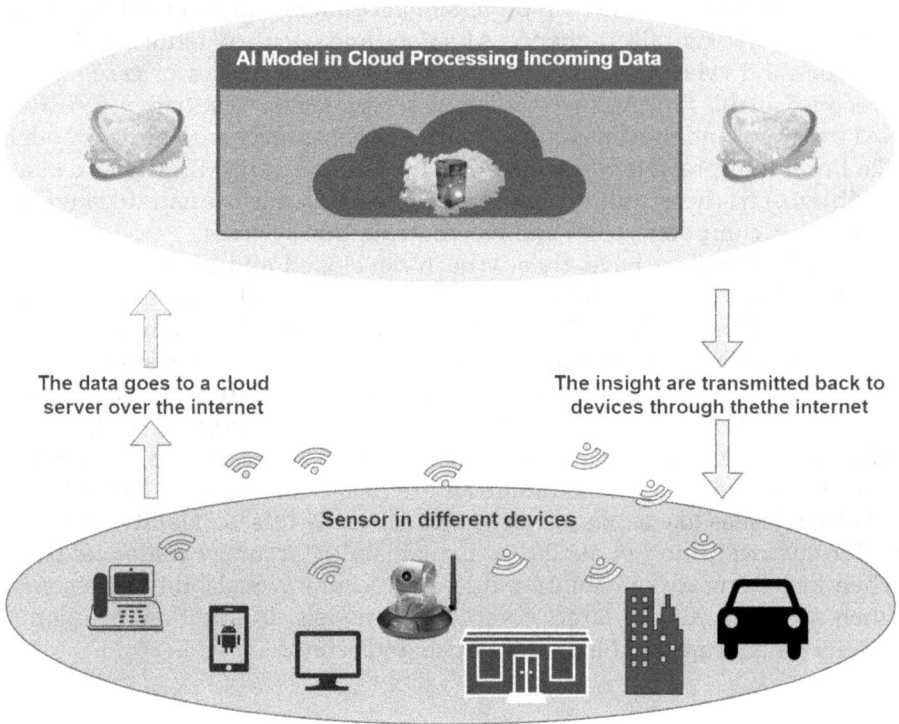

FIGURE 12.4
Edge AI Illustrations, demonstrating how AI is integrated with cloud models and sensors in different devices.

limitations of Edge AI cover device heterogeneity, data quality and security (LeCun et al., 2015). Device heterogeneity occurs when edge devices have varying computational resources and capabilities. Data quality issues arise when edge devices generate noisy or biased data. Security concerns include data privacy and edge device vulnerabilities.

Acceptability and Feasibility of AI

The AI Architecture has demonstrated significant potential across various sectors, however, its acceptability and feasibility among institutions and the general populace require further discussion. Over the last decade, the deployment of AI systems has gained traction worldwide, laying the foundation for the widespread adoption of AI technologies. However, some of the advanced technologies integral to the full realisation of AI systems are still in their developmental stages, which may hinder the practical and large-scale deployment of AI. It is anticipated that future technological break-throughs will address these limitations, enabling more seamless integration.

In recent years, several emerging AI technologies have also sparked concerns among users due to the risks and ethical challenges they pose (Tippins et al., 2021; Gaur & Sahoo, 2022; Li et al., 2022; Guleria et al., 2023; Dwivedi et al., 2023; Salloum, 2024). For example, implementing AI-powered sur-veillance or monitoring systems, such as facial recognition and behavioural tracking, requires embedding sensing devices in various environments. These systems can track facial expressions and movements to assess perfor-mance or engagement in real time. While the intention is to enhance pro-ductivity or improve outcomes, privacy concerns are often raised (Dong et al., 2020). Critics argue that these technologies could infringe on personal privacy or even cause psychological discomfort, potentially leading to decreased user acceptance and negative impacts on performance. However, it is essential to recognise that these systems typically process abstracted data rather than raw video footage, ensuring that sensitive information is not mis-used. Additionally, storing data on local servers instead of relying on cloud infrastructure can reduce the risk of data breaches. To further mitigate risks, Dong et al. (2020) emphasised that robust cybersecurity measures should be integrated into AI systems, which can alleviate some of the privacy concerns of users and help build trust in these technologies.

Another common challenge to AI adoption is the resistance to new technol-ogies due to familiarity with traditional systems. Users who are accustomed to conventional methods may find AI systems complex and disruptive. This reluctance can negatively impact the acceptance and adoption of AI solutions. Historically, the acceptance of new technologies has required an adjustment period, as described by the Innovation Diffusion Theory (IDT) (Rogers et al., 2014). As long as AI developers adhere to user-centric prin-ciples, greater acceptance of AI systems by both institutions and the general populace is expected over time. The acceptance and adoption of AI technol-ogy are illustrated in Figure 12.5 through the Innovation Diffusion Theory. Specifically, the IDT categorises technology acceptance into five groups: innovators, who adopt AI when it is new; early adopters, who embrace AI upon recognising its benefits; early majority, who join when the advantages of AI are evident; late majority, who adopt AI once substantial help and support are available; and laggards, who adopt AI only when it becomes necessary.

Nevertheless, to address these concerns and enhance the acceptance and acceptability of AI systems, it is critical to incorporate feedback from end-users. The best practice in this regard is to conduct surveys or other forms of user outreach to gather insights on public perceptions (e.g., Cubric, 2020; Radhakrishnan & Chattopadhyay, 2020; Bedué & Fritzsche, 2022; Madan & Ashok, 2023; Bukar et al., 2024a, 2024b). The results can then guide efforts

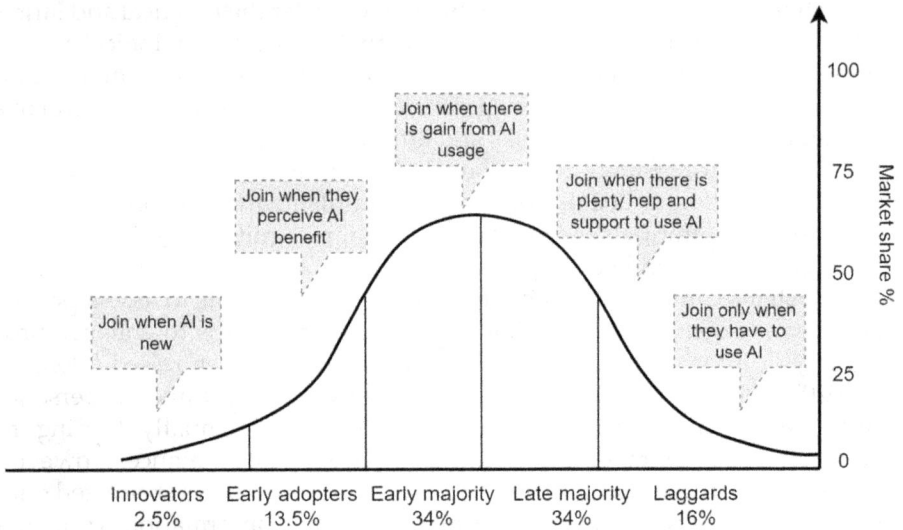

FIGURE 12.5
The acceptance and adoption of AI technology explained through the diffusion of innovation theory.

to adjust AI systems to align better with user preferences and alleviate concerns. By prioritising user-centric design and addressing ethical issues, AI systems can gain broader acceptance while meeting the needs of society.

Conclusion

In this chapter, the pivotal moment in technological evolution is evident by the applications of AI in various sectors. The myriad AI taxonomy and technologies driving AI forward highlighted the core and transversal classification of AI techniques. In particular, various methods were classified into reasoning, planning, learning, communication and perception models, as well as integration and interaction, services and ethics to philosophy. In addition, the course of emerging AI trends focuses on the dominant AI enablers and major achievements. Furthermore, various breakthroughs in machine learning algorithms to the proliferation of AI-powered applications have been marked by exponential growth and innovation. The landscape of AI is shaped by technological advancements such as XAI and Edge AI, and factors such as societal needs and economic forces. Accordingly, several trends are poised to reshape the AI landscape, acceptance and adoption behaviours, which cover the following:

- **Ethical AI**: As AI becomes increasingly integrated into society and civilisation, ensuring ethical considerations to guide its development and deployment will be paramount. From bias mitigation to transparency and accountability, ethical AI principles will underpin responsible AI innovation.
- **AI Democratisation**: The democratisation of AI tools and technologies will empower individuals and organisations across all sectors to harness the power of AI. Open-source platforms, cloud-based services, and low-code AI solutions will democratise access to AI capabilities, fuelling innovation and driving widespread adoption.
- **AI Augmentation**: Rather than replacing human workers, AI will augment human capabilities, enhancing productivity, creativity and decision-making across diverse domains. Human-AI collaboration will become the norm, enabling synergistic partnerships that leverage the strengths of both humans and machines.
- **AI Governance**: With AI's growing influence on society, policymakers will face the challenge of crafting robust regulatory frameworks to govern its ethical and responsible use. From data privacy and security to algorithmic transparency and accountability, effective AI governance will be essential to mitigate risks and foster trust.
- **AI for Good**: Harnessing AI for social good could be a driving force for innovation, with applications spanning healthcare, education, environmental sustainability and humanitarian aid. AI plays a crucial role in tackling some of the most urgent challenges facing the world today, such as precision medicine and personalised learning to climate modelling and disaster response.

Furthermore, despite the fact that the implementation of AI offers unprecedented opportunities to leverage its transformative potential for the advancement of society. However, along with these opportunities come formidable challenges that must be addressed, these include:

- **Ethical Considerations**: Balancing technological advancement with ethical considerations will be imperative to ensure that AI serves the greater good while minimising potential harm.
- **Workforce Transformation**: The integration of AI into various industries will necessitate reskilling and upskilling efforts to prepare the workforce for the jobs of the future.

- **Data Privacy and Security**: Protecting data privacy and security will be crucial as AI systems become more dependent on large quantities of sensitive information.
- **Algorithmic Bias**: Tackling algorithmic bias and promoting fairness and equity in AI decision-making processes will be vital to avoid reinforcing existing societal inequalities.
- **Regulatory Frameworks**: Developing agile and adaptive regulatory frameworks that keep pace with technological advancements will be crucial to fostering innovation while safeguarding public interests.

Accordingly, the discussion of this chapter showcases the current state of AI development. As society stands on the point of a transformative era defined by unprecedented technological innovation and societal change. It is necessary to embrace the AI emerging trends by navigating challenges and upholding ethical principles. This ensures individuals and organisations harness the full potential of AI to shape a more equitable, sustainable and prosperous future for all. Hence, "Charting the Future: AI in the Next Decade – Emerging Trends and Conclusions" serves as both a reflection on the past and a roadmap for the future, guiding humanity towards a future in which AI acts as a catalyst for positive change and the flourishing of humanity.

References

Adamson, G. (2020). Explainable Artificial Intelligence (XAI): A reason to believe? *Law Context: A Socio-Legal J.*, 37, 23.

Barocas, S., & Selbst, A. D. (2016). Big data's disparate impact. *California Law Review*, 104(3), 671–732.

Bedué, P., & Fritzsche, A. (2022). Can we trust AI? an empirical investigation of trust requirements and guide to successful AI adoption. *Journal of Enterprise Information Management*, 35(2), 530–549.

Bukar, U. A., Sayeed, M. S., Razak, S. F. A., Yogarayan, S., & Sneesl, R. (2024a). *Decision-Making Framework for the Utilization of Generative Artificial Intelligence in Education: A Case Study of ChatGPT*. IEEE Access.

Bukar, U. A., Sayeed, M. S., Razak, S. F. A., Yogarayan, S., & Sneesl, R. (2024b). Prioritizing ethical conundrums in the utilization of ChatGPT in education through an analytical hierarchical approach. *Education Sciences*, 14(9), 959.

Bukar, U. A., Sidi, F., Jabar, M. A., Nor, R. N. H., Abdullah, S., Ishak, I., ... & Alkhalifah, A. (2022). How advanced technological approaches are reshaping sustainable social media crisis management and communication: a systematic review. *Sustainability*, 14(10), 5854.

Caţă, M. (2015, September). Smart university, a new concept in the Internet of Things. In *2015 14th RoEduNet international conference-networking in education and research (RoEduNet NER)* (pp. 195–197). IEEE.

Chen, L. W., Chen, T. P., Chen, D. E., Liu, J. X., & Tsai, M. F. (2018). Smart campus care and guiding with dedicated video footprinting through Internet of Things technologies. *IEEE Access*, 6, 43956–43966.

Cubric, M. (2020). Drivers, barriers and social considerations for AI adoption in business and management: A tertiary study. *Technology in Society*, 62, 101257.

Dong, Z. Y., Zhang, Y., Yip, C., Swift, S., & Beswick, K. (2020). Smart campus: definition, framework, technologies, and services. *IET Smart Cities*, 2(1), 43–54.

Doshi-Velez, F., & Kim, B. (2017). Towards a rigorous science of interpretable machine learning. *arXiv preprint arXiv:1702.08608*.

Dwivedi, Y. K., Kshetri, N., Hughes, L., Slade, E. L., Jeyaraj, A., Kar, A. K., ... & Wright, R. (2023). Opinion Paper: "So what if ChatGPT wrote it?" Multidisciplinary perspectives on opportunities, challenges and implications of generative conversational AI for research, practice and policy. *International Journal of Information Management*, 71, 102642.

Erdt, M., Fernández, A., & Rensing, C. (2015). Evaluating recommender systems for technology enhanced learning: a quantitative survey. *IEEE Transactions on Learning Technologies*, 8(4), 326–344.

Gaur, L., & Sahoo, B. M. (2022). Explainable AI in ITS: Ethical concerns. In *Explainable Artificial Intelligence for Intelligent Transportation Systems: Ethics and Applications* (pp. 79–90). Cham: Springer International Publishing.

Guleria, A., Krishan, K., Sharma, V., & Kanchan, T. (2023). ChatGPT: ethical concerns and challenges in academics and research. *The Journal of Infection in Developing Countries*, 17(09), 1292–1299.

Jara, C. A., Candelas, F. A., Puente, S. T., & Torres, F. (2011). Hands-on experiences of undergraduate students in Automatics and Robotics using a virtual and remote laboratory. *Computers & Education*, 57(4), 2451–2461.

Jordan, M. I., & Mitchell, T. M. (2015). Machine learning: Trends, perspectives, and prospects. *Science*, 349(6245), 255–260.

Jouppi, N. P., Young, C., Patil, N., Patterson, D., Agrawal, G., Bajwa, R., ... & Yoon, D. H. (2017, June). In-datacenter performance analysis of a tensor processing unit. In *Proceedings of the 44th annual international symposium on computer architecture* (pp. 1–12).

Kenton, J. D. M. W.C., & Toutanova, L. K. (2019, June). Bert: Pre-training of deep bidirectional transformers for language understanding. In *Proceedings of naacL-HLT* (Vol. 1, p. 2).

Khan, W. Z., Ahmed, E., Hakak, S., Yaqoob, I., & Ahmed, A. (2019). Edge computing: A survey. *Future Generation Computer Systems*, 97, 219–235.

Krizhevsky, A., Sutskever, I., & Hinton, G. E. (2012). Imagenet classification with deep convolutional neural networks. *Advances in Neural Information Processing Systems*, 25.

Kwok, L. F. (2015). A vision for the development of i-campus. *Smart Learning Environments*, 2, 1–12.

LeCun, Y., Bengio, Y., & Hinton, G. (2015). Deep learning. *Nature*, 521(7553), 436–444.

Li, F., Ruijs, N., & Lu, Y. (2022). Ethics & AI: A systematic review on ethical concerns and related strategies for designing with AI in healthcare. *AI*, 4(1), 28–53.

Liu, Y., Ott, M., Goyal, N., Du, J., Joshi, M., Chen, D., ... & Stoyanov, V. (2019). RoBERTa: a robustly optimized BERT pretraining approach. arXiv e-prints. *arXiv preprint arXiv:1907.11692*.

Lubold, N., Walker, E., & Pon-Barry, H. (2016, March). Effects of voice-adaptation and social dialogue on perceptions of a robotic learning companion. In *2016 11th ACM/IEEE International Conference on Human-Robot Interaction (HRI)* (pp. 255–262). IEEE.

Madan, R., & Ashok, M. (2023). AI adoption and diffusion in public administration: A systematic literature review and future research agenda. *Government Information Quarterly*, 40(1), 101774.

Mayer-Schönberger, V. (2013). *Big data: A revolution that will transform how we live, work, and think*. Houghton Mifflin Harcourt.

Priya, P., Gopinath, B., Mohamed Ashif, M., & Yadeshwaran, H. S. (2023, April). AI Powered Authentication for Smart Home Security—A Survey. In *International Conference on Information and Communication Technology for Intelligent Systems* (pp. 227–237). Singapore: Springer Nature Singapore.

Qu, S., Li, K., Zhang, S., & Wang, Y. (2018). Predicting achievement of students in smart campus. *IEEE access*, 6, 60264–60273.

Radhakrishnan, J., & Chattopadhyay, M. (2020). Determinants and barriers of artificial intelligence adoption–A literature review. In *Re-imagining Diffusion and Adoption of Information Technology and Systems: A Continuing Conversation: IFIP WG 8.6 International Conference on Transfer and Diffusion of IT, TDIT 2020, Tiruchirappalli, India, December 18–19, 2020, Proceedings, Part I* (pp. 89–99). Springer International Publishing.

Ribeiro, M. T., Singh, S., & Guestrin, C. (2016a, August). "Why should I trust you?" Explaining the predictions of any classifier. In *Proceedings of the 22nd ACM SIGKDD international conference on knowledge discovery and data mining* (pp. 1135–1144).

Ribeiro, M. T., Singh, S., & Guestrin, C. (2016b). Model-agnostic interpretability of machine learning. *arXiv preprint arXiv:1606.05386*.

Rogers, E. M., Singhal, A., & Quinlan, M. M. (2014). Diffusion of innovations. In *An integrated approach to communication theory and research* (pp. 432–448). Routledge.

Salloum, S. A. (2024). AI perils in education: Exploring ethical concerns. *Artificial Intelligence in Education: The Power and Dangers of ChatGPT in the Classroom*, 669–675.

Samoili, S., Lopez, C., Gomez, G. E., De P. G., Martinez-Plumed F., & Delipetrev, B. (2020). AI WATCH. defining artificial intelligence.

Sánchez-Torres, B., Rodríguez-Rodríguez, J. A., Rico-Bautista, D. W., & Guerrero, C. D. (2018). Smart Campus: Trends in cybersecurity and future development. *Revista Facultad de Ingeniería*, 27(47), 104–112.

Satyanarayanan, M. (2017). The emergence of edge computing. *Computer*, 50(1), 30–39.

Silver, D., Huang, A., Maddison, C. J., Guez, A., Sifre, L., Van Den Driessche, G., ... & Hassabis, D. (2016). Mastering the game of Go with deep neural networks and tree search. *Nature*, 529(7587), 484–489.

Sutjarittham, T., Gharakheili, H. H., Kanhere, S. S., & Sivaraman, V. (2019). Experiences with IoT and AI in a smart campus for optimizing classroom usage. *IEEE Internet of Things Journal*, 6(5), 7595–7607.

Tippins, N. T., Oswald, F. L., & McPhail, S. M. (2021). Scientific, legal, and ethical concerns about AI-based personnel selection tools: a call to action. *Personnel Assessment and Decisions*, 7(2), 1.

Zhou, Z., Chen, X., Li, E., Zeng, L., Luo, K., & Zhang, J. (2019). Edge intelligence: Paving the last mile of artificial intelligence with edge computing. *Proceedings of the IEEE*, 107(8), 1738–1762.

Index

Pages in *italics* refer to figures and pages in **bold** refer to tables.

For Product Safety Concerns and Information please contact our EU
representative GPSR@taylorandfrancis.com
Taylor & Francis Verlag GmbH, Kaufingerstraße 24, 80331 München, Germany

www.ingramcontent.com/pod-product-compliance
Lightning Source LLC
Chambersburg PA
CBHW060343220326
41598CB00023B/2792